RADICAL HISTORY *Review*

Issue 93

Homeland Securities

TEACHING RADICAL HISTORY

REFLECTIONS

VISUAL ESSAYS

Editors' Introduction

The experience of editing this special issue of *Radical History Review* has been bracketed by two global disasters: the initiation of the war on terror precipitated by the September 11, 2001, attacks on U.S. soil and the December 26, 2004, tsunami in the Indian Ocean precipitated by an earthquake off Sumatra. Both caused tragic loss of life and were accompanied by a spontaneous outpouring of goodwill toward the survivors from nations and individuals around the world. As historically trained observers of the present, however, we know we must study the geopolitics of disaster even as we respond in human and individual terms to its tragedy. Disasters throw up new opportunities for old forces and interest groups, and settled power relations acquire new dynamics. We tend to refer to disasters, and the policies that follow in their wake, in terms of natural cycles, paradigm shifts, or watersheds. But the watershed metaphor can be misleading because it distracts us from the ways in which powerful players have reshaped existing relations and wrested new meanings from old. The instant displays of national and international solidarity called forth by disasters—whether labeled human-made or natural—often screen deeper geopolitical shifts and fractures. Formerly sedimented meanings are briefly up for grabs, and the most powerful global actors rush to reshape and appropriate their chains of signification.

September 11: Shifting Significations

In late September 2001, just two weeks after 9/11, we gathered at a *Radical History Review* editorial collective meeting with both horror and hope. Shelving our standard agenda for most of that day, we concluded that as historians with progressive pedagogical and professional commitments, we had a responsibility to bear witness to the shifting terrain of 9/11's human disaster and to respond by offering historically nuanced readings of our current predicament that would help us offer critical

Radical History Review
Issue 93 (Fall 2005): 1–10
Copyright 2005 by MARHO: The Radical Historians' Organization, Inc.

perspectives on, and radical alternatives to, the new world order whose political contours were shifting even as we spoke.

The first spate of commentaries had already begun to appear, and many were reading this moment as a watershed. The USA PATRIOT Act was passed by the U.S. Congress forty-five days after September 11, 2001, with virtually no debate. Although many elements of the surveillance society had long been part of state security practice and debated in public discourse, they were now cast in terms of security and freedom, suddenly interpellated into the lives of more people in more ways than ever before. What emerged were both newly obedient practices (a startlingly wide range of citizens agreeing, for example, to the exchange of liberties for safety, or voting to preserve marriage and family values) and newly creative resistances (local and international solidarities against the new normalcy grew almost overnight; the resistant people of the world were christened the world's second superpower on the front page of the *New York Times* on February 15, 2003). Everyday terms—*patriotism, French fries, freedom, feminism, the vote, the veil, evil,* and *courage*—and everyday practices—reading, teaching, speaking, consuming, migrating, meeting, photographing, and protesting—were reshaped and contested, most spectacularly and successfully by the neoconservative right wing, but also persistently, interstitially, and ingeniously by coalitions of resistance.

As with most watershed disaster narratives, the more we looked, the more we saw both continuity and change. The role of a history journal in documenting such a monumental contemporary event was far from clear: should we include the most recent readings of political developments, or broader historical analyses? What were disciplinary and methodological starting points for rethinking historical research in the light of this shifting new reality? How could we facilitate not only immediate reflections but also the creation of sustained research projects, given both the pressures of the everyday practices of resistance that swept us up—teach-ins, petitions, mobilizations, and debates—and the growing assault on progressive scholars? We invited articles that would address the need for a continued radical interrogation of our political moment, and our role in it. The September 2001 editorial collective meeting and our ongoing discussions, which extended to larger academic and activist communities, yielded the "Terror" issue (*RHR* 85), and an activist group that became known as Historians against War (HAW), initially organized in October 2002 and catalyzed by the February 2003 protest against the Iraq war. This issue builds on and stands in dialogue with both the "Terror" issue and the ongoing work of HAW. In our call for submissions, we asked people to help frame an open-ended discussion that we now invite you to continue:

The shift in U.S. domestic and international agendas in the wake of 9/11,
and the accompanying rhetorics of national defense, the war on terrorism,
and homeland security, establish a complex challenge for radical scholars

and activists. While the agencies and policies grouped under the rubric of
homeland security ostensibly address issues of the safety of this nation and
its citizens, its implications reach far beyond the borders of the United States
and raise both new and familiar questions about transnational mobility,
imperialism, nation, and citizenship. Increasingly, governments around the
world are adopting the discourse of national security to beef up their militaries,
quash dissent, and crack down on those considered alien to particular
conceptions of national identity. What is the role of radical historians and
engaged intellectuals under this "new normalcy"?

The Christmas Tsunami: Human and Strategic Mobilizations

On December 26, 2004, a massive earthquake off the coast of Sumatra created a
tsunami whose devastation crossed the Indian Ocean, causing the worst humanitarian disaster in recent memory. U.S. individuals moved far more quickly than
their rulers to send donations to the Asian victims of the tsunami, and it seemed as
if America's people would preempt its state, rising to internationalist sympathy in
the face of this disaster. Initially slow, but increasingly aware of the public relations
opportunities in a region of the world that reported high negative opinions of the
United States, the Bush administration accelerated its aid from nothing, in the first
days following the Christmas tsunami, to an ever more public display of concern
for its destitute victims. Images of friendly Marines delivering care packages to
thankful Asians promised to replace the disturbing snapshots of American soldiers
abusing Iraqi prisoners in Saddam Hussein's former prison, even as more evidence
of abuse was coming to light during specialist Charles Graner's court-martial. At
the same time, Alberto Gonzales, author of the infamous torture memo, stood
poised for confirmation as U.S. attorney general, and prisoners at the Guantánamo
Bay prison camp entered their fourth year of detention.[1] It seemed as if the imperial military machine had been forced to temporarily pause in the face of natural
disaster.

Behind the tsunami, commented a journalist in the *Asia Times*, "a power
game is also being played over who calls the shots and retains influence in the
Indian Ocean region, and by default the rest of Asia."[2] Japan announced $400 mil-
lion in aid to outdo the $350 million provided by the United States. India rushed
aid and military assistance to Sri Lanka, displaying its naval strength and announcing itself a donor rather than a victim nation. India and China jockeyed with and
against the United States to manage the balance of power in the Indian Ocean.
The Indian state's slogan of the 1970s, "Indian Ocean: A Zone of Peace," seemed
a quaint reminder of a time when both India and China had strategically negoti-
ated against U.S. military presence in the Indian Ocean and Asia. Now, despite
attempting to assert its autonomy from postdisaster donor nations, India feared that
a decline in U.S. military power in the Indian Ocean could mean greater Chinese

power; China feared that a withdrawal of U.S. troops from Asia might strategically empower Japan.[3]

Two of the worst-hit regions—the Tamil region of northern Sri Lanka controlled by the Liberation Tigers of Tamil Eelam, and the Aceh region of Indonesia—had been sites of militant resistance against their respective states. But with their people and resources devastated by the tsunami, the future of these movements could increasingly be scripted by the global geopolitical response. International solidarity movements exerted pressure on Western governments to stand with the Acehnese and against the Indonesian state; but Kofi Annan, under pressure from the Sri Lankan state, cancelled plans to visit the Tamil Tigers. Meanwhile, India's religious Right mobilized relief operations designed to carry anti-Islamic propaganda to the poorest classes of the subcontinent.

Homeland Insecurities

While all of these geostrategic equations have more complex histories than we have space for here, and none were created overnight by large ocean waves, they remind us that we are probably witnessing, in the wake of the tsunami, the largest buildup of U.S. military presence in and around Asia since the end of the Vietnam War, as well as the largest propaganda effort since September 11, 2001, to create a benevolent peace-time image of the U.S. military. Just as we complete an issue on the insecurities of the homeland, these histories in the making remind us of the need to view homeland insecurities in comparative transnational perspective.

Three feature articles reflect on ways in which the new world order offers a brutally revivified version of, and one unapologetically continuous with, older forms of control. Jasbir Puar reads the abuse of Iraqi prisoners at Abu Ghraib as an instance of the violence that has always been intrinsic to the civilizing mission. The U.S. media's constructions of Arab sexuality and shame, the rapid circulation of images in virtual networks, the complicit responses of liberal feminism and gay conservatism, and the exceptionalism argument the Bush administration used to explain the abuses at Abu Ghraib all come into play in Puar's reading of the intersections of homophobia, racism, sexism, Orientalism, new media, and the new imperialism. Jorge Mariscal also explores continuities with existing forms of racial oppression in the United States, tracking the ways in which white supremacy has received new strength in the past decade, now further fueled by fears of terrorism. Latino youth are targeted for army recruitment as economic decline traps Latino families in minimum-wage jobs, while racist anti-immigration rhetoric grows ever more shrill. Natsu Taylor Saito addresses the costs of homeland security through the lens of critical legal theory, rejecting the dichotomous choice of liberty or security. The real questions, she argues, are: Which sections of the population do the new security measures benefit? Who is being defined as a real American? In what ways are these new developments continuous with older state histories of sanctioned violence against people of color?

A cluster of interventions offers us examples of radical critique welded to experimental resistances, as well as glimpses of alternative histories and futures. As in any spontaneous pattern of resistance, we see multiple and often contradictory claims in this section, but all flow from resistant practices with which the authors have direct experience.

Maurice Wheeler writes about U.S. librarians' courageous and creative efforts to protect the privacy of their patrons' records against sweeping new state snooping activities in the wake of the PATRIOT Act. Wheeler reminds us that although public libraries are often ignored by both policy makers and intellectual elites, there is a significant thinking population whose main access to information and books is located in their public library. The toughest struggles, Wheeler warns, are still ahead. In the same vein, Beatriz da Costa and Claire Pentecost write about the disturbing case of the FBI investigation of the Critical Art Ensemble, one among many instances in which the PATRIOT Act appears to cast its shadow over creative expression, scientific-artistic collaborations, and public dissent.

In the aftermath of 9/11, networks of resistance developed—in answer to the need for national mobilization, as well as to the hunger for alternative news that could counter U.S. mainstream media narratives of a primitive Arab world filled with irrational terrorists and abject women. Essays by Barbara Abrash and Eric Hiltner, for example, find resistance to the floods of mainstream media propaganda in alternative, interstitial media technologies. Abrash explores the spontaneous creation of public spaces after 9/11, the proliferation of Internet news sites, and the possibilities of nonstandard narratives for resistant communication. Hiltner also talks about a spontaneous appropriation of media after 9/11 for ends ranging from public mourning to organized resistance. He argues that changes in video, audio, and Internet technology have democratized the space of technological communication just as the copy machine democratized print media. Francisco Balderrama tells the story of the unconstitutional deportation of Mexican Americans in the 1930s, thereby linking history with the present through moving accounts of the experience of masses of people whose actions resist the logic of the liberal state.

Two interventions take up feminist responses to the war on terror. Martha Howell reminds us of the hypocrisy of the U.S. state's rescue mission to save Afghan women and articulates a radical position that acknowledges caring as well as resistance. Howell's piece comments on the continuing relevance of Spivak's critique of gendered colonial practices in which "white men save brown women from brown men." Kath Weston argues that the legal politics of recognition for queerness should not seduce us into reinstating the alleged priority of biology and kinship. Tracing ways in which late-twentieth-century liberalism has interpellated LGBT citizens within a kinship narrative of familial inclusion, even as globalization impoverished many of them and right-wing groups maneuvered to strengthen homophobia, Weston warns that the law forecloses radical experiments in constructing families. Like Howell, Weston cautions us against accepting the neoliberal narrative, advocating the harder work of building crosscutting alliances that find common cause with other oppressed groups and resist the logic of the national security state.

A collection of reflections helps us locate ourselves professionally and politically, exploring the possibilities for old solidarities and new alliances. Much U.S.-based resistance after 9/11 expressed a dual concern: on the one hand, there was a sense of outrage at the intensity of the imperialist ideology that defined the post-9/11 American landscape; and, on the other, there existed a fragmentary but resilient sense of hope that we could build better, more hopeful narratives—of antijingoism and anti-imperialism, and of meaningful freedoms, spaces, and practices. The "Reflections" section offers a cross-section of concerns that have occupied progressive academics: the role of the military in civilian spaces; the right-wing assault on progressive historians and on area studies; the seductions of the new imperialisms for a range of political formations, including nationalist, feminist, and queer; and the role of intellectuals in resisting everyday forms of control and surveillance. Reading these reflections together, we see familiar tropes across disciplines and across historical periods, such as the notion that radicals have hijacked American higher education, which has long justified a silencing of academic freedom in the name of national security.

Ellen Schrecker reminds us of the antecedents of the gulf between the intellectual work of professional historians and conservative-populist understandings of the past by tracking the political links between Campus Watch, the attack on scholars of the Middle East, and prior campaigns against left-liberal historians of American and Soviet communism. As Schrecker points out, the knowledge practices of think tanks and foundations are slowly but surely becoming an institutional alternative to academic scholarship. Rogers Smith poses a challenge to the U.S. state to protect civil liberties in this brave new world of antiterrorism. Smith sees a tension between civil rights and national security and calls for the U.S. government to institute procedural safeguards lest citizens become disillusioned with the promise of American democracy. Priscilla Murolo suggests that recent disturbing trends, such as the establishment of the Northern Command, effecting federal troop deployment within national borders, are just the latest in a pattern that dates back more than two hundred years. She argues that the federal military has always participated in civilian law enforcement, primarily to police a controllable trade environment. Quincy Mills reminds us how powerful conversations can be when one challenges one community's constructions of another in the context of a militarized security state. His public conversations in black barbershops engage patrons in weekly political discussions through which he hopes to nurture the practices of participatory democracy. Jerry Atkin offers glimpses of the 2003 immigrant freedom ride that, four decades after the original Freedom Ride galvanized the civil rights movement, took immigrants on a ride across America to demand equal rights and to build solidarities across history, class, and race. As Atkin points out, there is a power "in the telling itself" of these stories that excavates alternative histories and possible futures. Poet Rachel Tzvia Back, resident of a Jewish village in western Galilee, was outraged when she received an information sheet one morning that warned the residents of her village about Arab "strangers." Reflecting on the Israeli state's manipulations of notions of native and stranger, she offers an eloquent call for solidarity and alliance among Arab and Jewish neighbors.

The range of vigorous and imaginative academic analyses that shaped post-9/11 activism is well represented by three wide-ranging interviews. Lawrence Jones interviews *Nation* correspondent and author Christian Parenti, who argues that 9/11 brought a quantitative rather than a qualitative shift in security regimes. He claims that the nature of electronic surveillance needs to be understood carefully. Parenti emphasizes the continuities in the history of surveillance, linking document databases and motion surveillance with the control of slave passes and manumission papers, early immigration protocols, and, more recently, the creation of Social Security numbers and mountains of detailed data on the poor by social service organizations. A culture of entertainment and fame now contribute, he argues, to the aestheticization of surveillance and the trivialization of its political cultural implications. Parenti regrets the difficulty of problematizing the surveillance culture and building resistance to it: "A culture where people are habituated to obedience, because they're habituated to surveillance, in a way precludes social change."

Lori Allen, Lara Deeb, and Jessica Winegar interview Rashid Khalidi, the Edward Said Professor of Arab Studies and director of the Middle East Institute at Columbia University, who explores connections among the war on terror, the persecution of scholars of the Middle East, the growth of an anti-intellectualist Huntingtonian paradigm, and faith-based approaches to politics. He argues, like Schrecker, that the state now seeks to supplant expertise with propaganda. Khalidi argues that the role of the academic in the face of propaganda is simply "doing what we do" (even while that becomes increasingly difficult), rather than descending into deceit and falsehood: "If we have any authority, it has to do with . . . trying to figure out what's going on in the world, and using that information to explain things."

Enrique Ochoa interviews Angelica Salas, the executive director of the Coalition for Humane Immigrant Rights of Los Angeles, reminding us that the scapegoating of immigrants has a long history and that the war on terror is simply a new guise for raids, deportations, and detentions—the kind of violence that has long terrorized immigrants and communities of color. Salas, translating for her immigrant family and friends from the age of four, came to see this world from the inside; she talks about how much more difficult organizing has become since the institutional shift from the Immigration and Naturalization Service to the Department of Homeland Security's Bureau of Citizenship and Immigration Services. Like Kath Weston, Salas reminds us that "we can't assume our alliances." While an essentializing position might assume that immigrant Latino issues would find natural support from Latino politicians, she argues that links to Korean immigrants, or Middle Eastern and South Asian men targeted by special registrations, as well as other connections far beyond definitions of immigrant communities, must be worked toward.

Each of the interviews raises the question of the role of the academic in continuing activist interventions in the post-9/11 world. Building on the theme of academic activism, our "Teaching Radical History" section includes a syllabus from Vivian Price. In recounting her experiences teaching about war, sex, and resistance in a women's studies class in 2003, Price reminds us of the continuing resistant possibilities in progressive teaching.

We are fortunate to include in this issue the extraordinary photographs of artist Connie Samaras, accompanied by Matias Viegner's commentary. Samaras and Viegner offer a visual/textual essay that moves from Los Angeles to Las Vegas to New York's Ground Zero, exploring the spectacular and intimate landscapes of homeland insecurities. We have also included an exceptional selection of photographic works by Kevin Noble and drawings by Conor McGrady that visually comment and expand on many of the themes explored in this issue. Like Samaras, Noble and McGrady are artist-activists working in a political climate marked by fear, surveillance, and social control. As McGrady explains in the artistic statement that accompanies his drawings, but which could also easily characterize Noble's photographs, "The aim of all the drawings is to raise questions relating to the control of space, to boundaries, and to ideas of how architecture is used as a divide to enforce social order."

Our "(Re)Views" section explores a rich cross-section of media that assess the impact of 9/11. Joseph Masco pays a visit to Washington, DC's International Spy Museum and talks to Oleg Kalugin, a former head of KGB operations in the United States—and now an American hero. Contrasting current incarnations of national security with nostalgic exhibits at the Spy Museum and former sites of Cold War–era espionage in the DC area, an account emerges of how the U.S. state is reimagining its own history in order to wage an unending global war founded on secrecy, covert action, and an unapologetically antidemocratic national security agenda. Masco's essay explores how the U.S. national security state shifted, but did not eliminate, the structural logic of the Cold War as it moved its intellectual and technological resources from countercommunist to counterterrorist agendas.

Marc Stein reviews two recent books that explore histories of the sexualization of U.S. national insecurity. As Kath Weston argued in her "Interventions" piece, it is important to understand the intertwined histories of homophobia, misogyny, xenophobia, and the role of the modern imperial state. David K. Johnson's *The Lavender Scare* recounts the history of the sexual policing of U.S. government employees; Eithne Luibhéid's *Entry Denied* addresses the history of the sexual policing of U.S. borders. Federal antisubversion campaigns from the 1940s through the 1960s targeted not only communists but also homosexuals. Anti-immigration campaigns in the nineteenth and twentieth centuries did not only focus on race, ethnicity, and class but also policed gender and sexuality. Working together, the U.S. national security state, the police, and welfare systems developed classed, gendered, racialized, and sexed visions of heteronormative citizenship. Burçak Keskin-Kozat reviews Mary Dudziak's edited collection *September 11 in History: A Watershed Moment?* The volume takes issue with the watershed metaphor, or the idea that 9/11 wrought a paradigmatic shift in U.S. politics. Instead, it pays attention to ways in which prior paradigms were reshaped in ever more antidemocratic ways. While Keskin-Kozat delivers a generally positive review, the questions she finally poses about this book's project are ones we would do well to consider seriously as we move forward: What accounts for the strong U.S.-focused analyses that characterize most of this work? Was 9/11 only an American event? What consequences has the war on terror had for the lives and families outside the United States, and what responses have emerged from other contexts?

With a few exceptions, the same critique could be made of this issue of *RHR*: Where are the subjectivities of those affected by this brutal war outside the borders of the United States? While U.S.-based resistance movements have made strong connections between repression at home and imperialism abroad, scholarly work that puts Arab, Muslim, and South Asian experiences with the war on terror in the foreground has yet to receive adequate attention and support. Compelling research topics also exist around the phenomenon of cross-national collaborations in the war on terror, such as in the strengthening of security discourses between the United States and Pakistan, or India and Israel.

As suggested by the pairing of the disasters of 9/11 and the South Asian tsunami, the story of homeland security is still emerging, and it is increasingly global in its reach and scope. Both real and imagined, domestic and transnational, homeland insecurities are being crafted through the rhetorics of national security, neoliberalism, and transnational discourses of cooperation that interpellate states, nongovernmental organizations, and the media. Although the weight of empire is formidable, we do, as most authors here suggest, have an opportunity to do, with integrity and perseverance, what we do best: understand and explain the world in a continual attempt to change it.

—Kavita Philip, Eliza Jane Reilly, and David Serlin

Notes

1. As counsel to president George W. Bush from 2001, Alberto Gonzales wrote post-9/11 memos supporting Justice Department assertions that wartime powers enabled the president to supersede antitorture laws. His most controversial memo, dubbed the "torture memo," advocated a presidential determination that the Geneva Convention Relative to the Treatment of Prisoners of War did not apply to al-Qaeda and Taliban because it "substantially reduces the threat of domestic criminal prosecution under the War Crimes Act" and argued that the war on terror "renders obsolete [the] Geneva [Convention's] strict limitations on questioning of enemy prisoners." He also supported the claim that the effects of an interrogation must include "injury such as death, organ failure, or serious impairment of body functions—in order to constitute torture." For a full text of the memos, see the Center for American Progress' Web site, www.americanprogress.org/site/pp.asp?c=biJRJ8OVF&b=246536 (accessed April 18, 2005). Calling attention, on January 10, 2005, to the third anniversary of detentions at the U.S. naval base in Cuba, Amnesty International noted: "The administration of President Bush has sanctioned detention conditions and interrogation techniques at Guantánamo Bay that violate international standards" (Amnesty International UK's Web site is available at www.amnesty.org.uk/news/press/15851.shtml, accessed April 18, 2005). On January 18, 2005, secretary of state designate Condoleezza Rice noted that "the tsunami was a wonderful opportunity" for the United States, that reaped "great dividends" on the diplomatic front. Reported by Agence France Press and reprinted in Common Dreams, at the Common Dreams News Center's Web site, www.commondreams.org/headlines05/0118–08.htm (accessed April 18, 2005; this site is no longer active).
2. Siddharth Srivastava, "Power Play in Tsunami's Wake," *Asia Times*, January 8, 2005, www.atimes.com/atimes/South_Asia/GA08Df03.html.
3. B. Raman, the retired additional secretary of the Cabinet Secretariat of India, wrote on January 4, 2005: "US naval ships and military personnel have started moving into the affected countries to organize the relief effort. It has been reported that about 1,300 U.S. Marines are likely to be deployed in Sri Lanka alone. . . . India has done well to reject US and West European offers of assistance." B. Raman, "The Tsunami: Some Security Aspects," South Asia Analysis Group, saag.org/papers13/paper1211.html (accessed April 18, 2005).

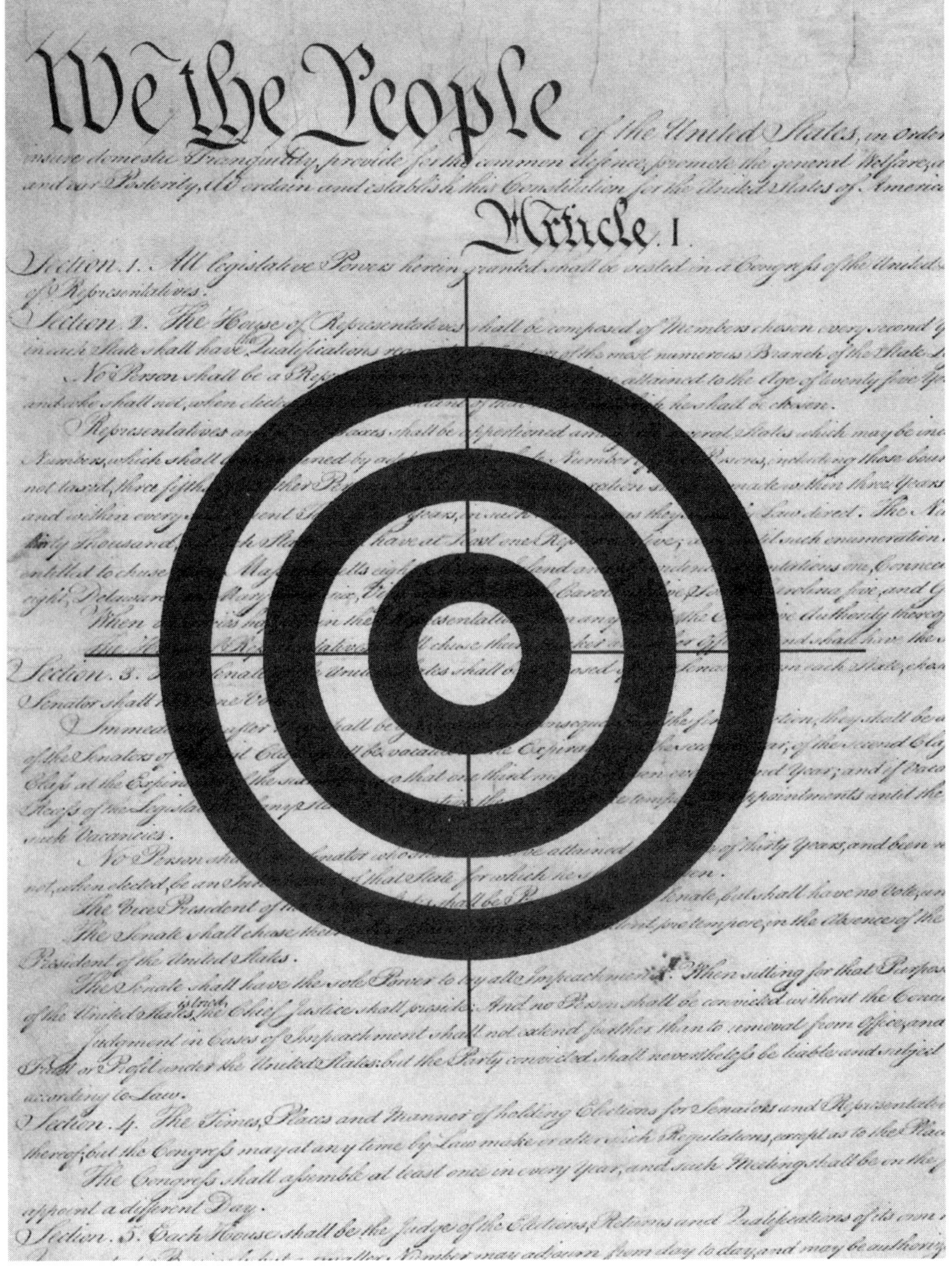

"We the People," Kevin Noble (2004)

"Spiral," Kevin Noble (1999)

On Torture: Abu Ghraib

Jasbir K. Puar

The torture of Iraqi prisoners at Abu Ghraib is neither exceptional nor singular, as many—Donald Rumsfeld and the Bush administration, the U.S. military establishment, and even good liberals—would have us believe. We need think only of the fact that so many soldiers facing prosecution for the Iraqi prisoner situation came from prison guard backgrounds, reminding us of incarceration practices within the prison industrial complex, not to mention the treatment of Palestinian civilians by Israeli army guards, or even the brutal sodomizing of Abner Louima by police officers in New York City. Neither has it been possible to normalize the incidents at Abu Ghraib as business as usual even within the torture industry. As public and governmental rage alike made clear, a line had been crossed. Why that line is so demarcated at the place of so-called sexual torture—specifically, violence that purports to mimic sexual acts closely associated with deviant sexuality or sexual excess such as sodomy and oral sex, as well as S/M practices of bondage, leashing, and hooding—and not, for example, at the slow starvation of millions due to U.S. sanctions against Iraq, the deaths of thousands of Iraqi civilians since the U.S. invasion in April 2003, or the plundering and carnage in Falluja, is indeed a spectacular question. The reaction of rage, while to some extent laudable, misses the point entirely—or, perhaps more generously, upstages a denial of culpability. The violence performed at Abu Ghraib is not an exception to, nor an extension of, imperialist occupation. Rather, it works in concert with proliferating modalities of force, an indispensable part of the so-called shock-and-awe campaign blueprinted by Israelis on the backs of Palestinian corpses. Bodily torture is but one element in a repertoire of techniques of occupation and subjugation that include assassinations of top leaders, house-to-house roundups

Radical History Review

Issue 93 (Fall 2005): 13–38

Copyright 2005 by MARHO: The Radical Historians' Organization, Inc.

often involving interrogations without interpreters, the use of tanks and bulldozers in densely populated civilian residential areas, helicopter attacks, and the trashing and forced closure of hospitals and other provisional sites.

The sexual humiliation and ritual torture of Iraqi prisoners enabled the Bush administration to forge a crucial distinction between the supposed depravity of Abu Ghraib and the "freedom" being built in Iraq. Days after the photographs from Abu Ghraib had circulated in the domestic and foreign press, President George W. Bush stated of the abused Iraqi prisoners, "Their treatment does not reflect the *nature* of the American people."[1] Not that I imagine our president to be so thoughtful or profound (though perhaps his speechwriters are), but his word choice is intriguing. Which one, exactly, of the acts perpetrated by American soldiers is inimical to the "natural" tendencies of Americans? Is it the behavior of the U.S. soldiers conducting the abuse? The ones clicking the digital shutter? Or is it the perverse behaviors forcibly enacted by the captured prisoners? What, exactly, is it that is "disgusting"—a word commonly used during the first few days of the prison scandal—about these photos? The U.S. soldiers who are grinning, stupidly waving their thumbs in the air? The depicted sex acts themselves, simulated oral and anal sex between men? Or the fact that the photos were taken at all?

Bush's efforts to refute the idea that the psychic and fantasy lives of Americans are depraved, sick, and polluted by suggesting instead that they remain naturally free from such perversions—not only would one never enjoy the infliction of such abuse but one would never even have the mindset or capacity to think of such acts—reinstantiate a liberal regime of multicultural heteronormativity intrinsic to U.S. patriotism. The state of exception surrounding these events is produced on three interrelated planes: that of the rarity of this particular form of violence (the temporality of emergency as excessive in relation to the temporality of regularity); that of the sanctity of the sexual and of the body (the site of violation as extreme in relation to the individual rights of privacy and ownership accorded to the body within liberalism); and that of the transparency of abuse (as overkill in relation to other wartime necropolitical [referring to the right to kill] violence and as defying the normative standards that guarantee the universality of the human in human rights discourses). Here is an extreme example, but one indicting on all three counts nonetheless: in May 2004, Rev. Troy Perry of the Metropolitan Community Churches (MCC) circulated a press release in reaction to incidents at Abu Ghraib in which he condemned "the use of sexuality as an instrument of torture, shame, and intimidation," arguing that the fact "that prisoners were forced to perform sexual acts that violate their religious principles and personal consciences is particularly heinous." The press release concluded by declaring that "MCC pledges to continue to work for a world in which all people are treated with dignity and equality and where sexuality is celebrated, respected and used for good."[2]

Hardly exceptional, as Veena Das argues, violence is not set apart from sociality, nor is sociality resistant to it: "Violence is actually embedded in sociality and could itself be a form of sociality."[3] Rita Maran, in her study of the application of torture in the French-Algerian war, demonstrates that torture is neither antithetical nor external to the project of liberation; rather, it is part and parcel of the necessary machinery of the civilizing mission. Torture is the underside, indeed, the accomplice of the civilizing mission. Furthermore, Maran, citing Roger Trinquier, notes that "torture is the particular bane of the terrorist,"[4] remarking that the "rational equivalency" plays out as follows: "As the terrorist resorts to extremes of violence that cause grievous individual pain, so the state replies with extremes of violence that, in turn, cause grievous individual pain."[5] Any civilizing mission is marked precisely by this paradox: the civilizing apparatus of liberation is exactly that which delimits the conditions of its possibility. Thus torture is at the very least doubly embedded in sociality: it is integral to the missionary/savior discourse of liberation and civilizational uplift, and it constitutes apposite punishment for terrorists and the bodies that resemble them. As I argue in this article, deconstructing exceptionalism and contextualizing the embeddedness of torture entails attending to discourses and affective manifestations of sexuality, race, gender, and nation that activate torture's corporeal potency.

The Production of the Muslim Body as Object of Torture

"Such dehumanization is unacceptable in any culture, but it is especially so in
the Arab world. Homosexual acts are against Islamic law and it is humiliating
for men to be naked in front of other men," Bernard Haykel, a professor of
Middle Eastern studies at New York University, explained. "Being put on top of
each other and forced to masturbate, being naked in front of each other—it's
all a form of torture," Haykel said.[6]

Those questioned for their involvement—tacit and explicit—in torture at Abu Ghraib cited both the lack-of-training and the cultural-difference argument to justify their behavior: "If we had known more about them, about their culture and their way of life" whined one soldier plaintively on the U.S. news, "we would have been better able to handle the situation." The monolith of Muslim culture constructed through this narrative (performatively reiterated by Bush's tardy apology for the Abu Ghraib atrocities, bizarrely directed at the token Muslim visiting at the time, King Abdullah of Jordan) aside, the cultural-difference line has also been used by conservative and progressive factions alike to comment on the particularly intense shame with which Muslims experience homosexual and feminizing acts. For this, the prisoners receive vast sympathy from the general public. The taboo of homosexuality within Islamic cultures figures heavily in the equation for why the torture has been so "effective"; this interpretation of sexual norms in the Middle

East—sexuality is repressed, but perversity is just bubbling beneath the surface—
forms part of a centuries-long Orientalist tradition, an Orientalist phantasmatic
that certainly informed the photographs of torture at Abu Ghraib. (A longer exposi-
tion on this subject would perhaps draw out the continuities between these photos
and the paintings of Delacroix and other photographs and art considered in Said's
Orientalism.) In "The Gray Zone," Seymour Hersh delineates how the U.S. military made particularly effective use of anthropological texts in order to determine
effective torture methods:

> The notion that Arabs are particularly vulnerable to sexual humiliation became
> a talking point among pro-war Washington conservatives in the months
> before the March 2003 invasion of Iraq. One book that was frequently cited
> was *The Arab Mind*, a study of Arab culture and psychology, first published
> in 1973, by Raphael Patai, a cultural anthropologist who taught at, among
> other universities, Columbia and Princeton, and who died in 1996. The book
> includes a twenty-five-page chapter on Arabs and sex, depicting sex as a taboo
> vested with shame and repression. "The segregation of the sexes, the veiling of
> the women . . . and all the other minute rules that govern and restrict contact
> between men and women, have the effect of making sex a prime mental
> preoccupation in the Arab world," Patai wrote. "Homosexual activity, or any
> indication of homosexual leanings, as with all other expressions of sexuality,
> is never given any publicity. These are private affairs and remain in private."
> The Patai book, an academic told me, was "the bible of the neocons on Arab
> behavior." In their discussions, he said, two themes emerged—"one, that
> Arabs only understand force and, two, that the biggest weakness of Arabs
> is shame and humiliation." The government consultant said that there may
> have been a serious goal, in the beginning, behind the sexual humiliation
> and the posed photographs. It was thought that some prisoners would do
> anything— including spying on their associates—to avoid dissemination of the
> shameful photos to family and friends. The government consultant said, "I was
> told that *the purpose of the photographs was to create an army of informants,
> people you could insert back in the population*." The idea was that they would
> be motivated by fear of exposure, and gather information about pending
> insurgency action, the consultant said. If so, it wasn't effective; the insurgency
> continued to grow.[7]

I quote these passages from Hersh's article at length to demonstrate how the intri-
cate relations between Orientalist knowledge production, sexual and bodily shame,
and espionage informed the context of Abu Ghraib. As Yoshi Furuhashi has astutely
pointed out, Patai's *The Arab Mind* actually surfaced in Edward Said's *Orientalism*
as an example of the contemporary conduits of Orientalism,[8] which also include
the knowledge formations of foreign and public policy, terrorism studies, and area

studies.[9] (We should add to Said's list the interrogation and intelligence-gathering industry: Titan Corporation and CACI International have been accused of "outsourcing torture" to Iraq and of refining, honing, and escalating torture techniques in order demonstrate proven results, thus winning lucrative U.S. government contracts and ultimately directing the illegal conduct at Abu Ghraib.)[10] Patai, who also authored *The Jewish Mind*, writes of the molestation of the male baby genitals by doting mothers, the routine beatings and stabbings of sons by fathers, the obsession with sex among Arab students (as compared to American students), and masturbation: "Whoever masturbates . . . evinces his inability to perform the active sex act, and thus exposes himself to contempt."[11] *The Arab Mind* constitutes a mainstay text in diplomatic and military circles, and the book was reissued in November 2001 with an introduction by Norvell B. De Atkine, director of Middle East Studies at the John F. Kennedy Special Warfare Center and School at Fort Bragg in North Carolina.[12] Clearly, not only is the lack of knowledge with respect to cultural difference irrelevant (for would knowing have ended or altered the use of these torture tactics?) but it is precisely through this knowledge that the U.S. military has been diplomatically instructed. It is exactly this unsophisticated notion of (Arab/Muslim/Islamic) cultural difference that military intelligence capitalized on to create what it believed to be a culturally specific and thus effective matrix of torture techniques. Furthermore, though originally the photographs at Abu Ghraib had a specific information-retrieval purpose, they clearly took on a life of their own, informed by what Slavoj Žižek recalls as the "'unknown knowns'—the disavowed beliefs, suppositions and obscene practices we pretend not to know about, even though they form the background of our public values."[13]

In another example of the transfer of information, the model of terrorism used by the State Department swerves between a pyramid structure and a network structure: the former represents a known, rational administrative format, one that is phallic and, hence, castratable; the latter represents chaotic and unpredictable alliances and forces. (The pyramid form also appears in the *Battle of Algiers* [1966, Italy/Algeria, dir. Gillo Pontecorvo], viewed for brainstorming purposes by the Pentagon in September 2003.) Perhaps it is mere coincidence that in several of the Abu Ghraib photos, Iraqi prisoners are arranged naked in human pyramids, in which they are seen to be simulating both the "passive" (feminized) prone position necessary to receive anal penetration and the "active" mounting stance of anal sex. What is significant here is not that the meaning of the pyramid has been understood and translated from one context to another, but rather that the transfer of information and its mimicry does not depend on contextual meaning to have symbolic and political effect.

Such transnational and transhistorical linkages—including unrelated but no less relevant examples drawn from Israeli surveillance and occupation measures, the behavior of the French in Algeria, and even the 2002 Gujarat pogrom in India—surge together to create the Muslim body as a particular typological object of torture.[14] During the Algerian war, for instance, one torture of Arabs "consisted of suspending them, their hands and feet tied behind their backs . . . with their head upwards. Underneath them was placed a trestle, and they were made to swing, by fist blows, in such a fashion that their sexual parts rubbed against the very sharp pointed bar of the trestle. The only comment made by the men, turning towards the soldiers present: 'I am ashamed to find myself stark naked in front of you.'"[15] This kind of torture directed at the supposed Muslim terrorist is not only subject to the normalizing knowledges of modernity that mark him (or her) both as sexually conservative, modest, and fearful of nudity (and it is interesting how this conceptualization is rendered both sympathetically and as a problem) as well as queer, animalistic, barbarian, and unable to control his (or her) urges. Thus the shadow of homosexuality is never far off. In *Brothers and Others in Arms: The Making of Love and War in Israeli Combat Units*, author Danny Kaplan, looking at the construction of hegemonic masculinity and alternative sexual identities in the Israeli military, argues that sexualization is neither tangential nor incidental to the project of conquest but, rather, is central to it: "[The] eroticization of enemy targets . . . triggers the objectification process."[16] This eroticization always inhabits the realm of perversion:

An instance where the image of mehablim [literally, "saboteurs"—a general term for terrorists, guerilla soldiers, or any Arab groups or individuals that operate against Israeli targets]—in this case, Palestinian enemy men—merges with another image of subordination, that of actual homosexual intercourse. It seems that the sexual-targeting drive of masculitary soldier could not resist such a temptation. This is one way to understand Shaul's account of one of the brutalities he experienced in the Lebanon War. During the siege on [Palestinian Liberation Organization, PLO] forces in Beirut, he was stationed next to a post where Israeli snipers observed PLO activity in city houses. Suddenly, something unusual appeared in the sniper's binoculars:

"One of them said to me, 'Come here; I want you to see something.' I looked, and I saw two mehablim, one fucking the other in the ass; it was pretty funny. Like real animals. The sniper said to me, 'And now look.' He aims, and puts a bullet right into the forehead of the one that was being fucked. Holy shit, did the other one freak out! All of a sudden his partner died on him. It was nasty. We were fucking cruel. Cruelty—but this was war. Human life didn't matter much in a case like this, because this human could pick up his gun and fire at you or your buddies at any moment."[17]

Kaplan concludes this vignette by remarking that despite the episode's brutal ending, the gender position of the active partner is what was ultimately protected:

"It is striking that even in this encounter it is the passive partner who gets the bullet in his ass, while the active partner remains unscathed."[18] This exemplifies the literalization of performativity whereby the faggot Muslim receives his torture as a faggot Muslim. Violence is naturalized as the inexorable and fitting response to non-normative sexuality. But not only is the Muslim body constructed as pathologically sexually deviant and as potentially homosexual, and thus read as a particularized object for torture, but the torture itself is constituted on the body as such: as Brian Axel has argued, "the performative act of torture produces its object."[19] The body informs the torture, but the torture also forms the body, thus suturing the double entrenchment of perversion into the circuitry of becoming. (So while it is questionable whether the acts of torture should be read as simulating "gay sex" acts, a conundrum I discuss later in this essay, they nonetheless perform an initiation, confirmation, or even conversion in the eyes of the perpetrators.) Furthermore, the faggot Muslim as torture object is splayed across five continents, prominently in Arab countries through the "transnational transfer of people" in a tactic called "renditions," the U.S. practice of holding terrorist suspects in third-country locations such as Saudi Arabia, Egypt, Morocco, Jordan, and, most recently, Syria, thereby sustaining a "worldwide constellation of detention centers" and rendering these citizenship-stripped bodies, about whom the United States can deny having any knowledge, as "ghost detainees."[20]

As the space of "illicit and dangerous sex,"[21] the Orient is the site of carefully suppressed animalistic and perverse homo- and hypersexual instincts. This paradox lies at the heart of Orientalist notions of sexuality that are reanimated through the transnational production of the Muslim terrorist as torture object. Underneath the veils of repression sizzles an indecency waiting to be unleashed. The most recent invocation of the perverse, deranged terrorist and his naturalized proclivities is found in this testimony by one of the prisoner guards at Abu Ghraib: "I saw two naked detainees, one masturbating to another kneeling with its mouth open. . . . I saw [Staff Sergeant] Frederick walking towards me, and he said, 'Look what these animals do when you leave them alone for two seconds.' I heard PFC England shout out, 'He's getting hard.'"[22] Note how the Iraqi prisoner, the one in fact kneeling in the submissive position, is referred to as "it." Contrary to the public debate recently generated on torture, which foregrounds the site of detention as an exemplary holding cell that teems with aggression, this behavior is hardly relegated to prisons, as an especially unnerving moment in Michael Moore's documentary *Fahrenheit 9/11* (United States, 2004) reveals. A group of U.S. soldiers are shown loading a dead Iraqi, presumably recently killed by them, covered with a white sheet onto a stretcher. Someone yells, "Look, Ali Baba's dick is still hard!" while others follow in disharmonized chorus, "You touched it, eeewww you touched it." Even in death, the muscular virility of the Muslim man cannot be laid to rest in some humane manner;

not only the Orientalist fantasy transcends death but the corpse's sexuality does, too—it rises from death, as it were. Death here becomes the scene of the ultimate unleashing of repression.

Wither Feminism

Despite the recurring display of revulsion for attributes associated with the feminine, the United States apparently still regards itself as the arbiter of feminist civilized standards. Writing in the *Gully*, a Lesbian, Gay, Bisexual, Transgender, Queer (LGBTQ) political news forum, Kelly Cogswell worries about homophobic and misogynist backlash, as if the United States had not already demonstrated its capacity to perpetuate their most extreme forms. "Images of men forced to wear women's underwear over their faces and engage in homosexual activity," Cogswell writes, "will also inflame misogyny and homophobia. Forget about Bush's anti–gay marriage stand in the United States. By tolerating this behavior in Iraq and elsewhere, his administration has made homosexuality abhorrent world-wide. The image of an American woman holding a prisoner's leash will be used as a potent argument against modernization and the emancipation of women."[23] Barbara Ehrenreich expresses similar concerns: "It was [Lynndie] England we saw with a naked Iraqi man on a leash. If you were doing PR for Al Qaeda, you couldn't have staged a better picture to galvanize misogynist Islamic fundamentalists around the world. Here, in these photos from Abu Ghraib, you have everything that the Islamic fundamentalists believe characterizes Western culture, all nicely arranged in one hideous image—imperial arrogance, sexual depravity, and gender equality."[24] It is surely wishful thinking to assume that U.S. guards, female or not, having forced prisoners to wear women's underwear, among other derogatory "feminizing" acts, would then be perceived by the non-West as a product of the West's gender equality. In fact, misogyny is perhaps most easily understood between captor and captive. Former prisoner Dhia al-Shweiri notes: "We are men. It's OK if they beat me. Beatings don't hurt us; it's just a blow. But no one would want [his] manhood to be shattered. They wanted us to feel as though we were women, the way women feel, and this is the worst insult, to feel like a woman."[25]

The picture of Lynndie England, dubbed "Lynndie the Leasher," leading a naked Iraqi on a leash (also being referred to as "pussy whipping") has now become a surface on which fundamentalism and modernization, apparently dialectically opposed, can wage war. One could argue that this image is about both the victories of liberal feminists, who claim that women should have equal opportunities within the military, and the failures of liberal feminists to adequately theorize power and gender beyond male-female dichotomies that situate women as less prone toward violence and as morally superior to men. Writes Zillah Eisenstein: "When I first saw the pictures of the torture at Abu Ghraib I felt destroyed. Simply heart-broken. I thought 'we' are the fanatics, the extremists; not them. By the next day as I continued to think about Abu Ghraib I wondered how there could be so many women involved in the atrocities?"[26] Why is this kind of affective response to the failures of Euro-American feminisms, feminisms neither able to theorize gender and violence nor able to account for racism within their ranks, appropriate to vent at this particular moment, especially when it works to center the Euro-American feminist as victim, her feminism having fallen apart? Another example: brimming with disappointment, Ehrenreich pontificates: "Secretly, I hoped that the presence of women would over time change the military, making it more respectful of other people and cultures, more capable of genuine peacekeeping. . . . A certain kind of feminism, or perhaps I should say a certain kind of feminist naiveté, died in Abu Ghraib."[27] Similarly, Patrick Moore articulates the death of a parallel yearning, as if gay male sexuality had never chanced on its own misogyny: "The idea that female soldiers are as capable as men of such atrocities is disorienting for gay men who tend to think of women as natural allies."[28] Nostalgically mourning the loss of the liberal feminist subject, this emotive convergence of white liberal feminists and white gay men unwittingly reorganizes the Abu Ghraib tragedy around their desires.

But the sight of England with her leash also hints at the sexual perversions associated with S/M, something not mentioned at all in the popular press. The comparisons now proffered between the depraved, cigarette-toting, dark-haired, pregnant-and-unmarried, racialized England (now implicated in making a pornographic film with another guard) and the heroic girl next door Jessica Lynch, informed by their working class background similarities but little else, speak also of the need to explain away the solid presence of female Abu Ghraib torturers as an aberration.[29] While the presence of women torturers should at least initially give us pause, it is a mistake to exceptionalize these women as well; the pleasure and power derived from their positions and actions cannot be written off as some kind of false consciousness or duping by the military, nor as what Eisenstein refers to as "white female decoys."[30] If, as Veena Das argues, violence is a form of sociality, then women are not only the recipients of violence but are actually connected to and benefit from forms of violence in a myriad of ways, regardless of whether they are the perpetrators of violence themselves.[31] That is to say, the economy of violence produces a circulation whereby no woman is strictly an insider or an outsider. Rather, women can be subjects of violence but also agents of it, whether it is produced on their behalf or perpetuated directly by them.[32] In this regard, three points are at stake: How do we begin to understand the literal presence of women, and possibly of gay men and/or lesbians, in both the tortured and the torturer populations? How should one explore the analytic of gender positionings and sexual differentiation beyond masculine and feminine? And finally, what do we make of the participation of U.S. guards in the photos, behind the cameras, and in front of computer screens, and of ourselves, as curious and disturbed onlookers?

Gay Sex?

Male homosexuality is deeply shameful in Arab culture; to force naked Arab
prisoners to simulate gay sex, taking pictures you could threaten to show, would
be far worse than beating them.
— Gregg Easterbrook, "Whatever It Takes"

Deploying a parallel homophobic logic, conservative and progressive pundits alike
have claimed that the illegal status of homosexual acts in Islamic law demarcates
sexual torture in relation to the violence at Abu Ghraib as especially humiliating.
Republican senator Susan Collins of Maine, for example, was skeptical that the U.S.
guards elected to inflict "bizarre sexual humiliations that were specifically designed
to be particularly offensive to Muslim men,"[33] while sexual humiliation became
constituted as "a particular outrage in Arab culture."[34] But from a purely military
security perspective, however, the torture was very effective and, therefore, completely justified.[35] Bush's administration claims that the torture in the forms it took
was particularly necessary and efficacious for interrogation because of the ban of
homosexuality in Islam. That "nakedness, homosexuality and control by a woman
might be particularly humiliating in Arab culture" has been a sentiment echoed by
many.[36]

Madhi Bray, executive director of the Muslim American Society, a nonprofit Islamic organization located in Virginia, says that Islam calls for "modesty in
dress"—"being seen naked is a tremendous taboo and a tremendous humiliation in
Muslim culture"—and that homosexuality, considered a sin, "only becomes a problem when it is flaunted, affecting the entire society."[37] Faisal Alam, founder and
director of the international Muslim LGBTIQ organization, Al-Fatiha, states that
"sexual humiliation is perhaps the worst form of torture for any Muslim." The press
release from Al-Fatiha continues: "Islam places a high emphasis on modesty and
sexual privacy. Iraq, much like the rest of the Arab world, places great importance
on notions of masculinity. Forcing men to masturbate in front of each other and to
mock same-sex acts or homosexual sex, is perverse and sadistic, in the eyes of many
Muslims." In another interview, Alam maintains that the torture is an "affront to
their masculinity."[38] In a very different context, Patrick Moore, author of *Beyond
Shame: Reclaiming the Abandoned History of Radical Gay Sex*, opines:

Because "gay" implies an identity and a culture, in addition to describing a
sexual act, it is difficult for a gay man in the West to completely understand
the level of disgrace endured by the Iraqi prisoners. But in the Arab world,
the humiliating techniques now on display are particularly effective because
of Islam's troubled relationship with homosexuality. This is not to say that
sex between men does not occur in Islamic society—the shame lies in the
gay identity rather than the act itself. As long as a man does not accept the
supposedly female (passive) role in sex with another man, there is no shame

in the behavior. Reports indicate that the prisoners were not only physically abused but also accused of actually being homosexuals, which is a far greater degradation to them.[39]

The Foucauldian act to identity telos spun out by Moore delineates the West as the space of identity, while the Arab world is relegated, apparently because of "Islam's troubled relationship to homosexuality," to the backwards realm of acts. The fiction of identity—not that identity is a fiction but, rather, that identity based on the concept of progressive coherence is—effaces men who have sex with men (MSM), such as those men on the down low (DL), so that the presence of gay- and lesbian-identified Muslims in the Arab world becomes inconceivable. But let us follow Moore's logic to its conclusion: since the acts are allegedly far more morally neutral for Muslims than they are for men in the West, being forced to do them in the obvious absence of an avowed identity should actually not prove so humiliating. Given the lack of any evidence that being called a homosexual is much more degrading than being tortured, Moore's rationalization reads as an Orientalist projection.

I want to underscore the complex dance of positionality that Muslim and Arab groups, such as the Muslim American Society and especially Al-Fatiha, must perform in these times, during which a defense through the lens of culture easily becomes co-opted into racist agendas. Gay conservative Andrew Sullivan, for example, capitalizes on the cultural-difference discourse, nearly claiming that the repressive culture of Muslim extremism is responsible for the potency of the torture, in effect blaming the victims. Islamophobia has become central to the subconscious of homonormativity.[40] In general, however, either deliberately or unconsciously, these accounts by LGBTQ progressives tend to uphold versions of normative masculinity—that is, being in the feminized passive role is naturalized as bad. This comes, perhaps, as an unintended side effect of the focus on homosexuality, which tends to reproduce misogyny in the effort to disrupt homophobia. Furthermore, in both conservative and progressive interpretations of the abuse at Abu Ghraib, we see the trenchant replay of what Michel Foucault termed the "repressive hypothesis": the notion that a lack of discussion or openness regarding sexuality reflects a repressive, censorship-driven apparatus of deflated sexual desire. (Indeed, considering the centrality of Foucault's *History of Sexuality* to the field of queer studies, it is somewhat baffling that some queer theorists have accepted at face value the discourse of Islamic sexual repression. That is not to imply that Foucault's work should be transparently applied to other cultural and historical contexts; rather, his insights deserve evaluation as a methodological hypothesis about discourse.) In Said's *Orientalism*, the illicit sex found in the Orient was sought out in order to liberate the Occident from its own performance of the repressive hypothesis. By contrast, in the case of Abu Ghraib, it is the repression of the Arab prisoners that is highlighted in order to efface the rampant hypersexual excesses of the U.S. prison guards.

This gives us a clear view of the performative privileges of what Foucault described as the "speaker's benefit": those who are able to articulate sexual knowledge appear to be freed, through the act of speech, from the space of repression. Given the unbridled homophobia demonstrated by the U.S. guards, it is indeed ironic, yet somehow also predictable, that in these accounts the United States nonetheless emerges as more tolerant of homosexuality (and less tainted by misogyny and fundamentalism) than the repressed, modest, nudity-shy Middle East. As Sara Ahmed notes, this hierarchy between open (liberal democracy) and closed (fundamentalist) systems obscures "how the constitution of open cultures involves the projection of what is closed onto others, and hence the concealment of what is closed and contained 'at home.'"[41]

What, then, is closed, and what is contained at home? In the gay press, the Abu Ghraib photos are continuously hailed as "evidence of rampant homophobia in the armed forces."[42] Aaron Belkin, for example, decries them as symbolic representations of "the most base, paranoid, or extreme elements of military homophobia,"[43] while Paula Ettelbrick, the executive director of the International Gay and Lesbian Human Rights Commission, maintains that "this sort of humiliation" becomes sanctioned as a result of the "don't ask, don't tell" policies implemented during the Clinton administration,[44] as if therein lies the brunt of the military establishment's cruelty, and not in the murders of thousands of civilian Iraqis. Humiliation becomes sanctioned because the military functions as a reserve for what is otherwise seen as socially unacceptable violence, sanitizing all aggression in its wake under the guise of national security. In these accounts, the homophobia of the U.S. military is pounced on, with scarce mention of the linked processes of racism and sexism. Patrick Moore, who admits that the photos "evoked in me a deep sense of shame as a gay man," in particular sets up the (white) gay male subject as the paradigmatic victim of the assaulting images, stating that "for closeted gay men and lesbians serving in the military, it must evoke deep shame."[45] But how prudent is it to foreclose unequivocally on the chance that there might be gay men or lesbians among the perpetrators of the torture at Abu Ghraib? To foreground homophobia over other vectors of shame is to miss that these photos are not merely representative of the homophobia of the military; they are also racist, misogynist, and imperialist. To favor the gay male spectator—here, presumably white—is to negate the multiple and intersectional viewers implicated by these images and, oddly, is also to privilege as victim the coherently formed white gay male sexuality in the West (and those closeted in the military) over acts-qualified bodies, not to mention the bodies of the tortured Iraqi prisoners themselves. Moore complicates this audience vectorship in another interview: "I felt the government had found a way to use sexuality as a tool of humiliation both for Arab men and for gay men here." The drawing together of (presumably straight) Arab men and (presumably white) gay men is yet another moment where the sexuality of Arab men is qualified as repressed and oriented toward premodern acts, the precursor to the identity-solidified space of "here."[46]

Further complicating this issue is the long-standing debate among LGBTQ communities about whether or not, and to what degree, the war on terror is in fact a gay issue. Mubarak Dahir, writing for the *New York Blade*, intervenes by arguing that the depiction of "gay sex" is central to the images: "The claim by some members of the gay and lesbian community that the invasion and occupation of Iraq is not a 'gay' issue crumbled last week when photos emerged of hooded, naked Iraqi captives at the Abu Ghraib prison near Baghdad being forced to simulate gay sex acts as a form of abuse and humiliation." And later: "As a gay man and as a person of Arab descent, I felt a double sting from those pictures. Looking at the blurred-out photos of hooded Iraqi prisoners being forced to perform simulations of gay oral sex on one another, I had to wonder what it was that my fellow Americans in uniform who were directing the scene found the most despicable: the fact that the men were performing gay sex, or that they were Arabs."[47]

Given the resounding silence of national and mainstream LGBTQ organizations, currently obsessed by the gay marriage agenda, the political import of Dahir's response on the war on terror in general, and on Abu Ghraib in particular, should not be dismissed. In fact, on May 28, 2004, in the midst of furious debate regarding sexual torture, the Human Rights Commission, the Servicemembers Legal Defense Network, and the American Veterans for Equal Rights jointly released "Fighting for Freedom," a press statement highlighting brave and patriotic LGBT soldiers in the military and announcing the release of *Documenting Courage*, a book on LGBT veterans. Driven by "stories [that] go unmentioned," both the statement and the book privilege the testimonial voice of authenticity. In the absence of any commentary about or position on Abu Ghraib, this might be read as a defensive move to restore honor to U.S. soldiers while reminding the public of the struggles LGBT soldiers face in the military, thus shifting the focus of victimhood away from Iraqi prisoners.[48]

Declaring that the torturous acts are simulations of "gay sex," however, invites other consequences, such as the response from Egyptian protestors in Cairo calling for the removal of the "homosexual American executioners,"[49] which reaffirmed that homosexuality is an unwanted import from the West. Such an accusation feeds nicely into Bush's anti–gay marriage agenda. Right-wing organizations such as Concerned Women for America have similarly condemned the torture as a direct result of homosexual cultural depravity. But are, in fact, the acts depicted in these photographs specifically and only referential of gay sex (and here, *gay* means "sex between men")? Is it the case that, as Patrick Moore argues, homosexuality has been deployed as the "ultimate tool of degradation," and as a "military tactic [that] reaches new levels of perversity"?[50] Certainly this rendition evades a conversation about what exactly constitutes the distinction between gay sex and straight sex, and also presumes some static normativity about gender roles as well. Saying that the simulated and actual sex scenes replicate gay sex is an easy way for all—mass media, Orientalist anthropologists, the military establishment, and even LGBTQ groups and organizations—to disavow the "perverse" procilivities inherent in heterosexual sex and the gender normativity immanent in some kinds of gay sex. (It should be noted that Amnesty International is among the few organizations that did not make reference to homosexuality, homosexual acts, or same-sex sexuality in its press release condemning the torture.)[51] These readings reproduce what Gayle Rubin calls the "erotophobic fallacy of misplaced scale." "Sexual acts," Rubin argues, "are burdened with an excess of significance";[52] this excess produces a misreading and perhaps even an exaggeration of the scale by which the significance of sex is a measure done that continually privileges humiliation (mental, psychic, cultural, social) over physical pain. In fact, it may well be that these responses by Westerners reveal what we might deem as the worst form of torture—that is, sexual torture and humiliation rather than extreme pain—more than any comprehension of the experiences of those tortured. The simulated sex acts must be thought of in terms of gendered roles rather than through a universalizing notion of sexual orientation. But why talk about sex at all? Was anyone having sex in these photos? (One could argue that in the photos, the torturers were turned on, erotically charged, and looked as one might when having sex.)

The focus on gay sex also preempts a serious dialogue about rape—the rape of Iraqi male prisoners, but also, more significantly, the rape of female Iraqi prisoners, the occurrence of which appears neither news- nor photograph-worthy. Indeed there has been a complete underreporting of the rapes of Afghani and Iraqi women both inside and outside of detention centers. As Trishala Deb and Rafael Mutis point out:

Women's rights advocates in the U.S. have made the distinction between sex and rape for a long time. By defining rape and sexual assault as an act of violence and not sex, we are placing the validity in the voice of the assaulted, and accepting their experience as central to the truth of what happened. . . . Again, what we understand by centering the perspective of the assaulted people is that there was no sex happening regardless of the act.[53]

Major General Anthony Taguba's report notes that among the some 1,800 digital photos, there are unreleased pictures of females being raped and women forced at gunpoint to bare their breasts, as well as videotape of female detainees forced to strip and rumors of impregnated rape victims.[54] Why are there comparatively few photos of women, and why have they not been released? Is it because the administration found the photos of women even more appalling? Or has the wartime rape of women become so unspectacular, so endemic to military occupation, as to render its impact moot? How, ultimately, do we begin to theorize the connections and disjunctures between male and female tortured bodies, and between masculinities and femininities?

Although feminist postcolonial studies have typically theorized women as the bearers of cultural continuity, tradition, and national lineage, in the case of terrorism the line of transmission seems always to revert to the male body. The locus of reproductive capacity is, momentarily, expanded from the female body to the male body. This expansion does not mark a shift away from women as the victims of rape and pawns between men during wartime. But the principal yet overriding emphasis on women's rape as a weapon of war can displace the importance of castrating the reproductive capacities of men. It is precisely masculinity, the masculinity of the terrorist, that threatens to reproduce itself. Writing about the genital and anal torture of Sikh men in Punjab, Brian Keith Axel argues that torture produces sexual differentiation not as male and female, but rather as what he calls national-normative sexuality and antinational sexuality:

> Torture in Punjab is a practice of repeated and violent circumscription that produces not only sexed bodies, but also a form of sexual differentiation. . . . National-normative sexuality provides the sanctioned heterosexual means for reproducing the nation's community, whereas antinational sexuality interrupts and threatens that community. Torture casts national-normative sexuality as a fundamental modality of citizen production in relation to an antinational sexuality that postulates sex as a "cause" of not only sexual experience but also of subversive behavior and extraterritorial desire ("now you can't be married, you can't produce any more terrorists" . . .). The form of punishment corresponds to the putative source of transgression: sexual reproduction, identified as a property of masculine agency within the male body.[55]

It is important to emphasize, of course, that there exist multiple national-normative sexualities and, likewise, multiple antinational sexualities, as well as entities that make such distinctions fuzzy. It is equally important to recognize that, for all of its insights, Axel's formulation cannot be entirely and neatly transposed onto the Abu Ghraib situation, as Punjabi Sikh detainees form part of both the Indian nation and the religious fundamentalist terrorists that threaten to undo that nation. In other words, for Punjabi detainees, torture works to finalize expulsion from the nation-state. What I find most compelling is Axel's formulation of national differentiation as sexual differentiation. However, I would argue that it is precisely feminizing (and thus not the categories of male and female, as Axel notes), and the consequent insistence of mutually exclusive positions of masculine and feminine, that strips the tortured male body of its national-normative sexuality. This feminizing divests the male body of its virility and, thus, compromises its power not only to penetrate and reproduce its own nation ("our" women) but to contaminate the Other's nation ("their" women) as well. Furthermore, the perverted sex of the terrorist is a priori cast outside the domain of normative national sexualities: that is to say, "the form of punishment," that is, meddling with penis and anus, "corresponds to the putative source of transgression," not only because of the desire to truncate the terrorist's capacity to sexually reproduce but also because of the (homo)sexual deviancy always already attached to the terrorist body. These two attributes, the fertility of the terrorist (in the case of Muslim men, always interpreted through polygamy) and the (homo)sexual perversions of the terrorist, are rendered with extra potency given that the terrorist is also a priori constituted as stateless, thus lacking national legitimization or national boundaries. In the political imagination, the terrorist serves as the monstrous excess of the nation-state.

Torture, to compound Axel's formulation, works not merely to disaggregate national from antinational sexualities—for those distinctions (the stateless monster-terrorist-fag) are already in play—but also, in accordance with nationalist fantasies, to reorder gender and, in the process, to corroborate implicit racial hierarchies. The force of feminizing, then, lies not only in the stripping away of masculinity, the "faggotizing" of the male body, or in the robbing of the feminine of its symbolic and reproductive centrality to national-normative sexualities. Rather, it is the fortification of the unenforceable boundaries between masculine and feminine, the rescripting of multiple and fluid gender performatives into petrified sites of masculine and feminine, the regendering of multiple genders into the oppressive binary scripts of masculine and feminine, and the interplay of it all within and through racial, imperial, and economic matrices of power. That is the real force of torture.

Axel writes that "torture casts national-normative sexuality as a fundamental modality of citizen production." But we can also flip these terms around: national-normative sexuality casts torture as a fundamental modality of citizen production. One could scramble this further still: citizen production casts national-normative sexuality as a fundamental modality of torture. And so on. The point is that in the metonymic chain linking torture, citizen production, and national-normative sexualities, torture surfaces as an integral part of a patriotic mandate to separate off the normative-national genders and sexualities from the antinational ones. As Joanna Bourke elaborates: "It is hard to avoid the conclusion that, for some of these Americans, creating a spectacle of suffering was part of a bonding ritual. Group identity as victors in an increasingly brutalized Iraq is being cemented: this is an enactment of comradeship between men and women who are set apart from civilian society back home by acts of violence. Their cruel, often carnivalesque rites constituted what Mikhail Bakhtin called 'authorised transgression.'"[56] The bonding ritual, culminating in an authorized transgression, is authorized not from above but between actors seeking to redirect animosity toward each other. In this sense, the bonding ritual of the carnival of torture—discussing it, producing it, getting turned on by it, recording it, disseminating the proof of it, gossiping about it—is the ultimate performance of patriotism. Here all internal tensions (the working class, "white trash" Lynndie, the African American sergeant, and so forth) are focused outwards, toward the hapless bodies in detention, so that a united front of American multicultural heteronormativity can be not only performed but, more important, affectively felt.

Technologies of Simulacrum

As voyeurs, conductors, dictators, and dominatrices, those orchestrating these acts, several of whom appear erotically riled in the Abu Ghraib photographs, are part of, not external to, the torture scenes themselves, sometimes even explicitly so. For example, convicted Specialist Jeremy Sivits, who took many of the photographs, testified that "Staff Sergeant Frederick would take the hand of the detainee and put it on the detainee's penis, and make the detainee's hand go back and forth, as if masturbating. He did this to about three of the detainees before one of them did it right."[57] This is hardly indicative of a detached, objective, distanced observer behind the camera, positioned only to capture the events via the click of the shutter. Reports of U.S. soldiers sodomizing Iraqi prisoners with chemical light sticks and broomsticks, and inserting fingers into prisoners' anuses, also fully implicate the U.S. guards and raise specters of interracial and intercultural sex. Less overtly, the separation of participant from voyeur becomes complicated by the pleasures of taking, posing for, and looking at pictures, especially as the use of cameras and videos as an intermediary tool of sexual pleasure inform varied practices (such as watching porn) between partners of all genders in all kinds of sex.

Many of the photos, originally cropped for damage-controlled consumption, are now revealing the presence of multiple spectators, bystanders, and participants. In the case of the widely disseminated and discussed photo of a hooded man made to stand on a box with wires attached like appendages to his arms, legs, and penis— a classic torture pose known predominantly to interrogation experts as the "Vietnam"—the full photograph reveals a U.S. soldier on the periphery, nonchalantly examining his digital camera. The Vietnam, explains Darius Rejali, derives from an amalgamation of the forced-standing techniques used by torturers in the British army (where it was known as the "crucifixion") and in the French army (where it was known as the "Silo") during the early twentieth century, and among those employed by U.S. police, Stalin's People's Commissariat for Internal Affairs (NKVD), the Gestapo in 1930s Germany, and South African and Brazilian police (who added the electrical supplement) in the 1970s.[58] In fact it is indeed this image, deemed by many to be the least sexually explicit and therefore less horrifying to view, that has been most reproduced around the world, its simulacra taking shape on billboards and murals and parodied through antiwar protest attire worn on the streets of Tehran, London, and New York and through fake iPod adverts done in hot pink and lime green. Performance artists, such as the New York City–based Hieronymous

Bang, use the American flag as a substitute for the black cloak. In Salah Edine Sallat's mural in Baghdad, the hooded prisoner on the box is paired with a shrouded Statue of Liberty holding up an electric gadget connected to the circuit breaker that threatens to electrocute them both.

To what can we attribute the now iconic status of this image? For starters, it is the only released photo to date that exposes almost no skin—only the legs and shins of the victim can be seen, preserving an anonymity of body that simultaneously incriminates the viewer less than some of the more pornography-like images and also radiates a distressing mystique. The hoods hark back to the white hoods of the Ku Klux Klan, but they also resemble veils. Indeed, the cloaking of nearly the entire body references another iconic image, that of the oppressed Muslim woman in her *burkha*, covered head to toe in black and in need of rescue. It is plausible, then, that this image of the Vietnam resonates as yet another missionary project in the making. It is the male counterpart to the Muslim-woman-in-*burkha* that liberal feminist organizations (like the National Organization for Women [NOW] and the Feminist Majority Fund), the Bush administration (especially Laura), and the conservative right-wingers who tout rhetorics of democracy and freedom love so well. There is another, more sinister reason why the photo echoes so acutely. Called "stealth torture that leaves no marks," the Vietnam is traceless, leaving the bodies of its victims undifferentiated from unscathed ones. As happens with cloaking, the body remains both untroubled and unseen, and "if it were not for the photographs, no one would know that it had been practiced."[59] The only evidence of the Vietnam comes in the form of the photograph. Its mass multiplication and mutations may speak to the need to document and inscribe into history and our optic memories that which otherwise leaves no visual proof. As Susan Sontag proclaimed, "the pictures will not go away."[60] Noting that "soldiers trained in stealth torture take these techniques back into civilian life as policemen and private security personnel," Rejali claims that the Vietnam is found throughout U.S. policing and imprisonment tactics,[61] another likely rationale for the intense reverberations of this photo.[62]

Claiming that "theatricality leads us to the crux of the matter," Slavoj Žižek argues that the pictures "suggest a theatrical staging, a kind of tableau vivant, which brings to mind American performance art, [Antonin Artaud's] 'theatre of cruelty,' the photos of [Robert] Mapplethorpe or the unnerving scenes in David Lynch's films."[63] The facile comparison of the evidence of brutal wartime violence to spaces of artistic production might put the reader on edge. Indeed, the Right is concocting similar conjectures: in the *American Spectator* George Neumayr writes, "Had Robert Mapplethorpe snapped the photos at Abu Ghraib, the Senate might have given him a government grant."[64] But the point, as I understand it, is not so much that these photos resemble works of art, but more that the pictures look indeed as if the U.S. guards felt like they were on stage, hamming it up for the proud parents nervously biting their lips in the audience. The affect of these photos is one of exaggerated theatricality; jovial and void of any somberness, it invites the viewer to come on and jump on stage as well. As Richard Goldstein points out, "One reason why these photos are such a sensation is that they are stimulating."[65]

Even more trenchant is the collapsing, in the Abu Ghraib photographs, of production and consumption, image and viewer, onto the same vectors, the same planes. There is no inside or outside here; rather, there are only movement, circulation, contingent temporalities, momentary associations and disassociations. One could argue that if there is anything exceptional about these photographs, it is not the actual violence itself but, rather, the capturing of this violence on film, the photographic qualities of which are reminiscent of vacation snapshots, mementos of a good time, victory at last, or even the trophy won at summer camp. Unlike images of the purportedly unavoidable collateral deaths of war, these photos divulge an irrefutable intentionality. We have proof, finally, of what we suspect might be true, not only in Iraq, Afghanistan, and Guantánamo Bay but in our very own detention centers and prisons.[66] These photos not only depict the techniques of torture; they also depict how both process (the photographing) and product (the pictures) constitute shaming technologies and function as a vital part of the humiliating, dehumanizing torture itself: the giddy process of documentation, the visual evidence of corporeal shame, the keen ecstatic eye of the voyeur, the haunting of surveillance, the dissemination of the images on the Internet, the speed of transmission—aphrodisiacs unto themselves, "swapped from computer to computer throughout the 320th Battalion,"[67] perpetuating humiliation ad nauseam.

Thus these images not only represent specific acts and allude to the procedural vectors of ever-expansive audiences but they also reproduce and multiply the power dynamics that made these acts possible in the first place. As Sontag famously asserted in the *New York Times Magazine*, "the photographs are us." Comparing the images to the photographs of black lynching victims, taken between 1880 and 1930, that depicted "Americans grinning beneath the naked mutilated body of a black man or woman hanging behind them from a tree," Sontag argues that a shift has occurred in the utility of photos. Once collectible items for albums and display in frames at home, photos are now "less objects to be saved than messages to be disseminated, circulated."[68] Obviously, technology has been a major catalyst in this transition from trophy to propaganda: the digital camera, sexy and absorbing software to assist in manipulating and perfecting images, and Internet sites that serve as virtual photo albums seem ubiquitous. It is a transition from stillness to proliferation, from singularity to fertility, like ejecting dandelion spores into the wind. More important, mobility, motility, speed, and performance function as primary erotic and addictive charges of modernity: clicking the send button marks the ultimate release of productivity and consumption; dissemination is the ultimate form of territorial coverage and conquest, one more layering of the sexual matrix. While the visages and corpses of American casualties in Iraq remain protected material—even the faces of deceased soldiers were considered unseemly in a television program honoring them—Iraqi bodies are accessible to all, available for comment, ridicule, shaming, scrutiny. If we were to honor Žižek's invocation of the theatricality of the Abu Ghraib photos, they would indeed qualify as what Cynthia Mahmood, writing about the display of tortured Sikh bodies in Sikh living rooms and *gurdwaras* (temples), calls "massacre art": "In their very gruesomeness, [they] assert themselves in a room; they are impossible to ignore, and intrude in conversation, meditation, and everyday activities. Their potency derives only in part from their blood; it also derives from their unwillingness to be masked, covered, or distorted."[69] Abu Ghraib's massacre art disrupts the caricature of the placid, Pleasantville-like aura of the American family room, the streaming images from the television set mesmerizing us into silence. They are potent not only for their naked honesty but also because they are the evidence of how much power we can actually, and stunningly, command over others. Unlike the reports of prison abuses compiled by Amnesty International, the Red Cross, and other humanitarian organizations, as well as the testimonies of hundreds of detainees and released prisoners, all easily ignored by the Bush administration, the photos and their circulatory modalities double as representation and information, as the representation of information, and the only information taken seriously and validated by corporate media sources.

Calling the torture an initiation, for those subjected, into the "obscene underside" of "American culture," Žižek avers: "Similar photos appear at regular intervals in the U.S. press after some scandal explodes at an Army base or high school campus, when such rituals went overboard."[70] Again, Žižek's limp analogizing effectively evacuates the political context of forced occupation and imperial expansion within which specificity and singularity must be retained. While the comparison to fraternity house hazing (I assume that Žižek means college campus rather than high school) or army pranks is not without merit—for certainly proliferating modalities of violence need and feed off one another—there is an easy disregard of the forced, nonconsensual, systemic, repetitive, and intentional order of violence hardly attributable to "rituals" that have gone "overboard." (We might also ask, in another essay perhaps, whether these acts of torture really reveal anything intrinsic or particular to "American culture," or whether they can instead be linked more broadly to war cultures and states of occupation at large.) Again, this slippery analysis is fodder for the conservative Right: Rush Limbaugh sanctioned a similar statement by a caller on his radio show by responding thusly:

Exactly my point. This is no different than what happens at [Yale University's secret fraternity] Skull and Bones initiation, and we're going to ruin people's lives over it, and we're going to hamper our military effort, and then we are going to really hammer them because they had a good time. . . . You know, these people are being fired at every day. I'm talking about people having a good time, these people. You ever heard of emotional release?[71]

Later, Limbaugh opined: "This is something you can see onstage at Lincoln Center from an N.E.A. grant, maybe on 'Sex and the City.'" Once more, the references to theatricality and staging draw together liberal and right-wing commentators, efface the power dynamics of occupation, war, and empire, and ultimately leave a distasteful sense of smugness or satisfaction—from Limbaugh—at having neatly trivialized something into next to nothing.

Conclusion

We now know more about Lindsey [*sic*] England and Charles Grainer (two of the accused military police) than we do about any of the people who were the prisoners in those pictures. We know very little of their own narratives, identities, or their perspective on the U.S. occupation. Given that, we have to remember that their own histories, genders, and sexualities are as complex as our own. The U.S. media has managed to once again make them subjects of a war that are marginal in their own story. And the question remains: for which culture would these acts of sexual assault, rape, and murder be less appalling?
— Trishala Deb and Rafael Mutis, "Smoke and Mirrors"

What emerges, then, from most interpretations in terms of narratives regarding homosexuality and its intersections with the violence at Abu Ghraib can be summed up thusly:

1. The sexual acts simulated are all specifically and only gay sex acts.

2. Homosexuality is taboo in Islamic cultures, making such acts the worst forms of humiliation for Muslims to endure. This insinuates that these forms of torture would be easier for other, less homophobic populations to tolerate (this appears preferable to a more expansive notion of bodily torture as violating for all) and discounts the presence of gay-identified Muslims in Arab societies, what Joseph Massad terms the "gay Arab international," while also obscuring those engaging in same-sex erotics even if not within the rubric of identity.[72]

3. American tolerance for homosexuality is elevated in relation to that of Islamic societies, as symptomatized by the unspecific, ahistorical, and generalized commentary on the taboo of homosexuality for Muslims.

4. The enactment of "gay sex" (consolidated around the act of sodomy) constitutes the worst form of torture, sexual or otherwise.

5. Iraqi prisoners, having endured the humiliation of gay sex, are subjects worthy of sympathy—an affective, emotive response more readily available than a sustained political critique of the U.S. occupation in Afghanistan and Iraq.

6. The question of race and how it plays out in these scenarios is effaced via the fixation on sexuality; gender likewise becomes effaced when the acts are said to originate from a homophobic military culture, instead of from a misogynist one.

7. Sexuality is isolated within the purview of the individual, as opposed to situated within an integrated diagrammatic vector of power.

8. The language favoring gay sex acts over torture once again casts the shadows of perversity outside, onto sexual and racial others, rather than contextualizing the processes of normalizing bodily torture.

9. Technologies of representation work to occlude the lines of connectivity (sexual, bodily, in terms of proximity, in terms of positionality) between captors and their prisoners.

Despite the widespread absence of sexuality in public debates about 9/11 and the war on terror, the "prisoner sexual abuse scandal," as it is now termed, vividly reveals that sexuality constitutes a central and crucial component of American patriotism. The use of sexuality—in this case, to physically punish and humiliate—is not tangential, unusual, or reflective of a state of exception. Of course, not all of the torture was sexual, and thus the odd acts—threatening dogs, for example—need to retain their idiosyncrasy. Nudity itself is not automatically and innately sexual; it must be made to signify erotics. Therefore the terms *scandal*, *sexual*, and *abuse* need to be semiotically decharged. This does not mean that this treatment is not sexual or abusive, but rather that such abuse is a commonplace occurrence in detention. Thus, following what Achille Mbembe describes as "necropolitics," in which systems of domination become increasingly "anatomical, tactile, and sensorial," we can say simply that sexualized bodily abuse is a normalized facet of prisoner life, and that the sexual is always already inscribed in necropolitics.[73] Furthermore, as postcolonial scholars such as Ann Stoler and Anne McClintock have aptly demonstrated, the sexual is part and parcel of the histories of colonial domination and empire building—conquest is innately corporeal. That is to say, this scandal, rather than being cast as exceptional, needs to be contextualized within a range of practices and discourses, perhaps ones less obvious than the Iraqi prisoner abuse, that pivotally links sexuality to the deployment and expansion of U.S. nationalism, patriotism, and, increasingly, empire. Despite the actions of those in charge of Abu Ghraib, perversity is still withheld for the body of the queer Muslim terrorist, insistently deferred to the outside. This outside is rapidly, with precision and intensity, congealing into the population of what Giorgio Agamben has called *homo sacer,* "those who can be killed with impunity since, in the eyes of the law, their lives no longer count."[74] Žižek considers this space "between the two deaths"—dead in the eyes of history but still alive for the countdown—as the fate of the prisoners at Abu Ghraib, the ghost detainees.[75] As with the systemic failure of U.S. military operations at the prison, not the fault of a handful of individuals but rather due to the entire assemblage of necropolitics, sexuality itself is not the barometer of exception, a situation out of control, an unimaginable reality. Rather, it constitutes a systemic, intrinsic, and pivotal module of power relations.

Notes

With thanks to Barbara Balliet, Patricia Clough, Inderpal Grewal, Nancy Hewitt, Louisa Schein, and David Serlin for their feedback on earlier drafts of this essay.

1. "Bush Voices 'Disgust' at Abuse of Iraqi Prisoners," *New York Times*, May 1, 2004; emphasis mine.
2. "A Pastoral Statement from Metropolitan Community Churches Statement by the Reverend Dr. Troy D. Perry," *Office of the Moderator*, May 2004, Metropolitical Community Churches home page, www.MCCchurch.org.
3. Thomas Cushman, "A Conversation with Veena Das on Religion and Violence, Suffering and Language," *Hedgehog Review* (Spring 2004), www.virginia.edu/iasc/hedgehog.html.
4. Roger Trinquier, *Modern Warfare* (New York: Praeger, 1964), xv.
5. Rita Maran, *Torture: The Role of Ideology in the French-Algerian War* (New York: Praeger, 1989), 82.
6. Seymour M. Hersh, "Torture at Abu Ghraib," *New Yorker*, May 10, 2004, 43.
7. Seymour M. Hersh, "The Gray Zone," *New Yorker*, May 24, 2004, 42; emphasis mine.
8. See Edward Said, *Orientalism* (New York: Vintage, 1979), 308–9, 311, 312, 349.
9. Yoshi Furuhashi, "Orientalist Torture," *Critical Montages*, May 20, 2004, montages. blogspot.com/2004/05/orientalist-torture.html.
10. The Center for Constitutional Rights has filed a lawsuit against private firms participating in the so-called torture conspiracy. See www.ccr-ny.org/v2/reports/report.asp?ObjID=c Bct36Qkps&Content=401. Trishala Deb and Rafael Mutis elaborate on the implications of outsourcing torture: "CACI is a corporation that generates over $930 million dollars in profit a year, 65% of its budget coming from government contracts. The question remains how these private contractors are accountable to US and international laws, not to mention the international public. Given the restrictions on access to information about the functioning of the war machine since the establishment of the USA PATRIOT Act and Department of Homeland Security, we have even less access to information and accountability regarding some of the most important and dangerous aspects of this permanent war. The relevance of this information is that it exposes one of the most insidious sides to this story the cycle of government expenditures on private contractors as enforcement agents in this war, and profits made by US corporations which are awarded those contracts. In this way the prison industrial complex is at once exposed and expanded; not only were severe crimes against humanity committed but at least one corporation has profited from those crimes. For those corporations who are being paid to provide interrogators and intelligence, war crimes are not a consideration, just a consequence." Trishala Deb and Rafael Mutis, "Smoke and Mirrors: Abu Ghraib and the Myth of Liberation," *Colorlife*, May 2004: 2.

11. Patai quoted in Emram Qureshi, "Misreading *The Arab Mind*," *Boston Globe*, May 30, 2004.

12. Ibid.

13. Žižek points out that it is not the known knowns, the known unknowns, or the unknown knowns that matter most here, but rather the unconscious, the knowledge that does not know itself. Slavoj Žižek, "What Rumsfeld Doesn't Know That He Knows about Abu Ghraib," *In These Times*, May 21, 2004, www.inthesetimes.com/site/main/article/what_rumsfeld_doesnt_know_that_he_knows_about_abu_ghraib/ (accessed May 30, 2004).

14. During February and March of 2002, over two thousand Muslims were killed and tens of thousands more were displaced from their homes in rioting by Hindus; the police were complicit with this violence, and the Hindu nationalist BJP is accused of premeditated orchestration of the pogroms. In regards to Muslim masculinity, the International Initiative for Justice writes: "Muslim men, in the Hindu Right discourse, are not seen as 'men' at all: they are either 'oversexed' to the extent of being bestial (they can satisfy four wives!) or they are effeminate and not masculine enough to satisfy their women. . . . [As] a symbol of the 'sexual superiority' the emasculated Hindu man must recover by raping and defiling Muslim women . . . there have been calls to Hindu men to join gyms and develop muscular bodies to counter the 'animal' attraction of the over-sexualized Muslim man. Of course, when Hindu men commit rape and assault their actions are not seen as bestial or animal-like but are considered signs of valor. Simultaneously, there is an attempt to show that Muslim men are not real men, but rather homosexuals or *hijras* (eunuchs)—considered synonymous and undesirable and are therefore unable to satisfy their women. As a VHP (Vishva Hindu Parishad) leaflet called *Jihad* (holy war) boasts:
    We have untied the penises which were tied till now
    Without castor oil in the arse we have made them cry
    Those who call religious war, violence, are all fuckers
    We have widened the tight vaginas of the bibis (women) . . .
    Wake up Hindus there are still Miyas (Muslim men) left alive around you
    Learn from Panvad village where their mother was fucked
    She was fucked standing while she kept shouting
    She enjoyed the uncircumcised penis."
Initiative for Justice, "Threatened Existence: A Feminist Analysis of the Genocide in Gujarat," December 19, 2002, 29–30, www.onlinevolunteers.org/gujarat/reports/iijg (accessed May 12, 2005).

15. Alistair Horne, *A Savage War of Peace* (London: Pan Books, 2002), 197–98.

16. Danny Kaplan, *Brothers and Others in Arms: The Making of Love and War in Israeli Combat Units* (New York: Harrington Park, 2002), 193.

17. Ibid., 193–94.

18. Ibid., 194.

19. Brian Keith Axel, "The Diasporic Imaginary," *Public Culture* 14 (2002): 420.

20. Dana Priest and Joe Stephens, "Secret World of U.S. Interrogation: Long History of Tactics in Overseas Prisons Is Coming to Light," *Washington Post*, May 11, 2004.

21. Said, *Orientalism*, 167.

22. Quoted in Hersh, "Torture at Abu Ghraib," 44.

23. Kelly Cogswell, "Torture and America: So This Is Us," *Gully*, May 13, 2004, www.thegully.com/essays/iraq/040513_torture_abu_ghraib.html.

24. Barbara Ehrenreich, "Prison Abuse: Feminism's Assumptions Upended," *Los Angeles Times*, May 16, 2004.

25. Quoted in Joe Crea, "Gay Sex Used to Humiliate Iraqis," *Washington Blade*, May 7, 2004.
26. Zillah Eisenstein, "Sexual Humiliation, Gender Confusion, and the Horrors at Abu Ghraib," Women's International League for Peace and Freedom, www.peacewomen.org/news/Iraq/June04/abughraib.html (accessed August 3, 2004).
27. Ehrenreich, "Prison Abuse."
28. Patrick Moore, "Gay Sexuality Shouldn't Become a Torture Device," *Newsday*, May 7, 2004.
29. "Most Americans believe the abuses were isolated instances, not common occurrences. They believe the perpetrators were acting on their own, not following orders. And by an overwhelming margin, the public sees the abuses as a violation of military policy, rogue crimes, not a policy. As a result, most Americans blame the soldiers who carried out the abuses and the officers supervising them, not Secretary Rumsfeld or President Bush." Reportage on polling results by William Schneider on Judy Woodruff's *Inside Politics*, CNN, May 10, 2004.
30. Eisenstein, "Sexual Humiliation, Gender Confusion, and the Horrors at Abu Ghraib."
31. Cushman, "A Conversation with Veena Das."
32. Das says: "A very good example of this is the idea that a woman gets higher status in society by being the hero's mother; or there are other examples in which a woman's honor may depend on the son's or husband's valiant performance in the world. There is a very subtle exchange of maleness and femaleness in these kinds of formations. So that, yes, you can get forms of sociality where violence is an exclusively male form of sociality from which women might be excluded or other forms of sociality in which she is incorporated within male forms of violence." Ibid.
33. Quoted in Esther Shrader and Elizabeth Shogren, "Officials Clash on Roles at Prison," *Los Angeles Times*, May 12, 2004.
34. David Stout, "Rumsfeld Offers an Apology," *New York Times*, May 8, 2004.
35. Al-Fatiha Foundation, "Al-Fatiha Condemns Sexual Humiliation of Iraqi Detainees, Calls for National LGBT Groups to Denounce Homophobic Human Rights Abuses," press release, May 10, 2004. Founder and director Faisal Alam opines: "As queer Muslims, we must condemn in the most forceful terms, the blatant acts of homophobia and sexual torture displayed by the US military. These symbolic acts of abuse represent the worst form of torture."
36. Michael A. Fuoco and Cindi Lash, "A Long Way from Obscurity," *Pittsburg Post-Gazette*, May 14, 2004.
37. Quoted in Crea, "Gay Sex."
38. Ibid.
39. Moore, "Gay Sexuality Shouldn't Become a Torture Device."
40. Andrew Sullivan, "Daily Dish," May 4, 2004, www.andrewsullivan.com.
41. Sara Ahmed, "Affective Economies," *Social Text*, no. 79 (2004): 134.
42. For example, see Joe Crea, "Gay Sex."
43. Quoted in ibid.
44. Quoted in Duncan Osborne, "Pentagon Uses Gay Sex as Tool of Humiliation," *Gay City News*, May 13, 2004, www.gaycitynews.com/5_13/pentagonusesgayssex.html. See also the press release from *Outrage!*, outrage.nabumedia.com/pressrelease.asp?ID=190 (accessed May 12, 2005).
45. Quoted in Osborne, "Pentagon."
46. Ibid.
47. Mubarak Dahir, "Gay Sex and Prison Torture in Iraq War," *New York Blade*, May 14, 2004.

48. Human Rights Campaign, www.hrc.org/Template.cfm?Section=Home&. CONTENTID =19413&TEMPLATE=/ContentManagement/ContentDisplay.cfm (this site is no longer active).

49. Patrick Letellier, "Egyptians Protest 'Gay' Abuse in Iraq; LGBT Groups Hit Out at 'Torture' Confusion," May 18, 2004, uk.gay.com/headlines/6271.

50. Moore, "Gay Sexuality."

51. Amnesty International, www.amnestyusa.org/iraq/iraq_index.html.

52. Gayle Rubin, "Thinking Sex: Notes for a Radical Theory of the Politics of Sexuality," in *Pleasure and Danger: Exploring Female Sexuality*, ed. Carol Vance (Boston: Routledge and Kegan Paul, 1984), 278–79.

53. Deb and Mutis, "Smoke and Mirrors."

54. Luke Harding, "The Other Prisoners," *Guardian*, May 20, 2004.

55. Axel, "The Diasporic Imaginary."

56. Joanna Bourke, "The Pornography of Pain," *Guardian*, May 9, 2004.

57. Quoted in Kate Zernike, "Accused Soldier Paints Scene of Eager Mayhem at Iraqi Prison," *New York Times*, May 14, 2004.

58. Darius Rejali, "A Long-Standing Trick of the Torturer's Art," *Seattle Times*, May 14, 2004.

59. Ibid.

60. Susan Sontag, "Regarding the Torture of Others," *New York Times Magazine*, May 23, 2004.

61. Rejali, "A Long-Standing Trick of the Torturer's Art."

62. Additionally, the Prison Litigation Reform Act of 1996 delimits what are deemed to be frivolous lawsuits, ensuring that prisoners must demonstrate signs of physical injury prior to claims of mental or emotional injury.

63. Žižek, "What Rumsfeld Doesn't Know."

64. George Neumayr, "The Abu Ghraib Collection," *American Spectator*, May 12, 2004.

65. Richard Goldstein, "Stuff Happens! Don't Call It Torture: It's Just a Broomstick up the Butt," *Village Voice*, May 5, 2004.

66. See, for example, Bob Herbert, "America's Abu Ghraibs," *New York Times*, May 31, 2004; and Nina Bernstein, "Two Men Charge Abuse in Arrests After 9/11 Terror Attack," *New York Times*, May 3, 2004.

67. Seymour M. Hersh, "Chain of Command," *New Yorker*, May 17, 2004, 39.

68. Sontag, "Regarding the Torture of Others," 28.

69. Cynthia Keppley Mahmood, *Fighting for Faith and Nation: Dialogues with Sikh Militants* (Philadelphia: University of Pennsylvania Press, 1996), 189.

70. Slavoj Žižek, "What Rumsfeld Doesn't Know That He Knows about Abu Ghraib," *In These Times*, May 21, 2004, www.inthesetimes.com/site/main/article/what_rumsfeld_doesnt_know_that_he_knows_about_abu_ghraib/ (accessed May 30, 2004).

71. Quoted in Sontag, "Regarding the Torture of Others," 28.

72. Joseph Massad, "Re-Orienting Desire: The Gay International and the Arab World," *Public Culture* 14 (2002): 361–85. Accessed online May 12, 2005, at www.newschool.edu/gf/publicculture/backissues/pc37/massad.html.

73. Achille Mbembe, "Necropolitics," *Public Culture* 15(2003): 34.

74. See Giorgio Agamben, *Homo Sacer: Sovereign Power and Bare Life* (Stanford, CA: Stanford University Press, 1998).

75. Žižek, "What Rumsfeld Doesn't Know."

Homeland Security, Militarism, and the Future of Latinos and Latinas in the United States

Jorge Mariscal

My purpose in this essay is to begin to outline the many ways recent developments in the United States affect one sector of the North American working class: the diverse Latino communities in the United States. Let me begin by reminding the reader that what I will be calling the "Latino community in the United States" is in fact a patchwork of heterogeneous groups with distinct identities, histories, and cultural traditions. Latinos are everywhere, no longer limited to the Southwest or New York City; there are Puerto Ricans and Dominicans on the East Coast, Salvadorans and Guatemalans on the West Coast, distinct Cuban communities in Florida and New Jersey, Mexicans along the southern border, and others in cities ranging from Raleigh, North Carolina, to Seattle, Washington.

More striking, perhaps, is the fact that more than half (51 percent) of all adult Latinos in the United States are first-generation immigrants (compare this to just a decade ago, when only 22 percent were foreign born and 78 percent were born in the United States).[1] An additional 20 percent are the U.S.-born children of those immigrants. Third- and fourth-generation Latinos (a generic term for all groups of Latin American descent) increasingly make for a minority, now constituting only roughly 25 percent of the Latino population. Of those 25 percent, only a fraction identify themselves as Chicano or Chicana, a fact that has cultural and political implications, as we shall see. Put another way, because the first generation is gener-

Radical History Review

Issue 93 (Fall 2005): 39–52

Copyright 2005 by MARHO: The Radical Historians' Organization, Inc.

ally preoccupied with economic survival, the sector of the Latino community committed to progressive change is almost always quite small and generally finds itself in the position of having to renew itself by drawing on continuous pools of new immigrants and their children.

The Latino subgroups with the longest history in the United States are, of course, Mexicans and Mexican Americans (a traditional term for ethnic Mexicans in the United States). Most of the West and the entire Southwest was once indigenous and later Mexican land conquered and occupied in a preemptive first strike (inspired by Providence itself according to the war planners) during the U.S. war against Mexico from 1846 to 1848. Since the time of the Treaty of Guadalupe Hidalgo, then, peoples of Mexican origin have made up an important part of the labor force that has contributed to the building of the United States.

Today even the Mexican group is crisscrossed by class, gender, and generational lines. The well-heeled Mexicans shopping at upscale malls in San Diego and El Paso have little in common with the migrant workers picking strawberries, packing poultry, or making expensive garments in sweatshops. The newly arrived immigrant is unfamiliar with the worldview of the second- or third-generation Chicano raised in the United States and schooled in the ways of U.S. popular culture, consumer capitalism, and race-based discrimination. Increasingly, the third- or fourth-generation Chicano or Chicana (a term signifying more than anything else adherence to a militant political stance, whether a regressive ethnic nationalism or a liberal to left progressive agenda) has little in common with the third- or fourth-generation Hispanic (a generic term related to *Latino* but with conservative political overtones) who sees nothing wrong with the status quo and merely wants to grab his or her piece of the American dream.

The 2000 census teaches us several interesting facts about the way Latinos are contributing to the changing face of the United States. First, more legal immigrants arrived in the decade of the 1990s than in any previous decade in U.S. history. The economic boom (or more accurately, the stock market bubble) of the Clinton years attracted large numbers of people from around the world, many of whom would discover only later that household incomes did not rise during the same period.[2] Second, the majority of these immigrants came from Latin America (approximately 51 percent; with 26 percent coming from Asian countries). And finally, Mexican immigrants, who made up the bulk of the Latin American group, are now spread out across the fifty states.

Let us take the example of the Old South or, as Trent Lott used to say, the Old Confederacy. According to the 2000 census, the increase in Latinos between 1990 and 2000 in North Carolina was 393.9 percent, 337 percent in Arkansas, 299.6 percent in Georgia, and 278.2 percent in Tennessee.[3] In Senator Lott's home state of Mississippi, the number of Latinos more than doubled during the 1990s. Whereas in 1990 only nineteen of the state's eighty-two counties had two hundred or more Latino residents, by 2000 more than half, or forty-eight, counties had two hundred or more Latinos. These numbers are probably too low given the census bureau's track record of undercounting Latinos.

For the most part, the new arrivals are workers searching for a better life; they do not have much education, and they are deeply attracted by the promise of economic opportunity north of the border. According to a recent survey, 83 percent of Mexican immigrants polled were confident that their children would be better off financially than they are.[4] The overwhelming majority of these immigrants will work hard, their children will become educated, and they will make significant contributions to our society. But the same study projects that by 2025, when Latino workers will make up 25 percent of the labor force, they will be less educated and earn significantly less than their "white" counterparts.

Because these new immigrants have yet to experience the disconnect between the promise of democracy and equality in this country and what the United States has actually delivered to working people of color over time, many of them will adopt an uncritical view of current events. If local and national authorities proclaim that war against Iraq is necessary and the mass media reinforces that message, many new arrivals will accept it as fact. Some will even join the armed forces or encourage their children to do so. What better way, they ask, to show our gratitude to the United States? What better way to get an education (assuming the recruiters' promises are true)? What better way to prove our patriotism and show that we, too, are real Americans?

Code Brown: Homeland Security and U.S. Latinos

What many of these immigrants do not know is that while they were arriving in this country or busy working to provide their children with greater opportunities, across the nation—but especially in California—a severe backlash against Spanish-speaking immigrants occurred that gave us Propositions 187 (elimination of social services for undocumented workers), 209 (elimination of affirmative action programs), and 227 (elimination of bilingual classes). Led by former governor Pete Wilson, conservatives who promoted these initiatives now claim that they were not anti-Mexican but only anti–illegal immigration. Yet from a Spanish-speaker's point of view, the attacks on bilingualism, for example, could only be interpreted as an overt act of hostility. This reaction was even more pronounced in the case of Proposition 187, which sought to eliminate the social safety net for immigrant families. By the end of the decade, the hate speech directed at Mexicans and immigrants in general reached critical mass, suggesting that the new century would be no less racist for Latino working people than the previous 150 years had been.[5]

In the summer of 2003, the wave of anti-immigrant rhetoric in California interfaced effortlessly with the conservative push to recall Democrat governor Gray Davis and efforts to undermine the candidacy of Lieutenant Governor Cruz Bustamante. Republican candidates Tom McClintock and Arnold Schwarzenegger teamed up with right-wing radio hosts and journalists to attack Bustamante for his brief affiliation while in college with the Chicano student organization Movimiento Estudiantil Chicano de Aztlán (MEChA). The Fox network (Bill O'Reilly, Sean Hannity, and others) joined the fray and piled on current MEChA members because of the organization's slogans adopted thirty years ago. The Schwarzenegger campaign took a less visible but no less aggressive stance towards MEChA in an effort to discredit Bustamante. According to an editorial in the San Diego *North County Times*, Schwarzenegger operatives contacted newspapers throughout the state, urging them to write anti-MEChA op-eds.[6]

In the attacks on MEChA, the full force of anti-Mexican bigotry and demographic fear come together. Among other things, *mechistas* were accused of being racist, separatist, a fifth column for the Mexican takeover of the Southwest, and somehow related to the KKK, Nazism, and communism. After publishing a defense of MEChA on the Web and in local newspapers, I was inundated with the fiery if confused discourse of the Far Right. Self-declared Hispanics or American Indians launched some of the more heated missives. Here is just one representative sample: "Why are you so full of hate and envy? I read your rhetoric and almost had to stop when I read 'white privilege.' As a fellow member of the population with 'Hispanic' roots, I am embarrassed by you and your, to borrow your style, LEFT-WING myopic hate group."[7] A noxious mixture of Cold War residue, nineteenth-century racist tropes, and hysteria about changes in the state's population, the attacks reveal a desire for a return to the pre–civil rights era, a time when colored people knew their place. As one letter writer warned me: "Your damm right there is some Anti-Mexican Racism going on. I am sick and tired of supporting illegal 'visitors' to my country. I am tired of my government kissing V. Foxes ass. You sit in your tax-supported ivory tower and accuse people like me of being racist while supporting the most racist la Rasa bunch of MEChas. If Arnold wins I have a feeling there is going to be a whole lot of shaking going on."[8]

After September 11, 2001, the number of Immigration and Naturalization Service (INS) abuses skyrocketed, primarily against Muslim and Arab people, but also against Latinos. In January 2003, INS Operation Game Day swept up hundreds of innocent workers in San Diego during preparations for the Super Bowl, many of them Mexican. In Missouri, where significant numbers of migrants from the Mexican state of Oaxaca now reside and work in the tourist industry, the INS, now known as the U.S. Citizenship and Immigration Services (USCIS), conducted roundups of innocent workers who had organized their community to start a Centro Latino where they hoped to discuss the possibility of forming a union.

The most infamous case involving a Latino and the war on terror is that of Jose Padilla, arrested in May 2002 and since held as an enemy combatant without access to legal counsel even though he is a U.S. citizen. The use of a 1909 Supreme Court decision on a union-busting case in Colorado to justify Padilla's detention is one of the less-well-known abuses of the Ashcroft Justice Department. Despite the ruling by the Second U.S. Circuit Court of Appeals in December of 2003 that the Bush administration lacked the authority to hold Padilla as an enemy combatant, the federal government appealed to the Supreme Court in order to retain custody. As of April 2005 Padilla was still in prison.[7]

Fueled by the fear of domestic terrorism and the rapidly shifting demographics I have described, an upgraded and potent form of white supremacy has taken shape over the past ten years. Writing for the Internet newspaper *World Net Daily* (where one finds "fair and balanced journalism" by conservative bomb-thrower Ann Coulter, for example) two months after September 11, Joseph Farah described radical Chicanos as "activists who see themselves as 'America's Palestinians' [who] are gearing up a movement to carve out of the southwestern United States. . . . The leaders of this movement are meeting continuously with extremists from the Islamic world."[8]

Recently, the raw material for this kind of Internet conspiracy fantasy found its way into the mainstream through the writings of Samuel Huntington and Patrick J. Buchanan. Huntington is best known for his so-called clash of civilizations analysis of the war on terror in which he not so cleverly disguises his concerns about domestic demographic changes within a Eurocentric caricature of Islam. In a preview of his new book *Who We Are: The Challenges to America's National Identity* (2004), he wrote:

The persistent inflow of Hispanic immigrants threatens to divide the United States into two peoples, two cultures, and two languages. Unlike past immigrant groups, Mexicans and other Latinos have not assimilated into mainstream U.S. culture, forming instead their own political and linguistic enclaves—from Los Angeles to Miami—and rejecting the Anglo-Protestant values that built the American dream. The United States ignores this challenge at its peril. . . . A plausible reaction to the demographic changes underway in the United States could be the rise of an anti-Hispanic, anti-black, and anti-immigrant movement composed largely of white, working- and middle-class males, protesting their job losses to immigrants and foreign countries, the perversion of their culture, and the displacement of their language. Such a movement can be labeled "white nativism."[9]

Several years earlier, it was conservative millionaire Ron Unz (the principal sponsor of Proposition 227) who had articulated a rough draft of the same complaint. Unz's analysis of the Los Angeles riots of 1992 cut directly to the white fear that animates an ever-expanding body of anti-Mexican writings. Unz wrote in the wake of the riots: "Suddenly, the happy multicultural California so beloved of local boosters had been unmasked as a harsh, dangerous, Third World dystopia. . . . the large numbers of Latinos arrested (and summarily deported) for looting caused whites to cast a newly wary eye on gardeners and nannies who just weeks earlier had seemed so pleasant and reliable. If multicultural Los Angeles had exploded into sudden chaos, what security could whites expect as a minority in an increasingly nonwhite California?"[10] Huntington's privileged location at Harvard University lends credibility to Unz's otherwise irrational claim and gives an Ivy League imprimatur to the latest form of neoracism.

In his best-selling *The Death of the West: How Dying Populations and Immigrant Invasions Imperil Our Country and Civilization*, Buchanan had dredged up conservative rhetoric from the 1960s to convince readers that MEChA posed a serious threat to national security. The organization, warned Buchanan, is "a Chicano version of the white-supremacist Aryan Nation . . . and is unabashedly racist and anti-American."[11] Quoting freely from the founding fathers but most approvingly from Teddy Roosevelt about the dangers of ethnic identities, Buchanan claimed: "With their own radio and TV stations, newspapers, films, and magazines, the Mexican Americans are creating an Hispanic culture separate and apart from America's larger culture. They are becoming a nation within a nation."[12] This same phrase—"nation within a nation"—to describe Latinos in the United States has been appropriated recently by more mainstream pundits like George Will.[13]

In San Diego, columnist Joseph Perkins, in a February 2002 op-ed, explained that the fear inspired by immigrants from Middle Eastern countries was related to the University of California's recent decision to grant in-state tuition to academically qualified undocumented students. Perkins wrote: "The president is talking about getting tough on immigrants in this country who overstay their visas. Meanwhile, California is getting soft on undocumented immigrants by offering them in-state college tuition rates. So much for securing the homeland against foreign infiltrators."[14] In Perkins's distorted thinking, the U.S.-educated children of Mexican workers morph into al-Qaeda sleeper cells determined to infiltrate America in order to destroy it. The racist logic that underlies such an argument seems self-evident. (The fact that Perkins is African American could make this a topic for another essay.)

Life Chances for Native-Born Latinos

Mexican American or Chicano and Chicana youth, that is, the children of families who have been in the United States for decades, if not centuries, continue to have a relatively limited range of life chances. Today, over one-third of all Latinos are under eighteen years of age. With a high school dropout rate around 40 percent and high rates of incarceration (in California, Latinos make up 36 percent of the prison population, but only 32 percent of the state population), many Latino youth see little hope for the future. For first-generation immigrants from Mexico, the situation appears desperate with a 61 percent high school dropout rate.[15]

The cost of a college education in California is rising sharply. Increased fees and artificially stringent admissions criteria will keep the number of Chicanos and Chicanas in the University of California system frozen below 10 percent for the foreseeable future. Recent changes in the California state college system will make access more difficult. Even at community colleges, where most Latino college students are found, there are proposals to double the fees. Among college graduates who attended graduate and professional programs in 2000, Latinos made up only 1.9 percent (compared to 3 percent African American, 3.8 percent whites, and 8.8 percent Asian). Of all doctorates earned in the United States in 2000, Latinos made up only 4 percent, and their numbers are declining.[16]

Across the board, economic conditions for Latinos have deteriorated since the 2000 election. Although Latinos have a high rate of participation in the labor force, over 11 percent of Latino workers live in poverty. About 7 percent of Latinos with full-time jobs were still living below the poverty line in 2001 (compared to 4.4 percent for African Americans and 1.7 percent for whites). The Economic Policy Institute recently noted that according to a variety of measurements, the United States currently finds itself in "the longest continuous stretch of job decline since 1944–46."[17] Since March 2001, the economy has lost 3 million private-sector jobs. What is clear from the data is that Latinos are working extremely hard but remain trapped in minimum-wage jobs. Many hold multiple jobs at low wages. Whatever economic "recovery" took place in early 2004 was limited to the financial sectors and did little to ameliorate conditions for working-class families.

Health care figures for Latinos are also striking. According to the National Center for Health Statistics, in the year 2001 only 49.7 percent of Latinos under sixty-five years of age had private health insurance, compared with 80 percent for Caucasians and 61.9 percent for African Americans. The Bush administration has opposed the Immigrant Children's Health Improvement Act that would expand federal health care in order to cover legal immigrant children and pregnant women. Ironically, green card holders are more than welcome to serve in the U.S. military, and many of the early casualties during the invasion of Iraq in March of 2003 were among the some forty thousand noncitizen soldiers who serve in today's ranks.

Latino Youth as the Pentagon's Target

Military recruiters, well aware that the economic situation for Latino youth is relatively bleak, have targeted this group as one of the primary objectives for their efforts in coming years. The recent "Strategic Partnership Plan for 2002–2007," written by the U.S. Army Recruiting Command, noted: "The Hispanic population is the fastest growing demographic in the United States and is projected to become 25 percent of the U.S. population by the year 2025." The plan goes on to state that "priority areas [for recruitment] are designated primarily as the cross section of weak labor opportunities and college-age population as determined by both [the] general and Hispanic population."[18] Not surprisingly, the top two recruiting battalion areas according to this document are Los Angeles and San Antonio.

The targeting of Latino youth for military recruitment was initiated by former secretary of the Army Louis Caldera (now president of the University of New Mexico) who once declared that "Hispanics have a natural inclination for military service" and that the Army could "provide the best education in the world."[19] The very notion that Hispanics constitute an ethnicity-based military caste would seem to belong to an earlier century, yet it is sustained by comments such as these made by Caldera and reiterated by the Mexican American commander in Iraq, Lieutenant General Ricardo Sanchez, who told *Hispanic* magazine: "When I became a soldier the ethics and the value system of the military profession fit almost perfectly with my own heritage. It made it very easy for me to adapt to the military value system."[20]

Given the overall economic context and the military's interest in Latino youth, we can be sure that the enlisted ranks will fill up with increasing numbers of Latinos. In 2002, a deputy assistant secretary of the Army told a San Antonio newspaper: "We know Hispanics represent approximately 22 percent of our recruiting market."[21] That means Latino youth are being targeted at about twice their rate in the general population. Nowhere is this more apparent than in Puerto Rico, where high unemployment rates facilitate military recruitment efforts. In 2002, the Army initiated the Foreign Language Recruitment Initiative designed to give recent immigrants crash courses in English, and President Bush signed Executive Order No. 13269 on July 3, 2002, in order to expedite the naturalization process for noncitizens in the U.S. military.

A careful reading of 2001 Department of Defense statistics reveals that of Latinos in all the service branches, 17.7 percent had "Infantry, Gun Crews, and Seamanship" occupations. Of those Latinos in the Army, 24.7 percent occupied such jobs, while 19.7 percent of Latinos in the Marine Corps had such jobs.[22] It is important to remember that in 2001 Latinos made up only 12.5 percent of the general population.

Visit any high school with a large Latino population, and you will find JROTC units, Army-sponsored computer games, and an overabundance of recruiters, often more numerous than career counselors. Although the Pentagon periodically claims that JROTC is not being used for recruiting purposes, the Army's own literature states that "Junior ROTC is a strategic initiative that allows us to present the idea of the military lifestyle to High School students. By mission JROTC attempts to create better citizens, but also emphasizes military values, and presents the idea of the military lifestyle."[23]

Two additional Pentagon-sponsored programs merit our attention. The increased presence of military recruitment programs in the nation's public schools is a little-known consequence of the Department of Defense's plans for maintaining manpower levels in coming decades. By targeting teachers, counselors, coaches, principals, and other school personnel known in Pentagon jargon as "influencers," each branch of the armed forces seeks to create a pool of unofficial recruiters who are in daily contact with young people and who can guide them toward military careers.

The centerpiece of these stealth-recruiting strategies is the Educator Workshop Program (EWP). According to the Marine Corps EWP Web site, teachers and others who participate in the program "get a basic understanding of the Marine Corps and are better equipped to advise their students about our career opportunities. These workshops dispel the myths about recruit training and the Marine Corps' mission by providing you with a first hand experience that is truly a once-in-a-lifetime opportunity."[24]

After being bused to boot camp, EWP participants are given a week-long glimpse of military life in a kind of ersatz shock and awe designed to instill enhanced respect in recruits. Experiences range from the initial harangues delivered by drill instructors to visits to weapons training activities, as well as the final act of the so-called Crucible, a seventy-two–hour ordeal that pushes recruits to the limits of their endurance and concludes with a patriotic spectacle complete with amplified anthems at the foot of a mock Iwo Jima memorial. The approximately forty educators from each recruiting area who participate every year are flown to either San Diego or Parris Island, lodged in nearby hotels, and reimbursed on their return with a $225 per diem.

The desired reaction from educators was expressed succinctly by Staff Sergeant Jesús Lora, a public affairs officer for the Marine Corps Recruit Depot in San Diego: "I've talked to one from last year's Educator Workshop and she said it was an experience that will be treasured forever. She now passes the experiences she felt last year and teaches it to her students."[25] This, of course, is precisely the point: the so-called influencers are expected to communicate their excitement about their well-controlled and sanitized "experience" of boot camp to their young charges.

But not all influencers are welcome in the workshops. An article written by a recruiter in Lansing, Michigan, advised EWP organizers to eliminate as workshop participants anyone with prior military experience. Because one of the goals of EWP is to "dispel all misconceptions about the Marine Corps that infiltrate the American society," military veterans are considered potentially disruptive given their firsthand knowledge of military values and practices.[26]

The Pentagon thus courts professional educators in order to exploit their influence over young people. In a complementary move designed to achieve the same result, military veterans are moved into school systems through the so-called Troops to Teachers program (TTT). Initiated as a Department of Defense (DOD) and Department of Education (DOE) collaboration in 1994, TTT seeks to place veterans in teaching positions across the country, with an emphasis on districts in poor and underserved areas. The No Child Left Behind act of 2001 will provide funding for TTT through the 2006 fiscal year. To date, over six thousand teachers have been placed, and another six thousand are currently in training or seeking employment. In California, where cash-strapped school systems such as Los Angeles and San Diego serve large African American and Latino communities, military veterans are given a six-week crash course and placed directly into the classroom.[27]

Given the crisis in state education budgets and ongoing teacher shortages, it would seem that there is nothing inherently wrong with a program that attempts to help veterans transition into careers in education. But the long-term impact of exposing children to military values and experiences coincides well with the recruiters' goal of "getting them while they're young." A recent *Washington Post* article on TTT captured the agendas of some of the veterans turned teachers:

Such teachers also can make good ambassadors for the military. When [George] Hartman [a former gunnery sergeant in the Marine Corps] took over his business education classroom from a former Navy man, he put in a call to his local Marine recruiter. "I said, 'I want calendars. I want pens. I want all this Navy stuff out of my classroom, and I want to put Marine junk in here,'" he said. . . . Chrystal Puryear, 33, a Head Start teacher at Davis Elementary in Southeast Washington, tends to talk about the military less with her students than with their parents. . . . "They don't think they have any options, and I tell them the military is always an option. They will teach you what you are capable of."[28]

Both the EWP and TTT programs form key elements in the ongoing effort to instill military values as collective common sense. A complete analysis of the wide array of related programs would require a separate article. Yet the so-called Take Charge! initiative designed by the Army Recruiting Command, for example, is disguised as a stay-in-school program. Across the nation, education officials are encouraging teachers to contact local recruiters about such programs. In 2003, the Wisconsin State superintendent of public instruction advised district administrators that "the Army also has two new programs you might consider integrating into instructional programs or other activities at school. One program addresses the history of the U.S. Army, and the other is a character development program based on Army values."[29]

The debacle of the American war in Southeast Asia produced a generation of young people wary of warrior masculinities, cheap patriotism, and foreign policy adventurism. The Bush administration's manipulation of September 11, exaggerated claims about the threat of Saddam Hussein's Iraq, and media complicity allowed many to wrap themselves in the flag once again. If the United States was to conduct itself as a missionary for free markets and democracy in the coming decades, a reserve force of foot soldiers for its legions would have to be continually replenished. What better institutional site for conducting such a campaign than the nation's dysfunctional public school systems, which have been thrown into chaos by massive budget cuts, overcrowding, and neglect?

Despite overwhelming obstacles and a multimillion-dollar Pentagon recruitment campaign, local communities are reacting to the presence of militarism in their school systems. Just last year, at historic Roosevelt High School in East Los Angeles, a group of students was so appalled at the intrusive behavior of military recruiters that they formed an organization called Students Not Soldiers and demanded the hiring of real career counselors. At California State University–Northridge, just north of Los Angeles, students and faculty have protested the university's contract with Army ROTC, a contract that brings Pentagon funding on campus and unlimited access to students for recruiters. In Puerto Rico, student members of the Frente Universitario por la Desmilitarización y la Educación (FUDE) (University Front for the Demilitarization of Education) recently established a civil disobedience camp at the University of Puerto Rico–Mayagüez in order to block the construction of a ROTC building.

These acts of resistance to the ongoing militarization of public education are rarely reported and not well known. Most Latino students and their parents, therefore, will fall prey to a limited range of opportunities (what we might call the economic draft or economic conscription) and the Pentagon's propaganda blitz about free money for college and travel. For all working-class youth with limited horizons, these appear as powerfully seductive messages.

As progressive scholars and activists, we must struggle to understand the pressures felt by working-class communities. It will not suffice to shake our heads in disapproval at their displays of uncritical patriotism, especially within the context of the culture of fear continually cultivated by governing elites. Homeland security for these communities comes together at the intersection of limited life chances, concerns about their children's future, and the militarization of the entire culture.

Conclusion

In his classic 1907 study of European militarism, Karl Liebknecht argued that the primary purpose of any standing army was to protect the interests of the capitalist elites or, in modern parlance, the corporate class. "The task of militarism," Liebknecht wrote, "is above all to secure for a minority, at whatever cost, even against the enlightened will of the majority of the people, domination of the state and freedom to exploit."[30]

Focusing his activism on the youth of his day, Liebknecht argued that the struggle against militarism must begin with the young workers in both the urban and rural areas of the nation. He emphasized: "We must not overlook the question of the education of young people, which is the most essential part of anti-militarist propaganda" (166). But the counterdiscourse of antimilitarism must reach beyond individuals: "We have to consider the question not only of the youths liable to military service, but also the parents, especially the mothers, who should be specially mobilized for educating the young people in anti-militarism" (174).

Almost one hundred years after Liebknecht delivered the lectures that would become his book, we clearly have much to learn from his insights. Updated with only a few changes of language for the new context, his *Militarism and Anti-militarism* offers us a precedent with which to analyze our own moment, an analysis that exposes the cynicism and greed of those who would govern the world in the name of free markets and democracy.

Liebknecht reminds us that the children of working families bear the brunt of militarism. It is not that working people are completely deceived by the flag waving and the patriotic rhetoric. On the contrary, they are painfully aware of the losses they must endure. He wrote: "The proletariat knows that the wars which are waged by the ruling classes impose on it heavy sacrifice of life and property for which it is rewarded with miserable pensions for the disabled, funds in aid of veterans, street organs and kicks of all kinds after it has done the work. The proletariat knows that in every war brutality and baseness are rampant amongst the peoples participating in it and culture is set back for years" (18).

With the United States engaged in protracted military commitments in Iraq and Afghanistan, and with domestic crises in education and health care, Latino communities are slowly awakening to the fact that a permanently militarized economy and culture will not benefit them or their children. If the homeland to be secured willingly seeks Latino youth for the ranks of its military while continuing to portray Spanish-speaking communities as a foreign threat to national identities, what will be the long-term gains for the vast majority of Latino working families? We can only hope that, in the great tradition of radical social movements and militancy that mark Mexican, Latin American, and Chicano histories, Latinos in the United States will continue to add their voices to the national and international chorus demanding a different future than the one envisioned by the oligarchs of the new imperialism.

Notes

1. Diane Schmidley, "The Foreign-Born Population in the United States: March 2002," *Current Population Reports* (2003).
2. See Robert Pollin, *Contours of Descent: U.S. Economic Fractures and the Landscape of Global Austerity* (London: Verso, 2003).

3. "The Road to a College Diploma: The Complex Reality of Raising Educational Achievement for Hispanics in the United States," *The Interim Report of the President's Advisory Commission on Educational Excellence for Hispanic Americans* (Washington, DC: U.S. Government Printing Office, 2002), 6.

4. Robert Suro and Jeffrey S. Passel, *The Rise of the Second Generation: Changing Patterns in Hispanic Population Growth* (Washington, DC: Pew Hispanic Center, 2003).

5. Otto Santa Ana, *Brown Tide Rising: Metaphors of Latinos in Contemporary American Public Discourse* (Austin: University of Texas Press, 2002).

6. "Our View: MEChA Issue Is a Red Herring," *North County Times* (San Diego), September 12, 2003, www.nctimes.com/articles/2003/09/12/opinion/editorials/9_12_0319_53_32.txt (accessed April 14, 2005). For my defense of MEChA, see Jorge Mariscal, "MEChA: The Right's Tool to Further Anti-Mexican Racism," *San Diego Union Tribune*, September 10, 2003.

7. Letter dated December 4, 2003.

8. Emphasis in original. Letter dated September 3, 2003.

7. Jerry Seper, "Top Court to Expedite Hearing," *Washington Times*, January 24, 2004, www.washtimes.com/archive/. I want to mention briefly the debate that took place in the United Nations immediately before the U.S. invasion of Iraq, specifically Mexico's antiwar position and the Bush administration's diplomatic pressure on and economic threats against the Vicente Fox government. In the February 27, 2003, issue of the *Economist*, it was reported that an American diplomat told Mexican officials that a Mexican "no" vote in the UN might "stir up feelings" against Mexicans in the United States. www.economist .com (accessed April 14, 2005).

8. Joseph Farah, "America's 'Palestinians,'" World Net Daily, November 15, 2001, www. worldnetdaily.com/news/article.asp?ARTICLE_ID=25337.

9. Samuel P. Huntington, "The Hispanic Challenge," *Foreign Affairs* online edition (2004), www.foreignpolicy.com/resources (accessed April 14, 2005). Also available at www .freerepublic.com/focus/f-news/1084558/posts (accessed April 14, 2005). Huntington had actually sketched out the same argument as early as 2002: "Mexican immigration is a unique, disturbing and looming challenge to our cultural integrity, our national identity, and potentially to our future as a country." Samuel P. Huntington, "Reconsidering Immigration: Is Mexico a Special Case?" *Center for Immigration Studies Backgrounder* (2002): 5. For a conservative Hispanic rebuttal of Huntington's thesis, see Gregory Rodriguez, "Mexican Americans Are Building No Walls," *Los Angeles Times*, February 29, 2004.

10. Ron Unz, "California and the End of White America," *Commentary* online edition (1999), www.commentarymagazine.com/Archive/ (accessed April 14, 2005).

11. Patrick J. Buchanan, *Death of the West: How Dying Populations and Immigrant Invasions Imperil Our Country and Civilization* (New York: St. Martin's, 2002), 125.

12. Ibid., 125–26.

13. George Will, "Making California Matter to the GOP," *San Diego Union-Tribune*, February 29, 2004.

14. Joseph Perkins, "Immigrant Sweep Needs a Broader Brush," *Coast News* (San Diego), February 14, 2002.

15. "The Road to a College Diploma," 7.

16. Peter Schmidt, "Academe's Hispanic Future," *Chronicle of Higher Education* online edition, November 28, 2003, chronicle.com/chronicle/v50/5014guide.htm.

17. "Weak Labor Market Results in Second Consecutive Year of Job Loss," Economic Policy Institute, January 9, 2004, www.epinet.org/content.cfm/webfeatures_econindicators_jobspict-01-2004.

18. "Strategic Partnership Plan for 2002-2007," U.S. Army Recruiting Command (Fort Knox: USAREC, 2001).

19. Louis Caldera, "U.S. Army Has Plenty to Offer Youth," *Los Angeles Times*, June 4, 1999; Sydney J. Freedberg Jr., "Not Enough GI Joses," *National Journal* online edition, August 14, 1999, nationaljournal.com/.

20. Quoted in Mark Holston, "Soldier of Fortune," *Hispanic* (December 2003), www.hispaniconline.com/magazine/2003/dec/CoverStory/index.html (accessed February 2, 2004).

21. Macarena Hernández, "Pentagon Courts Hispanics," *San Antonio Express-News*, October 10, 2002.

22. U.S. Department of Defense, "September 2001 Current Population Survey," Table B-30 ("Fiscal Year 2001 Active Component Enlisted Members by Occupational Area, Service, and Race/Ethnicity"). Data from Bureau of Labor Statistics and U.S. Census Bureau, www.defenselink.mil/prhome/poprep2001/appendixb/b_30.htm (accessed May 29, 2003).

23. "Strategic Partnership Plan for 2002-2007."

24. For a first-hand account by a Los Angeles teacher, see Arlene Inouye, "Educators go to Boot Camp," Draft Notices, March–April 2005 (San Diego: Committee Opposed to Militarism and the Draft), 1–4. U.S. Marine Corps Educator Workshop Program, ews.4mcd.usmc.mil/whyyou.asp (accessed April 14, 2005).

25. Jeff Janowiec, "Educators' Workshop: What All Recruiters Should Know," U.S. Marine Corps, www.usmc.mil/marinelink/mcn2000.nsf/main5 (accessed February 5, 2004).

26. Ibid.

27. California Troops to Teachers, coordinated by the Sacramento County Office of Education, www.scoe.net/troops/ (accessed April 14, 2005).

28. Rosalind S. Helderman, "Turning Troops into Teachers," *Washington Post*, January 19, 2004.

29. Elizabeth Burmaster, State Superintendent, "Memo to District Administrators," November 2003, State of Wisconsin, Department of Public Instruction, www.dpi.state.wi.us/dpi/esea/pdf/1103army.pdf (accessed April 14, 2005).

30. Karl Liebknecht, *Militarism and Anti-militarism*, trans. Alexander Sirnis (1907; New York: Dover, 1972), 20.

The Costs of Homeland Security

Natsu Taylor Saito

Shortly after September 11, 2001, twenty-one-year-old Kimberly Lowe was killed in Oklahoma by young white men in a pickup truck who, as they assaulted her, yelled out, "Go back to your country!" Since then, literally thousands of instances of discrimination, harassment, and physical assaults against Muslims, Arab Americans, and those of Middle Eastern descent have been reported.[1] Kimberly's case, however, proved particularly poignant for she was American Indian—Creek, to be specific. Her murder illustrates both the climate of fear and suspicion fostered by the so-called war on terror and how the Other in the United States has been constructed to exclude even those truly native to this land.

The harsh measures recently implemented by the U.S. government against both immigrants and U.S. citizens in the name of the country's collective well-being and national interests have rightly been criticized for their constrictions of civil liberties.[2] But the costs are much greater than those evoked by the question, as it is most often framed, of whether we are willing to sacrifice "some" liberties for a greater sense of security. The real question, I believe, is whether we are willing to sacrifice the very rule of law for the benefit of what turns out to be a fairly small sector of the population. This becomes apparent if we step back from the rhetoric of the war on terror and place these recent developments in the broader history of the use of "emergency" measures in what has become the United States. We also need to consider the concomitant limits on who is considered a "real" American, and whose homeland and whose security are being protected.

Radical History Review
Issue 93 (Fall 2005): 53–76
Copyright 2005 by MARHO: The Radical Historians' Organization, Inc.

The Aftermath of September 11

The war on terror—a war without geographic boundaries or a specific enemy, and therefore a war of global scope and indefinite duration—has been presented to us as one of "good" versus "evil," a struggle for the survival and advancement of "civilization." Those who are supposedly evil hate America and threaten national security, a term explicitly defined to include not only American lives but U.S. economic interests as well. In perhaps its most honest iteration, it is presented as a war to preserve "our way of life." "Good" is equated with "core American values," as identified in *The National Security Strategy of the United States of America*, a report presented by the White House to Congress in September 2002, as "the nonnegotiable demands of human dignity." These include free speech, equal justice, religious and ethnic tolerance, democratic forms of government, and the rule of law.[3]

The rule of law does not mean that a government can exercise power in any manner it wishes as long as it does so in the name of law enforcement; rather, it means that the laws that we trust the government to enforce must comport with broader notions of justice. Most fundamentally, this means that the law that is enforced must be both substantively and procedurally legitimate. It must be enacted in a procedurally legitimate fashion, equitably enforced, and remain substantively congruent with the basic principles that give the government its legitimacy—in this case the Constitution and the basic principles of international law. As the Supreme Court stated in 1803, it is our assurance that "this is a government of laws, not of men."[4]

Since the September 11 attacks on the Pentagon and the World Trade Center, racial profiling has been reintroduced as an acceptable practice, apparently on the theory that those from predominantly Arab or Muslim countries are generically, or perhaps genetically, predisposed to terrorism.[5] In the immediate aftermath of the attacks, the Justice Department began rounding up hundreds of noncitizen residents, most of them—perhaps all of them—men of Middle Eastern or South Asian origin. These men have literally disappeared: taken without notice from their homes or workplaces, held incommunicado, moved from prison to prison, questioned without charge, forbidden from contacting their families or lawyers. Plainly, these are practices we tend to associate with military dictatorships, not with democratic governments.[6]

Initially, the Justice Department proudly announced the numbers of those detained, though not their names or locations, under the assumption that this would make the public feel more secure. When that approach backfired and protests arose, the Justice Department stopped telling us even how many people it was holding. As of January 2005, about five thousand people have been detained. Almost none of these detainees have been charged with crimes, much less with terrorism, but thousands have been deported for technical violations of immigration laws.[7] Despite the government's refusal to tell us what is happening, we do know a bit about the conditions of the detainees' confinement. Rabih Haddad, a Muslim community leader from Detroit, reported being held in isolation, shackled, with lights on twenty-four hours per day, permitted outside his cell for only one hour per day (and then to a cage down the hall with a nonfunctioning exercise bicycle), and allowed only one fifteen-minute phone call to his family each month.[8]

Hady Hassan Omar's story was featured in the *New York Times Magazine* in October 2002. Apparently picked up because he had bought a plane ticket on a computer at the same Kinko's as one of the hijackers, he was held under similar conditions as Haddad, interrogated for months, and told he might never be released. Increasingly desperate, he tried to go on a hunger strike—he was then force-fed, and he finally tried to commit suicide. At this point he was released. This was not coincidental: according to one Washington official who spoke to a *New York Times* reporter on condition of anonymity, it is the government's theory that when people reach that point of total despair, "we can be pretty sure they're telling the truth."[9]

In addition to the detainees, the INS (Immigration and Naturalization Service) expedited the deportations of about six thousand people, also identified by age, gender, and country of origin, usually on the basis of secret evidence presented, if at all, in hearings closed to the public. Another five thousand young men from the Middle East or South Asia were asked to come in for "voluntary" interviews with the INS and FBI; and onerous new entry-exit registration procedures were implemented for visitors from certain countries. As hundreds of Iranians discovered in Los Angeles, many of those who tried to comply with these new requirements found themselves detained for several days since the INS was unprepared to process them.[10]

U.S. citizens, too, have been indefinitely imprisoned in military custody, without charge, hearing, access to counsel, or any other constitutional rights on the government's unsubstantiated assertion that they are "enemy combatants." Yaser Esam Hamdi and Jose Padilla, both U.S.-born citizens, have been held in this manner for nearly three years. They were kept in custody for more than two years before being allowed to even talk to their lawyers, and then only as a matter of military "discretion," not as a civil right. Hamdi, like John Walker Lindh, was captured in Afghanistan; but unlike Lindh, Hamdi did not receive a hearing in a civilian criminal court. One could argue that the only discernable difference in their cases was that while Lindh is a Euro-American, Hamdi is of Middle Eastern descent. The Supreme Court finally concluded, in the spring of 2004, that Hamdi, as well as the hundreds of noncitizens held without charge at the Guantánamo Bay naval base, were entitled to some minimal judicial hearing.[11] In response, the Justice Department, rather than having any sort of hearing on his detention, released Hamdi on the condition that he renounce his U.S. citizenship and return to Saudi Arabia.[12]

Jose Padilla, also known as Abdullah al-Muhajir, a Brooklyn-born Puerto Rican, was detained at O'Hare Airport in Chicago. While Justice Department officials assert that he had some connection to a so-called dirty bomb plot, he has never been able to see the evidence against him or present his side of the story to a court.[13] There may be other citizens similarly held—we do not know because the government will not tell us—but what we do know is that the executive branch is unilaterally deciding which citizens are protected by the Constitution and which are not. In Hamdi's case, the U.S. government chose to force him to become a noncitizen rather than abide by the Constitution.

These actions and many more have been taken in the name of "our security," presumably to protect both our physical safety and the freedom and democracy threatened by terrorists. At face value, however, they do not seem to embody those "nonnegotiable demands" for freedom, equal justice, or compliance with the rule of law articulated in *The National Security Strategy*. Indeed, they seem to embody the exact opposite. By way of explanation, we are told that we face a new and imminent threat, a different kind of threat requiring a different kind of response. But is the threat—or the response—really so new and different? Whose way of life is being threatened, and who is ultimately paying the price?

Parallels to the Japanese American Internment

In the first weeks after September 11, the media began reporting on the families of the disappeared: wives and children who came home to discover that their husbands or fathers had vanished; frantic inquiries to local police and hospitals that yielded no information; occasional phone calls from the men who reported that they were being moved from state to state, held in maximum security prisons and questioned without knowing why; many summarily deported without seeing their homes again. Hearing these reports, a deep uneasiness lodged itself in the pit of my stomach, and stories from my childhood came flooding back.

I remembered my father talking about how he came home from junior high in Aberdeen, Washington, in December 1941 to find that his widowed mother had disappeared and FBI agents were ransacking the house; how it took his brother and sister three weeks to figure out that she was being held in the Seattle jail as a "dangerous enemy alien"; how, after interrogation, she was cleared in January but was not released until after Easter, just in time for the family to pack what they could carry and, under armed guard, board a darkened, dirty train that took them across the desert to the internment camp at Tule Lake in northern California, where they remained for several years. This happened, of course, to 120,000 Japanese Americans—men and women, children and old people. Members of the older generation were still Japanese citizens, but more than seventy thousand of those imprisoned were U.S. citizens by birth.[14]

It is hard not to be struck by the parallels—the targeting of a group solely on the ground that ethnicity or national origin somehow links them to an "enemy." In World War II, the U.S. government *knew* that Japanese Americans did not pose a threat to national security—the FBI and military intelligence had long held Japanese American communities under surveillance and had consistently reported that they posed no threat. In fact, they reported that the Japanese government was much more likely to use white spies and saboteurs because they would be much less obvious.[15] Nonetheless, these agencies had compiled lists of all political, religious, and business leaders in the community—such as my grandmother, for example, who was targeted because she ran a small import-export store—and everyone on those lists was rounded up and interrogated immediately after Pearl Harbor and then either released or sent to special internment camps following individual hearings. *After* this process of targeted individual screenings, the entire community—every person of Japanese descent on the West Coast—was incarcerated pursuant to President Roosevelt's Executive Order No. 9066 on a completely unsupported assertion of "military necessity."[16] The national security card, invoked on a racialized basis, simply trumped the Constitution.

This situation finds its parallel in the thousands of detentions following September 11, except that typically the recent detainees have been denied hearings. Even though this process has not yielded any terrorists, many residents who posed no threat to the national security have been deported on the basis of technical immigration violations. Just as much is now made about immigrants threatening the national security, during World War II much was made of the fact that the older generation of Japanese Americans were "enemy aliens." While this was technically true, the argument ignored the fact that these people were prevented from becoming citizens by racial restrictions on naturalized citizenship, as well as the fact that two-thirds of those incarcerated were U.S.-born citizens. All persons of Japanese descent, even babies in orphanages, were portrayed as a threat,[17] just as Muslims and Arab Americans, long before September 11, 2001, were portrayed in the media and popular culture—consider movies like *The Siege* (dir. Edward Zwick, 1998) as inherently prone to be terrorists or at least sympathizers or supporters of terrorism.[18]

During World War II, this purported concern with security applied only to those racially identified as Other, *not* to German or Italian Americans. Similarly, white terrorists have not been targeted since September 11. Witness how the anthrax threat virtually disappeared from the news after a white scientist was identified as the primary suspect.[19] Or consider the case of Timothy McVeigh, convicted of the 1995 bombing of the Murrah Federal Building in Oklahoma City—until then the largest terrorist attack on American soil, resulting in the deaths of 168 men, women, and children. McVeigh received an open trial with full constitutional protections, and we certainly did not see sweeping investigations of white supremacist groups or a mass incarceration of the racist Right. Instead, the Oklahoma City bombing became part of the rationale for implementing the harsh anti-immigrant provisions of the Illegal Immigration Reform and Immigrant Responsibility Act and the Anti-Terrorism and Effective Death Penalty Act, both of which passed in 1996.[20]

The internment of Japanese Americans is now generally acknowledged to have been a mistake but—as Supreme Court chief justice William Rehnquist put it in his recent book, *All the Laws but One*—an understandable one given that the United States found itself at war.[21] In 1988, Congress passed the Civil Liberties Act, which attributed the internment to "racial prejudice and wartime hysteria" and provided an official apology and the payment of $20,000 to each surviving internee.[22] This, of course, was merely symbolic for it came nowhere near compensating those interned for their loss of property, much less the resultant trauma and disruption of lives. Because of this acknowledgment, until a few years ago it was generally assumed that such a thing—the mass incarceration of U.S. citizens or residents on the basis of race or presumed political loyalty—could never happen again.

But could it? The Supreme Court opinions, which in 1943 and 1944 upheld the internment against constitutional challenge, have never been overturned and thus remain "good law."[23] No laws have been passed to prevent mass internments; in fact, from 1950 to 1971, Title II of the National Security Act explicitly authorized the government to create internment camps. The president still has the ability to order such incarcerations; and, if recent assertions of executive power such as the order authorizing military tribunals provide any indication, he would not hesitate to do so. In addition, numerous laws have been passed in the name of fighting the so-called wars on crime or drugs which allow preventive detention and dramatically curtail the rights of detainees.[24]

Official acknowledgment of a wrong, even if accompanied by an apology and some kind of compensation, is meaningless if no structural change prevents its recurrence. In fact, these days it appears that the internment of Japanese Americans during World War II is increasingly used to justify post–September 11 measures, the message now being that even though the government previously took "extraordinary" actions in times of war, everything in the end turned out fine. Unless we want to allow one massive wrong to become the excuse for more and potentially greater violations of the Constitution and of fundamental human rights, we have to be very clear that the internment of Japanese Americans was neither a response to actual national security concerns nor an aberration.

Conflating Race, Immigration, and Security Issues

Both the Japanese American internment and the current racialization of Arab Americans as terrorists reflect the historic conflation of race, perceived foreignness, and threats to the national security. Japanese immigration to the United States began in the late 1880s, following a successful nativist campaign to exclude Chinese workers. The Japanese, like the Chinese, were deemed Other—racially inferior, inassimilable, untrustworthy—and kept foreign in as many ways as possible. They were routinely discriminated against, segregated, denied naturalized citizenship on racial grounds, excluded from many professions, and prohibited from owning land because they were "aliens ineligible to citizenship."[25] Despite all of this, they encouraged their children, U.S. citizens by birth, to assimilate. As my father has said, "We were Christians and Boy Scouts; we grew up saying the Pledge of Allegiance at school every day: 'with liberty and justice for all.'" Despite the structural obstacles placed in their way, the older generation soon owned small businesses and turned wasteland into productive farms, often putting the land in the name of their U.S.-citizen children.

Yet immigrants' success at assimilating, rather than their inability to do so, generated great resentment, both from white labor, which saw them as unfair competition, and white farmers, who wanted their land. Nativist groups such as the Native Sons of the Golden West, one of whose prominent members was future California governor and U.S. Supreme Court chief justice Earl Warren, put constant pressure on the federal government to exclude and ultimately to intern Japanese Americans and, when they succeeded, managed to profit handsomely from the forced dispossession of Japanese property.[26]

We see, of course, many parallels between the history of Asian American labor and migration and the push-pull dynamics of contemporary Mexican immigration.[27] The very concrete nature of this connection was brought home to me a few years ago when I went for the first time to Tule Lake, to see where my family had been interned. I had expected to find a few remnants of crumbling barracks in that isolated desert terrain, and instead was shocked to see rows of small, identical, newly constructed houses, surrounded by a barbed wire fence. Driving around the compound, I eventually came to a gate, where a large sign dispelled my confusion: "State of California Migrant Labor Camp."

When we look at the treatment of immigrant groups of color in the United States, we see that while the motivation both to bring in and to exclude has generally been economic, the rhetoric used to deny them rights and benefits has not only been framed in racialized terms; these terms, in turn, are linked to the rhetoric of national security. The oft-evoked goal of "preserving 'our' way of life" thus has both a racial and a more explicitly political dimension. This is interesting because the United States is consistently characterized as a nation of immigrants—a framing necessary to maintain an appearance of legitimacy, given that it is, in fact, a settler-colonial state occupying someone else's land—but, at the same time, immigrants are the first to be attacked as threatening to the social, economic, and/or racial status quo.[28]

The founding fathers were, of course, immigrants—illegal immigrants, one might accurately assert—but they and their descendants have assumed the mantle of the "real Americans." And they have done what they could to ensure that those deemed American looked like them. In 1790, the first Congress passed a law that limited naturalized citizenship to "free white persons"—a racial restriction not entirely eliminated until the Immigration and Nationality (McCarran-Walter) Act of 1952.[29] Interpreting this phrase in 1923 to find Bhagat Thind, a "high caste Hindu," ineligible to naturalization, the Supreme Court succinctly summarized who was to be an American:

The words of familiar speech, which were used by the original framers of the law, were intended to include only the type of man whom they knew as white. The immigration of the day was almost exclusively from the British Isles and Northwestern Europe, whence they and their forebears had come. When they extended the privilege of American citizenship to "any alien being a free white person" it was these immigrants—bone of their bone and flesh of their flesh—and their kind whom they must have had affirmatively in mind.[30]

The Supreme Court had already made very clear in its 1857 *Dred Scott v. Sanford* decision that African Americans were not only *not* citizens but not even "people" under the Constitution as originally framed.[31] Birthright citizenship only came after the Civil War, with passage of the Fourteenth Amendment in 1868, and most American Indians were not U.S. citizens until citizenship was unilaterally imposed on them in 1924.[32] Using economic and literacy tests, as well as country quotas based on the 1890 census, immigration of northwestern Europeans (those of so-called Aryan or Anglo-Saxon stock) was encouraged; southern and eastern European immigration was discouraged and immigration from most of the rest of the world essentially banned.[33] From the beginning, those truly native to this land, those brought as chattel slaves, and immigrants of color became the Other. Those who thus deemed themselves real Americans justified the dispossession of the native peoples by asserting their superior right to the continent's land and resources, a notion embodied in the popular doctrine of Manifest Destiny.[34] They characterized indigenous resistance to this dispossession as threatening the national security, thus rationalizing a military policy of outright extermination combined with the forced removals of native peoples from their homelands and their incarceration in what can only be accurately called concentration camps.[35]

Throughout U.S. history, any movement that has threatened the hegemonic control of this small sector of the settler population has been labeled a threat to the national security. Where possible, "foreigners" have been blamed; the term *un-American* thus has both a literal and a figurative dimension. According to the master narrative, Catholic immigrants from southern and eastern Europe were untrustworthy because of their supposed primary allegiance to the Pope. Labor organizing was the work of foreign agitators, and immigrants were to blame for the popularity of anarchist and socialist movements in the late nineteenth century and early decades of the twentieth century.[36] In turn, those who voiced dissent politically have been cast as disloyal, un-American, and under foreign influence. As early as 1798, the first Alien and Sedition Acts were passed in response to the Federalists' claim that the Jeffersonians were agents of France attempting to bring the French Revolution's "reign of Terror" to the United States.[37] Those who fought for the abolition of slavery were deemed "seditious";[38] those who opposed the war fought to "pacify" the Philippines from 1898 to 1902 were accused of treason.[39] As socialist labor leader Eugene Debs, convicted under the Espionage Act for his outspoken opposition to World War I, noted on his way to prison, "It is extremely dangerous to exercise the constitutional right of free speech in a country fighting to make the world safe for democracy."[40]

In the 1950s and 1960s, civil rights and antiwar organizations were inevitably labeled communist front groups and, more generally, *anyone* advocating social or political change was deemed a threat to the national security.[41] As the Senate Select Committee on Intelligence (also known as the Church Committee) reported in the mid-1970s, this procedure was used as an excuse by the FBI and numerous other federal agencies to engage in thousands of counterintelligence operations against U.S. citizens, using means that were lawful only when employed against spies, saboteurs, and other such "agents of foreign powers." Used as they were against citizens, they were not only illegal but also unconstitutional; to quote the Church Committee, they were "abhorrent in a free society."[42]

In many ways the recently enacted so-called USA PATRIOT Act is attempting to legitimize this war to preserve the status quo and, one might add, thereby make it easier to finance.[43] Political protest is now interpreted as domestic terrorism; and, under the proposed Patriot II, the government is seeking the power not only to declare such activity un-American but also to literally strip Americans associated with certain organizations of their citizenship, as it has already done with Yaser Hamdi.[44] It is this conflation of those who are supposedly not-American with that which is allegedly un-American—and the further conflation of "our security" with the established order, that is, the status quo—that we must consider as we turn to post–September 11 developments in the United States.

Whose Homeland?

First, we need to ask: *whose* homeland is being defended? The underlying presumption is—as it was for Congress when it enacted the Chinese exclusion laws in the 1880s, or for the Supreme Court when it decided that neither Dred Scott nor Bhagat Thind were citizens—that this is a *white* country or, as the proponents of Manifest Destiny phrased it, a nation that represents the highest form of Anglo-Saxon civilization and that must be protected from the corruption of the uncivilized Other.

While the language used to justify exclusionary policies is now often less direct—or, one might say, more obfuscatory—the presumptions have not changed. We can see this illustrated by the recent anti-immigrant movement in California, where there has been a resurgence of nativist sentiment in the face of demographic trends indicating that the population most often identified as white may soon constitute a minority. Thus, for example, in affluent Orange County, just south of Los Angeles, the population in 1980 was almost 80 percent white, whereas in 2000 it was about 51 percent white, 31 percent Latino, and 14 percent Asian, with over 40 percent of its residents speaking a language other than English at home, a change that has generated much support among the white population for restrictions on immigration.[45]

But one might also ask: why is 1980 treated as a historical benchmark? The county was, after all, established in the 1880s and named after its numerous orange groves. Who was planting and nurturing those orange trees? Who was picking and loading the fruit? Chinese labor in the process of being excluded and replaced by Japanese labor? Mexican migrant workers? In other words, could Orange County ever have become Orange County without these outcast immigrant Others?

While much of the concern about immigrants in Orange County has focused on Mexican Americans, it is worth remembering that California was part of Mexico until the United States annexed it in 1848. Under the Treaty of Guadalupe Hidalgo, those Mexicans who wanted to remain in California were guaranteed all the rights of U.S. citizenship—if they wished to accept it (though, tellingly, *not* all the rights of white Americans).[46] Regardless of citizenship, they were also guaranteed recognition of their title to the land. But history reveals that the Land Act of 1851 effectively nullified this promise, encouraging Anglo homesteading on Mexican land and forcing Mexican landowners to go through a difficult and costly procedure of proving their ownership using U.S.-approved documentation in hearings conducted in English. Prior to 1860, all land in California worth more than $10,000 was in Mexican hands; by 1870, that number had been reduced by three-quarters, and by 1880, Mexicans were virtually landless in California.[47] In the meantime, by 1851, all native Mexicans had been excluded from the state Senate and, by the 1880s, virtually no one with a Spanish surname held public office. Arguing to the California legislature for exclusion of Mexicans from the mines, G. B. Tingley of Sacramento described Mexicans and other Latinos as follows: "Devoid of intelligence sufficient to appreciate the true principles of free government; vicious, indolent, and dishonest, to an extent rendering them obnoxious to our citizens; with habits of life low and degraded; an intellect but one degree above the beast of the field, and not susceptible of elevation; all these things combined to render such classes of human beings a curse to any enlightened community."[48] In this kind of climate, it is not surprising that Mexicans soon found themselves strangers in their own land.

But we could go back even further in California history to find precedents for such attitudes. Those now referred to as Mexican are the descendants of the indigenous populations of this land and of their Spanish colonizers. Spain controlled California and the other Mexican territories until 1821, but the Spanish, too, were immigrants. Orange County's first long-term European settlement was the Mission of San Juan Capistrano, founded by Father Junipero Serra in 1776. By the time Serra died in 1784, there were nine Franciscan missions in California and, like other Spanish missions in the Americas, they were essentially forced labor concentration camps in which the American Indians' fate was described by the Spanish colonizers themselves as "worse than that of slaves."[49] It was these Indians, not their colonizers, whose sweat and blood went into the initial conversion of California into the agricultural mecca it would become. The life expectancy of those held in the missions was only ten to twelve years at best; those who attempted to escape were restrained or hunted down. Ironically, because the old and the young were first to die, those who survived were relatively productive, generating significant profits for the Spanish. Overall, the indigenous population of what is now California was reduced by perhaps 75 percent by the time the Spanish withdrew in 1821.[50]

There were as many as eighty American Indian nations in California when the European colonizers arrived. A large-scale Anglo invasion was underway by the mid-to-late 1840s, and with it came a determined campaign of extermination, most of it in the form of so-called private actions, massacres by settlers fueled first by official scalp bounties and then by bounties offered by business consortiums. Dryden Laycock, a settler in Round Valley, claimed that, beginning in 1856, the first year of white settlement, groups of Round Valley settlers would go out "two or three times a week" and kill "on an average, fifty or sixty Indians on a trip," and that these raids continued for five years.[51] In the view of those engaged in this process, American Indians were reduced to a form of insect life. As professional Indian killer H. L. Hall instructed his colleagues, they should kill native infants as well as adults, because "a nit grows up to be a louse," a genocidal metaphor invoked a century later by SS *Reichsführer* Heinrich Himmler when he compared the extermination of Jews to the "delousing" of Europe.[52] The genocidal policies of the California settlers were remarkably successful. According to historian David Stannard, the native population of California dropped from eighty-five thousand in 1852 to thirty-five thousand just eight years later; by 1890, this number was less than eighteen thousand and continuing to drop.[53] The Juanenos, the people indigenous to Orange County, along with numerous other California nations, were declared extinct by the U.S. government in 1970—officially "terminated" by the terms of what is known as the Pitt River Land Settlement. The descendents of the Juanenos are still fighting today for their existence to be officially recognized by the government.[54]

Thus, in California, as in the rest of what has become these United States, Euro-American settlers in large measure created the way of life that their descendants are now so concerned with preserving through the slaughter of American Indians, the dispossession of Mexican landowners, and the exploitation of Asian and Latino labor. This process allowed Euro-American whites to consolidate their control over enormous resources and use the power of the state to ensure their security—or, more precisely, to ensure their immunity from the consequences of their actions.

Whose Security?

As this very brief overview indicates, the consolidation of this country must be seen in terms of its history of dispossessing the Other. The original immigrants—the colonial settlers—dispossessed (and, one could even argue, *consumed*) the native peoples of California, physically confining them and often literally working them to death. Of course, in somewhat different ways, the more than four hundred other indigenous nations of this continent were similarly dispossessed. The state of Mexico was literally dispossessed of half its territory, only to then have its people consumed as migrant labor. Chinese, Japanese, Koreans, Filipinos, and other Asians were also considered disposable labor and, as we noted in discussing the Japanese American internment, dispossessed when they managed to establish an independent economic base. All this formed part of the internal consolidation of the American state, and it was followed by U.S. expansion overseas. The Kingdom of Hawai`i was overthrown in 1893 and annexed in 1898.[55] In what was explicitly termed an imperial expansion, the Philippines, Puerto Rico, Guam, American Samoa, and the U.S. Virgin Islands were occupied at the turn of the twentieth century and, in fact, all of these territories except the Philippines remain under U.S. control today.[56]

Those now insisting on the necessity of repressive measures in the name of security are those who have visited this dispossession on others. It was the self-proclaimed Anglo-Saxon settlers who managed such large-scale and complete dispossession of the Other, but somehow it has always been the victims who are portrayed as the threat. The realities that underlie the current world order are rejected in a process that projects the attributes of the colonizers' history and resulting character onto the Other. Now, in an extension of this process, we see anyone who can be associated with brown-skinned terrorists by virtue of religion or national origin treated as potential terrorists themselves. This development is used, in turn, to justify events like the invasion of Iraq, a country of brown-skinned Others declared a threat to U.S. national security (a claim rejected by virtually all the rest of the world) and from whom the U.S. is systematically dispossessing land and natural resources.[57]

Who is really benefiting from this? We are led to believe that the vaunted American way of life depends on this exercise of U.S. global hegemony, that our economic prosperity and the lifestyles that come with it are in jeopardy. In fact, however, an increasingly narrow elite is benefiting from this process. We have seen, of course, how much corporations like Halliburton have profited from the war in Iraq.[58] This is important not simply because a few large corporations and their stockholders are benefiting greatly from the war on terror but because it is reflective of the more general reality that 1 percent of the U.S. population controls 40 percent of the country's collective wealth and that the United States, in turn, with only 5 percent of the world's population, consumes 25–30 percent of the resources of the planet.[59] So we have to ask: are we collectively benefiting from this war on terror, or are our fears, constantly inflamed by media coverage, merely exploited to entrench the economic and political security of that 1 percent?

Many thoughtful scholars and analysts have pointed out that the U.S. government's actions overseas are generating more resentment and anger against the United States, not less. There were no documented ties between Iraq and al-Qaeda before the U.S. invasion; now there are reports of hundreds of al-Qaeda members crossing the border to join the Iraqi resistance.[60] Here at home, instead of working respectfully with Muslim and Arab American communities, the federal government has engaged in the surveillance of mosques, the roundups of community leaders, and wholesale deportations. Can this *really* be making us safer?

The Real Costs of Protecting "Our Way of Life"

Just as we must consider who benefits from the war on terror, we must also consider the real costs of implementing policies to achieve what is deemed homeland security. As indicated in my very brief overview, immigrants have been the focus of national security debates throughout U.S. history. Those perceived as foreign are regularly portrayed not simply as not-American but as un-American, probably disloyal, and always potential enemies. In the 1940s Americans of Japanese descent saw themselves transformed into the enemy overnight; immediately after that, in the context of the Cold War, the Chinese, who had been friends to the U.S. during World War II, were now considered potential enemies. And it continues to this day. Vietnamese, Cambodian, and Laotian refugees—most of whom are in the United States only because they became allies in the U.S. war against Indochina during the 1960s and 1970s—are assaulted as if they were the enemy. Of course, there has also been a new wave of hate crimes directed at many other immigrant and ethnic communities since September 11.

My point here is not that such violence continues to be perpetrated against peoples of color, but that it is still sanctioned. We no longer have official scalp bounties, and lynching is theoretically illegal, but racially motivated attacks are consistently treated as understandable. The murder of Kimberly Lowe, an American Indian, becomes another statistic of the war on terror. The racing of certain groups as the enemy continues as we move into an era of increasingly harsh measures taken in the name of the war on terror. Security concerns are raised by one privileged sector of immigrants who have targeted both the indigenous peoples of this continent and subsequent immigrant groups as threatening their primacy as self-appointed real Americans.

Interestingly, in the context of these post–September 11 measures, we see immigrants framing both sides of the debate. At one end of the spectrum, for example, stands Viet Dinh, a Vietnamese refugee who settled in Orange County, California, and who has been portrayed as the poster boy for the American dream. After graduating from law school, he went to work for the Justice Department and became the primary architect of the PATRIOT Act.[61] At the other end of the spectrum we see Hai Duc Le, also a Vietnamese immigrant, who became one of the first targets of the act when, in June 2002, a pipe bomb exploded in his car, and he was charged with using a weapon of mass destruction. While there were five state felonies and misdemeanors under which Le could have been charged, none carried a penalty greater than seven years. Under the PATRIOT Act, however, he faced a thirty-five-year sentence.[62] Most lawyers would agree that while such prosecutions did not form part of the stated intent of the PATRIOT Act, nothing in the law prevents its use in this manner. It is not a coincidence, I believe, that the law is being tried out in a case against a relatively powerless immigrant Other, someone unlikely to have the resources to generate a high-profile challenge to the act's unconstitutionality.

The PATRIOT Act was written by an immigrant and is being field-tested on immigrants, but its reach extends to all of us. It is the most visible, but there have been dozens of similarly draconian laws passed since September 11, giving the government an arbitrary ability to lock up more Americans for longer periods of time and effectively nullifying our constitutional rights in the name of protecting freedom and democracy. We are not safer as a result. Plenty of laws existed before September 11 that criminalized terrorist activity, and those desperate enough to fly planes into buildings are not going to be deterred by more laws. What is being deterred is our collective ability to influence the government purporting to represent us. Those who attend antiwar meetings are receiving federal grand jury subpoenas and visits from the FBI; those who criticize government policy find themselves on no-fly lists; and those who organize political protests face criminal prosecution as domestic terrorists.[63]

To allow this to happen is to sanction state repression. What is being preserved is not "our" security, but the privilege, real or imagined, of one narrow sector of the settler population. What is being sacrificed are not the few liberties we rarely exercised anyway, but the very principles that supposedly define the American way of life. The ratcheting up of police and intelligence powers since September 11 has not made us, collectively, any more secure. Instead, they have further entrenched the status quo and, in the process, have made most of us much less secure. In considering how, or even whether, to respond to these developments there are, I believe, two vital questions concerning the costs of this kind of homeland security.

First, is this really the kind of world we want to preserve? As we look around, the world does not look like such a pretty place. Untold numbers of children die of malnutrition and preventable diseases every day.[64] Millions of all ages are killed in ongoing wars, most of them waged by states against the peoples whose lands they are occupying.[65] In this generation alone, 250 languages and their attendant cultures, knowledge, and worldviews will disappear, along with hundreds of plant and animal species.[66] Vast swaths of land have been rendered uninhabitable by the relentless quest for "progress." In many American cities, we cannot drink the water or safely breathe the air.[67] The gap between rich and poor is increasing, both globally and in the United States.[68] Here at home we have the poorest public education and health care in the industrialized world.[69] Every night thousands of homeless people sleep on the streets.[70] The United States has the world's second highest incarceration rate, and 80 percent of everyone in this country charged with a felony is too poor to afford a lawyer.[71] Currently, approximately one in every three black men in the United States between the ages of eighteen and twenty-five is either in prison, has done prison time, or is destined to do so before he turns twenty-six—that is approximately double the prospect of a black man of the same age group in South Africa at the height of apartheid.[72] Latinos in the United States also suffer disparate rates of incarceration, as do American Indians.[73] Do we really need to be locking up more people? Regardless of the differences we may have about the kind of world we want to leave for our children, and what we are willing to do to get there, are we really willing to give up our ability to have a say in this process? Because that is what we are talking about: giving up the fundamental rights embodied in the Constitution, indeed, the rule of law itself, and thereby relinquishing any hope we have for a voice in the government acting in our name. Are we really willing to relinquish this for a blind faith that those currently in charge will do the right thing?

I have briefly touched on the undermining of constitutional rights in the name of security. Having consolidated itself internally in the ways described above, the United States is now projecting this same order globally, and international law is similarly being undermined. In *The National Security Strategy*, George W. Bush informs us that there is now a "single sustainable model for national success"—the American one, of course—and that the U.S. government is committed to maintaining the country's "unprecedented and unequaled strength and influence in the world" by ensuring that U.S. military power is so overwhelming that no one would dare consider challenging it. International law and cooperation are to be supplanted by what Bush terms a "distinctly American internationalism that reflects the union of our values and our national interests."[74] In other words, the system that has evolved in the United States in the manner referred to above is what the country's leaders are attempting to impose on the entire planet, in our name.

In piecemeal fashion, some of these problems are beginning to be recognized. Lawsuits have been brought to challenge indefinite detentions. Hundreds of local governments have voted to reject the PATRIOT Act, and a federal judge recently held some of its provisions unconstitutional.[75] But the problem cannot be fixed by tinkering with the law, for it is not the specifics of the PATRIOT Act, or any other particular executive measure, but the abandonment of international law in favor of U.S. unilateralism and the abandonment of constitutional principles at home that are the real problem.

In 1901 the Supreme Court ruled that the protections of the Constitution need not be extended to the newly acquired territory of Puerto Rico. Writing for the majority, Justice Henry Billings Brown acknowledged that this raised concerns about the imposition of arbitrary power on the inhabitants of the colonized nation. However, he assured the nation that such fears about the probability of despotism were unwarranted, for "there are certain principles of natural justice inherent in the Anglo-Saxon character which need no expression in constitutions or statutes to give them effect or to secure dependencies against legislation manifestly hostile to their real interests."[76] Will we allow the rule of law to be subverted, allow the executive and legislative branches of government to disregard both the Constitution and international law, on the assurance that we will be protected by these "principles of natural justice inherent in the Anglo-Saxon character"?

Douglas Porpora, in his book *How Holocausts Happen*, notes, "As long as we continue to go to work or pay our taxes or otherwise conduct business as usual, we contribute to the continued functioning of the various social systems to which we belong. . . . Perhaps, however, our sense of that complicity will awaken us from the everydayness in which we routinely slumber away our lives. Perhaps it will stir us to recognize that something extraordinary is afoot, demanding that we behave in ways beyond the ordinary."[77] Do we wish to live in a world ruled by a self-anointed elite, defined by its pursuit of profit, with all the racist, colonialist, genocidal, and ecocidal horrors that entails, or would we rather live in a world governed by a system of law in which the arbitrary authority of the state is constrained by a citizenry empowered by genuinely inalienable rights—in other words, one truly reflective of freedom and democracy? This is the question with which we are faced and which we, by our action or our quiet complicity, are in the process of deciding.

Notes

A version of this essay was first presented as part of the "Changing Face of Orange County" lecture series at the University of California, Irvine, on February 25, 2004. I am particularly grateful to Ward Churchill for his assistance in the preparation of that lecture.

1. See "Fight Hate and Promote Tolerance," *Hate in the News: Violence against Arab and Muslim Americans*, www.tolerance.org/news/article_hate.jspid412 (accessed January 15, 2004); Stephen Lee, "U.S. Intervention in the Middle East, the 'War on Terror,' and Domestic Hate Crimes: An *Amerasia Journal* Chronology," *Amerasia Journal* 27–28 (2001/2002): 295, 311–16. Kimberly Lowe's story is listed with Oklahoma hate crimes.
2. See Nancy Chang, *Silencing Political Dissent: How Post–September 11 Anti-terrorism Measures Threaten Our Civil Liberties* (New York: Seven Stories, 2002); David Cole, *Enemy Aliens: Double Standards and Constitutional Freedoms in the War on Terrorism* (New York: New Press, 2003).

3.   *The National Security Strategy of the United States of America* (Falls Village, CT: Winterhouse, 2002). For additional articulations of the good-versus-evil philosophy, see the collection of post–September 11 speeches by George W. Bush in *We Will Prevail* (New York: Continuum, 2003).

4.   *Marbury v. Madison*, 5 U.S. (1 Cranch) 137, 163 (1803). The distinction was perhaps best described by Ernst Fraenkel in *The Dual State*, written in 1940, describing the transition in the German government from a normative state, "endowed with elaborate powers for safeguarding the legal order," to a prerogative state, defined as a "governmental system which exercises unlimited arbitrariness and violence unchecked by any legal guarantees." See Michael Stolleis, *The Law under the Swastika: Studies on Legal History in Nazi Germany* (Chicago: University of Chicago Press, 1998), 8, 193 n. 3. For a more general discussion, see Berta Esperanza Hernandez-Truyol, "The Rule of Law and Human Rights," *Florida Journal of International Law* 16 (2004): 167.

5.   See Farah Brelvi, "Un-American Activities: Racial Profiling and the Backlash after Sept. 11," *Federal Law* 48 (2001): 68.

6.   See Natsu Taylor Saito, "Will Force Trump Law after September 11? American Jurisprudence Confronts the Rule of Law," *Georgetown Immigration Law Journal* 17 (2002): 1, 6–10, 27–28.

7.   See David Cole, "The Priority of Morality: The Emergency Constitution's Blind Spot," *Yale Law Journal* 113 (2004): 1753; see also David Firestone and Christopher Drew, "A Nation Challenged: The Cases; Al Qaeda Link Seen in Only a Handful of 1,200 Detainees," *New York Times*, November 29, 2001; Chang, *Silencing Political Dissent*, 69–87.

8.   Letter from Rabih Haddad to Mr. Thayer, a member of the Chicago Coalition against War and Racism, January 27, 2002. See also *Detroit Free Press v. Ashcroft*, 195 F. Supp.2d 937 (E.D. Mich. 2002), holding that Haddad's hearing should be open to the press. On conditions generally see Reuters, "Group Reports Mistreatment of Detainees," *New York Times*, March 15, 2002; Chisun Lee, "A Prison Where Detainees Disappear: Black Hole in Brooklyn," *Village Voice*, July 2, 2002.

9.   Matthew Brzezinski, "Hady Hassan Omar's Detention," *New York Times Magazine*, October 27, 2002.

10.   See David Cole, "Enemy Aliens," *Stanford Law Review* 54 (2002): 953, 975; Dan Eggen and Cheryl W. Thompson, "U.S. Seeks Thousands of Fugitive Deportees: Middle Eastern Men Are Focus of Search," *Washington Post*, 8 January 2002; Robert S. White, "New Post–9/11 Registration Procedure for Foreign Workers, Students, and Visitors," *Illinois Bar Journal* 91 (2003): 253.

11.   On the Guantánamo detainees, see Michael Ratner and Ellen Ray, *Guantánamo: What the World Should Know* (White River Junction, VT: Chelsea Green, 2004).

12.   Eric Lichtblau, "U.S. to Free 'Enemy Combatant,' Bowing to Supreme Court Ruling," *New York Times*, September 23, 2004. Contrary to the headline, the Supreme Court did not mandate his release, only that he be given a hearing. See *Hamdi v. Rumsfeld, U.S.*, 124 S. Ct. 2633 (2004). For background, see Melysa H. Sperber, "John Walker Lindh and Yaser Esam Hamdi: Closing the Loophole in International Humanitarian Law for American National Captured Abroad While Fighting with Enemy Forces," *American Criminal Law Review* 40 (2003): 159; Alejandra Rodriguez, "Is the War on Terrorism Compromising Civil Liberties? A Discussion of Hamdi and Padilla," *California Western Law Review* 39 (2002): 379.

13. See Rodriguez, "Is the War Terrorism Compromising Civil Liberties?"; Samantha A. Pitts-Kiefer, "Jose Padilla: Enemy Combatant or Common Criminal?" *Villanova Law Review* 48 (2001): 875; *Rumsfeld v. Padilla*, 124 S. Ct. 2711 (2004) (holding that the case was brought in the wrong jurisdiction).

14. For good general histories of the internment, see Michi Nishiura Weglyn, *Years of Infamy: The Untold Story of America's Concentration Camps* (New York: Morrow, 1976); and Roger Daniels, *Concentration Camps USA: Japanese Americans and World War II* (New York: Holt, Rinehart and Winston, 1972). My family's story can be found in Klancy Clark de Nevers, *The Colonel and the Pacifist: Karl Bendetsen, Perry Saito, and the Incarceration of Japanese Americans during World War II* (Salt Lake City: University of Utah Press, 2004).

15. See U.S. Congress, Commission on Wartime Relocation and Internment of Civilians (CWRIC), *Personal Justice Denied: Report of the Commission on Wartime Relocation and Internment of Civilians* (Seattle: University of Washington Press, 1982), 54–55.

16. See Peter Irons, *Justice at War: The Story of the Japanese American Internment Cases* (New York: Oxford University Press, 1983), 63.

17. Colonel Karl Bendetsen (aka Bendetson), the primary architect of the internment, informed a Maryknoll priest in charge of an orphanage that all children who "have one drop of Japanese blood in them" were to be sent to the camps. Weglyn, *Years of Infamy*, 76–77.

18. See generally Jack G. Shaheen, *Reel Bad Arabs: How Hollywood Vilifies a People* (New York: Olive Branch, 2001); on the parallels between the racing of Asian and Arab Americans, see Natsu Taylor Saito, "Symbolism under Siege: Japanese American Redress and the 'Racing' of Arab Americans as 'Terrorists,'" *Asian Law Journal* 8 (2001): 8.

19. See Frank James, "FBI Hits Wall in Anthrax Investigation: Suspect Profile Is Only Clue Agency Has after Two Years," *Chicago Tribune*, March 2, 2004; "Profile: Pat Clawson Defends Steven Hatfill Who Is Being Investigated by the FBI as a Possible Suspect in Anthrax Mailings," *NBC News Today*, August 15, 2002.

20. On McVeigh, see, generally, Stephen Jones and Jennifer Gideon, "*United States v. McVeigh*: Defending the 'Most Hated Man in America,'" *Oklahoma Law Review* 51 (1998): 617; on the repressive measures enacted in 1996, see David Cole and James X. Dempsey, *Terrorism and the Constitution: Sacrificing Civil Liberties in the Name of National Security*, 2nd ed. (New York: New Press, 2002).

21. William H. Rehnquist, *All the Laws but One: Civil Liberties in Wartime* (New York: Knopf, 1998).

22. 50 U.S.C. sec. 1989 *et seq.* The act is reproduced in Leslie T. Hatamiya, *Righting a Wrong: Japanese Americans and the Passage of the Civil Liberties Act of 1988* (Stanford, CA: Stanford University Press, 1993), 206–22.

23. For an excellent analysis of the Supreme Court opinions in the challenges brought by Gordon Hirabayashi, Minoru Yasui, Fred Korematsu, and Mitsuye Endo, see Eugene V. Rostow, "The Japanese American Cases—A Disaster," *Yale Law Journal* 54 (1945): 489. On the cases, brought in the mid-1980s, in which lower federal courts vacated the convictions of Hirabayashi and Korematsu but did not change the precedent set by the Supreme Court, see Peter Irons, ed., *Justice Delayed: The Record of the Japanese American Internment Cases* (Middletown, CT: Wesleyan University Press, 1989).

24. I discuss these developments in more detail in Natsu Taylor Saito, "For 'Our' Security: Who Is an 'American' and What Is Protected by Enhanced Law Enforcement and

Intelligence Powers?" *Seattle Journal for Social Justice* 2 (2003): 23, 40–57; Saito, "Whose Liberty? Whose Security? The USA PATRIOT Act in the Context of COINTELPRO and the Unlawful Repression of Political Dissent," *Oregon Law Review* 81 (2002): 1051, 1078–111.

25. See Ronald Takaki, *Strangers from a Different Shore: A History of Asian Americans* (New York: Little, Brown, 1989); Sucheng Chan, *Asian Americans: An Interpretive History* (Farmington Hills, MI: Twayne, 1991). On the alien land laws, see Keith Aoki, "No Right to Own? The Early Twentieth-Century 'Alien Land Laws' as a Prelude to Internment," *Boston College Law Review* 40/*Boston College Third World Law Journal* 19 (1998): 37.

26. See, generally, Roger Daniels, *The Politics of Prejudice: The Anti-Japanese Movement in California and the Struggle for Japanese Exclusion* (New York: Atheneum, 1968); on Warren, see Sumi Cho, "Redeeming Whiteness in the Shadow of Internment: Earl Warren, *Brown*, and a Theory of Racial Redemption," *Boston College Law Review* 40/*Boston College Third World Law Journal* 19 (1998): 73.

27. For background on Mexican immigration issues, see Joseph Nevins, *Operation Gatekeeper: The Rise of the "Illegal Alien" and the Making of the U.S.-Mexico Boundary* (New York: Routledge, 2002).

28. On the genocidal policies undergirding the settling of the continent and on the fact that the United States, even by its own laws, lacks legal title to much of the territory, see Ward Churchill, *A Little Matter of Genocide: Holocaust and Denial in the Americas, 1492 to the Present* (San Francisco: City Lights, 1997); and Ward Churchill, "Charades, Anyone? The Indian Claims Commission in Context," in *Perversions of Justice: Indigenous Peoples and Angloamerican Law* (San Francisco: City Lights, 2003), 125–52.

29. See Ian F. Haney Lopez, *White by Law: The Legal Construction of Race* (New York: New York University Press, 1996).

30. *United States v. Bhagat Singh Thind*, 261 U.S. 204, 213 (1923).

31. *Dred Scott v. Sanford*, 60 U.S. (19 How.) 393 (1857). See Don E. Fehrenbacher, *The Dred Scott Case: Its Significance in American Law and Politics* (New York: Oxford University Press, 1981); and A. Leon Higginbotham Jr., *Shades of Freedom: Racial Politics and Presumptions of the American Legal Process* (New York: Oxford University Press, 1996).

32. In *Elk v. Wilkins*, 112 U.S. 94 (1884), the Supreme Court held that American Indians were not U.S. citizens by virtue of birth in the territory. Those who accepted land under the Allotment Act of 1887 were generally required to also accept citizenship, while the remainder were deemed citizens under the Citizenship Act of 1924. See Blue Clark, *"Lone Wolf v. Hitchcock": Treaty Rights and Indian Law at the End of the Nineteenth Century* (Lincoln: University of Nebraska Press, 1994).

33. A literacy test was imposed by the Immigration Act of 1917, national origins quotas by the Immigration Act of 1924. See Bill Ong Hing, *Defining America through Immigration Policy* (Philadelphia: Temple University Press, 2004), 51–70.

34. It postulated that "Anglo-Saxons are endowed as a race with innate superiority, that Protestant Christianity holds the keys to Heaven, that only republican forms of political organization are free, that the future—even the predestined future—can be hurried along by human hands, and that the means of hurrying it, if the end be good, need not be inquired into too closely." Frederick Merk, *Manifest Destiny and Mission in American History: A Reinterpretation* (New York: Knopf, 1963) 32–33; see also Reginald Horsman, *Race and Manifest Destiny: The Origins of American Racial Anglo-Saxonism* (Cambridge, MA: Harvard University Press, 1981).

35. See Ward Churchill, *Struggle for the Land: Native North American Resistance to Genocide, Ecocide, and Colonization* (San Francisco: City Lights, 1999); also see his *A Little Matter of Genocide*.

36. See Howard Zinn, *A People's History of the United States* (New York: HarperColophon, 1980), 206–89; Robert Justin Goldstein, *Political Repression in Modern America: From 1870 to 1976*, 2nd ed. (Urbana: University of Illinois Press, 2001), 3–101.

37. Richard O. Curry, introduction to *Freedom at Risk: Secrecy, Censorship, and Repression in the 1980s*, ed. Curry (Philadelphia: Temple University Press, 1988), 5; Chang, *Silencing Political Dissent*, 22.

38. See Michael Kent Curtis, "The Crisis over the Impending Crisis: Free Speech, Slavery, and the Fourteenth Amendment," in *Slavery and the Law*, ed. Paul Finkelman (Lanham, MD: Rowman and Littlefield, 1997), 160–205.

39. See Stuart Creighton Miller, *"Benevolent Assimilation": The American Conquest of the Philippines, 1899–1903* (New Haven, CT: Yale University Press, 1982), 77, 156–66; see also Daniel B. Schirmer and Stephen Rosskamm Shalom, eds., *The Philippines Reader: A History of Colonialism, Neocolonialism, Dictatorship, and Resistance* (Boston: South End, 1987), 5–33.

40. Quoted in Ramsey Clark, "Introduction: Notes on War and Freedom," in *Freedom under Fire: U.S. Civil Liberties in Times of War*, ed. Michael Linfield (Boston: South End, 1990), xvii; see also *Debs v. United States*, 249 U.S. 211, 214 (1919).

41. See Ward Churchill and Jim Vander Wall, *Agents of Repression: The FBI's Secret Wars against the Black Panther Party and the American Indian Movement*, 2nd ed. (Cambridge: South End, 2002); Ward Churchill and Jim Vander Wall, *The COINTELPRO Papers: Documents from the FBI's Secret War against Dissent in the United States*, 2nd ed. (Cambridge: South End, 2002); Saito, "Whose Liberty?" 1078–104.

42. U.S. Senate, Select Committee to Study Government Operations with Respect to Intelligence Activities, *Final Report: Intelligence Activities and the Rights of Americans*, 94th Cong., 2d sess., 1976, S. Rep. 755, 8.

43. USA PATRIOT Act (Uniting and Strengthening America by Providing Appropriate Tools Required to Intercept and Obstruct Terrorism) of 2001, October 26, 2001; see John W. Whitehead and Steven H. Aden, "Forfeiting 'Enduring Freedom' for 'Homeland Security': A Constitutional Analysis of the USA PATRIOT Act and the Justice Department's Anti-Terrorism Initiatives," *American University Law Review* 51 (2002): 1081.

44. The proposed Domestic Security Enhancement Act of 2003, leaked to the press in February 2003, is available with Justice Department comments at www.publicintegrity.org/dtaweb/downloads/Story_01_020703_Doc_1.pdf. Section 501 includes the citizenship-stripping proposal. (This site no longer active.)

45. On the demography, see California State University at Fullerton Web site, www.fullerton.edu/cdr/cities/Orange%20County.pdf (accessed August 20, 2004).

46. See David J. Weber, ed., *Foreigners in Their Native Land* (Albuquerque: University of New Mexico Press, 1973), 163–64; Juan F. Perea, "A Brief History of Race and the U.S.-Mexican Border: Tracing the Trajectories of Conquest," *UCLA Law Review* 51 (2003): 283, 294; Richard Griswold del Castillo, "Manifest Destiny: The Mexican-American War and the Treaty of Guadalupe Hidalgo," *Southwestern Journal of Law and Trade in the Americas* 5 (1998): 31. See also Rodolfo F. Acuña, *Occupied America: A History of Chicanos*, 3rd ed. (New York: HarperCollins, 1988).

47. Juan F. Perea et al., eds., *Race and Races: Cases and Resources for a Diverse America* (St. Paul, MN: West Group, 2000), 289–90; see also Malcolm Ebright, *Land Grants and Lawsuits in Northern New Mexico* (Albuquerque: University of New Mexico Press, 1994).

48. Quoted in Acuña, *Occupied America*, 113–14. See also Horsman, *Race and Manifest Destiny,* 208–48.

49. David J. Weber, *The Spanish Frontier in North America* (New Haven, CT: Yale University Press, 1992), 236–70, quote at 261.

50. Ibid., 261–65.

51. Ward Churchill, "'Nits Make Lice': The Extermination of North American Indians, 1607–1996," in Churchill, *A Little Matter of Genocide,* 129, 187–88; see also Lynwood Carranco and Estle Beard, *Genocide and Vendetta: The Round Valley Wars of Northern California* (Norman: University of Oklahoma Press, 1981).

52. Churchill, "Nits Make Lice," 229; see also Robert Jay Lifton, *The Nazi Doctors: Medical Killing and the Psychology of Genocide* (New York: Basic Books, 1986), 477.

53. David E. Stannard, *American Holocaust: Columbus and the Conquest of the New World* (New York: Oxford University Press, 1992), 134–46.

54. See Florence Connolly Shipeck, *Pushed into the Rocks: Southern California Indian Land Tenure, 1769–1986* (Lincoln: University of Nebraska Press, 1988); Alberto L. Hurtado, *Indian Survival on the California Frontier* (New Haven, CT: Yale University Press, 1988).

55. See, generally, Ward Churchill, "Stolen Kingdom: The Right of Hawai'i to Decolonization," in Churchill, *Perversions of Justice,* 73–123; Ward Churchill and Sharon H. Venne, eds., *Islands in Captivity: The Record of the International Tribunal of the Rights of Indigenous Hawaiians* (Cambridge: South End, 2004).

56. See Arnold H. Leibowitz, *Defining Status: A Comprehensive Analysis of United States Territorial Relations* (The Hague: Martinus Nijhoff, 1989); Christina Duffy Burnett and Burke Marshall, eds., *Foreign in a Domestic Sense: Puerto Rico, American Expansion, and the Constitution* (Durham, NC: Duke University Press, 2001).

57. See Noam Chomsky, *Hegemony or Survival: America's Quest for Global Dominance* (New York: Henry Holt, 2003); for a history of such U.S. military actions and violations of international law, see Ward Churchill, *On the Justice of Roosting Chickens: Reflections on the Consequences of U.S. Imperial Arrogance and Criminality* (San Francisco: AK Press, 2003).

58. See David Ivanovitch, "Pentagon May Divide Halliburton Contract: The $7.5 Billion Assignment May Be Sliced into Six Smaller, More Manageable Pieces," *Grand Rapids Press,* September 9, 2004; Sheila O'Flanagan, "Iraq War Turns Handsome Profit for Halliburton," *Irish Times,* July 2, 2004; Jackie Spinner and Mary Pat Flaherty, "Halliburton Reports $85 Million Profit from Iraq Operations," *Washington Post,* March 9, 2004.

59. Edward N. Wolff, *Top Heavy: A Study of the Increasing Inequality of Wealth in America* (New York: New Press, 1996), 7; Arlie Russell Hochschild, "A Generation without Public Passion," *Atlantic Monthly,* February 2001: 62–63. The article cites a 30 percent consumption rate and also notes that the U.S. produces 25 percent of the world's pollution. See also the 2000 Statistical Abstract of the United States, "Energy Consumption and Production by Country, 1990 and 1998," table 1390, www.census.gov/prod/2001pubs/statab/sec30.pdf (accessed November 11, 2003). (Note that in 1998 the United States accounted for approximately 25 percent of the world's energy consumption.)

60. See Agence France Presse, "Iraq Invasion a 'Major Blunder' in Fight against Al-Qaeda: Expert," September 8, 2004; Douglas Jehl, "U.S. Qaeda Detainee Disowned Claims about Iraq," *International Herald Tribune,* August 2, 2004. For current ties, see, for example, Salah Nasrawi, "Al-Qaida–Linked Group Gives Italy Fifteen Days to Withdraw from Iraq," *Canadian Press,* August 1, 2004; "Iraq Is Now a Battle Ground for al Quaida," *Birmingham Post* (UK), July 30, 2004.

61. Dina Bunis, "Dinh to Leave Attorney General's Office to Return to Academia: Fullerton High Graduate Is Top Vietnamese-American in Field of Law," *Orange County Register*, May 15, 2003.

62. Mike Anton and Christine Hanley, "Making a Federal Case of an O.C. Pipe Bomb: Legal Experts Say the PATRIOT Act Charges against Two Brothers after a Blast inside a Car Reflect a Kind of Legal Vigilance since Sept. 11," *Los Angeles Times*, June 19, 2003; see also Christine Hanley, "Brothers Indicted on New Pipe-Bombing Charges," *Los Angeles Times*, July 3, 2003. The PATRIOT Act has been used in a number of other cases not related to terrorism. See Eric Lichtblau, "U.S. PATRIOT Act Being Used in Many Nonterrorism Cases," *International Herald Tribune*, September 29, 2003; Eric Lichtblau, "PATRIOT Act Being Used in an Array of Crimes," *Milwaukee Journal Sentinel*, September 28, 2003.

63. See, for example, "Knock at the Door: FBI Agents Have Been Targeting Protesters for a Little Visit," *Akron Beacon Journal*, August 24, 2004; Eric Lichtblau, "Message Sent to Political Protesters: 'We're Watching You,'" *Grand Rapids Press*, August 22, 2004; Peter Shinkle and Karen Branch-Brioso, "Surveillance by FBI Intimidates Protesters," *St. Louis Post-Dispatch*, August 19, 2004; "Feds' 'No-Fly' System Needs an Upgrade," *Boston Herald*, September 25, 2004; Agence France Presse, "US Moves toward Giant Airline Passenger Screening System," September 22, 2004.

64. According to a recent UN report, "We the Children: Meeting the Promises of the World Summit for Children," one of every twelve children will die before age five, almost all from preventable causes. United Nations, press release, April 18, 2002.

65. See Bernard Neitschmann, "The Fourth World: Nations versus States," in *Reordering the World: Geopolitical Perspectives on the Twenty-First Century*, eds. George J. Demko and William B. Wood (Boulder, CO: Westview, 1994), 225–42 (noting that less than two hundred international states occupy, suppress, and exploit more than five thousand nations and peoples and that, since World War II, state-nation conflicts have produced the most numerous and longest wars, as well as the greatest number of civilian casualties and refugees).

66. See Daniel Nettle and Suzanne Romaine, *Vanishing Voices: The Extinction of the World's Languages* (New York: Oxford University Press, 2000), 40 (noting that 12 percent of the world's languages have less than 150 speakers); Joby Warrick, "Mass Extinction Underway, Majority of Biologists Say," *Washington Post*, April 21, 1998 (noting that at least one in eight plant species is threatened with extinction, and that nearly all biologists polled attributed the losses to human activity); The Turning Point Project, "Extinction Crisis," www.turnpoint.org/extinction.pdf (noting that species are dying at ten thousand times their natural extinction rate) (accessed February 11, 2003; site is no longer active).

67. See Alternative Energy Institute, "Effects of the Current and Future Population on . . . ," available at www.altenergy.org/2/population/effects/effects.html (noting that desertification is claiming 29 percent of the earth's landmass) (accessed March 28, 2003; this site is no longer active); Ward Churchill, "Geographies of Sacrifice: The Radioactive Colonization of Native North America," in Churchill, *Struggle for the Land*, 239–91 (describing federal plans to turn American Indian lands contaminated by uranium mining into "National Sacrifice Areas").

68. The richest 1 percent of the world's population receives as much income as the poorest 57 percent and, according to a recent United Nations annual human development report, fifty-four countries are now poorer than they were a decade ago. Overall human

development, as measured by an amalgam of income, life expectancy, and literacy, also fell in twenty-one countries during the 1990s. Larry Elliott, "The Lost Decade," *Guardian* (UK), July 9, 2003, citing the United Nations annual human development report.

69. See "Statistics on Adult Literacy," *Orange County Register,* September 22, 2002 (also noting that the United States holds forty-ninth place in world literacy), available on Westlaw at 2002 WL 5460682; U.S. Newswire, "Report: State Spending on Prison Grows at Six Times Rate of Higher Ed," August 22, 2002, available on Westlaw at 2002 WL 22070708; Krieger, "Economic Justice"; "System Overload: Pondering the Ethics of America's Health Care System," *Issues in Ethics* 3 (1990) (noting that the United States is "unique among the industrialized democracies" in retaining a "free market" health system), www.scu.edu/Ethics/publicaitons/iie/v3n3/system.html.

70. Paul Shepard, Associated Press, "'State of Cities' Study Released," June 19, 1998 (quoting Andrew Cuomo, U.S. secretary of housing and urban development); see also Haider Rizvi, Inter Press Service, "Hungry in a Wealthy Nation," March 26, 2003, quoting Anurandha Mittal of the Institute for Food and Development Policy and noting also that the United States spends only $16 billion per year on welfare. The Census Bureau reported 32.9 million Americans in poverty in 2001, 13.4 million with incomes less than half the official poverty level. See Robert Pear, "Number of People Living in Poverty Increases in US," *New York Times,* September 25, 2002.

71. "Anger Grows as U.S. Jail Population," *BBC News,* February 15, 2000; U.S. Department of Justice, "Defense Counsel in Criminal Cases," special report, November 2000, NCJ 179023; Southern Center for Human Rights, *Promises to Keep* (Atlanta: Southern Center for Human Rights, 2002).

72. See Ward Churchill, "Introduction: The Third World at Home," in *Cages of Steel: The Politics of Imprisonment in the United States,* ed. Churchill and J. J. Vander Wall (Washington, DC: Maisonneuve, 1992), 12; Marc Mauer, *Race to Incarcerate* (New York: New Press, 1999), 121; see also Michael A. Fletcher, "'Crisis' of Black Males Gets High-Profile Look: Rights Panel Probes Crime, Joblessness, Other Ills," *Washington Post,* April 17, 1999; David Cole, *No Equal Justice: Race and Class in the American Criminal Justice System* (New York: New Press, 1999); Jerome G. Miller, *Search and Destroy: African American Males in the Criminal Justice System* (Cambridge: Cambridge University Press, 1996).

73. On Latinos, see Mary Romero, "State Violence and the Social and Legal Construction of Latino Criminality: From El Bandido to Gang Member," *Denver University Law Review* 78 (2001): 1081. On American Indians, see Rennard Strickland, "'You Can't Rollerskate in a Buffalo Herd Even If You Have All the Medicine': American Indian Law and Policy," in *Tonto's Revenge: Reflections on American Indian Culture and Policy* (Albuquerque: University of New Mexico Press, 1997), 53; Ward Churchill, "Unraveling the Codes of Oppression," in *Fantasies of the Master Race: Literature, Cinema, and the Colonization of American Indians,* 2nd ed. (San Francisco: City Lights, 1998), xiv–xix.

74. *The National Security Strategy of the United States of America.*

75. More than 350 local governments, including New York City, as well as the states of Alaska, Hawai`i, Maine, and Vermont, have approved so-called Anti-PATRIOT Acts. See Susan Elan, "Legislators Vote against PATRIOT Act," *Journal News* (White Plains, NY), September 15, 2004; Alphonso A. Castillo, "Town Board Vote: Civil Rights as a Local Issue," *Newsday,* September 19, 2004. In January 2004 a federal judge in Los Angeles struck down the PATRIOT Act's prohibition on "providing expert advice or assistance"

to terrorist organizations as unconstitutionally vague. See Alan Bock, "Question the PATRIOT Act Series," *Orange County Register,* January 28, 2004. On April 6, 2004, the American Civil Liberties Union filed a lawsuit challenging a provision of the PATRIOT Act, but could only make a redacted version of its suit public, and then after intense negotiations with the Justice Department. See Alan Bock, "'Patriot' Games? Mend It or End It? A Better Question Is Why Bush Wants to Make the PATRIOT Act an Election Issue," *Orange County Register,* May 9, 2004.

76. *Downes v. Bidwell,* 182 U.S. 244, 280 (1901); see also Efren Rivera Ramos, "The Legal Construction of American Colonialism: The Insular Cases (1901–1922)," *Revista Juridica Universidad de Puerto Rico* 65 (1996): 225, 246–47.

77. Douglas V. Porpora, *How Holocausts Happen: The United States in Central America* (Philadelphia: Temple University Press, 1990), 185–86.

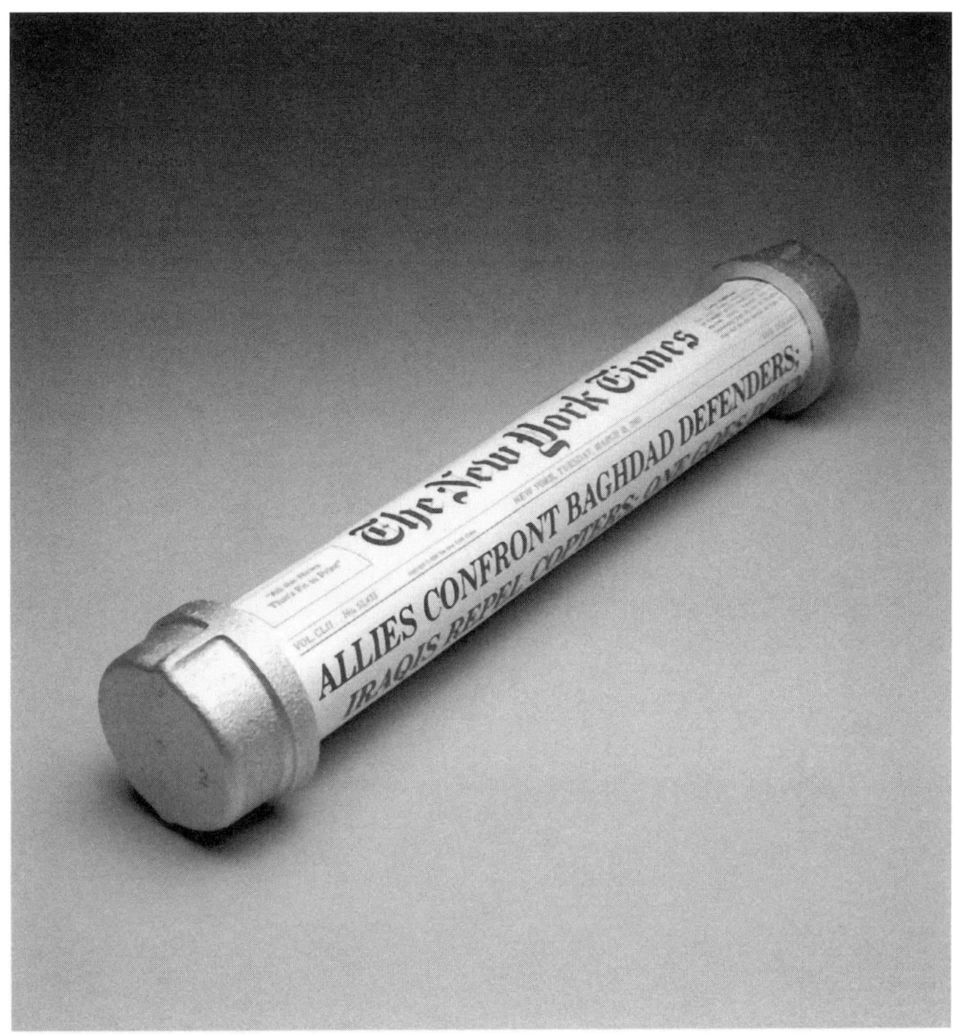

"Times," Kevin Noble (2004)

The Politics of Access:

Libraries and the Fight for Civil Liberties

in Post-9/11 America

Maurice B. Wheeler

The terrorist attacks across the United States on September 11, 2001 were a critical turning point in this nation's history. A total of 2,800 deaths were attributed to the three terrorist acts of that day. Not since the bombing of Pearl Harbor has an event captured Americans' attention and fostered such national preoccupation. No contemporary diplomatic, health, economic, or social issue has stopped the nation in its tracks and caused such wide-sweeping changes in the way we conduct our daily lives.

As of December 2001, over 450,000 people had died of HIV-related causes in the United States, but even AIDS never got our immediate attention.[1] It was estimated that 556,500 people would die of cancer in 2003,[2] and the *Journal of the American Medical Association* reported in 2000 that 250,000 people each year die from physician error or medical facilities–related causes.[3] Although all these numbers are significantly larger than the number of people who died on September 11, our national response has been marginal in comparison to our indignation about the 9/11 deaths. Perhaps this is because the way those victims perished struck at the core of our national identity and challenged our perceptions of our own freedom and liberties.

The terrorists' actions not only destroyed lives; they shattered our illusions of safety and challenged the arrogance that often accompanies positions of superiority.

Radical History Review
Issue 93 (Fall 2005): 79–95
Copyright 2005 by MARHO: The Radical Historians' Organization, Inc.

In an effort to protect the freedom and liberties of its citizens, the U.S. government instituted wide-ranging executive orders, emergency interim regulations, and new laws that negate constitutional guarantees and take away many liberties. Through passage of the USA PATRIOT Act (Uniting and Strengthening America by Providing Appropriate Tools Required to Intercept and Obstruct Terrorism), the Bush administration and Congress have set a course for the destruction of civil liberties that drafters of the U.S. Constitution and Bill of Rights would shudder to consider.[4]

Section 215 of the PATRIOT Act pertains to governmental agencies' access to business records and has been of great concern for librarians. Since the passage of the legislation, librarians have struggled to find appropriate ways to respond to the new demands placed on them by the federal government's unrestrained access to library users' records. Although the act does not specifically refer to libraries, as expected, it has been used to obtain library users' circulation records. While this level of access has serious implication for libraries, the act also contains other disturbing provisions that affect librarians. Because the range of interpretation and implementation of the new laws remains to be fully seen, there is uncertainty regarding their true impact on library operations, access to personal information, and the free flow of information and ideas in our society. It is certain, however, that libraries—and our societal expectation of normalcy—will continue to be affected by new ways of, and new reasons for, accessing information. A report issued by the General Accounting Office in May 2004 reported nearly two hundred data-mining projects either operational or in planning stages in federal government agencies. Many of these projects are based on data obtained from private-sector databases that make the information personally identifiable. Such studies have compelled Senator Daniel Akaka to call for a review of "agency practices and existing law to ensure that the privacy rights of individuals are not violated through the development of new technology."[5]

Although Americans' concepts of civil liberties, constitutional rights, and freedoms are being challenged, the uncertainties of constitutional law and political and professional boundaries leave us unable to predict the future with confidence. This article places librarians' concerns regarding section 215 of the PATRIOT Act within the context of the Bill of Rights and the current national political milieu. It also addresses issues beyond the current scope of librarians' immediate concerns, because these are likely to become issues of greater significance with the passage of time. I discuss librarians' collective national and local responses to the act to highlight the diversity of legal, political, and operational dilemmas presented by the passage and implementation of the PATRIOT Act.

History Repeats Itself

The gradual erosion of citizens' liberties is not new in America. To suggest that former U.S. attorney general John Ashcroft and others in the current Bush administration are the first national politicians to trample on the rights of citizens for their supposed protection and the good of the country is inaccurate. These kinds of measures had been employed long before September 11. The difference now is that the PATRIOT Act seems to have legalized the previous and continued transgressions of key governmental law enforcement agencies.

For many librarians, these new laws and regulations serve as uncomfortable reminders of past eras in our country's history, when certain groups in our society were prevented from using public libraries because of their ethnicity,[6] or when the federal government targeted library employees and users. Prior to the *Brown v. Board of Education* Supreme Court decision of 1954, African Americans had no legal basis to demand access to public libraries. During the McCarthy era of the late 1940s and early 1950s, homosexual librarians at the Library of Congress were identified and fired.[7] From the early 1970s until the late 1980s, librarians also quietly endured the Library Awareness Program, a counterintelligence program that tracked the library use of people primarily of Eastern European or Russian descent. In 1987, a librarian at Columbia University reported to the American Library Association (ALA) that Federal Bureau of Investigation (FBI) agents had demanded that she assist in identifying people who were possible KGB agents. Not only did her actions expose that operation, but it was also discovered that the FBI had conducted similar operations in libraries across the country dating as far back as the early 1960s.[8] The Columbia University librarian was asked to participate in exactly the kind of "fishing" expedition that many Americans now fear will result from the PATRIOT Act. When an FBI spokesperson, Susan Schnitzer, was asked to define what the librarians were being asked to look for, she replied, "It's hard to define: anything not quite right." After a Freedom of Information Act (FOIA) petition was filed in July 1987 by the National Security Archives, the FBI issued a report in May 1988 revealing that library directors were being asked to provide the circulation records of people "with Eastern European or Russian-sounding names." Only public outrage and political attention caused the abandonment of the Library Awareness Program.[9] As a result, the ALA Council adopted the so-called Policy on Confidentiality of Library Records. While all U.S. states recognize the importance of privacy and confidentiality in maintaining library patron records, federal law has yet to designate these records as privileged.

Professional and National Concerns

The PATRIOT Act raises significant problems that have challenged the professional ethics of this nation's librarians. Issues related to library users' privacy have caused the library profession to aggressively enter the national controversy generated by this hastily enacted legislation. Despite expressing initial concerns about various aspects of the PATRIOT Act, librarians have collectively restricted their reactions and responses primarily to the issue of FBI agents' access to library patrons' records.

The foundation of librarians' protestations is the right to privacy. The conundrum facing Americans is that one finds no right to privacy explicitly expressed in the Constitution. The acknowledgment of what seems like a fundamental exclusion begs the question of whether privacy is indeed a fundamental right. In fact, expectations about the right to privacy are based on an aggregate of laws, not the U.S. Constitution or its amendments. Nevertheless, Americans have come to expect a certain level of privacy as representative of the democracy in which they live. The scope of powers of search and surveillance that federal agents can now exercise as provided by the Patriot Act is unprecedented in our history. U.S. Representative Bernie Sanders of Vermont, an outspoken critic of the PATRIOT Act, states that "the right to read without government surveillance is a cornerstone of our democracy." But most important, he reminds us that First Amendment freedoms mean "nothing without a correlative freedom to read."[10] The First Amendment notwithstanding, a person's speech can still be challenged, sometimes even through the judicial system. Yet few Americans have ever considered that governmental agencies could scrutinize what they read.

Librarians' challenges and opposition to the PATRIOT Act can perhaps be best understood when placed in the context of the Bill of Rights. Provisions of the PATRIOT Act's section 215 are currently of greatest concern, as they stand in direct violation of or opposition to the First and Fourth Amendments to the U.S. Constitution. Amendment 1 reads as follows: "Congress shall make no law respecting an establishment of religion, or prohibiting the free exercise thereof; or abridging the freedom of speech, or of the press; or the right of the people peaceably to assemble, and to petition the Government for a redress of grievances." This amendment is perhaps the one most frequently invoked in the United States. It assures that Americans are free to express their ideas without fear of reprisal, regardless of the content or context of those ideas. It also attempts to create an environment in which people are free to express their political opinions openly. Because the new category of so-called domestic terrorism in the PATRIOT Act broadens the definition of terrorism, the line between free speech and illegal or criminal activity has become unclear. This ambiguity will likely diminish the free expression of political views that are unpopular or without mainstream support.

According to the American Civil Liberties Union (ACLU), "Section 215 violates the First Amendment because it allows the government to easily obtain information about, for example, the books people read, the Web sites they visit, and the religious institutions they attend and support."[11] Librarians throughout the country now live with the increased likelihood that the FBI will appear at any moment with an order to provide records of customer's library usage, not only for materials borrowed but also for records of Web sites visited or e-mails sent from library computers.

A residual effect of the challenges to citizens' freedom of speech is that limits will be placed on the public's access to information and ideas. Ultimately, the free exchange of ideas and information will be hampered, and political debates and criticism will be diluted. The consequences are even more serious when considering that future generations of adults may become reluctant to explore their intellectual curiosities or express their opinions openly. It does not seem so far-fetched to imagine that people will eventually hesitate before faxing a letter to the editor of a newspaper, calling in to a radio program, sending an angry e-mail to an elected official, or making a negative remark about a politician. Perhaps they will hesitate, and perhaps they should. Citizens across the country have been given the loud and clear message that publicly expressed negative opinions about President Bush are not tolerated. Federal agents have interrogated high school students without their parents after the students made nonviolent, but negative, comments regarding the president. A student in Ohio was even questioned for wearing an anti-Bush T-shirt.[12]

There have been other periods in our nation's history when the FBI was encouraged to investigate American citizens for exercising free speech. The reverend Martin Luther King Jr. had long been scrutinized by the FBI, but surveillance of him increased significantly after he began to express his opposition to the Vietnam War.[13] The difference now is that such actions appear to be supported by law. The FBI has free reign to monitor individuals and groups based on their political affiliation, regardless of the protections that the First Amendment provides.

There has been a nationwide resurgence in the use of public libraries as community centers. As such, libraries frequently host political forums, meetings, and events sponsored by organizations and individuals with a variety of political persuasions. A minority of the public continues to object to public library purchases of certain books and to particular groups meeting in libraries. Generally, thus far, library directors and administrators have not been forced to restrict the use of facilities to certain groups. However, librarians frequently find themselves in the difficult position of becoming pawns in the highly political game of public funding.

Under the PATRIOT Act, assembling for the purpose of criticizing the government could now be considered a crime, even when violence is not advocated. Although advocacy of "non-imminent" violence was ruled as protected speech by the Supreme Court in 1969, the PATRIOT Act appears to be in conflict with that ruling.[14] Of primary concern is that actions by the federal government presented as protections and security measures could also prevent the American public from having free access to information and ideas.

Amendment 4 reads: "The right of the people to be secure in their persons, houses, papers, and effects, against unreasonable searches and seizures, shall not be violated, and no Warrants shall issue, but upon probable cause, supported by Oath or affirmation, and particularly describing the place to be searched, and the persons or things to be seized." The PATRIOT Act increases the search and surveillance authority of federal agents through the business records section, section 215, of the Foreign Intelligence Surveillance Act (FISA). Some aspects of this authority are not new; FISA already provided access to records of specific types of businesses. The new provisions, however, allow searches to extend to "any relevant tangible item, including books, records, papers, documents, and other items."[15] Libraries, bookstores, and newspaper organizations are not specifically mentioned in FISA, yet librarians have focused on the examples listed in the act: books and records. They are fearful that patrons' reading and internet activities can be examined, unchecked, by FBI agents. The provision in the PATRIOT Act overrides the laws that all but two states in the United States have put in place to protect the confidentiality of library records.[16] Even more frightening, this authority can be applied to any business. Imagine the kinds of information that would be circulated among FBI agents if newspaper or television investigative reporters' notes were seized. Regardless of whether the information could be verified or corroborated, the implications are almost too horrible to imagine. In addition, the act also prohibits alerting someone to the fact that the FBI is investigating their reading habits, Internet activity, or bookstore purchases. Although the Supreme Court ruled in 2002 that an individual has the right to purchase books anonymously, the PATRIOT Act negates the intent of that ruling.[17] Because notification of citizens targeted by the investigations is forbidden, they have no chance to challenge the legality of the investigations. Regarding the gag order, the FBI has stated that librarians can only discuss the court order with an attorney to acquire assistance with processing the subpoena;[18] notification of anyone else is prohibited. Yet in most cases the law requires a search warrant, which gives librarians little or no time to confer with legal counsel. A search warrant, unlike a subpoena, can be acted on by agents immediately. In such a case, the librarian will have to comply immediately, or risk facing criminal charges.

Another disturbing factor is the apparent ease with which a search can be conducted. All that is needed to conduct an investigation or surveillance is the approval of the attorney general, although a court order is required in cases in which the investigator plans to conduct surveillance without notifying the parties being monitored or investigated.[19] This requirement of judicial review provides absolutely no protection for citizens because if an agent requests the court order stating that the investigation means "to protect against international terrorism or clandestine intelligence," the judge must grant permission. He or she has no authority to exercise discretion in issuing the warrant, and the proceedings are conducted in secret. In essence, a court order can be obtained to access library or other business records without demonstrating any level of probable cause or wrongdoing, and no one will know about it.

In addition, the act provides agents with the authority to track electronic communications, including e-mail and Internet activity. How will a librarian, or any person, be able to justify having innocently logged onto a Web site that the FBI is tracking, or should they even need to justify their Web activity? In the absence of any level of interrogation, and without his or her awareness, a librarian could become the object of a secret investigation that is baseless, as well as professionally and personally destructive. The notion of librarians having to turn over Internet use logs to agents seems disturbing enough, but the new electronic tracking and surveillance authority is extremely troubling. Dialing, routing, and signaling information can all now be legally tracked. The law requires agents to stop short of actually reading the content of e-mail messages. However, technologically, it remains impossible to separate routing information from the e-mail message itself. In 2001, the Justice Department issued a field guide to assist agents in becoming familiar with the new laws.[20] It seems absurd to expect that agents will not read messages in the process of tracking.

The new roving wiretap authority that the act provides also means that if a person is being investigated, any electronic communications that the person is likely to use may be tapped. Surveillance could include business telephone and computer lines at the person's place of employment and any public equipment the person uses, such as library public-use computers. Most alarming is the absence of constraints on the scope and duration of these activities, giving possible access to records or information about people who were not initially intended targets of the search.[21] Without strict guidelines and oversight, there is no guarantee that computer activity or telephone calls will not be tracked and recorded at times when in use by people other than the intended person. In the case of a library computer lab, if the intended person does not have a favored computer, all of the computers become suspect and may be monitored.

Hunkered Down, Prepared, and Defiant

Librarians' actions in defiance of the Patriot Act are based on personal convictions and the professional code of ethics to which they are committed. Excerpts from the code reveal the basis of the conflict:

American Library Association Code of Ethics:
Ethical dilemmas occur when values are in conflict. The American Library
Association Code of Ethics states the values to which we are committed
and embodies the ethical responsibilities of the profession in this changing
information environment.

• We have a special obligation to ensure the free flow of information and ideas to present and future generations.

• We protect each library user's right to privacy and confidentiality with respect to information sought or received and sources consulted, borrowed, acquired, or transmitted.[22]

Long before the PATRIOT Act became law, librarians were working in Washington to change its proposed wording and modify the provisions in section 215. They were ultimately unsuccessful, but they have not gone away quietly. The ALA joined with various organizations to form a coalition for the purpose of fighting the act through the judicial system. Millions of dollars have been spent in legal fees and other costs related to what everyone knew in advance would be a difficult and protracted battle.

The ACLU's first official challenge to the PATRIOT Act came on July 30, 2002, and charged that section 215 of the act violates citizens' and residents' rights to privacy, due process, and free speech by allowing the FBI to search library, business, and bookstore records in terrorist investigations without publicly disclosing that it has done so. Subsequent to the filing, the ACLU distributed posters informing the public about the PATRIOT Act, as well as about the fact that librarians were forbidden from informing them when their reading records were being accessed. It also directed any questions to John Ashcroft.[23]

While the library association participates in the struggle on the national level, librarians have determined that, locally, their best strategy is to be well informed and prepared and to find innovative, creative, and lawful means of continuing to conduct business. Those means include educating the public about the PATRIOT Act and librarians' concerns; assuring that collections are balanced in presentation of controversial subject matter; revising policies, procedures, regulations, and mission statements; and assuring that staff on all levels are trained and confident in their ability to handle any situation that might occur. That training and confidence, of course, will only come through working with skilled and knowledgeable professionals. Therefore, engaging the services of highly skilled legal counsel and training specialists has proven essential.

Libraries can and should change the way they do business in response to the issues under discussion here. Doing so may be considered simple, but in fact policy changes require attitudinal, operational, and procedural changes, as well as significant time for considering vital questions and issues. For example, if the policy change is to limit the amount of data maintained on a user, what are the institutional and legal implications? How was the data used in the past, and will the absence of that data in the future negatively affect operations? Will data created prior to the policy change be deleted, and is that deletion a violation of local or state laws?

Shortly after 9/11 and the passage of the PATRIOT Act, a survey conducted by the *Library Research Center* (LRC) at the University of Illinois revealed that few libraries had changed their policies on access to library usage materials and Internet usage. Although sixty public library staff and boards had been provided with information and instructions on how to respond to federal agent inquires, fewer than one out of ten had actually revised or created a policy in response to passage of the act.[24] Three years later, the findings would be vastly different. Throughout the country, not only have policies changed but ways of conducting everyday business have been modified. Librarians have found legal ways to continue conducting business without compromising their values or breaking the law. Although changes in policies and procedures have varied by location and political climate, frequent responses have included:

- Periodically washing backup tapes and files

- Restricting access to specific information to certain levels of staff

- Minimizing the number of patron records maintained

- Deleting traceable information at the end of all computer sessions (including cookies)

- Retaining no records after a book or item has been returned, unless an overdue fine has not been paid

- Recording only Internet site usage information, not user information specific to individuals

- Prominently displaying notification of what identifiable library patron information is being maintained

Librarians have been catalysts in the struggle against the PATRIOT Act because they have been able to harness some of their outrage, indignation, and concern by working actively through appropriate channels and thus have facilitated change. Because of the public's high regard for libraries, librarians have tremendous political clout, which they yet have to fully utilize. Not all librarians in the country agree with the library association's very public posture in the fight against the act. While many are concerned about the valid dangers that face our nation and the inappropriate measures taken to maintain a sense of national security, they are, politically, reluctant to bite the hand that feeds them.

Librarians are not lemmings, they are not easily duped, and they do not all dance to the same beat. Nevertheless, finding common ground on which to build collective responses is paramount. With the passage of time, if the public's resistance to the PATRIOT Act continues to diminish, a major concern for those engaged in resistance and criticism is that in the event of another major terrorist attack in this country, even more liberties will be lost in the government's response to that event.

Rhetoric and Retaliation

Despite sharp criticism, John Ashcroft offered no apology or concession for what he saw as appropriate security measures. Instead, he attacked the PATRIOT Act's critics with the same rhetorical fervor with which he defended the legislation itself,[25] calling on the nation's media to help "dispel fears about" the act.[26] Attributing the intense criticism of the PATRIOT Act to disinformation, Ashcroft attempted to belittle librarians by suggesting that they allowed themselves to be conned by the ALCU and others, thus stimulating "baseless hysteria" about the FBI's use of the PATRIOT Act in surveillances related to the public's reading habits.[27]

In a series of speeches intended to quell the growing criticism against the PATRIOT Act, Ashcroft continuously lampooned librarians and insulted the intelligence of many Americans by reiterating his assertion that the search warrant powers under the act have greater safeguards than grand jury warrants. Ashcroft mockingly quipped that the ALA believed "the FBI is not fighting terrorism. Instead, agents are checking how far you have gotten on the latest Tom Clancy novel."[28]

The current Bush administration has gotten a reputation of having a "take no prisoners" posture in political confrontations, so it seems unsurprising that librarians came under attack. Despite the fact that the president's wife is a librarian, it was far too easy for Ashcroft to summon the stereotype of librarians as easily conned and better off sticking to what they know: books. Although not everyone agrees with librarians' position on the issues, even supporters of the PATRIOT Act who believe that "librarians are providing a sanctuary for terrorists" acknowledge that librarians have become an important political force. Paul Walfield declares almost nostalgically that "ALA librarians are not the quiet, unassuming stereotypes you see on TV and in the movies."[29] Many in the library profession saw the attacks as affirmation of the existence of a chink in the proverbial armor. Emily Sheketoff, executive director of the library association's Washington office, stated that "if [Ashcroft is] coming after us so specifically, we must be having an impact,"[30] and John Berry relished the fact that librarians' leadership in raising critical issues about the PATRIOT Act have been "important enough to be a problem," and he encouraged them "to keep up the pressure and activism."[31] In the library association's official response, ALA president Carla Hayden, director of the Enoch Pratt Public Library in Baltimore, characterized Ashcroft as "openly contemptuous of those who seek to defend our Constitution" and challenged him to release aggregate information about the number of libraries visited using the expanded powers created by the PATRIOT Act.[32]

Despite Ashcroft's declaration that the FBI has neither the time nor the inclination to track the public's reading habits, the Justice Department for two years refused to release the information that Hayden requested, despite several FOIA petitions. By way of explaining such refusals, Elaine Scarry reports that "in October 2001 Attorney General Ashcroft sent a memo to many government departments telling them that if they declined to answer Freedom of Information Act requests, the Justice Department would support them."[33] In a telephone conversation with Hayden subsequent to the ALA's response, Ashcroft agreed to release the requested data. On September 18, 2003, he stated that "the number of times Section 215 has been used to this date is zero."[34]

For most people in the profession, that claim reduced Ashcroft's credibility even further. Less than five days after he proclaimed that section 215 had not been used to access library business or patron records, the California Library Association reported the results of a survey that appeared to contradict his claim. The survey revealed that since September 11, 2001, federal agents had contacted fourteen libraries in California with formal requests for patron record information.[35] Sam Morrison, the now retired director of Florida's Broward County Library, never hid the fact that FBI agents contacted his office soon after 9/11, although he said the FBI specifically instructed him not to reveal any information about the request.[36]

In addition, the research activities conducted in libraries by the LRC at the Graduate School of Library and Information Science beginning in 2001 were well known. Startlingly, results of an October 2002 survey mailed to 1,505 public libraries serving populations of over 5,000 revealed that 219 libraries voluntarily cooperated with law enforcement requests to provide information about library patrons' internet activities and reading habits. The surveys revealed that staff at 225 other libraries had declined voluntary cooperation.[37] In a survey of 585 public and private libraries in Illinois during the fall of 2003, seven public libraries reported having received requests for patrons' or circulation records from the FBI, and a total of eight libraries reported having been approached with a request related to a national security investigation. Fourteen libraries declined to answer some of the questions for fear of violating the law, although the survey did not seek information specific to the issuance of any section 215 orders or warrants.[38]

What accounts for such a drastic contradiction? Either Ashcroft's assertion was either factually inaccurate and intentionally misleading, a fabrication created to deceive the public for the sake of national security, or the contradiction is a matter of interpretation and semantics. In this highly nuanced political environment, perhaps in the absence of legal counsel, librarians may not have made distinctions between FISA physical search orders and other types of methods such as simple requests or criminal search warrants. If presented with what is clearly a valid search warrant by an FBI agent or law officer, in the current climate a librarian would probably assume it to be a FISA warrant. The results are, nevertheless, the same: the desired records and information are handed over.

Bill Olds, a former columnist for the *Hartford Courant,* began writing about section 215 when he learned that FBI officers had entered the local library, seized the hard drive of a computer, and exited, apparently without providing any explanation to the staff. The local FBI office responded with what Olds perceived as indignation when he was told that the hard drive had been seized because of an ordinary criminal investigation, not an alleged terrorist investigation.[39]

Therein lies a major problem with the legislation. Because the investigations are shrouded in extraordinary secrecy, agents can easily hide or disguise their actions, and librarians may be reluctant to ask questions. The intimidation resulting from the circumstances may shield agents from having to invoke section 215 provisions because they get the desired results without it.

No one really knows how many times library records have been requested in investigations related to homeland security since 9/11. Without accurate data, Congress and the public have no way of knowing if federal agents are abusing their new powers. Nonetheless, Justice Department spokespersons continue to deny, and even mock, the notion of an interest in library records, while librarians across the country continue to report activities directly contradicting Justice Department claims.

Why Libraries Are at Risk

Public libraries have struggled against social and political marginalization for over a century in this country. For policymakers and the social elite, libraries in many cities have become the place of last resort for information and access, and they remain a political afterthought except in times of crisis. Although librarians' success at providing services and collections that address the needs of a broad range of intellectual, educational, and recreational needs has endeared them to many, memories fade and allegiances shift quickly. Nevertheless, a portion of the country's population depends daily on public library services for their basic informational needs.

There are two values that keep people coming to libraries each day: trust and dependability. Not only do people depend on libraries to provide access to the materials and information they need; they also trust that they can carry out their activities in the library with a certain level of privacy and confidentiality. That is what Americans expect from libraries, institutionally, and that is what libraries have come to represent. When library users can no longer trust that libraries are able to protect their most private intellectual and informational explorations, they will stop coming. When libraries can no longer protect users' rights to educate and inform themselves with anonymity and confidentiality, a core and foundational aspect of their institutional identity will have been lost.

Librarians must continue to find creative ways to take a stance and challenge what is seen as wrong or detrimental to their existence. If not, they risk sending a message to the public that their trust has been misplaced. When libraries cannot be trusted with or protect the information about what their customers read, they have not only lost part of their identity but also their credibility. Recommendations have been made for librarians to post signs warning the public that library users' records can be obtained by federal agents. This approach continues to reinforce the perception that the library is helpless to protect itself and its customers. If signs are posted, they should take a different approach: the signs should identify what steps the library has taken to protect the public's right to privacy.

Without proactive measures, including courageous defiance, what can librarians expect next? Will the homeland security agents tell librarians which books they cannot purchase, or will they be told who cannot have access to certain materials? Despite the challenges posed over time to intellectual freedom in the United States, prior to 9/11, the answer to those questions would certainly have been a resounding no. Now it seems questionable. Will right-wing conservatives link access to information to shifting social norms? Is access to books such as *Daddy's Roommate*, written by Michael Willhoite, to blame for the changes in attitudes that led to the recent Supreme Court decision eliminating antisodomy laws? The implications do not seem so far fetched. One has to only recall the drastic budget cuts affecting the arts several years ago when politicians decided that they were offended by what others created or identified as art.

Unfinished Business

Because the PATRIOT Act was hurriedly created and passed with little congressional debate, the sunset provisions were essential for revisiting its most troublesome aspects. The initial law required the sunshine provisions to be reapproved by December 31, 2005. However, any international terrorism investigations underway by that date may continue indefinitely without any impediment.[40] The debate continues in Congress related to access to information and terrorism, but now it is pursued on a piecemeal basis. PATRIOT Act 2, the Domestic Security Enhancement Act of 2003, was apparently abandoned because details of its contents were leaked to the media, causing its contents to be debated in the media before official legislative debates began.[41] That proposed legislation sought to solidify as law many of the issues in the first act that were troublesome and had sunset provisions. However, many of those measures are likely to be recycled and to reappear in future proposals.

Legislation has been initiated by various congresspersons and senators to invalidate or limit certain provisions of the PATRIOT Act. Bills currently under consideration include:

• Protecting the Rights of Individuals Act (seeks to restore some of the liberties lost by passage of the PATRIOT Act and creates protective measures that prevent actions and methods adopted by the presidential administration and Justice Department without congressional approval)[42]

• Safe Act (significantly limiting the measures currently in section 215 of the PATRIOT Act, including exempting librarians, restricting the Justice Department's access to other business records, restricting federal agents' use of the so-called sneak-and-peak provisions in section 213, and increasing the requirement for probable cause in surveillance operations)

• Library, Bookseller, and Personal Records Privacy Act (significantly restricting federal agent's ability to obtain a person's library reading records or business transactions currently allowed in section 215 of the PATRIOT Act)

• Restoration of Freedom of Information Act (restoring the public's ability to obtain information on government agency activities)

• Freedom to Read Protection Act (exempting libraries and bookstores from section 215 of the PATRIOT Act)[43]

Lest anyone think that the toughest struggles are over, consider a few recent developments. Reports filed in May 2004 indicated that the Justice Department sought to expand an FBI subpoena power currently so secret that a lawsuit challenging it was kept quiet.[44] The ACLU disclosed in late April 2004 that it filed a lawsuit challenging the FBI's methods of obtaining business records. However, the ACLU was prohibited from even revealing the existence of the lawsuit. Filed on April 6, 2004, the case was sealed to avoid violating secrecy provisions contained in the PATRIOT Act. Only a redacted version of the lawsuit was permitted to be released after several weeks of negotiations with government officials.[45] At issue was the FBI's practice of issuing letters requiring businesses and organizations to submit business records, including telephone logs, e-mail, and electronic records containing financial and other personal information. Issued independently by FBI field offices since 9/11, these letters were considered a type of administrative subpoena currently "not subject to judicial review unless a case comes to court." The ACLU contends that "electronic communication service providers" should be able to notify the people whose information has been revealed.[46]

Conclusion

Despite presumed good intentions, not all measures established to protect U.S. citizens since the terrorist attacks of September 11, 2001, can be viewed as positive. Presidential executive orders, new regulations, and the PATRIOT Act have made it easier for governmental agencies to investigate, identify, and prosecute would-be terrorists. However, in the process, many rights and liberties that Americans take for granted have been quietly eliminated or reduced. The ALA and many of its members have emerged as leaders in challenging and bringing some these ill-advised provisions to the attention of politicians and the public. Yet their attentions have primarily focused on a narrow aspect of the PATRIOT Act. Although the focus of attention has centered on the critical issue of protecting library user records, the greatest risk for libraries and the public is not whether federal agents have access to libraries' business records. While librarians' efforts in the fight for the right to privacy for library users are not misplaced, the future may prove that equal attention is required to highlight additional issues that can be linked to American values and constitutional privileges of equivalent importance such as freedom of access to information (regardless of its controversial nature), the right to assemble, and the criminalization of free thought and free speech.

The greatest challenge seems to come in the form of broad information-related issues that librarians and others have thus far failed to raise with significant zeal. The diminished access to governmental information, which includes revised FOIA policies and the removal of Web-based government information, has scarcely received librarians' attention. Although the PATRIOT Act does not specifically address these issues, they should not be perceived as ancillary in importance. Perhaps issues such as the manipulation of information and public opinion will prove more difficult to challenge, but they are nonetheless important. In order to be fully effective, librarians must embrace a newly emerging role as national leaders on information-related issues beyond matters that narrowly affect library operations. Clearly, librarians are willing to fight for the basic human values and rights on which this country was built, and their engagement on a variety of levels in the overall struggle to prevent additional loss of liberty in the name of protection has made a tremendous difference.

Notes

1. Arialdi M. Miniño, Elizabeth Arias, Betty L. Smith, Kenneth D. Kochanek, and Sherry L. Murphy, "Deaths: Final Data for 2000," *National Vital Statistics Reports* 50 (2002), www.cdc.gov/nchs/data/nvsr/nvsr50/nvsr50_15.pdf.

2. Ahmedin Jemal et al., "Cancer Statistics, 2003," *CA Cancer Journal for Clinicians* 53 (2003): 5–26, caonline.amcancersoc.org/cgi/content/full/53/1/5.

3. Christopher M. Hughes et al., "How Many Deaths Are Due to Medical Errors?" *JAMA* 284 (2000): 2187.

4. USA PATRIOT Act HR 3162, title 2, section 215; Amending the Foreign Intelligence Surveillance Act (FISA), title 5, section 501(a)(1), leahy.senate.gov/press/200110/USA.pdf (accessed May 4, 2004).

5. Daniel Akaka, published statement regarding Government Accounting Office report "Data Mining: Federal Efforts Cover a Wide Range of Uses" (GAO-04-548), www.gao.gov. Akaka statement is available at akaka.senate.gov/~akaka/releases/04/05/2004527449.html (accessed May 27, 2004).

6. Maurice Wheeler and Debbie Johnson-Houston, "A Brief History of Library Service to African Americans," *American Libraries*, February 2004, 42–45.

7. Louise S. Robbins, "Loyalty Investigations in the Library of Congress, 1947–1956: No 'Communists or Cocksuckers,'" *Library Quarterly* 64 (1994): 365–85.

8. Herbert N. Foerstel, *Surveillance in the Stacks: The FBI's Library Awareness Program* (New York: Greenwood, 1991).

9. Ann Beeson and Jameel Jaffer, *Unpatriotic Acts: The FBI's Power to Rifle through Your Records and Personal Belongings without Telling You* (New York: ACLU, 2003), 10.

10. Bernie Sanders, "The Patriot's Act Threat to Libraries," *American Libraries*, February 2003, 32.

11. Beeson and Jaffer, *Unpatriotic Acts*, 7.

12. George Paine, "Secret Service Questions Student for Anti-Bush T-Shirt," December 11, 2002, www.warblogging.com/archives/000379.php.

13. Morton Halperin et al., *The Lawless State: The Crimes of the U.S. Intelligence Agencies* (New York: Penguin, 1976).

14. *Brandenburg v. Ohio*, 395 U.S. 444 (1969), www.bc.edu/bc_org/avp/cas/comm/free_speech/brandenburg.html (accessed August 5, 2003).

15. Congressional Research Service (CRS) Report for Congress, Code RS21441, February 26, 2003. Charles Doyle, "Libraries and the USA PATRIOT Act," CRS, Library of Congress, www.ala.org/Content/NavigationMenu/Our_Association/Offices/ALA_Washington/Issues2/Civil_Liberties,_Intellectual_Freedom,_Privacy/The_USA_Patriot_Act_and_Libraries/CRS215LibrariesAnalysis.pdf (accessed August 5, 2003).

16. American Library Association Office of International Freedom, "Confidentiality and Coping with Law Enforcement Inquiries: Guidelines for the Library and Its Staff" (April 2004), www.ala.org/Template.cfm?Section=Intellectual_Freedom_Issues&Template=/ContentManagement/ContentDisplay.cfm&ContentID=21654.

17. Dean Schabner, "Defining the Right to Read: Librarians, Booksellers Take on Feds over Patriot Act Provisions," ABC News, abcnews.go.com/US/story?id=90681&page=1 (accessed April 18, 2005).

18. Statement of Congressman Sanders on 6/23/2003 Regarding: Freedom to Read Protection Act, bernie.house.gov/statements/20030623160151.asp (accessed April 18, 2005).

19. Ibid.

20. United States Department of Justice, Computer Crime and Intellectual Property Section (CCIPS), "Field Guidance on New Authorities that Relate to Computer Crime and Electronic Evidence Enacted in the USA PATRIOT Act of 2001," www.usdoj.gov/criminal/cybercrime/PatriotAct.htm (accessed August 5, 2003).

21. Elaine Scarry, "Resolving to Resist: Local Governments Are Refusing to Comply with the Patriot Act," *Boston Review* online edition, www.bostonreview.net/BR29.1/scarry.html (accessed May 5, 2004).

22. "American Library Association Code of Ethics," adopted by the ALA, June 28, 1995, www.ala.org/ala/oif/statementspols/codeofethics/coehistory/codeofethics.pdf (accessed April 18, 2005).

23. "ACLU Makes First Patriot Act Challenge," *American Libraries*, September 2003, 14.

24. Graduate School of Library and Information Science, University of Illinois at Urbana-Champaign, "Public Libraries and Civil Liberties: A Profession Divided," alexia.lis.uiuc.edu/gslis/research/civil_liberties.html (accessed April 18, 2005).

25. Dan Eggan, "Ashcroft *Derides* Patriot Act Critics," *Washington Post,* September 19, 2003.

26. "Statement of Congressman Sanders," bernie.house.gov/statements/20030623160151.asp (accessed April 18, 2005).

27. "Ashcroft Mocks Librarians in Patriot Act Defense," *American Libraries*, November 2003, 10.

28. Ibid.

29. Paul Walfield, "The ALA Library: Terrorist Sanctuary," May 8, 2003, www.frontpagemag.com/Articles/Printable.asp?ID=7704.

30. Quoted in Eric Lichtblau, "Ashcroft Mocks Librarians and Others Who Oppose Parts of Counterterrorism Law," *New York Times*, September 15, 2003.

31. John Berry, "High Profile, Strong Image." *Library Journal*, December 2003, 8.

32. Quoted in "Ashcroft Mocks Librarians in Patriot Act Defense," 10.

33. Scarry, "Resolving to Resist."

34. Quoted in "Ashcroft Mocks Librarians in Patriot Act Defense," 10.

35. "FBI Visited Sixteen California Libraries since 9/11," *American Libraries*, November 2003, 11.

36. "FBI Monitoring Library Records in Terror Probe," www.freedomforum.org/templates/document.asp?documentID=16468 (accessed April 18, 2005).

37. "Public libraries and Civil Liberties," alexia.lis.uiuc.edu/gslis/research/civil_liberties.html.

38. David Mehegan, "Reading Over Your Shoulder," *Boston Globe*, March 9, 2004, bernie .house.gov/documents/articles/20040309103150.asp.

39. Scarry, "Resolving to Resist."

40. Ibid.

41. Shannon McCaffrey, "Patriot Act May Expand," May 22, 2004, bernie.house.gov/documents/articles/20040525204431.asp.

42. "ACLU Applauds Wyden Sponsorship of Bill to Roll Back USA Patriot Act," www.aclu-or .org/issues/terrorism/murkwydenbill/murk_wyden.htm (accessed April 18, 2005).

43. Scarry, "Resolving to Resist."

44. McCaffrey, "Patriot Act May Expand."

45. Dan Eggen, "Patriot Act Suppresses Challenge to Patriot Act," *Washington Post*, April 29, 2004: A17.

46. Ibid.

Digital Democracy, Digital History:
"9–11 and After"

Barbara Abrash

The attack on the World Trade Center marked a watershed moment between utopian hopes for open communication and the chilling of free speech, ushered in with the passage of the USA PATRIOT Act. On September 11, 2001, and in the days following, the utopian potential was briefly, strangely, realized in lower Manhattan, as people spontaneously created networks of communication, using every available form of technology from disposable cameras to the Internet, in order to connect, record, and grieve.

The 1990s were years of intense activity and belief in the liberating potential of old and new media technologies. The transnational HIV/AIDS movement, anti–World Trade Organization actions, and human rights campaigns are just a few examples of the activism enabled by readily available small-format video and digital technologies, which opened new circuits of connection, reconfiguring global and local, physical and virtual worlds.

In April 2001, the Center for Media, Culture, and History at New York University, which has a long-standing interest in the relationship between alternative media and cultural activism, invited an international group of media theorists and activists to explore emerging practices in a transforming media landscape. The participants in that meeting cited the need for a series of Web-based "virtual case books," each one organized around a specific issue. HIV/AIDS was to be the first subject. As events would have it, the first virtual case book came to be "9–11 and After" (www.nyu.edu/fas/projects/vcb), a Web project that maps the social uses of

Radical History Review
Issue 93 (Fall 2005): 96–100
Copyright 2005 by MARHO: The Radical Historians' Organization, Inc.

media technologies in lower Manhattan in the aftermath of the attack on the World Trade Center.[1] As we wrote in the introduction,

> Because of our location in lower Manhattan, we were particularly struck by the almost instantaneous proliferation of small and ephemeral media, particularly on the city streets. Candles, flowers, messages, posters, photos, vigils, performances, demonstrations, and singing transformed the cityscape in ways that corresponded to the altered consciousness of city residents. These became the media through which people sought loved ones, created memorials, expressed sorrow and grief, and told stories in an effort to comprehend and communicate such a traumatic and unprecedented experience. Downtown streets and parks, especially Union Square, became spontaneous sites of public gathering. Further distinguishing this public tragedy were the ways in which this kind of expression also took place virtually on the Internet, over cell phones, through radio. The virtual and physical realms came together unexpectedly.

We were troubled to note that this creative outpouring of public expression, with its great diversity of concerns and opinions, remained largely absent from national media coverage. After a stumbling start, the media contained the meanings of September 11 in a patriotic narrative of a nation on its way to war. And while there were many critiques of mass-media coverage, there was little discussion of the social and political significance of the practices we were witnessing.

"9–11 and After: A Virtual Casebook" brings together essays, Web sites, images, and interviews that frame, exhibit, and archive this public display of social expression. Field reports from places as distant as India, Amsterdam, and Palestine show how communities far from Ground Zero maintained connections through the Internet. In addition to eyewitness accounts, we explore the role of photography, museum exhibitions, memorials, video, and audio in giving shape and meaning to inchoate experiences.

September 11 has served to emphasize the fact that the telecommunications umbrella has made public events part of the texture of our individual lives.[2] In essays and interviews, "9–11 and After" shows the spontaneity and speed with which public spaces were improvised and claimed. Here Is New York: A Democracy of Photographs (www.hereisnewyork.org), which opened in a storefront in SoHo in early October 2001, is one example. In an interview, co-organizer Charles Traub describes this impromptu gallery space that became a site of witness, grieving, and exchange. Crowds lined up at its doors to view the thousands of photographs of the disaster on its walls and in its digital archives—photographs made by professionals and amateurs alike and exhibited without attribution. The space was at once a town hall, a chapel, a trauma center. It was, says Traub, "reality enabled by the virtual world."

City Lore, an organization that celebrates the cultural heritage of New York City, quickly joined neighborhood efforts to preserve and document the ephemeral material that the New York City Parks Department soon began clearing from public sites. Partnering with the New-York Historical Society, City Lore produced Missing: Streetscape of a City in Mourning (www.citylore.org), an exhibition of the photographs, found poetry, shrines, drawings, sculpture, and other expressions that filled parks, streets, and Web sites. The exhibition itself became a site of memory and storytelling. Says cocurator Marci Reaven, "Stories root you. They help establish a relationship with the swirling world around you. How to weave this extraordinary event into the fabric of your life?"

Barbara Kirshenblatt Gimblett has likened the streets of New York in the days after September 11 to one great public art project. Her essay "Kodak Moments, Flashbulb Memories: Reflections on 9/11" reminds us that this "spectacle that was photographed incessantly and seen instantaneously across the globe" will be remembered in images. But will it be in the endlessly replayed television images of falling towers and billowing smoke, or in the proliferation of Kodak moments—the meanings of which are multiple, ambiguous, and impossible to contain?[3]

In her essay "Witnessing 9–11," Diana Taylor speaks of those who watched the towers in flames as "witnesses without a narrative" and describes the impulse to take pictures as a way of bridging the gap between seeing and knowing, of making sense of incomprehensible experiences, of finding a way to form the threads of narrative.

The virtual casebook traces this complex and continuous process of narrative making in which personal accounts blend into social narratives and public stories—and the events of September 11 become history. The question is: Whose history will it be? What will count as evidence? Will it represent the subjectivity of those who lived it? Here, archives and the ways in which they select, organize, and display their holdings play a crucial role.

The September 11 Digital Archive,[4] which is committed to telling the "history of all the people in their own voices," took up the challenge of organizing and preserving personal stories, cartoons, oral histories, e-mails, and digital folk art: digital shrines, memorial quilts, animations, videos, and altered photographs. The archive "uses electronic media to collect, preserve, and present the history of the September 11, 2001 attacks in New York, Virginia, and Pennsylvania and the public responses to them." It is designed as a resource for historians, both professional and nonprofessional. Project directors Andrea Vasquez and Fritz Umbach, in their belief that "information in itself is not powerful—how it is shaped, who decides, and how it is circulated are crucial,"[5] state, "We are archiving raw material for the construction of counternarratives to nationalistic, patriotic, vengeful responses."

Meg McLagan reports on the Television Archive (www.televisionarchive

.org), a Web site that streams September 11 programming from nineteen sources around the world. As she says, "Given TV's centrality as an arena of political conflict and public debate in contemporary democratic societies, it is essential that citizens have free access to this form of primary source material."[6] The Television Archive challenges restrictive copyright claims by offering a contract that allows the non-commercial use of materials so long as the original source is identified. The Television Archive thus constitutes both a significant resource and an innovative intervention in the politics of information control.

While they offer unparalleled opportunities for archiving and research, digital forms also present significant challenges. How to select, preserve, and index such vast amounts of material? The digital archives that house the ephemera are themselves fragile—Web sites disappear (many of the URLs provided in "9–11 and After" have ceased to exist), and digital technologies quickly become obsolete. For the historian, evidence that is fragmented, often unattributed, and recombinant raises questions of credibility and historical truth, as well as profoundly challenging conventions of linear narrative.

How will the events of September 11 be remembered and told? As Pat Aufderheide points out, mainstream television news quickly settled on a tone of "therapeutic patriotism" that claims to heal but can also obscure remembering.[7] "9–11 and After" demonstrates a range of grassroots documentation and a multiplicity of voices, opinions, and information that challenge both official stories and traditional approaches to history.

This project provides fertile ground for exploring two key questions: Can we consider the Web a potential site of cultural resistance—a memory place where stories, both grassroots and mainstream, are shared, contested, and circulated over time? And, what do the open and inventive practices of testimony, documentation, and political expression that flowered in response to traumatic events suggest about new ways of writing history—digitally and otherwise?

Notes

All quotes in the text, unless otherwise identified, are taken from "9-11 and After: A Virtual Case Book," www.nyu.edu/fas/projects/vcb. Special thanks to Pat Aufderheide and Faye Ginsburg.

1. Barbara Abrash and Faye Ginsburg, eds., "9–11 and After." The project was funded by the Rockefeller Foundation.
2. David Garcia, "Defining Tactical Media."
3. An expanded version of this essay appeared in *TDR* (Spring 2003): 11-48.
4. The September 11 Digital Archive (www.911digitalarchive.org) is a project of the American Social History Project/Center for Media and Learning at the City University of New York (CUNY) Graduate Center and the Center for History and New Media, George Mason University. It was funded by the Alfred P. Sloan Foundation.

5. Andrea Vasquez and Fritz Umbach, "The September 11 Digital Archive," interview by the author.

6. Meg McLagan, "Archival Interventions," www.nyu.edu/fas/projects/vcb/case_911_ HTMLcontent.html (accessed May 13, 2005).

7. Pat Aufderheide, "Therapeutic Patriotism and Beyond," Television Archive, January 28, 2002, www.tvnews3.televisionarchive.org/tvarchive/html/article_pa1.html.

Insurgent Media

Eric Hiltner

Look out, corporate media, insurgent media has arrived! It is incisive, courageous, passionate, diverse, and invincible. Recent changes in video, audio, and Internet technology have done for independent media what the copy machine did for print media: democratize the medium. News and information production is becoming more decentered as groups from around the globe search for the means to communicate with the outside world. Now these groups can make media for and by themselves. While this is an advantage, it also proves a challenge to use the technology in the most appropriate ways. Its variation is not limited by the constraints of profit, religion, nation, or ideology, though most media still conforms to constitutional and legal restraints. Yet how does insurgent media compare to corporate media?

One can see two currents in moving-image media today, one in the mainstream, the other in the alternative sphere. The mainstream current is moving vertically, concentrating power into fewer corporations, eating up smaller markets, and eliminating competition; the alternative media, especially Indymedia, is moving horizontally, embracing diversity and spreading like wildfire across the globe as the technology to make videos gets better and less expensive. Yet is it possible for those with less training, money, and access to distribution to make a difference? Guerrilla media—media that makes what it can with what it has, media made under difficult conditions, or media made for itself by itself—struggles to show itself in an ocean of glossy, spectacular, sugar-coated, and money-driven corporate media. So does guerrilla media have a chance? Perhaps it can succeed if it makes contact with people in a personal way. Screenings that connect an artist with the audience create a personal impact that can help dissolve the distance between the media and

Radical History Review
Issue 93 (Fall 2005): 101–106
Copyright 2005 by MARHO: The Radical Historians' Organization, Inc.

the audience. Another option is to use the Internet to tell the stories of people who are typically excluded from the dominant media. Even though some groups may not have computers for all their members to use, groups in remote locations could collectively watch images from around the world on the Internet. Over the past five years, Indypendent Media Centers (IMC) have been set up on all continents and could become the biggest news organization in the world. Since this kind of movement does not have the means to move vertically, it has to move horizontally. So although corporate media has the vertical advantage of access, money, and production quality, alternative media is closer to the source, is made with the fuel of passion, persistence, pain and struggle, and can integrate action and media in ways uncommon in the dominant media. Activists use the Internet to give up-to-the-minute reports on policy activity at demonstrations; Web-based user groups spread information from member to member in a fast and easy way, while people in different countries can synchronize global actions. Americans' visual palette reflects changes in the economic, cultural, and political environment. As cable and satellite access spreads, Americans gain access to a broader variety, quality, and quantity of media. While some say that media is all the same or that it is unidirectional communication that precludes audience response, positive offerings do exist. But it requires discipline and active searching to find them. C-Span and lecture watchers do not constitute the typical target audience for alternative media. Those most likely to search for, and be inspired—ideally, to action—by insurgent media are those who have suffered from the racist, sexist, and homophobic nature of the system: students who have yet to benefit from the system; unemployed workers suffering in the global economy; or the elderly who have not had their needs met. One of the goals of radical media is, in fact, to enable those alienated from mainstream media to create, produce, and spread their own projects.

Indymedia has created a nonprofit franchise model for groups around the world to produce radical media for local and international distribution through the Internet. Ideally, nonprofit franchise models would spread to housing, health care, permaculture, and do-it-yourself living that resists the codes of the dominant reality. While Big Noise Tactical, which takes as its aim the production and distribution of passionate and revolutionary videos in communities of resistance, and the Guerrilla News Network (GNN), creating mini documentary music videos that combine experts and precise production, are centered in New York, Indymedia resists such temptations.

Aftermath: Unanswered Questions of 9/11 (2003) was made by the Guerilla News Network. It provides crucial information for people who want to know how it came to pass that the world's most advanced, well-funded intelligence agencies and government could not thwart the worst terrorist attack on U.S. soil in history. What did the government know before the attacks happened? Why has George W.

Bush not fired those who made the mistakes? Why did the Air Force not follow standard operating procedures that would have shot down the planes before they hit the World Trade Center (WTC)? These are critical questions, and it is rare to see a film address them in such a crisp, light, and inspiring style. The film is a must-see for every patriotic American who dares to defend his or her liberties, for those who dare to demand accountability from the administration for 9/11, and for those who want to see a concise, exciting exploration of the main issues pertaining to the 9/11 attack.

A challenge for anyone making a video on a particular subject is engaging the audience in a visual and intellectual way. Often in this genre of videos, we see talking heads without much action. *Aftermath* demonstrates how to captivate and hold an audience. Slow-motion images float on and off the screen, counterpointed by a bass track punctuated with subtle, dancing high notes. Like Beat generation avatars, the ideas gradually lift into a plateau of renegade intellectual subversion, slowly erasing the ideas that have justified the slaughter of tens of thousands of people. The cuts weave documents and text around commentators who challenge the administration's words with a set of facts that typically never come together in one document. Flying, flowing, and invading images expand on a screen without edges, undermining a terrain of government deception exposed by those who refuse to keep their mouths shut. This video defies those in power who want us to shut up, put up, and die for the corporate profit war machine. The video becomes a means for keeping the subject active in a format that is usually passive.

Neoliberal politics were sold to the world as the means to end poverty, increase economic growth, and create jobs; yet for many people, globalization means a life-and-death struggle to barely meet needs. As wealthy corporations and governments scheme to extract the most from those with the least, people become desperate for change. The harsh economic, social, and political realities in Argentina, South Africa, Korea, Palestine, and Mexico can fuel the kind of powerful resistance movements that are the subject of the Big Noise Tactical video titled *The Fourth World War*. Seventy-four action-packed minutes of courage and rebellion from around the world form a collage of insurgencies that refuse to submit to corporate and national domination.

Clashes in *The Fourth World War* begin in Argentina in 1976, when the military dictatorship took power. Eventually thirty thousand people disappeared as the government purged and terrorized an entire generation. Within a few moments the video zigzags from South Africa to Palestine and back to Argentina, showing police beatings, street clashes, and protesters fighting the repressive state apparatus. After dozens of years and thousands of people murdered, the opposition dismantles the military dictatorship in Argentina. The battles in the video now move from city streets to a remote area of Mexico. One scene shows Zapatistas defying the Mexican army by crossing a fence into an army compound, surrounding soldiers with big machine guns, and forcing them to leave without any violence. The tension appears palpable as we watch peasant women, children, and men swarm heavily armed soldiers, telling them to leave. Eventually the soldiers leave the compound without any apparent bloodshed. This video also features a number of violent battles with the police. While these are potent ways to respond to oppressive institutions, most of the time the state holds an advantageous position and people are seriously wounded. Furthermore, getting rid of the oppressor is only the beginning of the problem; the issue of meeting people's needs after such drastic changes is often overlooked. Still, too often people are left with little choice but to resist in ways that leave them exposed to the brutality of the nation-state. What globalization has meant for many people even in the United States is that they lose their jobs only to see them go to workers who must endure the harshest labor conditions on the planet.

Videos can function in two ways: to provide information that may sway viewers to the videomaker's perspective, or to arm the converted with the means to convince, persuade, or provoke others to resist the status quo. Because the videos discussed here are often made outside of institutions and the mainstream, they generate diverse formats. Such is the case for *Ammo for the Info Warrior* (dir. Guerilla News Network, 2002), a DVD that features nine different shorts exploring an acentered, cell-oriented opposition to domination and control. Functioning as independent units, these digestible, incisive cuts provide potent means for undermining the credibility of the system. In the first video, Ralph Nader asks people to run their own lives, or suffer having others run them for them. Backbeats add momentum to the ideas as the countdown to the end of power begins: "We can have the concentration of wealth and power in the hands of a few or we can have democracy; we can't have both," he argues. Later he deconstructs the evening news: "nine minutes of ads; three minutes of street crime; no corporate crime; one minute of chitchat between the hosts; four minutes of weather; four minutes of sports—and that's what happened in your town?" The quotes break for more beats as the video explores a genre that combines music video with big bites that devour wealth and power.

In another news video on the same DVD, the brutality of the U.S. empire, the excesses of science, and the criminal tactics of the CIA are exposed as snapshots of how power operates in and outside of the United States. Psychological warfare, inherited from the Nazis, evolved into CIA experiments with LSD, shock mistreatment, and sensory deprivation. These experiments were designed to control large numbers of people; without corporal punishment or the use of hallucinogens, public relations firms do a very similar job, primarily by manipulating media. *PR Watch*'s John Stauber appears in a section of the film that outlines how 40 to 60 percent of news coverage is turned into public relations, an invisible form of propaganda meant to garner public support for the government or large corporations.

The apocalyptic absurdities of the current historical epoch are explored in Norman Cowie's *Scenes from an Endless War* (2002). The film juxtaposes the terrifying contradictions that become evident as soldiers gloat over their killing machines while corporate media mock those who oppose or criticize the war effort. The relentless march of the military to create killing machines that perform "without risk to personnel or major assets" is the ideal of the superpower nation-state. These weapons are presented by Donald Rumsfeld, Paul Wolfowitz, Dick Cheney, and Bush, the architects of the latest assault on the world. Cowie encapsulates these leaders of terror in a black shroud of the dominant media, a spectacular world in which lies pass as truth and no one is accountable for his or her actions. The media, the weapons manufacturers, and government leaders have crafted a universe in which killing without consequence is idolized. Opposition to the war in the form of protests, statements from victims' families, and workers at the 9/11 sites combine to show perspectives uncommon in the dominant media. About halfway through the video, a figure, a prominent leader, stops, and the text begins to flow. The image and text froze my awareness as I felt terror running and screaming through my bones. That scene drove home the power of images to paralyze and terrorize people into submission, but also the power of images to freeze and expose those in power for who they are. This video, which constitutes a set of distinct statements, exposes the contradictions inherent in the diabolical age we live in. The cynical manipulations of the Bush administration spell death and misery for tens of thousands, perhaps even millions. This video spins the war-machine media and its leaders on their heads, exposes fascinations with diabolical killing machines, and provides evidence that not everyone is marching lockstep with the administration.

Immediately after 9/11, Union Square in New York City blossomed into a zone of popular expression and bewildered emotions. Candles, flowers, teddy bears, notes, photos, and peace symbols decorated the street, adding a bit of cheer and color to the somber situation. In a state of shock and grief, people came to the square to make collective sense of the colossal calamity. *9.11*, produced for the Indypendent Media Center with the help of NYC-IMC, Paper Tiger TV, a video collective in the city, and Big Noise Tactical, captured the event for the rest of the world to witness. The images drift around the trauma of the moment as people share sentiments, thoughts, and reactions to the massive attack. One woman demanded immediate retribution, another refused to let her grief become an excuse to justify more killing, and others felt the need to dig deeper to figure out why it happened and what could be done to prevent another attack. Then the images move to the Middle East to offer reasons for the attacks. Perhaps it is because the United States supports corrupt and brutal dictatorships in the Middle East that ignore human rights and democratic principals, or maybe people did not like how Americans overthrew the elected government of Iran in 1953, or the way the United States supports Israel's relentless land grabbing and brutality in Palestine, or how the United States claims to practice and support democracy and human rights while actually pursuing the opposite in order to secure access to profits and resources. Would any of this have happened if such abuses had been headlines backed up by strikes, protests, and calls for impeachment? The leaders failed to protect us, but they may have succeeded in their goals. The perpetual war has served the administration well. It can argue that as long as we find ourselves in a state of war in which an enemy threatens the public, all money and priorities must be put into security matters and the war machine, not health care, housing, food, or education, and certainly not diplomacy. Many statements from people at Union Square demanded less war and more peace.

Fresh, raw, and chaotic footage from near Ground Zero and Paper Tiger commentators come together in the video called *Turning Tragedy into War.* Calling into question the need for a military solution, providing reasons to use caution, and looking at the social and economic roots of 9/11 are some of the things the commentators do to counter the cries for revenge. Clips from the dominant media show the media-military connections that ignore background information that could help deescalate tensions. Some of the footage shown did offer reasons for the attack, but it was presented in a skeptical and discounting manner. As the orientation of the camera turns onto the Middle East, we as the audience begin to see the foreign policy mistakes that have added fuel to the fires of the terrorists and may have been the precursors to the current morass. As long as people ignore the underlying reasons for these conflicts and until people get a sense of the global priorities of the U.S. government, any rational solution will prove impossible.

The giant world of media has expanded as radical media groups begin to explore the potential of low-cost digital video production and distribution over the Internet. Video collectives in New York have created media that call into question the means and ends of globalization, the post 9/11 security state, and oil empire building in the Middle East. Whether this voice can be heard and have an effect in an ocean of other media grabbing for peoples' attention is a difficult question. Perhaps the odds are against them, but hearing any voice at all is a bright spot in dark times. Once can imagine that radical media groups are a mirror of radical media groups in other countries that struggle to get their message out with a fraction of the resources, while enveloped in a universe of other media contradicting what they are saying. Without these groups, the stories of millions would never be heard or seen by anyone else. They serve humanity, and for this I am grateful.

The Emergence of Unconstitutional Deportation and Repatriation of Mexicans and Mexican Americans as a Public Issue

Francisco E. Balderrama

At the California State Senate Hearings on Unconstitutional Deportation and Coerced Immigration on July 15, 2003, Emilia Castañeda painfully remembered arriving, as a young girl during the Great Depression, at the train station in Los Angeles with her father and brother. Los Angeles County had ordered her father to appear for expulsion to Mexico. While the family prepared to board, Los Angeles County officials advised Emilia and her brother that they could stay in Los Angeles if they declared themselves orphans and become wards of the state. Yet Emilia insisted that she was "no orphan," stating, "I have my father."

The officials dismissed her pleas for her family to stay, placing Emilia and her brother—who were both American citizens—with their father on the train to Mexico. They were expelled with few resources. "I think all we had was the trunk with maybe a few dishes, our blankets, and a few of our clothes." The family's arrival in and adaptation to Mexico involved severe hardship and suffering. "I wasn't used to that kind of life," Emilia remembered. "And I was probably unhappy and depressed." In recalling those days of despair, Emilia wondered why she and her family "had been sent out from our country to a strange country where we didn't belong."[1]

This tragic episode was not an isolated case. More than one million legal U.S. residents and American citizens of Mexican descent suffered the same terrible fate of unconstitutional deportation and coerced immigration. Contemporary

Radical History Review
Issue 93 (Fall 2005): 107–10
Copyright 2005 by MARHO: The Radical Historians' Organization, Inc.

scholars and activists should be familiar with this dark chapter of American and Mexican history as they grapple with the complex challenge of homeland security and the accompanying resurgence of nativism. This history provides an opportunity to understand the role of the Other, especially in regard to citizenship and transnational migration.

Unconstitutional deportation and coerced immigration of the Mexican population was commonly known as "repatriation" during the Great Depression. Repatriation implied that individuals were voluntarily returning to Mexico, leaving the United States of their own free will. Los Angeles County, however, initially employed the word *deportation* to describe its campaign of rounding up Mexicans and Mexican Americans for shipment to the border. But legal counsel advised the county that the right to deport was a function reserved for the federal government. So Los Angeles County, home to the largest concentration of Mexicans and Mexican Americans in the United States, invoked the term *repatriation* when rounding up the Mexican population. Chicago, Detroit, Denver, and other American cities joined Los Angeles in naming their campaigns with a euphemism. The procedure was also praised as a way to ensure that jobs would become available for "real" Americans and as a way to cut welfare costs during this period of massive unemployment. However, it turned out to be a foolish policy; Mexicans across the country never comprised more than 10 percent of those on welfare.

Economist Paul Taylor, anthropologist Manuel Gamio, and sociologist Emory Bogardus first reported the repatriation phenomenon as it occurred during the Depression years. Not until the 1970s, however, with the emergence of the study of Chicano history, did other scholars investigate repatriation. Abraham Hoffman's *Unwanted Mexicans in the Great Depression: Repatriation Pressures, 1929–1939* uncovered repatriation policy in Los Angeles, while Mercedes Carreras de Velasco's *Los Mexicanos que devolvió la crisis, 1929–1932* (*The Returned Mexicans from the Crisis of 1929-1939*) sketched the Mexican government's reaction.[2] Additional studies of the Depression called attention to repatriation. George Sánchez's *Becoming Mexican American: Ethnicity, Culture, and Identity in Chicano Los Angeles, 1900–1945* has interpreted repatriation as an influence on cultural and ethnic identity; Camillie Guerin-Gonzales's *Mexican Workers and American Dreams: Immigration, Repatriation, and California Farm Labor, 1900–1939* looks at how the American dream became a justification for exploitation and ousting of Mexicans.[3] More recently, Fernando Saúl Alanis Enciso has defined the formulation of Mexican policy for repatriation.[4]

These studies acknowledge the importance of repatriation even though the topic remains a relatively unknown story. *Decade of Betrayal: Mexican Repatriation in the 1930s* by Francisco E. Balderrama and Raymond Rodríguez "provided the first comprehensive treatment chronicling the treatment of the Mexican community by American and Mexican authorities during the Great Depression."[5] The study combines extensive archival and oral history sources to describe and analyze the impact of the repatriation phenomenon on Mexican and Mexican American men, women, and children on both sides of the border.

California State senator Joseph Dunn was "both shocked and intrigued" after reading *Decade of Betrayal* and decided to convene the Select Committee for Civic Participation in July of 2003.[6] The hearings led to bills for extending the statute of limitations to permit claims by repatriates and for establishing a state commission to investigate the repatriation. Congresswoman Hilda Solis also declared her intention to sponsor hearings in the U.S. Congress. The Mexican American Legal Defense and Education Fund (MALDEF) joined the movement seeking justice for survivors by filing a lawsuit—*Emilia Castañeda vs. the State of California, Los Angeles County, and the Los Angeles Chamber of Commerce* (2003).

The hearings, filing of the suit, town hall meetings, and press conferences have created extensive media attention. Newspaper coverage has included the *Los Angeles Times*, July 15 and July 16, 2003; the *Sacramento Bee*, July 16, 2003; the *San Jose Mercury*, July 17, 2003; London's *Guardian*, July 17, 2003; and the Orange County *Register*, July 19, 2003. The Spanish-language *La Opinión* gave the most exclusive attention to deportation-repatriation of the 1930s with a four-page treatment on July 13 and follow-up articles on July 14 and July 15. Furthermore, National Public Radio stations in Santa Monica, Pasadena, and Santa Barbara have produced a number of programs. Stories on repatriation also aired on Spanish-language television channels 34 and 52 and the English-language station 7.

On Thanksgiving Day, November 27, 2003, the *Public Broadcasting News Hour with Jim Lehrer* was the first national television news program to present the dark chapter of Mexican unconstitutional deportation and repatriation to the American public. Repatriation survivor María Ofelia Acosta testified how her parents—legal residents of the United States—and their American-born children were rounded up for shipment to Mexico. "I could have gone to school . . . my sisters and brothers. I could have had a better life," she lamented. Acosta is convinced that recent legal action on behalf of the survivors for reparations will never remedy the injustice: "No money can pay for that."

Acosta joins other survivors such as Emilia Castañeda, Ignacio Piña, Rubén Jimenez, and José López in wanting the American public to know about this injustice. These women and men are organizing support for the legal suit and new legislation by speaking at community forums, professional conferences, and union groups, as well as on television and radio programs. At these public events the survivors frequently state that they hope knowledge about this great injustice will prevent other ethnic or racial groups from suffering the same kind of mistreatment, especially during difficult times of social unrest and economic crisis. Detroit repatriation survivors and their families have delivered this same message in their documentary *Los Repatriados: Exiles from the Promised Land*, which focuses on repatriates from the Midwest.[7] These testimonies provide new evidence and insight into the repatria-tion experience, especially regarding adjustment to life in Mexico and, for many, their experiences on returning to the United States. These new testimonies provide important evidence that merits serious examination and careful analysis.

By seeking justice in the public arena, the survivors of repatriation have con-tributed to the empowerment of themselves, their families, and their communities. Many family members are relieved that at long last the injustice suffered by a parent or grandparent is now being addressed. For some it has been the lifting of a burden and an opportunity to begin the healing process for the survivors and their loved ones. Survivors and their families have also become students of Mexican repatriation history. They have read the limited secondary literature and have searched for pri-mary documents. Moreover, they are encouraging historians to continue their work because they value the scholarship on unconstitutional deportation and coerced immigration. More important, they have used this knowledge to construct a context for understanding their individual family experience. The survivors and their fami-lies therefore have transformed their private experience of repatriation injustice to the public issue of unconstitutional deportation.

Whatever the outcome of the lawsuit, pending legislation, or future govern-mental inquiries, it is unquestionable that the survivors of repatriation and their fam-ilies have emerged to claim their rightful place in American and Mexican history.

Notes

1. California Senate Select Committee on Citizen Participation Hearing, "Examination of Unconstitutional Deportation and Coerced Emigration of Legal Residents and U.S. Citizens of Mexican Descent," July 15, 2003.
2. Abraham Hoffman, *Unwanted Mexican Americans in the Great Depression: Repatriation Pressures, 1929–1939* (Tucson: University of Arizona Press, 1974); Mercedes Carreras de Velasco, *Los Mexicanos que devolvió la crisis, 1929–1932* (Mexico City: Secretaría de Relaciones Exteriores, 1974).
3. George Sánchez, *Becoming Mexican American: Ethnicity, Culture, and Identity in Chicano Los Angeles, 1900–1945* (New York: Oxford University Press, 1993); Camille Guerin-Gonzales, *Mexican Workers and American Dreams: Immigration, Repatriation, and California Farm Labor, 1900–1939* (New Brunswick, NJ: Rutgers University Press, 1994).
4. Fernando Saúl Alanis Enciso, "El gobierno de México y la repatriación de mexicanos de Estados Unidos, 1934–1940" (PhD diss., El Colegio de Mexico, 2000); and more recently, *El Valle del Rio Bravo, Tamaulipas, en la Decada de 1930* (Ciudad Victoria: El Colegio de Tamaulipas-El Colegio de San Luis, 2004).
5. Francisco E. Balderrama and Raymond Rodríguez, *Decade of Betrayal: Mexican Repatriation in the 1930s* (Albuquerque: University of New Mexico Press, 1995), 4.
6. "Examination of Unconstitutional Deportation and Coerced Emigration," July 15, 2003.
7. Information about the film is available from Fronteras Norteñas, PO Box 44859, Detroit, MI 48246.

Of Patriots and Profits: New Tools for Keeping Academic Research in Line

Beatriz da Costa and Claire Pentecost

How much is the federal government policing scientific research? How has this policing changed existing government-research relations within the academic research sector? The recent FBI investigation of Professor Steven Kurtz and the internationally acclaimed artists' collective Critical Art Ensemble (CAE) inspired us to take a closer look at the current administration's use and misuse of the expanded government and law enforcement powers granted by the USA PATRIOT Act. Since the investigation of Kurtz was initially articulated through the framework of terrorism, this essay asks if the USA PATRIOT Act was used to enable that investigation. But we also want to extend the analysis of this case in particular to inquire about the ways in which the USA PATRIOT Act has had an impact on bona fide research conducted within American educational institutions. Under the rubric of biosafety and biodefense, the USA PATRIOT Act introduces new regulations applicable to biology labs and the institutions that house them. How are these regulations and their violation relevant to the Kurtz case?

The Case

On the morning of May 11, 2004, Steve Kurtz, a professor at the State University of New York at Buffalo and a founding member of CAE, woke up to find that Hope Kurtz, another founding member of CAE and his partner of twenty-seven years, was not breathing. He called an emergency medical team, but they were unable to revive her. Later it was determined that she had died of heart failure. Because

Radical History Review
Issue 93 (Fall 2005): 111–21
Copyright 2005 by MARHO: The Radical Historians' Organization, Inc.

this was an unexpected death of a relatively young woman, the local police came to investigate the scene.

In the large hall outside the bedroom, police noticed a table laden with scientific equipment in plain view. Like all police in the United States, the Buffalo police now think terrorism when confronted by something difficult to explain. Kurtz accounted for the equipment, explaining that, as an artist, he used it to create educational events through which the public could become more familiar with commercially applied science. The police searched the house for several hours and then notified the FBI. The next day, as Kurtz was leaving home to make funeral arrangements, three carloads of FBI agents pulled up in front of his house and detained him for extended questioning. Still in shock over the death of his wife, and assuming he had nothing to hide, Kurtz was fully cooperative. His detention lasted twenty-two hours, or until the afternoon of the next day, when finally, by way of cell phone, he was able to get in touch with a lawyer who immediately told him that his detention was illegal and that he should walk away. The FBI informed Kurtz that he was free to go, but told him that he could not go home. The FBI—working with the Department of Homeland Security, the Joint Task Force on Terrorism, the Department of Alcohol, Tobacco, and Firearms, the Immigration and Customs Enforcement, and the Niagara County Sheriff's office—had closed Kurtz's street with police cars, fire engines, and medical emergency personnel while they sent in a team of agents in hazmat suits to search the house for biohazardous materials. Five days later, Kurtz was able to return to his house after the Buffalo Health Department and the FBI had determined that nothing there was dangerous or illegal. Nevertheless, the FBI had confiscated his scientific equipment, computers, notes, a shelf of history books about science, epidemiology, and biowarfare, Kurtz's passport and other personal documents, as well as Hope Kurtz's body. So far, only Hope's body, a few books, and most of his personal documents have been returned. His passport, having been turned over to the federal clerk, can be obtained for work-related reasons only with permission from his probation officer.

Investigators, if they had looked, would have been able to find scores of public sources, in print and on the Web, on the work of the CAE, a seventeen-year-old collective of artists of various specializations dedicated to exploring the intersections between art, technology, radical politics, and critical theory. Over the past seven years, the CAE has developed a body of work addressing the politics of biotechnology. The collective's work manifests itself in the form of book projects, installations, public performances, and direct-action projects. As part of its performance and installation work, the collective often uses the materials of science itself, including laboratory equipment and wetware (bacteria) to address issues that arise around the commercial application of developments in the life sciences. Those materials have included transgenic forms of *E. coli* bacteria, a cryo-tank for keeping frozen

DNA samples, and an entire mobile DNA extraction laboratory. In these projects, the CAE promotes hands-on experience with the materials of science as a way to demystify scientific research and process and related politics. Usually this kind of knowledge and experience is reserved for experts and takes place behind laboratory doors closed to the public.

Having few educational tools in this area, the general public typically has had to rely on the media for its only source of information with respect to biotechnology, a field rapidly transforming our lives. The CAE seeks to open the laboratory doors in order to provide nonspecialists with a sense of agency in regard to the life sciences and stimulate an informed public debate surrounding issues related to contemporary uses of biotechnology.[1] For instance, a CAE project called "Free Range Grains" includes a complete DNA extraction laboratory equipped to test food products for the presence of genetic modification. In public places such as cultural centers and museums, the CAE sets up the lab to test common brand-name foods like cornflakes or corn chips. Audiences are able to see the whole process, talk to the artists while they work, and learn about the issues surrounding genetically modified foods.

Apparently the long history and public visibility of the CAE's work did nothing to convince the FBI and the Justice Department that Steve Kurtz is a responsible artist with a highly credited professional track record and no intent to harm the public. Within barely a week, two members and collaborators of the CAE were served with federal subpoenas while preparing an art exhibition at the Museum of Contemporary Art in Massachusetts. The artists were ordered to appear in front of a federal grand jury investigating Kurtz on possible violations of the Biological Weapons Statute (HR 3162), expanded by the USA PATRIOT Act of 2001.

Over the course of the next month, eight more individuals known to the authors received subpoenas. These were members and associates of the CAE, as well as colleagues and one student of Kurtz's. The majority of the subpoenaed subjects exercised their Fifth Amendment rights since in addition to serving as witnesses in the case, they were also potential subjects of the investigation. Because grand jury proceedings are secret, it remains unclear who else has been served court orders or who may have testified. In addition to the individuals, Autonomedia, a press based in New York City and the publisher of the CAE's five books, received a subpoena to present all correspondence and business documents related to the accused.

The Role of the USA PATRIOT Act

Prior to October 2001, federal law prohibited the development, production, transfer, or possession of any biological agent, toxin, or delivery system for use as a weapon.[2] The USA PATRIOT Act expanded this law by prohibiting possession of a biological agent, toxin, or delivery system "of a type or in a quantity that, under the circumstances, is not reasonably justified by a prophylactic, protective, bona fide research, or other peaceful purpose." The lines quoted here are the lines quoted in a text attached to the subpoenas. Penalties for noncompliance include large fines and imprisonment for up to ten years.

Furthermore, the USA PATRIOT Act also restricts access to certain materials. Restricted persons may not possess, ship, or receive any biological agent or toxin listed as a so-called select agent. Select agents include lethal pathogens such as samples of the Ebola virus. The phrase *restricted persons* means any individual who

A) is under indictment for a crime punishable by imprisonment for a term exceeding one year
B) has been convicted in any court of a crime punishable by imprisonment for a term exceeding one year
C) is a fugitive from justice
D) is an unlawful user of any controlled substance (as defined in section 102 of the Controlled Substances Act (21 U.S.C. 802))
E) is an alien illegally or unlawfully in the United States
F) has been adjudicated as a mental defective or has been committed to any mental institution
G) is an alien (other than an alien lawfully admitted for permanent residence) who is a national of a country to which the Secretary of State, pursuant to [applicable law], has made a determination (that remains in effect) that such country has repeatedly provided support for acts of international terrorism [currently Cuba, Iran, Iraq, Libya, North Korea, Sudan, or Syria]
H) has been discharged from the Armed Services of the United States under dishonorable conditions.[3]

This section of the act makes quite clear the terms on which a person may be accused of violation. The U.S. Department of Justice could have easily ascertained, without a grand jury investigation, whether or not Kurtz was a restricted person or if he was in possession of any select agents. Despite the language attached to the subpoenas, however, the prosecutor of this case, U.S. attorney William Hochul, has publicly maintained that the accusations have nothing to do with the USA PATRIOT Act. Indeed, this was proven true when, on June 30, 2004, Hochul finally secured charges from the grand jury investigation. Kurtz, along with Robert Ferrell, a professor of genetics at the University of Pittsburgh and a longtime colleague and collaborator, was indicted for two counts each of mail fraud and wire fraud. In this particular case, wire fraud refers to the use of the Internet and credit cards to purchase the bacteria; mail fraud refers to the use of the U.S. Postal Service to receive and send the materials. Mail fraud and wire fraud are federal crimes carrying sentences of five years each. Since each of the defendants is charged with two counts of each crime, both are facing the possibility of twenty-year sentences. Interestingly enough, the laws on which these charges are based have nothing to do with bioterrorism; they have to do with property. What, then, did Kurtz and Ferrell actually do to earn such charges?

Public Threat, Private Interests

Certain biological samples are regulated because they pose health risks, but all commercially available samples, both the potentially dangerous and the certifiably safe, are regulated as property. University labs enter into agreements, called Material Transfer Agreements or MTAs, with the companies from which they buy biological agents. The scientist in charge of a laboratory at a university or research institution will sign a contract saying the lab will not share, sell, or give away the materials transferred. This is especially sticky when one considers that bacteria reproduce themselves.

For a new CAE project, Ferrell helped Kurtz obtain samples of three harmless bacteria commonly used in biology labs and occurring naturally in our environment. Typically, researchers buy these samples from companies like American Type Culture Collection, which produces biological samples for research labs and educational institutions. As evidenced by the e-mails between Kurtz and Ferrell quoted in the indictment, Kurtz wanted to be sure the supplies he was getting were as safe as possible, because he knew that some variations on these bacteria could, in fact, be pathogenic. This is especially significant as Hochul, despite Kurtz's documented concern, continues to cast the case as an issue of public safety.

The moment that Ferrell used his University of Pittsburgh contract with American Type Culture Collection to obtain $256 worth of bacteria samples, which he then mailed to Kurtz, Ferrell broke what was essentially an intellectual property contract. According to the U.S. attorney's office, Kurtz obtained these materials under the fraudulent representation that they would be used only in Ferrell's lab. As far as we know, this is the first time such charges have been applied to MTAs. These are contractual agreements surrounding the sale and purchase of a material whose reproduction, once in the hands of the consumer, is difficult to control.

In the established culture of biological research, sharing samples and other materials freely is the norm. By all accounts from scientists, it forms part of the cooperative approach to knowledge that until recently has characterized most scientific fields. It is about as common as sharing music has become to a generation of listeners. But while the lawsuits that have resulted from the sharing of recorded music are prosecuted by the industry against the consumer, in this case the government has stepped in to escalate the questionable interpretation of a contract agreement to the very serious federal charges of mail and wire fraud. Neither the American Type Culture Collection nor the employers of the two professors—the University of Pittsburgh and the State University of New York at Buffalo—filed complaints or concerns regarding the collaborative efforts and resulting exchanges between Ferrell and the CAE. Thus we must look further into the relationship of science and commerce to understand why the government wants to pursue this case.

Material transfer agreements are signed by the head scientist in any given laboratory, but they are also handled by technology transfer offices, which also take care of patents. The phrase *technology transfer* refers to the transfer of research results from universities to the commercial sector. The growth of these offices in universities is a bureaucratic sign of the increasing involvement of private interests in scientific research. This influence is working from both inside and outside the scientific community in the form of patents that can be obtained on living materials produced or modified in the lab, as well as the processes used on them. A large part of the growth of these offices is attributable to the Bayh-Dole Act of 1980, conceived as an incentive to national technological advancement that made it much easier for scientists (and universities) to patent, and thus profit from, their own research. Increasingly, it has also made it difficult to separate the kinds of research scientists actually decide to do from how much money they stand to make.

The money is potentially very big. The so-called life sciences have become one of the big investment areas of our time, with the pharmaceutical industry for several years claiming the top profit-making capacity in the world. Scientists partner with investors or venture capitalists to create small start-up companies that develop discoveries into marketable products. Often the most successful ventures from this level grow, go public, and are bought out by a larger corporation. Effectively, scientific research has come to play a substantive role in driving the postindustrial economy. The mechanism by which scientists have the opportunity to make more money than ever anticipated is the same mechanism that enables neoliberal market forces to control the direction of research at public institutions. To get a picture of how these forces have affected research in the life sciences, consider the following: according to the *Human Development Report 2001*, published by the United Nations Development Programme, 1,223 new commercial drugs were released worldwide between 1975 and 1996, but only 13 were developed to treat tropical diseases.[4] Drugs aimed at the problems of an impoverished population—and hence poor markets—are much less likely to command the research and development resources that an affluent market enjoys.

In addition to the lure of patents imagined down the pipeline, more and more scientists conducting research at public institutions are encouraged to forge partnerships with private corporations. The presumption is that these joint ventures offer the best way to drive scientific progress; competition is good for scientists and good for society because it drives the economy. Of course, like the patent system, reliance on such funding shapes the very questions that science sets out to ask. But it also reshapes the way in which scientists work. Research done in the interest of commercial development and likely to be patented or used in trade secrets is as jealously guarded as research used in secret military projects.

The most publicly controversial case of corporate funding in a public university was the five-year research agreement between plant biologists at the University of California at Berkeley and the biotechnology company Novartis (now part of Syngenta), which expired in November 2003. The deal awarded the members of Berkeley's Department of Plant and Microbial Biology access to trade secrets, principally in genetics, and $25 million. In return, Novartis had the right to negotiate licenses on inventions by faculty members who participated in the agreement, even if the work had been financed with federal funds. Given that the agreement stood at the center of fierce controversy from the beginning, the concrete results seemed somewhat anticlimactic as no dramatic discoveries were made during the contract period and Syngenta did not license a single invention. The strategic alliance, as it was called, between Berkeley and Novartis included money to commission an independent evaluation of the exchange, which was released in August 2004. Executed by a group of social and natural scientists at Michigan State University, the study reports that the agreement became a lightning rod for divisions within the College of Natural Resources and a new kind of Achilles heel for the credibility of both the department and the university. Relations among faculty members within the college "continue to be a serious problem," the report observes. "Such a poor state of collegiality hinders the productive capacity of the college as a whole and the quality of education that it is able to provide."[5]

One of the flash points for divisions within the Department of Plant and Microbial Biology at Berkeley was the tenure case of Ignacio Chapela, an assistant professor and outspoken critic of the deal. The Novartis deal "played a very clear role and an unsatisfactory role in the tenure process" of Chapela, said Lawrence Busch, a professor of sociology at Michigan State University, who headed the evaluation.[6] More than two hundred academics and others have called for an investigation of the tenure denial for Chapela. As of this writing, the Academic Senate's Committee on Privilege and Tenure is investigating whether he received due process, but his term of employment expired on December 31, 2004.

In the wake of this corporate-academic controversy, it is hard not to connect Chapela's extended troubles with the fact that it was he who, along with graduate student David Quist, discovered the presence of transgenic corn in Oaxaca, Mexico. This discovery ignited an international conflagration, not only because the planting of genetically modified corn is illegal in Mexico but because Oaxaca is considered the center of genetic diversity among maize plants. Apparently the United States has been dumping such corn, used for animal feed and human consumption, into the Mexican market for years.

The report does not indicate whether the Berkeley-Novartis strategic alliance actually influenced the direction of research at the school. However, in an editorial in the Berkeley *Daily Planet*, Andrew Paul Gutierrez and Miguel A. Altieri illuminate the dark continent of questions that were outright ignored by the evaluation:

> The report . . . assumes at Berkeley that the rise of biotechnology and the fall of applied agricultural fields such as biological control, plant pathology, soils and others is just part of the natural progress of science; a mere part of the process of modernization. In fact, according to the review, the "deal" appears consistent with the universities adjusting to the emerging norms of university-based economic development and gives the impression that science at Berkeley is protected from the influence of politics and corporate power.[7]

Whatever ethical issues are raised by the Berkeley-Novartis alliance, one could argue that the controversy is a symptom of a crisis in the mission of universities nationwide. Of the various possible mandates for universities in the early twenty-first century—providing conditions for independent research, creating knowledge, educating elites or the masses, training specialists for a changing job market, and stimulating the economy—only the last one of these seems to be gaining ground, normalized quickly and silently as intellectual property regimes and corporate funding opportunities take hold within academic culture. But the post-9/11 high-security defense paradigm adds yet another priority and is reforging an old set of relations between the state, corporations, and research institutions. The working and intellectual restrictions imposed on the life sciences have been tightening as a result of economic interests, and they are tightening even more by the conscription of the life sciences into military service.

Defending Concentrated Capital

Since 2000, there has been a sixfold increase in annual spending for biodefense in the United States. Much of this money is used to construct several new level-three and level-four biosafety laboratories in different parts of the country. Because these new facilities are designed to conduct research into very deadly infectious pathogens, they are capital-intensive complexes with very high-tech security systems that have to be maintained around the clock. All employees in these labs with access to the pathogens, from scientists to custodial staff, require background checks, and their daily routines are subject to intense surveillance. Research in universities is also becoming skewed toward biodefense in order to take advantage of new funding streams, so that labs in educational institutions will also be subject to high security restrictions affecting the culture of the entire institution and making it more hostile to the free and open sharing of research materials and information.

An earlier case, similar to that of the Kurtz/Ferrell prosecution, had already begun to dramatize the possible consequences of researchers who run afoul of regulations or interests powered by the judiciary. On January 14, 2003, Thomas

Butler, a leading authority on infectious diseases at Texas Technical University in Austin, called the FBI to report thirty missing vials of plague bacteria from his research laboratory. Under the pressure of FBI agents, Butler admitted the following night that he himself had accidentally destroyed the bacteria, a statement that he retracted shortly thereafter. The FBI investigation that followed examined his life and research activities: he was charged with lying to the FBI, smuggling plague bacteria into the country, and illegally transporting biological agents. Butler was acquitted of the former two charges but found guilty of the latter. His record shows a thirty-year career in infectious-disease research, often pursued at great personal risk. Drafted by the Navy during the Vietnam War, Butler treated plague patients overseas. In the early 1980s, he was actively involved in HIV research at a time when few scientists would dedicate their time and energy to research on the growing AIDS epidemic. Butler later returned to bubonic plague research and engaged in research relationships with hospitals located in Tanzania.

Since his legal troubles began, letters of protest on Butler's behalf have been publicized by the Infectious Diseases Society of America, the National Academy of Sciences and Institute of Medicine, the New York Academy of Sciences, and a group of four nobel laureates, to name but a few supporters. These official statements refer to the deleterious effects of the complex regulations following from the USA PATRIOT Act, and the heightened security accompanying escalated biodefense, on the practice of science. Many of Butler's supporters caution the government that such gross disproportion between the convicted offense and the punishment meted out is intimidating to scientists and, more specifically, that it will discourage scientists from working in the areas of biodefense and infectious disease research.

What has gone largely unremarked in the Butler case is the nature of the work he was doing and the program in which he was working at Texas Tech. According to a report by the Sunshine Project, Butler was working in a large and secretive biodefense program that received 70 percent of its funding from the U.S. Army Soldier Biological Chemical Command (SBCCOM), as well as other grants provided by the Air Force. The program at Texas Tech "engages in other kinds of research on bioweapons agents and toxins. This includes types of work that have drawn international criticism of the U.S. because they push the envelope of acceptability under the Biological Weapons Convention."[8] The report points out that the mishandling of vials of pathogens is not just a threat to public health but a gross political liability to the United States internationally.

It so happens that the materials obtained by Ferrell and shared with Kurtz were acquired for a new CAE project about exactly this same issue: to raise public awareness about U.S. policies concerning biodefense. This is the kind of discussion our government and its corporate backers do not want us to have. A real public debate on this subject would include a number of currently suppressed considerations. For example, according to many analysts, the threat of bioterrorism is actually very unlikely because, from a weapons-development perspective, most biological agents, with the exception of anthrax, are unstable, hard to work with, and more troublesome than explosives and chemical toxins. The problem with an aggressive biodefense program is that it remains essentially indistinguishable from an aggressive bioweapons program. Indeed, because researchers in the new level-four biosafety labs are developing deadly new pathogens in order to figure out how to defend against them, these facilities may actually increase the likelihood of previously unknown and lethal microbes.[9] In the only bioterrorism scare in the United States, the anthrax anonymously sent through the mail shortly after 9/11 was found to be genetically identical to one developed in a U.S. government defense lab, and three years after that discovery the government still cannot locate the perpetrator.[10] As shifts in federal budgets already demonstrate, biodefense spending comes at the expense of research into common infectious diseases that kill millions of people every year. The ultimate effect of such programs is the militarization of public health and the corporatization of all things military. Contracts to build and maintain high-security facilities, not unlike the enormous financial advantages gained by Halliburton and other private contractors from U.S. military operations in Iraq, are extremely lucrative, and the wealth derived from them is concentrated among the very few.

The writings published by the CAE offer a well-developed critique of this economic system. The collective also provides guidelines for empowering people and the means by which ordinary citizens can resist predatory corporate concerns. Nowhere has the CAE advertised terrorist or related activities that could be of harm to individuals. The subpoena of Autonomedia's records is just one indication that the government finds the CAE's ideas highly relevant to this case. This subpoena was made possible through section 215 of the USA PATRIOT Act, which relieves the government of providing probable cause to believe that the person whose records it seeks is involved in any kind of criminal activity. Records of any person living in the United States may be requested without providing a reason or justification. Those served with section 215 orders are prohibited from sharing that information with anyone else. The American Civil Liberties Union (ACLU) points out that these types of requests are likely to be used against persons living in the United States who exercise their First Amendment rights.[11] Autonomedia's subpoena was deactivated toward the end of the grand jury hearings after the New York Civil Liberties Union (NYCLU) sent a letter of complaint to the prosecuting attorney. It was precisely on the basis of First Amendment rights that the NYCLU ultimately discouraged the Department of Justice from pursuing the subpoena.

Comparing a string of judicial abuses under the Bush administration to the McCarthy era is not the only relevant hearkening to a Cold War mentality. The threat of terrorism has justified the retrenchment of a military-industrial complex in which government and corporate structures collude to concentrate material and human resources in a disciplinary paradigm dedicated to profit and social control. The USA PATRIOT Act is only one instrument in this new old order. In the case against Kurtz and Ferrell, the license granted to government power—codified in the USA PATRIOT Act but taking many forms ultimately legitimated through the public's concern for security—is used to support an economic system in which the government is devoted to protecting the rights of large corporations to develop a maximum opportunity for financial reward and a minimum responsibility toward the public good.

Notes

1. For more information regarding the Critical Art Ensemble's work, see www.critical-art.net.
2. U.S. Code, Title 18—Crimes and Criminal Procedure, Part I—Crimes, Chapter 10— Biological Weapons, Sec. 175, Prohibitions with Respect to Biological Weapons, uscode .house.gov/uscode-cgi/fastweb.exe?getdoc+uscview+t17t20+221+1++%28biological% (accessed May 17, 2005).
3. USA PATRIOT Act of 2001 (H.R. 3162), Title VIII, Section 817, Expansion of the Biological Weapons Statute. The entire text of the PATRIOT Act and other U.S. legislation can be found in the THOMAS database of the Library of Congress, thomas.loc. gov/ (accessed May 17, 2005).
4. United Nations Development Programme, "Making New Technologies Work for Human Development," in *Human Development Report 2001* (New York: Oxford University Press, 2001), 3.
5. Institute for Food and Agricultural Standards (IFAS), Michigan State University, "External Review of the Collaborative Research Agreement between Novartis Agricultural Discovery Institute, Inc., and the Regents of the University of California," July 13, 2004, 129, www.msu.edu/user/ifas/docs/Berkeley_Final_Report_071204.pdf.
6. Goldie Blumenstyk, "Peer Reviewers Give Thumbs Down to Berkeley-Novartis Deal," *Chronicle of Higher Education*, July 30, 2004, A25.
7. Andrew Paul Gutierrez and Miguel A. Altieri, "Some Reflections on the Berkeley-Novartis Report," *Berkley Daily Planet*, August 10, 2004.
8. The Sunshine Project, "The Thomas Butler Case: Some Unreported Information and Reasons for the Department of Justice's Prosecution," news release, October 28, 2003, www.sunshine-project.org.
9. For examples, see Judith Miller, "New Germ Labs Stir a Debate over Secrecy and Safety," *New York Times*, February 10, 2004; Dan Vergano and Steve Sternberg, "Anthrax Slip-Ups Raise Fears about Planned Biolabs," *USA Today*, October 13, 2004; and "What Exactly Is the Army Up To?" *Deseret Morning News*, July 25, 2004.
10. Rick Weiss and Susan Schmidt, "Capitol Hill Anthrax Matches Army's Stocks," *Washington Post*, December 6, 2001.
11. The ACLU provides excellent background material on section 215 of the USA PATRIOT Act. For more information, see www.aclu.org.

Families in Queer States:
The Rule of Law and the Politics
of Recognition

Kath Weston

What happens to a politics of recognition aimed at securing legal rights and remedies from the state when the nation-state to which subjects appeal for recognition is engaged in the rather nasty business of undermining the rule of law? What does it mean that people in many parts of the world have appealed to states to grant standing to their legally nonexistent yet fiercely intimate relationships at the very historical moment when multinational corporations with an investment in global trade have had to renegotiate their relationships with nation-states bent on fostering the logic of permanent (anti–terrorist) war? What are the implications of "homeland security" for a politics that demands legal protections for queer families, only to find that powerful states have begun to queer their own relationship to the law, the U.S. refusal to recognize the authority of the International Criminal Court offering only a case in point?

The politics of recognition for "alternative" families has emerged along with the economic transformations associated with neoliberal (free trade) ideologies elaborated under the auspices of the national security state. Debate about same-sex marriage, informal adoptions, and the possibility of ties made of stronger stuff than shared parentage can be heard from São Paolo to Johannesburg, from Delhi to the Pine Ridge reservation, in courtrooms, neighborhoods, homes, bazaars. What made the pursuit of recognition for such relationships at the turn of this last century more

Radical History Review
Issue 93 (Fall 2005): 122–41
Copyright 2005 by Kath Weston

than a notional development was the globalized, juridical form that it often took: a bid to secure legal status for queer relationships, broadly conceived, under the signs of family, kinship, partnership, and marriage.

In the aftermath of 9/11, pursuit of state recognition for social ties that fall into the interstices of legal frameworks appears to be gathering momentum, especially for those ties that can be codified as something akin to gay marriage. My purpose in this essay is less to stage an argument about the significance of these developments than to explore the ironies implicit in demands for legalization of queer relationships at a historical juncture when nominally democratic states have queered their own relationship to the law in the name of fighting terrorism. What sorts of protection does legalization afford when issued by a state prepared to dance a sort of legal two-step, circumventing laws it finds inconvenient while relying on legal technicalities to further its objectives? In the process, I hope to contribute to a better understanding of the part played by recourse to law on all sides of social struggles involving the national security state. The essay also calls attention to the importance of building alliances between sectors of social justice movements concerned with kinship and sexualities, on the one hand, and organizations that engage issues of sovereignty, antifascism, and democratization, on the other.

Before turning to examine the claims that have brought queer relationships before the law, consider the context: efforts to gain legal recognition for queer and GLBT (gay, lesbian, bisexual, and transgender) relationships are historically intertwined with a politics that exceeds family issues, a politics of state banditry and warmed-over imperial ventures. In the United States following 9/11, the age-old right to habeas corpus came under attack, as did the right to a lawyer and lawyer-client confidentiality. Torture and assassination, especially abroad, began to be debated on their supposed merits and were implemented following allegations rather than trials. Bombs dropped on Afghanistan and Iraq instituted a kind of collective responsibility for terrorist attacks or imagined threats that abjured courts and rules of evidence. Suspicion (of terrorist activities) became reason enough for detention, exclusion from air travel, even assassination. Quasi-legal schemes and initiatives that would previously have been unimaginable proliferated, from the doctrine of preemptive war to regulations proposing to expand the grounds for stripping individuals of citizenship. Racism and anti-immigrant sentiment fueled the apathy with which many people in the United States greeted the indefinite detention, without charge, of thousands of noncitizens, many from majority Muslim countries, in the name of fighting terror. As the insidious reach of administrative categories such as *enemy combatant* and *security detainee* extended to U.S. citizens, the legal protections associated with citizenship appeared increasingly precarious.[1]

More was involved than a movement of the state, or this state, into lawlessness. In many overdetermined senses, any dichotomy between law-abiding and lawabjuring cannot hold when the same state that denies certain prisoners the right to appear before a judge also combs the law books for centuries-old legal statutes that can be applied in ways never anticipated by their framers. The resurrection of an 1872 law regulating "sailor-mongering" to prosecute Greenpeace activists, the deportation of noncitizens in chains on visa technicalities (sometimes produced by the state's failure to process paperwork in a timely fashion), and the shameful appeal to a 1913 antimiscegenation statute to block nonresident same-sex marriages in Massachusetts all illustrate appeals to law by agents of a state that has proven the law's uncertain guardian.[2] The application of this search-the-law-books strategy to same-sex marriage suggests why it is that political struggles staged as bids to secure legal rights for queer families (in the broadest sense of queer as "different-from") need to engage debates about the deployment and rule of law.

A more refined formulation of the questions that open this essay, then, would ask about the implications for a politics of legal recognition when states do not upend the law in any overt fashion, but instead continue to utilize legal arenas to rationalize and legitimate state policy, even as agents of the state endeavor to operate outside less congenial laws. This is the refigured relationship of law to the state that yielded the Bush administration's claim that indefinite detention at the U.S.-run prison camp in Guantánamo, Cuba, was not illegal because the camp lies outside federal jurisdiction and therefore beyond judicial review. This is the refigured relationship of law to the state that explains the government's eager embrace of a court ruling that immigrants out of status can be imprisoned in secret. This is the refigured relationship of law to the state that marked the Senate hearings called in 2003 to consider whether to draft a constitutional amendment to deny same-sex couples access to marriage before such access had ever been granted. Since 9/11, legal rationales for state policy have coexisted rather comfortably with the disavowal of legal responsibility for violence inflicted in the course of state-sponsored interrogations, administration proposals to monitor judges who award light sentences, rejection of international treaty responsibilities, the privatization of prisons, and the practice of holding many avowedly apolitical prisoners in conditions unfit for a living being.

Although these examples concern the United States, it would be dangerously reductive to understand the queering of the state's relationship to the law as restricted to this country, much as some early analyses simplistically equated globalization with Americanization. Whatever leadership the United States has demonstrated in attempting to place the machineries of the state beyond the machineries of legislative and judicial review, the United States certainly does not stand alone. One has only to bear witness to the worldwide spread of detention centers for immigrants and asylum seekers, the acquiescence of innumerable countries to the U.S. demand to include biometric data on passports, or the global incitement to escalate orders for military hardware.

Nor are these developments without historical antecedents. Giorgio Agamben has argued that the proliferation of concentration camps under the Nazi regime can be traced to an earlier internment of communist militants by social-democratic governments that gave the color of law to internment by citing the doctrine of *Schutzhaft* (protective custody). *Schutzhaft*, in turn, derived from mid-nineteenth-century Prussian legislation drafted in response to a state of emergency. Once the state of emergency, or exception, takes on the trappings of the permanent and the everyday, space opens for the camp, authorized by a jurisprudence of exceptionality that can remain in place even if the declared emergency abates: "The state of exception thus ceases to be referred to as an external and provisional state of factual danger and comes to be confused with juridical rule itself."[3] In the era of an ill-defined, temporally unbounded so-called war on terrorism, there is a great deal here that needs to be taken to heart for any meaningful analysis of kinship and family politics, within or across borders.

In considering the relationship of a politics of recognition to the rule of law it is also important to bear in mind that a certain queering of the nation-state has entailed the movement of key decision-making processes outside the purview of institutions of liberal democracy, if not outside the law per se. Details of trade policy, toxic waste disposal, labor regulations (or lack thereof), visa requirements, lending practices, food-inspection regimes, and so on are now often set without reference to legislators, voters, or judges. What could be more basic to family life as conceived by most people in the United States than decent food, the opportunity to live together in the same country, the loan that secures shelter, and enough hours away from work to share a meal? Yet debates about queer families rarely examine the impact of extrajudicial moves by the state on these conditions, even as legal rights have come to preoccupy millions who seek intimacy with justice.

Looking to Law

At the turn of this latest century, GLBT people in most countries had obtained remarkably few legal protections, even in basic rights categories such as housing and employment. They could be fired at will for getting involved with someone of the same sex, for taking hormones, or simply for claiming an identity other than heterosexual. They could be denied shelter without much hope of redress. Under certain circumstances, they could be forcibly detained and separated from their partners, denied an inheritance, stripped of parental rights, and refused visits in jails or hospitals from people they considered close relations.

Attempts to respond to such injustices by seeking legal recognition for queer sorts of relationships have been as noteworthy for where they have emerged as for where they have not, and for which sorts of relationships they bring before the law and which sorts they leave locked away in the less-codified rooms of friendship and family life. As early as 1999, for instance, the South African Constitutional Court found that country's Aliens Control Act discriminatory for awarding rights to married heterosexual couples that it denied to lesbian/gay couples. Four years later, in Argentina, organizers solicited international support for a bill introduced during the 2003 legislative session in Santa Fe province that proposed to recognize civil unions as a legal category. The same year, Costa Rica's National Insurance Institute circumvented laws that restricted marriage to male-female couples by affirming the eligibility of same-sex partners and their families for social security.

At that point the Vatican felt compelled to issue a twelve-page document calling on Roman Catholic lawmakers to oppose any legislation providing recognition for same-sex marriage or supporting the violence allegedly visited on children when states allowed gay men and lesbians to adopt.[4] Canadian courts made headlines by laying the groundwork for legalization of marriage between two women or two men, even as Croatia busily passed its own same-sex civil union law. In countries such as Belgium and the Netherlands, legalization of gay marriage (but only for residents vetted by the state) was already yesterday's news.

While many activists in countries of the global South also engaged the politics of recognition, they had reason to proceed cautiously. As heirs to a colonial legal apparatus that had wreaked havoc on intimate relationships by acknowledging and codifying them in inequitable ways, some questioned the advantages of legal recognition per se. In the name of protection, laws promulgated to better the lot of women had ended up disenfranchising them from private property rights regimes installed by colonial administrations. In the name of respect for traditions that were never given as such, but rather became defined and fixed in place under colonial law, a certain fluidity in social relations that had allowed scope for same-sex intimacies diminished. In its place appeared classificatory schemes that reified as they legalized marriage, reified as they criminalized "unnatural acts" and erased same-sex eroticism from narrations of the histories of colonized space.[5] A workshop on same-sex marriage scheduled for the twenty-second World Conference of the International Lesbian and Gay Association in Manila in 2003 offered one forum for beginning to address the complexities of this legal legacy.

The degree to which assumptions about family are woven into legal rights and representations can be gauged from the plethora of family-related matters brought before legislatures and the bench by those who have decided to look to law to sanction and protect queer and GLBT relationships. To give greater texture to the abstraction called the politics of recognition, consider the following vignettes drawn from case law and legislation introduced in the United States during the quarter of a century after the categories of gay (not yet "queer") families and chosen families entered common parlance. Each reflects the historical shift, circa the mid-1980s, in which GLBT people in the United States began to lay claim to the concept of family and the practice of kinship. Each reflects, as well, a move by leading GLBT community organizations to focus on family-related issues. This new emphasis on family was not something unique to GLBT people, but rather something informed by a politicization of kinship in the larger society, a politicization to which GLBT claims on family contributed in turn.[6]

From the beginning, equal access to housing occupied a key position in legal struggles in which GLBT people cited the significance of family and/or kinship ties. In New York City, for example, a landlord had threatened Jeanette Santos, Ivonne Santiago, and their children with eviction from their state-subsidized studio apartment on grounds of overcrowding. The couple contended that the landlord, who knew they were waiting for a larger apartment in the same complex to open up, had shown discriminatory treatment because other four-person households in small units had been allowed to stay. In 1998 the landlord settled out of court and moved the Santos-Santiago family to the top of the waiting list for new apartments.[7]

Rights of inheritance and survivorship represent another key arena in which GLBT people in the United States have sought legal recourse over the past two decades. Larry Courtney, whose partner worked as a flight attendant on one of the planes that crashed into the World Trade Center towers in 2001, had to sue for workers' compensation survivor benefits after he was denied compensation on the basis that he was not married to his (male) partner.[8] Even a marriage certificate, however, was not enough to protect J'Noel Gardiner. The Kansas State Court of Appeals reversed a lower court ruling on an inheritance case that sought to prevent Gardiner from recovering a spousal share of her husband Marshall Gardiner's estate. In this case the courts had responded to a petition filed by Marshall's son, who argued that because J'Noel had had sex reassignment surgery, the marriage had not been legitimate. This despite the fact that Marshall had known all along about the surgery, which had occurred before the marriage. This despite J'Noel's possession of a state-issued driver's license validating the change in her legal status to female. The court of appeals remanded the case for a full hearing to determine whether J'Noel "was male or female at the time the individual's marriage license was issued and the individual was married, not simply what the individual's chromosomes were or were not at the moment of birth."[9]

Other prominent cases involved a quest for legal standing for the purpose of making medical decisions and resolving medical disputes. When Neal Conrad Spicehandler died after routine surgery on a broken leg, his mother joined his partner of sixteen years, John Langan, in filing a wrongful death suit against the New York hospital that performed the surgery. The hospital requested dismissal of the suit, contending that Langan had no legal standing to sue, despite the fact that the couple had traveled to the state of Vermont to legalize their relationship in the form of a civil union. In a 2003 ruling, the judge hearing the case held that same-sex couples recognized as such by the State of Vermont should be treated as legally joined in the State of New York. A declaration of opposition to gay marriage by the president of the United States followed in the wake of this decision.

While child custody cases have long been a battleground for GLBT rights advocates, in *Perdue v. Mississippi State Board of Health*, Lambda Legal Defense, a nonprofit organization, took the unusual step of filing suit on behalf of a four-year-old. In this case the State of Mississippi had refused to issue a birth certificate to Talie Goldstein-Perdue because his parents, who adopted him out of state, were lesbians. Lack of a birth certificate leads to difficulties in registering for school, securing a passport, and many other aspects of living in a document-driven world.[10] One larger issue here: can having queer parents render a person effectively stateless?

Love Sees No Borders, another nonprofit organization, reported that restrictions on movement across territorial borders after 9/11 were "seriously affecting" same-sex couples whose members held citizenship papers issued by different nation-states. Although the Immigration and Naturalization Service (INS) in 1990 had finally agreed to lift its ban on "homosexuals" from other countries entering the United States, more than a decade later GLBT people in binational couples continued to live precariously contingent lives, relying on extensions for nonimmigrant visas that had become increasingly difficult to obtain. According to "Patricia," a Brazilian citizen in a committed relationship with a U.S. national, "For some U.S. citizens, the heightened xenophobia has only fueled their fears. These citizens aren't necessarily afraid of losing their families to violent acts of terrorism; they are gay couples from different countries that fear the U.S. government's effort to separate them."[11] As a result of stepped-up deportations and freezes and delays in obtaining visas, some U.S. citizens in long-term relationships had to separate from their partners or give up established lives to obtain visas to enter the country in which the partner held citizenship. If neither country would issue a visa, the couple's only alternative to forced separation would be to leave the nation that represents itself as the land of freedom to seek asylum in a third country that recognizes the validity of same-sex relationships. With asylum seekers increasingly imprisoned in many parts of the world until their cases are adjudicated, this alternative might also entail parting from one another.

HR 690, the Permanent Partners Immigration Act introduced during the 2002 legislative session, sought to address some of these problems by adding the term *permanent partners* (of whatever sex) to federal definitions of family in the United States. That bill languished in subcommittees. Undaunted, a group of legislators offered Senate Bill 1510, the Permanent Partners Immigration Act, in the next session as an amendment to the Immigration and Nationality Act of 2003. An unquestioned premise in the debate attached to this legislation: it is the state's province to classify, as well as arbitrate, who shall count as family.

No discussion of queered kinship at the turn of the latest century would be complete without consideration of gay marriage, a synecdoche that often stood in for the broad range of issues entailed in the politics of legal recognition for GLBT families. In the 2002 Massachusetts gubernatorial race, Democratic candidate Shannon O'Brien announced that, if elected, she pledged to sign a gay marriage bill forwarded to her by the legislature (an unlikely event, given the composition of that legislative body). Alternatively, she promised to pursue state sanction for the quasi-marriage category called civil union. Her opponent, who won the race, immediately denounced this position, emphasizing his opposition to gay marriage in any form and calling same-sex marriage a threat to the institution of marriage itself.

Then, in a landmark ruling, the Supreme Judicial Court of the Commonwealth of Massachusetts ordered in 2003 that same-sex couples be granted marriage licenses in accordance with the court's interpretation of the state constitution. As conservative groups mobilized to put a referendum on the 2006 ballot that would restrict marriage to male-female unions, municipalities in Massachusetts celebrated the first legal marriages of lesbian and gay couples in the United States.

During the decade that preceded this ruling, a strange phenomenon passed largely without comment: same-sex couples in the United States were frequently told to go ahead and marry if they wanted to marry. This often well-meaning advice rested on the common, but at that time utterly false, perception that two women or two men in the United States could have legally married in some state, somewhere. This utopian vision was noteworthy for its tendency to credit developments that had not developed and to presume legal victories that had not occurred.

What do these scenarios have in common, apart from the fact that most of them would scarcely have been imaginable a mere half century ago? Each vignette depicts a politics of recognition that seeks legitimacy through the state. Many of the cases involve appeals to courts of law. When the courts failed to confer legal standing on relationships that people considered family, they sometimes sought remedies in legislative arenas and, to a lesser extent, through appeals to government agencies to revise regulations. Throughout, they had to contend not only with well-funded opponents who resisted state recognition for GLBT relationships but also with allies whose political energies were sapped by the comforting fantasy that legal status had already been attained.

Of course, GLBT people in the United States were far from united in embracing the new focus on family matters. Some worried that a strong emphasis on family might reinforce old hierarchies, divert resources from other important arenas of social struggle, and/or subordinate grassroots politics to the machineries of the state. Social critics urged closer attention to the sedimented associations and historical deployment of terms such as *marriage* that most people thought they already understood.[12] Wise counsel, perhaps, but one that has yet to figure prominently in the queering of twenty-first-century politics.

Before returning to examine the outcomes of these struggles in the context of the homeland security state, it is important to explore more of the history and the limitations of the politics of legal recognition as pursued over the course of the past twenty years in the United States by many GLBT people, their allies, and their advocates. The next section of the essay should resonate for North Americans who fought against Jim Crow laws only to find that legal status and legally mandated equality put no end to racial discrimination—only to find, in other words, that formal equality can sometimes provide legal cover for provisions that have a harsh, ongoing, and deleterious impact on the oppressed.

En Route to a Politics of Recognition

What led so many GLBT people toward the end of the twentieth century to embrace the concept of family, if not always kin? It was during the 1980s that lesbians and gay men in North America began to speak widely of chosen families, the families they saw themselves creating as adults. Some of the recognition they sought, and continue to seek, is social: for example, the opportunity to put up pictures at work of the friends, lovers, and children in their lives just like heterosexual coworkers, without being accused of flaunting their sexuality. Much of the recognition they sought, and continue to seek, takes the form of legal protections: for example, the right to rent an apartment without being told a lie ("it's already rented") by a landlord who objects to same-sex relationships, who suspects that the applicant's partner has changed gender, or who cannot reconcile fatherhood with gay identity.

Of course, GLBT people had been having children, raising children, forming couples, introducing lovers to their parents, and forging close daily bonds with friends well before they started talking about chosen families in the 1980s. Previously, however, these practices had had little place in discussions of family because GLBT people were, to a great extent, ideologically excluded from kinship. When young people came out, parents commonly worried that a gay life would doom their children to growing old alone. GLBT people were often perceived as essentially single even when they had partners, as not fully social or socialized people because they appeared to lack family responsibilities. Few coworkers stopped to wonder if a lesbian employee might need that raise because she was paying child support to a former partner or sending money to her lover's mother in El Salvador. Gay people were not widely understood to be family people, and family people were supposed to be, by definition, heterosexual.[13]

Race compounded with class, nation, and gender in these assessments. An African American woman in a relationship with another woman, for instance, had to grapple with ideologies that attempted to exclude her from family and kinship in more than one sense. Popular versions of the racist Moynihan Report, which assailed black kinship ties as pathological when they were acknowledged to exist at all, dovetailed all too neatly with the message of a resurgent conservative movement that mistakenly equated gay with nonreproductive and no reproduction with no family.

While the emergence of GLBT families often tends to be discussed as the product of a community, GLBT claims on family did not develop in a hermetically sealed environment, much less a vacuum. The claims that GLBT people made on family and kinship were intimately related to a renewed focus on family issues in the larger society. I have in mind here more than the family values debates of the late twentieth century, which often targeted GLBT people as a threat to a mythically unified construct called "the family." The 1980s were years of heated controversies over surrogate parenthood, in vitro fertilization, open adoptions, legal charges of fetal endangerment, a rise in both single-parent families and the blended families produced by heterosexual divorce and remarriage.

Preoccupation with family issues emerged as households experienced the impact of corporate profit taking and deregulation of the economy. Falling real wages dramatically exacerbated the problem of finding affordable child care in the United States, since many households had to send all adult members into the waged workforce to pay the bills. The business strategy of improving productivity not only through technological innovation but by requiring more work from fewer bodies cut into the time that people could spend with relatives, uninterrupted by workplace demands. No wonder they were worrying. No wonder they were talking about family.

Even retailers picked up on the family theme. In 1994 the Body Shop mail-order catalog featured the Year of the Family Soap, manufactured to commemorate the declaration of the Year of the Family by the United Nations. Despite the soap's superficially androgynous appearance, the height, size, and positioning of four figures merged into a single bar could easily be read as a biologically related nuclear group: father, mother, shorter/younger daughter and taller/elder son, available in one fabulous color, white. "Like our Endangered Species soaps, it is made at Soapworks," the company's advertising proclaimed. What began as a paean to diversity resolved itself into the family as endangered species. By making this link, the socially conscious Body Shop Corporation figured families through biological/animal connection, subtly associating kinship ties with biological ties in the very way that GLBT organizations would mobilize against.

This was the political and economic landscape out of which GLBT claims to family arose. As early as the mid-1980s, GLBT organizations had taken issue with the idea that after coming out people would have to live the rest of their lives alienated from the kinship networks in which they had grown up, without any opportunity to go on to create kinship ties of their own. Ten years on, the country witnessed a discursive shift in which many people who identified as gay, lesbian, bisexual, and transgender recast some of their most intimate ties of belonging as family and demanded recognition for those ties as such.

The ties put forward for recognition at the turn of this century did not represent some sort of substitute for the families in which GLBT people had grown up. Nor did they mark the invention of a brand-new family form that broke completely with a nebulous something called the traditional family. Although people tended to speak of the families they saw themselves making as chosen, the choices made were inevitably constrained.

To speak of GLBT families as substitute families would imply, incorrectly, that all GLBT people lose the families in which they grow up and therefore need to find a replacement. To speak of GLBT families as an alternative family form is no less a misnomer because it leaves undisturbed fantasies of a nuclear family as the real family to which queer forms of family are imagined to represent an alternative. There were, of course, those who experienced the pain of being disowned for claiming a GLBT identity or for "acting queer," sometimes having to make their own way in the world at a young age. Yet in the majority of cases, people maintained ties with relatives after coming out, weaving new relationships into the fabric of the old.

The relationships brought before the courts for recognition in the closing decades of the twentieth century were neither completely new nor freely chosen. The very language of chosen families employs a predictable, pervasive cultural rhetoric of voluntarism that draws on individualized notions of freedom and will. Kinship may be constructed, but that does not make it a blank slate on which actors—be they transgender, gay, bisexual, or straight—can write whatever they please. Queer sorts of families configure relationships, however creatively, from historically available materials. Those ties do not break with what has come before in any wholesale way, but rather incorporate aspects of religious, cultural, national, racial, ethnic, and other salient legacies.[14] How could it be otherwise?

To appreciate the magnitude of the discursive shift through which GLBT people began making claims on family, consider that antigay conservatives were not the only ones who had insistently positioned homosexuals outside of the realm of kinship. Gay liberationists of the 1970s, along with some feminists, had formulated a critique of the family as an oppressive institution irretrievably riddled with gender and age hierarchies. In the eyes of these critics, coming out meant coming into a certain kind of freedom from the imperative to form family ties. Gay liberationists differed from their conservative opponents primarily in that they saw this as a good thing, because many thought it represented a move in the direction of equality.[15] Other lesbians and gay men, mostly of color, contended that family and kinship should be embraced as historically intertwined with racial, cultural, and ethnic identities in North America. Cherríe Moraga, for instance, argued eloquently for allegiance to *familia* and identified forms of whiteness tacitly encoded in the gay liberationist position.[16]

Years later, when GLBT organizations sought to locate their constituencies inside kinship, right-wing organizations tailored their rhetoric to position homosexuals back outside the door. During the 1990s groups with names such as the Coalition for Family Values sponsored antigay legislation, implying that coalition members had families (and values), whereas GLBT people did not. A decade earlier, the Moral Majority had circulated similar exclusionary rhetoric using inflammatory headlines such as "Homosexual Diseases Threaten American Families."

One way that GLBT people countered these representations was by appropriating the terms of debate, sometimes using camp to give representations of family a lighthearted twist. In the San Francisco of the early 1990s, for example, GLAAD (the Gay and Lesbian Alliance against Defamation) paid for a billboard near City Hall that showed an interracial lesbian couple, arms around each other, one of the women obviously pregnant. The caption read, "Another Traditional Family." During the same period, a postcard made its way through the U.S. mail. The front of the card pictured a white man in an even whiter bridal gown, all dignity, all camp, with a comic-book bubble coming out of his mouth that had him speaking the line, "Mother always taught me traditional values."

The historical shift that placed family issues at the center of GLBT politics and associated gay rights with claims to kinship represented much more than a rhetorical move. The changes desired were never merely ones of nomenclature: substitution of *spouse* or *partner* for *boyfriend, parenting* for *child care, family of friends* for *homies* and *buddies.* By asserting claims to kinship, GLBT people could simultaneously make claims on material conditions that included country of residence and resources allocated through state-certified marital or biogenetic connection. In the process, they called attention to symbolic aspects of blood and marriage that worked to naturalize certain forms of kinship in European and North American societies.

One by-product of the GLBT movement's call in the 1980s for everyone to come out was precisely to denaturalize kinship in some of the ways that an anthropologist might. When people systematically contemplated telling relatives about the meaningful same-sex intimacies in their lives, they often reflected on the potential for supposedly permanent blood ties to be alienated. Before coming out, they worried about the possibility, however remote, that relatives might reject them, based on religious objections or negative preconceptions about what it means to be GLBT or queer. What if my mom disowns me? What if my cousin says that as far as he's concerned, we're not related? What if I end up "losing" biological ties that I thought could never be undone? In light of questions like these, "blood" ties appeared rather similar to other intimate ties of belonging—friendship, living together, marriage— in that they could be severed. For many GLBT people, as for many anthropologists, the belief that biology provides the only possible foundation for kinship, much less relatedness, began to seem a profoundly cultural move.

This does not mean that biology disappeared altogether from GLBT reckonings of kinship. By the late 1990s, a few lesbian mothers who had wanted their partners to be recognized as coparents changed their tune after the couples broke up. At that point, they resorted to playing biology as a trump card of sorts, going to court to deny visitation to the ex on the grounds that the ex had no "blood" connection to the child.

Nevertheless, by encouraging people to come out and subjecting the permanence of biological ties to review, the GLBT movement had inadvertently helped open the space to pose the question, what makes a family? Of course, the answer to that question was and is not fixed, for GLBT people or anyone else. The responses are multiple and emerge from historically changing conditions. What perhaps mattered most was not so much the answer to the question but rather the posing of the question, which created occasions for the recognition and adjudication of queer sorts of differences in the configuration of daily intimacies.

The Lure of Legality: Intimacy with Justice

What social and material resources were at stake when GLBT people pursued state recognition for their intimate relationships? A few examples from a very long list: In some parts of North America, insurance companies will not issue state-mandated automobile coverage to legally unrelated people living at the same address, even when they can show joint ownership on a vehicle's title. For many, this is more than a matter of driving. It is a matter of getting to work, and hence an exclusion with deep implications for class and survival, as well as sexuality. Or consider the gay man who cannot avoid probate on the death of his partner—the privilege of any heterosexual spouse—and so risks having the house in which he and his partner lived being sold out from under him. Or the woman who cannot pick up her lover from work because her lover's employer objects to hiring queers and the household needs that income. Or the bisexual man who ends up in a hospital emergency room after a long illness and is whisked away from the family of friends who have fed him and bathed him, cleaned his bottom and walked his dog. In hospital policies that restrict visitation to family members, such relationships are invisible. His family of friends might never see him again.

The threats to intimacy posed by unrecognized relationships gained currency among GLBT people through cautionary tales of people who had sought legal recourse or restitution in the aftermath of tragedies like these. For people living a heterosexual life, who sometimes asked in a bemused voice what the "big deal" was about being queer, the consequences of a lack of legal standing were far from evident. Someone with privilege, by definition, need not notice the benefits that privilege brings. Or to notice the implications for a person who lacks the same standing, precisely because the privileged life goes on smoothly, without disruption. Or, for that matter, to understand how under current law any relationship in the United States can be disadvantaged, even threatened, when unsecured by the legal protections that adoption, "blood" ties, and marriage afford. To give but one example: When Radmilla Cody, former Miss Navajo Nation, was remanded to prison for failing to report her boyfriend's drug dealing, the disposition of the case turned on the informal status of their relationship in the eyes of the state. Had the heterosexual couple possessed a marriage certificate, everything would have been different. As his state-certified spouse, she would have had no legal obligation to testify against him.[17]

At the same time, GLBT organizations bringing family issues before the law have tended to downplay the complex, unequal application of the protections and privileges that the law is supposed to secure. In a political system that routinely denies noncitizens constitutional protections, all the while eroding distinctions based on citizenship, it could be argued that marriage, for instance, is not a single institution that evenly confers legal rights on all who can avail themselves of it.[18] How is a noncitizen, resident in the United States on a visa, who has registered a domestic partnership with a municipality supposed to fill out federal immigration forms that offer only two choices, single or married? How is he to sleep in the aftermath of this forced choice, knowing that technicalities in recent years have become a vehicle used to facilitate deportations? How is marriage or citizenship to prevent a Native or Chicana lesbian from being caught up in the racial profiling that informs immigration sweeps in the U.S. Southwest and being summarily dumped, without money or identification, on the Mexican side of the border? These are inequities that often escape the attention of GLBT people whose relationships lack legal status but who enjoy privileges tied to other aspects of their state-patrolled bodies and state-documented lives.

A certain naivety born of longing as much as privilege informs any expectation that justice rides into town on the horse of legal status. "The appeal to the state," writes Judith Butler, "is at once an appeal to a fantasy already institutionalized by the state, and a leave-taking from existing social complexity in the hope of becoming 'socially coherent' at last."[19] In the process of tying the politics of recognition so tightly to legalities, it can be argued that something has been lost.

Homeland Insecurity

To the extent that GLBT people look to legal battles for confirmation of what it means to them to have family, do family, or even fight for family, a focus on state recognition can undermine kinship practices that have no hope of gaining legal standing and narrow the range of intimacies that people create. Under the type of legal system that prevails in the United States, judgments are established through case law. Case law appeals to precedent. A reliance on previous rulings compels attorneys to construct an argument, however creatively, with reference to conflicts adjudicated in very particular pasts. When bids for legal recognition can only move forward by citing cases already ruled on by the courts, many disputes over relationships will prove impractical, if not impossible, to bring before a judge. As a result, many ways of making family and creating kin are missing from the docket.

When GLBT people went to court in the 1990s to argue for the legitimacy of nonbiological parental ties, for instance, they sometimes used an in loco parentis argument. Adults who had raised and supported a child contended that they were acting as parents and therefore should have parental rights vis-à-vis that child, regardless of biogenetic connection. While theoretically in loco parentis doctrine can apply to any adults in the child's life, or even to institutions (as it has in the past for colleges), in practice GLBT claims that invoke in loco parentis have restricted themselves to gaining parental status for a limited number of adults in the child's life. Why should this be so? The focus on father and mother in legal precedent leaves little room for numbers in excess of two: little room for aunts, for cousins, for religious or political communities that take collective responsibility for children, for larger-than-nuclear households.

There are few if any pages in U.S. case law that yield directly relevant precedent for people who come from parts of the world where a mother's brother is supposed to maintain a key relationship with her child, sometimes taking more responsibility for the child than the mother's partner. Nor is there much room in U.S. case law for the gay man who has cared for a child two weekends a month since the child's birth, serving as an uncle of sorts but without any prospect of formal visitation rights. Nor are there precedents for kinship ties fashioned of friendship, despite a long history of GLBT people according friendship a special place in their hearts. Legalization of same-sex marriage would do little to strengthen the position of any friend, non–biologically related *tío* (uncle), or mother's brother who felt compelled to turn plaintiff. Wherever precedent rules in this legal system, "blood" ties and a nuclear model of family looms large.[20]

When the numbers concerned are precisely two, couples in so-called unconventional living arrangements may find little status for their relationships in even the progressive laws that organizations have worked so hard to pass. Suppose there are two people in a long-term committed relationship who both believe that the relationship will fare better and last longer if the partners do not live together. As currently written, domestic partnership legislation typically requires proof of coresidence for a specified period of time. At the very moment that the legal status of domestic partnership opens up the questions of what constitutes kinship and what makes a family, it forecloses the question of what makes a household. No bold new experiments in daily living there.

In their important book, *Left Legalism/Left Critique*, Wendy Brown, a political theorist and culture critic, and Janet Halley, a professor of law, examine the emphasis on legal remedy that characterized progressive political projects in North America in the late twentieth century. Recourse to law, they argue, sometimes unintentionally fostered developments very much at odds with the changes originally sought.[21] This is a conversation that those engaged in a politics of recognition for queer relationships very much need to join. In times such as these, the limitations of such a politics concern much more than the fate of intimacies that cannot gain the imprimatur of the courts.

Take a Look Around: A Different Politics of Recognition

People struggling to gain meaningful recognition for intimate ties cannot afford to misrecognize the historical moment in which they work. When the executive branch claims extrajudicial prerogatives while legislators accede and judges flinch, legal strategies for social change cannot be enough. Political developments that threaten the rule of law, or threaten to replace a rule of law with a rule of technicalities, undermine the protections associated with painstakingly acquired legal rights, but they also open new possibilities for GLBT people to join together with other constituencies that have been forced to reconsider their focus on law in response to the changing character of appointments to the bench.

Far from conserving precedent, judges at the highest level in the United States have endangered—to give but one example—a two-hundred-year history of treaty law, case law, and legislative intent that dealt with Native American nations as sovereign entities with which federal and state governments had to parley. Addressing an audience of Native people in 2002, U.S. Supreme Court justice Stephen Breyer advised that it would be unwise to bring tribal sovereignty cases to the Supreme Court until the composition of the court changed.[22] What, then, for queer kinship and GLBT families?

When laws are arbitrarily invoked and ignored with impunity, they provide recognition and legitimacy primarily for the already powerful. Since 9/11, North Americans have grown accustomed to news of detentions without due process, searches without warrants, cavalier dismissals of international treaties, warmongering that finds its justification in the ability to convince you that "it's all right for me to hit you first if I fear that you might be thinking about hitting me someday." What will it matter to have queer families recognized before the law if law does not prevail? So it is that sovereignty rights, civil liberties, the latest word on troop movements, the growing public acceptance of torture, the lovers separated by newly inscribed borders, have all become queer issues.

At a time when many have warned that the United States is retreating from the rule of law, there is an urgent need to build nonkinship solidarities with groups working in these areas.[23] If GLBT people are to secure and defend even the most elementary protections for their intimate relationships, given the politics of this day, then both the coalitions and the arenas in which they seek justice must multiply and move beyond a politics of bringing family issues, narrowly conceived, before the law. GLBT organizations already have an impressive history of making common cause in the fight for more expansive, nuanced interpretations of intimate relationships. During the 1980s and 1990s, they worked in alliance with senior citizens groups to pass domestic partnership legislation by arguing that employee health benefits should extend to any financial dependent. They filed amicus briefs in court cases involving heterosexuals when those cases had a bearing on the legal calculus of determining who should count as kin. In the same spirit, they supported the rights of unmarried heterosexual couples to visit one another in the hospital and the rights of mothers to visit in prison the children they had raised but never formally adopted. In the same spirit, they now must consider what part they will play in efforts to uphold legal process and oppose reckless imperial ventures.

The task at hand is not only organizational but theoretical as well. Social justice movements across the spectrum require a better understanding of shifts in the articulation of nation-states to legal and corporate forms in order to contend with the endlessly morphing shape of global capital flows and the failure of tried-and-true tactics for political protest to generate their anticipated effects.[24] These are shifts, perhaps, in the very character of the nation-state, which turns out to be not-one.

Those whose relatives languish in the limbo of indefinite detention, those who have had their closest ties scrutinized by governments, those who have passed through the criminal justice system, those who go home at night to neighborhoods subjected to paramilitary-style policing and the constant threat of being thrown up against the wall by a policeman who is not their friend: immigrants, refugees, the poor, people of color, whose daily lives are permeated by such experiences, tend to understand all too well the double-edged character of appealing to the state, be it for recognition, resources, or both. More than most, they may not survive a misplaced confidence in the law. Whatever legal status people with queer sorts of families manage to secure for their relationships, recent developments have ensured that they will remain subject to the worldwide proliferation of a national security state with an investment in fostering insecurity. In the legally ambiguous shadow of the new imperialism, those who find themselves and their families in queer sorts of states might do better to move toward forms of organizing that question the justice of allocating resources fundamental to life—food, housing, peace, work, travel, health care—through kinship in the first place.

Notes

With appreciation for the invitation extended by Anthony Petro and the Alliance for Diversity at Georgia State University in 2002 that incited the first draft of this essay. My thanks also to Geeta Patel and David Wilkins for agreeing to read a later version, to Kumkum Sangari and Sheba Chhachhi for that provocative conversation, and to Yvonne Lassalle for her excellent editorial suggestions.

1. David Cole and James X. Dempsey, *Terrorism and the Constitution: Sacrificing Civil Liberties in the Name of National Security* (New York: New Press, 2002); Michael Welch, *Detained: Immigration Laws and the Expanding I.N.S. Jail Complex* (Philadelphia: Temple University Press, 2002); Moustafa Bayoumi, "How Does It Feel to Be a Problem?"

in *Asian Americans on War and Peace*, ed. Russell C. Leong and Don T. Nakanishi (Los Angeles: UCLA Asian American Studies Center Press, 2002), 81–89; Linda Greenhouse, "Word for Word/*Rumsfeld v. Padilla*: The Supreme Court Asks, Who Will Guard the Guardians?" *New York Times*, May 9, 2004.

2. Pam Belluck, "Governor Moves on Non-Massachusetts Couples," *New York Times*, May 19, 2004; Pam Belluck, "Governor Seeks to Invalidate Some Same-Sex Marriages," *New York Times*, May 21, 2004; Adam Liptak, "Typical Greenpeace Protest Leads to an Unusual Prosecution," *New York Times*, October 11, 2003. The sailor-mongering law, Liptak explains, was drafted to discourage proprietors from "luring crews to boarding houses" and brothels by climbing onto ships on the way into port. Greenpeace activists had boarded a cargo ship arriving in Florida to call attention to the illegal importation of mahogany.

3. Giorgio Agamben, *Homo Sacer: Sovereign Power and Bare Life*, trans. Daniel Heller-Roazen (Stanford, CA: Stanford University Press, 1998), 168. See also Achilles Mbembe, "Necropolitics," *Public Culture* 15 (2003): 11–40.

4. Frank Bruni, "Vatican Exhorts Legislators to Reject Same-Sex Unions," *New York Times*, August 1, 2003.

5. See, for example, Veena Talwar Oldenburg, *Dowry Murder: The Imperial Origins of a Cultural Crime* (New York: Oxford University Press, 2002); and Rudi C. Bleys, *The Geography of Perversion: Male-to-Male Sexual Behavior Outside the West and the Ethnographic Imagination, 1750–1918* (New York: New York University Press, 1995).

6. Kath Weston, *Families We Choose: Lesbians, Gays, Kinship*, 2nd ed. (New York: Columbia University Press, 1997); Judith Stacey, *In the Name of the Family: Rethinking Family Values in the Postmodern Age* (Boston: Beacon, 1996). On the politicization of kinship during this period, see Rayna Rapp, "Toward a Nuclear Freeze? The Gender Politics of Euro-American Kinship Analysis," in *Gender and Kinship: Essays Toward a Unified Analysis*, ed. Jane Fishburne Collier and Sylvia Junko Yanagisako (Stanford, CA: Stanford University Press, 1987), 119–31.

7. *Phipps v. Santiago* (New York State Court, settled 1998). See the case summary on the Web site of Lambda Legal, whose attorneys represented Santiago and Santos. www.lambdalegal.org/cgi-bin/iowa/cases/record?record=62 (accessed April 19, 2005).

8. *In re: Workers' Compensation Claim of Larry Courtney*, New York State Workers' Compensation Board, filed 2001. See case summary on Web site of Lambda Legal, www.lambdalegal.org/cgi-bin/iowa/cases/record?record=183 (accessed April 19, 2005).

9. *In the matter of the estate of Marshall G. Gardiner*, No. 85,030, Kansas State Court of Appeals, May 11, 2001. The judgment is listed on the Web site of the Kansas Supreme Court/Kansas Court of Appeals, www.lambdalegal.org/cgi-bin/iowa/cases/record?record=193 (accessed April 19, 2005).

10. *Perdue v. Mississippi State Board of Health*, Cause No. G-2001-1891 S/2, Chancery Court of the First Judicial District of Hinds County, Mississippi, March 5, 2003.

11. Gabriel Dean, "Exiled from Main Street: U.S. Immigration Laws Compel Some Gay Americans to Leave Country," *Creative Loafing Atlanta*, September 11, 2002, www.atlanta.creativeloafing.com/2002-09-11/feature.html (accessed April 19, 2005).

12. John Borneman, "Until Death Do Us Part: Marriage/Death in Anthropological Discourse," *American Ethnologist* 23 (1996): 215–38; Ellen Lewin, *Recognizing Ourselves: Ceremonies of Lesbian and Gay Commitment* (New York: Columbia University Press, 1998); Ruthann Robson, "Resisting the Family: Repositioning Lesbians in Legal Theory," *Signs* 19 (1994): 975–96. For a sense of the differing positions taken by GLBT

people regarding marriage, see Thomas B. Stoddard, "Why Gay People Should Seek the Right to Marry," *Out/Look: National Gay and Lesbian Quarterly* 2, no. 2 (1989): 9, 14–17.

13. Weston, *Families We Choose.*

14. Kath Weston, "Made to Order: Family Formation and the Rhetoric of Choice," in *Long Slow Burn: Sexuality and Social Science* (New York: Routledge, 1998), 83–93.

15. For example, Guy Hocquenghem, *Homosexual Desire,* trans. Daniella Danqoor (1978; Durham, NC: Duke University Press, 1993); Barrie Thorne, "Feminism and the Family: Two Decades of Thought," in *Rethinking the Family: Some Feminist Questions,* ed. Thorne and Marilyn Yalom (Boston: Northeastern University Press, 1992), 3–30.

16. Cherríe Moraga, *The Last Generation: Prose and Poetry* (Boston: South End, 1993); and Cherríe Moraga, *Loving in the War Years: Lo Que Nunca Pasó por Sus Labios,* 2nd ed. (Boston: South End, 2000).

17. For background on the case, in an article that takes her criminalization as fait accompli, see Larry Di Giovanni, "Diné in Shock over Cody's Crimes," *Gallup Independent,* December 11, 2002.

18. On heightened state scrutiny, constitutional protections, and citizenship, see David Cole, *Enemy Aliens: Double Standards and Constitutional Freedoms in the War on Terrorism* (New York: New Press, 2003); Eithne Luibhéid, *Entry Denied: Controlling Sexuality at the Border* (Minneapolis: University of Minnesota Press, 2002); and Welch, *Detained.*

19. Judith Butler, "Is Kinship Always Already Heterosexual?" in *Left Legalism/Left Critique,* ed. Wendy Brown and Janet Halley (Durham, NC: Duke University Press, 2002), 243.

20. Here my argument differs, in its attention to precedent and legal process, from Borneman's in "Until Death Do Us Part." Borneman treats "the relentless debate about 'families' in both anthropology and popular culture" as a "disguise" for "what is actually at stake: social and legal recognition and protection of marriage" (216). On the contrary: gay marriage, far from constituting the preeminent object of queered familial desire, has come to dominate representations of queer families due in part to the pursuit of those forms of recognition that can themselves hope to be acknowledged by the law.

21. Brown and Halley, *Left Legalism/Left Critique.*

22. Kevin Gover, "We Shouldn't Have (Indian) Trust in the Supreme Court," *Indian Country Today,* August 21, 2002. Justice Breyer's warning was scarcely allayed by the court's double take on sovereignty in its 2004 ruling in *U.S. v. Lara.* See David Wilkins, "Justice Thomas and Federal Indian Law—Hitting His Stride?" *Indian Country Today,* May 5, 2004. "Termination, even wrapped in a black robe, is still termination," testified David Getches, a professor at the University of Colorado at Boulder Law School, before the Senate Committee on Indian Affairs (quoted in Jim Adams, "Campaign against 'Terminators in Black Robes,'" *Indian Country Today,* October 16, 2002). See also Getches's "Beyond Indian Law: The Rehnquist Court's Pursuit of States' Rights, Color-Blind Justice, and Mainstream Values," *Minnesota Law Review* 86 (2001): 267–362.

23. See John Mohawk, "Abandoning the Principle of Law Is the Wrong Way to Go," *Indian Country Today,* April 7, 2004; Barbara Olshansky, *Secret Trials and Executions: Military Tribunals and the Threat to Democracy* (New York: Seven Stories, 2005); and John W. Dean, "How the War on Terrorism Is Shrinking Congressional Powers," parts 1 and 2, FindLaw's Legal Commentary, writ.findlaw.com/dean/20021011.html (accessed April 19, 2005). Dean argues that the expansion of executive powers in the United States at the turn of the twenty-first century contravened provisions of the U. S. Constitution. On implications of the abrogation of international law, see John Gray, "Power and Vainglory,"

Independent, May 22, 2004. On grassroots opposition to these developments, see Elaine Scarry's careful analysis of municipal resolutions that have authorized resistance to the 2001 USA PATRIOT Act, "Resolving to Resist: Local Governments Are Refusing to Comply with the Patriot Act," *Boston Review* (February/March 2004), www.bostonreview .net/BR29.1/scarry.html. According to Scarry, "The documents consistently register the view that both the people and the laws of the country are endangered. Together the local resolutions constitute a treatise on self-governance and the rule of law."

24. I am indebted to Kumkum Sangari and Sheba Chhachhi for clarifying the urgency of this point.

The Women Bush Forgot

Martha Howell

Just after the United States went into Afghanistan and had more or less routed the Taliban, Laura Bush, wife of George W. Bush, a former school teacher, mother, and homemaker who generally stays very far from political view, went on the radio, taking the president's place in his Saturday morning address to the nation. She spoke for a long time, detailing the suffering the Afghan women had endured under the Taliban—denied schooling, driven from the workplace, subjected to beatings, sexual abuse, and generally bad treatment at the hands of husbands, brothers, and fathers—all symbolized by the odious *burka*, the blue shroud women were compelled to don if they ventured away from the patriarchal domain. Mrs. Bush then went on to celebrate our armies, her husband, and America for having brought freedom to these women, a liberation best represented by their release from the *burka*.

The American media picked up this heart-warming story and immediately sent camerapeople and microphones to Kabul and elsewhere to photograph smiling women walking to market with faces exposed, serious girls in classrooms gratefully learning to read and write, and female doctors or nurses joyfully returning to the hospitals and clinics in which they could continue the useful work for which they had been trained.

For long months these images were played and replayed on TV and remanufactured every time a reporter arrived in Kabul, and the administration continues to congratulate itself for its humanity, its concern for women, its love of freedom, a love so passionate it extends even—perhaps especially—to women. In his 2002 State of the Union address, President Bush crowed that "the mothers and daughters of Afghanistan were captives in their own homes. . . . Today they are free."

Radical History Review
Issue 93 (Fall 2005): 142–46
Copyright 2005 by MARHO: The Radical Historians' Organization, Inc.

Just before the invasion of Iraq in 2003, an article appeared in the respected, if deeply conservative, financial daily, the *Wall Street Journal*, written by a woman who proudly located herself among the Bush admirers.[1] It not only echoed the story of the administration's gallantry but it attacked women, dismissively labeled feminists, for their failure to support Bush's war; in other words, for their refusal to recognize that the coming Iraq invasion was good for women. Some feminists, the author claimed, preached an idiotic "women are good/men are bad" sermon, refusing, she implied, to acknowledge that women are capable of evil and that men can do good. Others cowardly hid behind laws and bureaucracies, afraid to fight for what they knew was right, while they clung to the false hope that freedom could come to people afraid to engage the heroic struggle for it. Worst, however, were the "postcolonial" feminists nestled in universities like my own who, she suggested, blamed Western imperialism for the harm done to women in places like Afghanistan. These, she insisted, have even "been known to defend forced marriage, polygamy, and even female circumcision." In her final salvo against such scholars, our author ridiculed my own colleague Gayatri Spivak, who has famously characterized much of Western "do-good-ism" around the world as "white men saving brown women from brown men."[2]

There are so many distortions, lies, cruelties, and cynicism imbedded in this rhetoric that it is hard to know where to begin to unravel them. Let me try, however, by focusing on women themselves, the ostensible subject of this narrative spun by the Bush administration, put into the mouth of Mrs. Bush, and paraded in the pages of the *Wall Street Journal*. I will focus not just on the women of Afghanistan, but on women around the world—women in Pakistan and Saudi Arabia and Iraq, women in Africa and Asia, women in Europe, women in South America, and women in the United States. And let me try to use a few facts about some of these women as a wedge to deconstruct not just the rhetoric but the political culture of America today, an America in which over half of the people supported unilateral action in Iraq, in which a stunning percentage—over 40 percent—of people thought and appear still to think that Saddam Hussein was behind al-Qaeda, in which our administration talked itself into believing that Hussein had massive stockpiles of biological and chemical weapons and was poised to use them, and in which the voices of protest were then and are now too easily disregarded, labeled unpatriotic, or ridiculed.

Fact number 1: Before September 11, Western feminists, joining women around the world, had long been pleading for more global attention—from Western governments, and in particular from the U.S. government—to the sufferings of the Afghan women. I myself signed and circulated many petitions; I heard lectures and read articles in academic journals about their plight. We begged our own government to give no support to the Taliban until they ceased the policies of abuse, to bring all pressure to bear to promote change. We got no response, except the occasional handwringing from the Clinton administration. The Bush administration, in fact, extended aid to the Taliban until four months before 9/11. Our mainstream press barely covered the issue. Even the *New York Times*, our newspaper of record, gave considerably more coverage to the Taliban's destruction of ancient Buddhist statuary than it did to the plight of women in the country, and Western governments did more to protest that travesty than they ever did to protest a thousand wife beatings, ruthless claustrations, or forced marriages.

Fact number 2: Women in Afghanistan today are not liberated. Some have, indeed, returned to school and jobs, especially in Kabul, where the Karzai regime has some control and where Western journalists spend most of their time, and I am sure these women—most of them from the old educated middle class—are glad. And if so, so am I. But most Afghan women are not in school; they are huddled in a dangerous countryside—or even in Kabul—without adequate food, shelter, or medical services, uncertain what the future will bring, afraid for their children, suspicious of the Americans and of the peace they claim to have imposed. They are not certain whether it is safe to drop the *burka*, resentful of being forced to do so by the pressure of Western ideas of freedom and, in many cases, not at all convinced that they want to live without the veil. Some, in fact, cannot imagine their lives without the *burka*. The American media seldom talks about these women because they do not exactly represent the new Afghanistan the Bush administration wants us to believe is in the making and for which it wants to take full credit. These women are also ignored because they raise interesting and difficult questions about what freedom might mean in the particular context of Afghanistan today and in their specific lives—or, more disturbing still, what freedom might mean in ours.

Only recently have some cracks appeared. Today, as I update this piece for *Radical History Review*, an op-ed piece appeared in the *New York Times* acknowledging what many of us knew then, what many more know now: the Bush administration is not interested in the women of Afghanistan. Nicholas Kristof, a regular columnist for the paper who had once, as he admits, "strongly backed the war in Afghanistan," now feels "betrayed, as do the Afghans themselves." He goes on to say that "we [the Bush administration] lost interest in Afghanistan and moved into Iraq. . . . Mr. Bush has refused top security outside Kabul. . . . the Taliban is having a resurrection in the countryside." All this, he laments, "has had a particularly devastating effect on women. . . . Even now, in the new Afghanistan we oversee, they [women] are being kidnapped, raped, married against their will to old men, denied education, subjected to virginity tests and imprisoned in their homes. We failed them."[3]

Fact number 3: Women in secular Iraq did not wear *burka*s under Saddam and by and large did not suffer the same form of patriarchal dominance from which the Bush administration claimed they had freed Afghan women. What Iraqi women suffered then and suffer still is illness, malnutrition, even starvation, and fear—for which the United States has itself a great deal to answer. It is not only because the sanctions the United States insisted on for twelve years prior to the invasion did nothing to disempower Saddam and everything to inflict harm on the Iraqi people. Nor is it only because the American Army has, as promised just before the invasion—and here I paraphrase from the *New York Times*, which reported the comments of a high Defense Department official—"[reduced] Baghdad to rubble. It will be another Hiroshima." No, it is not those sins alone for which we have to answer. It is also the fact that we are, in important ways, responsible for Saddam—he was once useful to the United States, and once the country armed and supplied him.

Fact number 4: The cruelties suffered by Afghan women—boundless as they were—are suffered in many places in the world, frequently in the very countries the United States counts as its friends and allies—in Pakistan, Saudi Arabia, Nigeria, the former Zaire, Algeria, Peru, Chile—and we do nothing, and say nothing officially. In the Gaza Strip we sit by as Israeli weapons destroy entire families and decimate what is left of communities. In Bosnia and Serbia we watched as women suffered mass rape and murder, as children were disemboweled before their mothers' eyes, as family homes were destroyed, and ancestors' graves desecrated. Only Kosovo finally moved us, finally. But even then, it was only after months of inaction.

Now I am enough of a realist to know that no Western government, not even ours—which counts itself powerful enough to run the world—can rid the world of evil, and that seeking to do so might, in fact, do more harm than good. Our attack on Iraq could be used to exemplify such hubris. But I consider it a great a crime to pretend that our actions in Afghanistan or Iraq had or have anything important to do with our government's concern for women. It is truly evil to wage war in the name of women when we so obviously care so little about them—as women or as citizens.

Fact number 5: The Bush administration is no friend of women as a group. It is ruthlessly raping our environment, thereby desecrating the patrimony of the next generation. It feeds the rich and the military and favored industries while it ravages the budgets of schools, medical institutions, and child-care facilities. It denies the world adequate birth control supplies and education while it refuses to take on the battle against AIDS (or acknowledge its consequent, if indirect, responsibility for the millions of motherless orphans AIDS has left in its wake). It schemes to make abortion illegal. Together these actions add up to a systematic assault on motherhood itself, the very thing the administration piously claims it honors and which, it says, feminists would ridicule and undermine. No, it is the Bush administration that seeks to make effective mothering impossible; it is the Bush administration that will not allow that motherhood, like fatherhood, is a sociocultural institution, not a purely biological fact. It is feminists, not Bush, who recognize that motherhood is the serious business of society, not a rhetorical black hole into which we dump primal longings for the maternal breast. We know what a hard job it is to mother (or father), what kind of skills, material resources, and communal support it takes to be a good parent, how desperately our civilization, any civilization, depends on one generation's commitment to the next. We know that women must be positioned to play a powerful, determining part in the process of making good mothering possible, and not be used as a rhetorical device to divert scrutiny from the real agenda. We know that a real commitment to freedom for women would respect women's right to name and claim the resources they need.

Fact number 6: Feminists have not "forgotten" the women of Afghanistan, as the *Wall Street Journal* columnist charged and as the Bush administration likes to imply. Feminists take serious account of them. Those feminists who marched under banners saying "women say no to war: invest in caring, not killing" (a banner derisively quoted in the *Wall Street Journal* article to demonstrate the stupidity of "women are good" feminists) were not sanctimoniously insisting that women are good and men bad. They were calling on all their fellow citizens, men and women alike, to recall what is best about our humanity and to cultivate those qualities necessary for our survival as humans. These are not women's values; they are human values, and if by marching as women they reinforced a traditional cultural association between women and caregiving, they were only reminding us that we dare not assign these values to a nonpolitical space inhabited by women alone. As for those feminists who "hide behind laws," in the words of our journalist, they were not in retreat. They, unlike Bush, had learned from history; they knew what war does, what an endless unraveling of civilization it can unleash, and that a war sailing forth on a sea of untruths, bribes, and bullying can have no good outcome. They knew what our invasion of Iraq would bring—to Iraqis, to the community of nations on which world peace depends, and to our own nation's capacity for justice. As for the endlessly scorned postcolonial feminists, these intellectuals were in fact cleverly revealing the big lie at the heart of Laura Bush's little radio talk: the speech was not really about Afghan women; rather, it was a broadcast of an imperialist narrative in which "white men save brown women from brown men"—and then wantonly abandon them to fates still more cruel.

Notes

1. Kay S. Hymowitz, "The Women Feminists Forgot," *Wall Street Journal*, March 7, 2003.
2. Gayatri Chakravorty Spivak, "Can the Subaltern Speak?" in *Marxism and the Interpretation of Culture*, ed. Cary Nelson and Lawrence Grossberg (Urbana: University of Illinois Press, 1988), 271–313.
3. Nicholas D. Kristof, "Afghan Women, Still in Chains," *New York Times*, February 14, 2004.

"Breeding Ground," Conor McGrady (2003). Gouache on paper

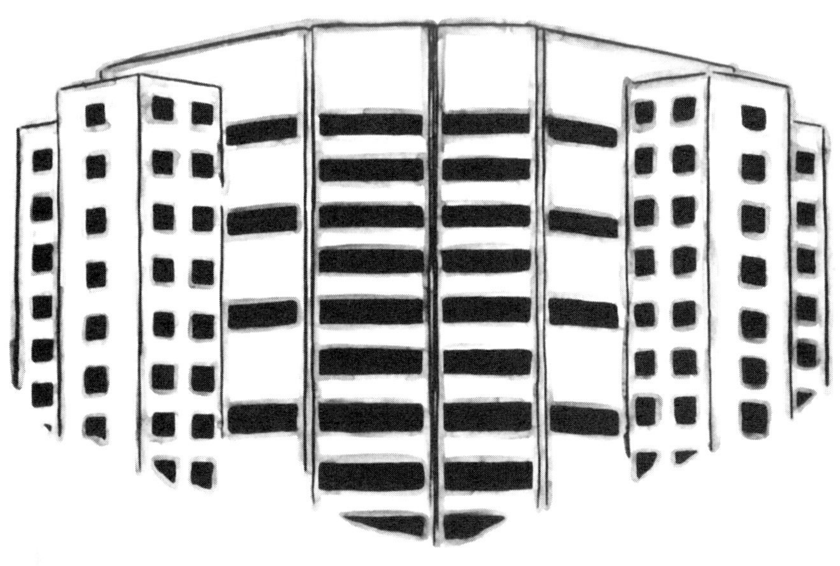

"Edifice," Conor McGrady (2003). Gouache on paper

War, Sex, and Resistance

Vivian H. Price

There should be a space for women's studies students to learn about, analyze, and vent their feelings about the U.S. invasion of Iraq within feminist perspectives. This idea drove my design for a senior seminar in women's studies at the University of California at Irvine in the spring of 2003, in the shadow of the war on Iraq. I was inspired by the legacy of teach-ins that legitimized critical examination of U.S. foreign policy; I also wanted to give students an academic arena for writing a pivotal paper at the conclusion of their study in the Department of Women's Studies.

It is useful for students to have ways to connect their experience and feelings to theoretical perspectives and, at the same time, to develop an understanding of how others relate their own lives to what they believe. This view led me to seek out sources for examining ideas about the relationship between gender, race, and war in popular culture, including film, newspaper articles, and Web sites. I felt students would be able to express themselves more openly if they moved back and forth between popular texts and scholarly literature from several disciplines that provided historical and psychological perspectives on colonialism and resistance.

My syllabus began with readings and visual texts that examined social constructions of femininities and masculinities, along with issues of sexuality and family and political authoritarianism. From there we moved to texts that explored how women's issues have been manipulated by liberal democracies to justify the supposed Western rescue of colonial subjects. We looked specifically at Japan and Hawai`i, then at Islamic countries, reflecting on Orientalism. Some of these texts also looked at patriarchy and aggression in non-Western cultures, so as to make clear that the issue of sexual exploitation and militarism is not uniquely American.

Radical History Review
Issue 93 (Fall 2005): 149–57
Copyright 2005 by MARHO: The Radical Historians' Organization, Inc.

It seemed worthwhile to read feminist works reviewing reactions to 9/11 and the war on Afghanistan by subjects in multiple locations. These provided important reflections on U.S. aggression prior to the invasion of Iraq. Two collections of feminist essays, Susan Hawthorne and Bronwyn Winter's *September 11, 2001: Feminist Perspectives* and M. Jacqui Alexander, Lisa Albrecht, Sharon Day, and Mab Segrest's *Sing, Whisper, Shout, Pray! Feminist Visions for a Just World*, offered discussions of a range of subjects, as well as background on Middle Eastern conflict considering women's struggles within Afghanistan and Palestine in conjunction with the development of political struggle. An outstanding paper by Cheryl Mattingly, Mary Lawlor, and Lanita Jacobs-Huey, "Narrating September 11: Race, Gender, and the Play of Cultural Identities," offered students methodological, theoretical, and substantive insights into community activism and oppositional ways of thinking. The authors are social activists and scholars, and they write about a group of African American women who have been meeting for a number of years around questions of justice. Their article appeared in a special issue of *American Anthropologist* on reactions to 9/11, and it was one of many online texts I assigned so that students could use university electronic access to texts rather than having to buy an additional reader. It also served as a bridge text that led us back to looking at issues of racism in the United States, questions of welfare, incarceration, and the camouflaging of U.S. history that appears especially submerged when this government asserts its hegemonic role in democratizing the world.

The last few weeks of the course were organized around sites of resistance. One class was devoted to looking at media representations of pro- and antiwar images. Another class focused on surveying and analyzing antiwar Web sites. A final class was dedicated to essays and films. Readings from *Sing, Whisper, Shout, Pray!* included Audre Lorde, "Oberlin College Commencement Address, May 29, 1989"; Becky Thompson, "Multiracial Feminism"; and Juliana Pegues, "Strategies from the Field: Organizing as an Asian American Feminist." Other works included Yoko Fukumura amd Martha Matsuoka's "Okinawa Women's Resistance to US Militarism" and Jennifer Abod's award-winning film, *The Edge of Each Others' Battles: The Vision of Audre Lorde*, on multiracial and transnational feminist organizing.

Designing the class syllabus was an important way for me to integrate my academic and activist commitments. While I created a syllabus that strongly questioned the motives for U.S. intervention in Iraq, I placed this questioning within a broader critical framework. My vision of academic freedom is one that encourages questioning dominant views, but it does not require the student to mimic a political view to please the instructor. I also imagined that while most students would be feminists, as they were all women's studies majors, they would still have varying ideological frameworks. I wanted them to understand a Gramscian approach to hegemonic ideology so that they would become more conscious of what passes for common sense and be more alert to the power of contesting dominant views.

As the quarter began, I found that my students felt concerned about the war and looked forward to having more informed views. Many of them shared feelings of confusion about the nature of the war, feeling frustrated and powerless. They comprised a diverse group, including students from Afghanistan, Poland, India, and El Salvador, as well as U.S.-born white, Latino, Asian, and African American students. Most of them came from working-class or middle-class families. Some of them were activists, but most were not politically radical.

Transformations

I organized the class so that pairs of students would be responsible for presenting an analysis of several of the assigned texts each week, while I would frame the material and summarize points from the readings or visual texts that were not covered. Students were asked to come prepared with at least one question or issue to discuss with the rest of the class, to turn in three reaction papers, and to write a final paper.

Sut Jhally's film *Tough Guise: Violence, Media, and the Crisis in Masculinity* (1997), based on Jackson Katz's presentations on the constructions of violent masculinity in popular culture, was a great place to start because it immediately got students immersed in an analysis of the relationship between gender representation and state-sponsored violence. Steven Hill's Web site GI Joe K-I-S-S-I-N-G Barbie: Competitive Economics, Competitive Sex, on male and female doll models, provided a good companion piece for making the intimate connection between notions of femininity and masculinity and the military, and this fit well with Cynthia Enloe's "Masculinity as a Foreign Policy Issue."

Making accessible Wilhelm Reich's *The Mass Psychology of Fascism* proved somewhat more difficult. Reich's book contains a fascinating analysis of the reinforcing relationship between the hierarchy of the family and the authoritarian state, but it is embedded in historical and psychological language alien to most undergraduates. I think it does work as a political benchmark for later feminist analyses about gender, family, and authoritarianism, but perhaps other readings are better to use. Possible options include Friedrich Engels, *The Origin of the Family, Private Property, and the State*; Gayle Rubin, "Thinking Sex: Notes for a Radical Theory of the Politics of Sexuality"; and Heidi Hartmann, "The Unhappy Marriage of Marxism and Feminism: Towards a More Progressive Union." Enloe's books are critical for making the connections between gender issues and the military, particularly her *Bananas, Beaches, and Bases: Making Feminist Sense of International Politics*. Her *Maneuvers: The International Politics of Militarizing Women's Lives* might also be excerpted to bring in other language for these concepts. Class assignments also incorporated newspaper articles to bring out questions of media coverage, issues of inequality, and the issue of family and community support for members in the military. Analyzing public media texts on the rationale for the war after explaining Gramscian theories about the constant struggle for consent helped to build a view of hegemonic contestation about public support for the war. It might have been helpful to assign texts by and about Antonio Gramsci as well, such as his *Letters from Prison*, and Web pages such as Monica Stillo and David Gauntlett's The Life and Work of Antonio Gramsci (www.theory.org.uk/ctr-gram.htm#hege).

The films were great ways to use a popular medium to broaden and diversify the ideas about relationships between gender and state domination. It was important to show that other colonial countries deployed sex and sexuality as a way to support war psychology, as in the example of Japanese exploitation of comfort women during World War II. I was also interested in looking at the multiplicity of intersections of race, gender, nationality, sexuality, and so on. Classes later in the quarter built on the relation of colonial domination to sex and sexuality, emphasizing the difference between the rhetoric of American notions of female equality and practices that subverted resistance and local knowledge.

Because this was a senior seminar, students began this class with some background in women's studies. But their feelings about the war, in particular the debates about the suppression of women in Islamic countries, and the American justification of liberating women in the Middle East were ambivalent. On the whole, they questioned the war but had an uneven sense of the relationship between issues of gender and the war against terrorism. Laying a foundation regarding this relationship was very useful. Mire Koikari's essay "Exporting Democracy? American Women, 'Feminist Reforms,' and Politics of Imperialism in the U.S. occupation of Japan, 1945–1952" explores how the United States manipulated the notion of feminism in the occupation of Japan, and it proved particularly compelling in part because of the way historical distance sharpens one's ability to see contradictions. Reading this article in conjunction with watching *Our Job in Japan* emphasized the role of cultural imperialism in rationalizing U.S. occupations.

Orayb Aref Najjar, "Still 'A Difficult Journey Up the Mountain'? Palestinian Women's National versus Gender Politics, 1919–2002," and Charles Hirschkind and Saba Mahmood, "Feminism, the Taliban, and the Politics of Counter-insurgency," interrogated the representation of women and the veil through Western eyes and offered feminist entries into discussing the Israeli occupation of Palestine, as well as background on the wars in Afghanistan and Iraq, and provided short articles on reactions to 9/11 from multiple locations.

Having students pair up and give presentations worked well. Some of the students seemed more familiar with the particular history and concepts discussed than others; and some were more forthcoming than others about their evaluations of the material relative to reflecting on their own political views. I encouraged students to summarize the arguments of writers, identify controversies among the authors, and analyze the strengths and weaknesses of the arguments before reacting to them. Since the war was unraveling, protests were being held, and the media was filled with discussions about the war in Iraq as the class was happening, we often spent some time translating the material in view of current events. Students talked about how their conversations about the war, and sometimes even about the material we were examining in class, played out in their interactions at work, in other classes, and with their families. I found their reflection papers becoming more and more thoughtful.

Many of the students became very ambitious about their final projects; some felt overwhelmed and frustrated because they found too much material; still others balked at the problem of making an argument. In the end, the majority of papers were of a high caliber. Our final session was a presentation of several of the papers at a Department of Women's Studies year-end reception for faculty, family, and friends. Several of the students volunteered to present their work. One of them wrote about the U.S. military's sex camps that ring bases in East Asia, and the resistance movement that is engaged in challenging these practices. Another wrote about issues of sexuality and repression in the United States and their relationship to authoritarianism. Their papers were well received, and I felt proud and inspired. The class grew close over the ten weeks that we met, and we were able to talk about many of our differences and about what was going on in the world.

WOMEN'S STUDIES SENIOR SEMINAR: FEMINIST PERSPECTIVES ON WAR AND JUSTICE

Course Description

The topic of this class varies from year to year. The course serves as a space for undergraduate students with a background in women's studies to address pressing contemporary issues, as well as to review and apply theories studied in previous classes. This quarter the topic will be feminist perspectives on war and justice. Women's involvement in peace and antiwar movements has a long history, yet women have also been deeply involved both as the pretext for war and as ardent supporters of war. This class will focus on several questions regarding dominant culture's appropriation of feminist discourse to rationalize the use of violence while at the same time reinforcing masculinist ideologies. We will also look at the feminist discourse about war on various combat zones, not only on the so-called battlefront but also in neighborhoods and homes. We will ask the following questions: How and why are gender and race implicated in justifications and representations of war? How do neocolonial projects utilize feminist discourse in the rationalization of the use of violence? In what ways do critical feminist rearticulations of war present alternative concepts of justice?

Final Paper

There will be a final paper in lieu of a final exam. Your final paper will be a research paper that makes an argument about feminist perspectives on war and justice. You may use any of the material offered in the syllabus, but your paper must also use at least TWO ACADEMIC SOURCES and ONE MEDIA SOURCE not assigned in this class. Use the bibliographies in the assigned texts to locate your additional academic sources, or contact the professor for advice. You may be creative in your choice of media sources: you might use articles from newspapers of record, or you might choose a popular film or other mass-media production that takes up the issues relevant to feminist perspectives on war and justice. Final papers must be analytical and make use of the theoretical tools you will be exposed to in this class. They will be ten to twelve pages in length (typed, double-spaced, ten- or twelve-point font) and will be due by 10 a.m. on the day of the final for the class. The final paper will account for 20 percent of your final grade.

Required Texts

Susan Hawthorne and Bronwyn Winter, eds., *September 11, 2001: Feminist Perspectives* (North Melbourne, Australia: Spinifex, 2002).
M. Jacqui Alexander et al., eds., *Sing, Whisper, Shout, Pray! Feminist Visions for a Just World* (Fort Bragg, CA : EdgeWork, 2003).
Selected articles PDF, online and electronic reserves.
Selected videos.
Please watch your e-mail and the Web site for updated information on readings and videos.

Syllabus

Week 1

Gender, Race, and Class Underpinnings of a Military Nation/Construction of Masculinities— Protector, Competitor, and Aggressor
Steven Hill, GI Joe K-I-S-S-I-N-G Barbie: Competitive Economics, Competitive Sex, www.giantleap.org/envision/compsex.htm (accessed January 3, 2003).
Sut Jhally, *Tough Guise: Violence, Media, and the Crisis in Masculinity* (Northampton, MA: Media Education Foundation, 1999).
Sut Jhally, *Representation and the Media* (Northampton, MA: Media Education Foundation, 1997).
Cynthia Enloe, "Masculinity as a Foreign Policy Issue," in Hawthorne and Winter, *September 11, 2001*, 254–59.

Week 2

Sexuality, Race, and Class and the Military
Kathleen T. Rhem, "Officials Say Draft Not Necessary," *Air Force Link*, January 13, 2003, www.af.mil/news/story.asp?storyID=11403661.
Maria Tomchick, "Dodge It," *Eat the State!* February 17, 1999, eatthestate.org/03–22/DodgeIt .htm.
Tom Gorman, "Hopis, Navajos Come Together in Support of Missing Soldier," *Los Angeles Times*, March 29, 2003, www.latimes.com/news/nationworld/nation/la-war-lori29mar29,1, 3909505.story.

Stephanie Simon, "A Town's Military Conflict," *Los Angeles Times*, March 29, 2003, www.latimes.com/news/nationworld/iraq/homefront/la-war-army29mar29.

Surveillance Camera Players, scripted images from Willhelm Reich's *The Mass Psychology of Fascism*, www.notbored.org/reich.html (accessed January 2003).

Willhelm Reich, *The Mass Psychology of Fascism*, trans. Vincent R. Carfagno (New York: Farrar, Straus and Giroux, 1970).

Dai Sil Kim-Gibson, dir., *Silence Broken: Korean Comfort Women* (NAATA Distribution, 1999).

Vivian Ducat, *Hawaii's Last Queen* (PBS Home Video, 1997).

N̄a Maka o ka ʻĀina, dir., *Act of War: The Overthrow of the Hawaiian Nation* (Cross Current Media, National Asian American Telecommunications Association, 1993).

Haunani-Kay Trask, "Self-Determination for Pacific Island Women: The Case of Hawaii," in Alexander et al., *Sing, Whisper, Shout, Pray!* 138–50.

Week 3

Liberal Democracy and the Liberation of Women

Reed Johnson, "A Feminist Decries Pacifists' Rubbish," *Los Angeles Times*, March 24, 2003.

Mire Koikari, "Exporting Democracy? American Women, 'Feminist Reforms,' and Politics of Imperialism in the U.S. Occupation of Japan, 1945–1952," *Frontiers*, 23 (2002): 23–47.

Information and Education Division, War Department, *Our Job in Japan* (Army Pictorial Service, Signal Corps United States War Dept., 1945).

Ratna Kapur, "Un-veiling Women's Rights in the 'War on Terrorism,'" *Duke Journal of Gender, Law, and Policy* 211 (2002): 211–36.

Week 4

Orientalism and the Subject/Object of Muslim Women/Greater Islam and the Palestine-Israeli Dichotomy

Lila Abu-Lughod, "Do Muslim Women Really Need Saving? Anthropological Reflections on Cultural Relativism and Its Others," *American Anthropologist* 104 (2002): 783–90.

Lisa Albrecht, "From the First Intifada to the Second Intifada: Notes from an American Jew," in Alexander et al., *Sing, Whisper, Shout, Pray!* 103–14.

Orayb Aref Najjar, "Still 'A Difficult Journey Up the Mountain'? Palestinian Women's National versus Gender Politics, 1919–2002," in Alexander et al., *Sing, Whisper, Shout, Pray!* 181–211.

Optional Reading: Charles Hirschkind and Saba Mahmood, "Feminism, the Taliban, and the Politics of Counter-insurgency," *Anthropological Quarterly* 75 (2002): 107–22.

Week 5

Feminist Responses and Reflections on September 11

Cheryl Mattingly, Mary Lawlor, and Lanita Jacobs-Huey, "Narrating September 11: Race, Gender, and the Play of Cultural Identities," *American Anthropologist* 104 (2002): 743–53.

"Lurching through These Frightening Days," in Alexander et al., *Sing, Whisper, Shout, Pray!* 116–24.

Rosalind P. Petchesky, "Phantom Towers: Feminist Reflections on the Battle between Global Capitalism and Fundamentalist Terrorism," in Alexander et al., *Sing, Whisper, Shout, Pray!* 15–29.

Madeleine Bunting, "Women's Voices Silenced in the Enthusiasm for War," in Hawthorne and Winter, *September 11, 2001*, 26–27.

Barbara Lee, "Why I Voted against War," in Hawthorne and Winter, *September 11, 2001*, 38–39.

Makere Stewart, "I Too Am a Muslim, a Hindu, an Arab," in Hawthorne and Winter, *September 11, 2001*, 42.

Harawira Theresa Wolfwood, "Resistance Is Creative: False Options and Real Hope," in Hawthorne and Winter, *September 11, 2001*, 43–47.

Judith Ezekiel, "Un Pavé dans la Mare; or, Rocking the Boat: September 11 Viewed from France," in Hawthorne and Winter, *September 11, 2001*, 100–103.

Tum Rigoberta Menchú, "Letter to President George W. Bush," in Hawthorne and Winter, *September 11, 2001*, 104–5.

Barbara Kingsolver, "No Glory in Unjust War on the Weak," in Hawthorne and Winter, *September 11, 2001*, 106–8.

Week 6

Feminist Responses and Reflections on September 11 Continued

Jen Couch, "So the Party Is Over? The Global Justice Movement after September 11," in Hawthorne and Winter, *September 11, 2001*, 48–52.

"Transnational Feminist Practices against War," in Hawthorne and Winter, *September 11, 2001*, 58–63.

"Revolutionary Association of Afghanistan Appeal to the UN and World of the Women Community," in Hawthorne and Winter, *September 11, 2001*, 163.

Montserrat Boix, "Women's Networks: Islamists' Violence and Terror," in Hawthorne and Winter, *September 11, 2001*, 165–70.

Valentine M. Moghadam, "Women, the Taliban, and the Politics of Public Space in Afghanistan," in Hawthorne and Winter, *September 11, 2001*, 260–84.

Arundhati Roy, "The Algebra of Infinite Justice," in Hawthorne and Winter, *September 11, 2001*, 331–38.

Nahla Abdo, "Eurocentrism, Orientalism, and Essentialism: Some Reflections on September 11 and Beyond," in Hawthorne and Winter, *September 11, 2001*, 372–92.

Ronit Lentin, "Feminist Snapshots from the Edge: Reflections on Women, War, and Peace Activism in Israel after September 11," in Hawthorne and Winter, *September 11, 2001*, 393–411.

Evelyne Accad, "The Phallus of September 11," in Hawthorne and Winter, *September 11, 2001*, 412–25.

Catharine A. MacKinnon, "State of Emergency," in Hawthorne and Winter, *September 11, 2001*, 426–31.

Diane Bell, "Good and Evil: At Home and Abroad," in Hawthorne and Winter, *September 11, 2001*, 432–49.

Bronwyn Winter, "If Women Really Mattered," in Hawthorne and Winter, *September 11, 2001*, 450–80.

Week 7

Internal Colonies: War within the United States and the Struggle for Multiracial Feminism

Linda Burnham, "Racism in U.S. Welfare Policy: A Human Rights Issue," in Alexander et al., *Sing, Whisper, Shout, Pray!* 58–76.

Angela Y. Davis, "Masked Racism: Reflections on the Prison Industrial Complex," in Alexander et al., *Sing, Whisper, Shout, Pray!* 52–57.

Winona LaDuke, "Akwesasne: Mohawk Mother's Milk and PCBs," in Alexander et al., *Sing, Whisper, Shout, Pray!* 158–71.

Cherríe L. Moraga, "A Xicanadyke Codex of Changing Consciousness," in Alexander et al., *Sing, Whisper, Shout, Pray!* 91–102.

Mab Segrest, "On Being White and Other Lies: A History of Racism in the United States," in Alexander et al., *Sing, Whisper, Shout, Pray!* 243–85.

Merle Woo, "Josephine and Me: Teaching about Racism in Women's Studies," in Alexander et al., *Sing, Whisper, Shout, Pray!* 221–30.

Week 8

Media Representations of War, Antiwar Movements, Women as Warriors

Artistic representations: What makes an image pro-war or antiwar?

Historical: Pablo Picasso, *Guernica*; Käthe Kollwitz

Contemporary: Barbara Kruger; Sebastião Salgado

Mobilizing art: Art for a Change; Women in Black

Suggested antiwar films to watch in Media Resource Center: *Hearts and Minds* (dir. Peter Davis, US, 1974); *Dr. Strangelove* (dir. Stanley Kubrick, US, 1963); *In the Year of the Pig* (dir. Emile de Antionio, US, 1968); *Flame* (dir. Ingrid Sinclair, US, 1996); *Maria's Story* (dir. Pamela Cohen and Catherine M. Ryan, US, 1990).

Suggested pro-war films: *First Blood (Rambo)* (dir. Ted Kotcheff, US, 1982); *Top Gun* (dir. Tony Scott, US, 1986).

Week 9

Examination of the Antiwar Movement

Leila Rupp, *Worlds of Women: The Making of an International Women's Movement* (Princeton, NJ: Princeton University Press, 1997); on reserve.

Mark Barringer, "Vietnam Anti-war Movement in the United States," in *Modern American Poetry: Online Journal and Multimedia Companion to Anthology of Modern American Poetry*, ed. Cary Nelson, 2000, www.english.uiuc.edu/maps/vietnam/antiwar.html.

Women's International League for Peace and Freedom, www.wilpf.org.

United for Peace, www.unitedforpeace.org.

Code Pink, www.codepink4peace.org.

Surveillance Camera Group, reason.com/hod/sr090601.shtml.

All sites accessed January 28, 2003.

Week 10

Transnational Feminism

Jennifer Abod, dir., *Edge of Each Others' Battles* (Profile Productions and Women Make Movies, US, 2002).

Audre Lorde, "Oberlin College Commencement Address, May 29, 1989," in Alexander et al., *Sing, Whisper, Shout, Pray!* 530–38.

Becky Thompson, "Multiracial Feminism," in Alexander et al., *Sing, Whisper, Shout, Pray!* 397–424.

Juliana Pegues, "Strategies from the Field: Organizing as an Asian American Feminist," in Alexander et al., *Sing, Whisper, Shout, Pray!* 425–37.

Yoko Fukumura and Martha Matsuoka, "Okinawa Women's Resistance to US Militarism," in *Women's Activism and Globalization*, ed. Nancy Naples and Manisha Desai (New York: Routledge, 2002), 239–63.

"University," Kevin Noble (1994)

History in Red—and White and Blue

Ellen Schrecker

The Cold War is over, but the struggle over its history has yet to subside. When the Soviet Union collapsed in 1991, the new Russian government opened up the records of its predecessor. Since then scholars have used these materials, as well as those from the former Soviet bloc countries in Eastern and Central Europe, to rewrite the history of the past half century.[1] Though most of that work explores the inner workings of the Soviet sphere, because the Moscow archives also held the records of foreign communist parties, the history of American communism is being revised as well—and revised in a contentious process that makes it clear that for at least some historians, the Cold War is still quite hot.

The main protagonists in this intellectual civil war, John Earl Haynes, an archivist at the Library of Congress, and Harvey Klehr, a political scientist at Emory University, were among the first and most prolific scholars to use the new materials. Both men had already written several books about the American Communist Party (CP); and Haynes, in particular, had been servicing the scholarly community for years by compiling a quarterly survey of contemporary research for the Historians of American Communism organization.[2] Their initial forays into the former Soviet archives resulted in two books of documents that revealed the close ties between the Kremlin and the American CP—*The Secret World of American Communism* (1995) and *The Soviet World of American Communism* (1998).[3] These publications also provided new support for the allegations of espionage that had stoked the anti-communist furor of the early Cold War, for among the dozens of documents on the party's undercover work that Haynes and Klehr reprinted were some that bolstered

Radical History Review
Issue 93 (Fall 2005): 159–69
Copyright 2005 by MARHO: The Radical Historians' Organization, Inc.

Elizabeth Bentley's tarnished account of her adventures as the courier for a Soviet spy ring in Washington, DC.

In 1995, a few years after the Moscow archives opened, the American government, under the prodding of Senator Daniel Patrick Moynihan, declassified the Venona Project—a decades-long undertaking by the National Security Agency to decrypt and decipher thousands of KGB telegrams intercepted during World War II.[4] Although some information about the project had surfaced in the 1980s, it was so highly secret in its early days that even President Harry S. Truman never knew his counterspies were reading the Soviets' mail. The code breakers could not retrieve all the Russian texts, but the ones they did decipher revealed that Soviet intelligence officers had been running dozens of American agents. Not only did the Venona messages implicate Julius Rosenberg and the federal bureaucrats Elizabeth Bentley had fingered but they also revealed some hitherto unknown spies like the young Manhattan Project physicist Theodore Hall. In addition, they showed how deeply the American CP had been involved in recruiting and managing these agents. Soon there were several books, one by Haynes and Klehr among them, that incorporated the Venona materials into the story of Soviet espionage.[5]

Meanwhile, several other scholars, including the Hiss case chronicler Allen Weinstein whose publisher paid an undisclosed sum for the privilege, got access to the KGB's records. Since no one else can see those files, the research of Weinstein and his Russian collaborator raises questions. Even so, their findings are consistent with what we have learned from the Venona decrypts and other Moscow archives.[6] New information has also surfaced in the memoirs of former Soviet officials.[7] Naturally, it would be preferable if the KGB were more forthcoming and if the GRU, the Soviet military intelligence agency for which Alger Hiss almost certainly worked, would also release its records. Nonetheless, by the end of the 1990s, enough evidence about the KGB's espionage operations had accumulated to convince most historians in the field, myself included, that about one hundred (and possibly more) American communists spied for the Soviet Union and that the party abetted those efforts.[8]

Case closed. Or so one would assume. A few holdouts may be waiting for the GRU's archives to open before throwing in the towel on Hiss, but it is hard to imagine that any reputable scholar from now on would argue that Julius Rosenberg was innocent or deny the validity—if not all the details—of Bentley's story. Future researchers might want to look more closely at some of the key KGB agents or try, if they can ever see the requisite Soviet records, to assess the impact of that espionage, which may well be exaggerated. But as far as most historians are concerned, the debate is over. From the 1930s until the Cold War put them out of business, at least a hundred American communists spied for the Soviet Union. So, nu? Now let's get on with using the new records to assess the party's other activities and its impact on the rest of American society. Espionage forms only part—and a small part—of that story. That being the case, it is hard to understand why Haynes and Klehr published *In Denial*, a 233-page book criticizing the historical profession's treatment of American communism and Soviet espionage.[9]

Sour grapes may be one reason. The two authors seem to have been distressed by the reception their earlier work received in the nation's two main historical journals. Dominated by scholars Klehr and Haynes label revisionists, both the *American Historical Review* (*AHR*) and the *Journal of American History* (*JAH*) had either overlooked the pair's recent volumes or else did not grant them the same favorable treatment they received elsewhere in the media.[10] This was not a new phenomenon, they insisted; the pages of *AHR* and *JAH* had been closed for decades to the work of such traditionalist historians as themselves.[11] That allegation resonates with the long-standing contention of other conservative historians that the historical profession subordinates conventional political and diplomatic history to the more trendy cultural or social varieties. Much of the evidence that Klehr, Haynes, and the others cite for this discrimination relates to the absence of papers in those fields at the annual meetings of the Organization of American Historians (OAH) and the American Historical Association (AHA).[12] Having served on an OAH program committee in the early 1990s, I witnessed no such discrimination. We were eager to mount panels in military, political, and diplomatic history, but received few if any proposals for them. And, in any event, such complaints overlook the plethora of titles in those areas that the nation's academic presses—surely a major component of the historical establishment—publish every year. What historians would not rather have their books published by Yale University Press, as Haynes and Klehr's have been, than present papers at the OAH?

Professional grudges all to one side, it is clear that *In Denial*'s authors have a partisan agenda. They want to alert the public to the "intellectually sick situation" reigning within the historical profession.[13] As they see it, their unhappy experiences with the profession's main institutions reveal "how an alienated and politicized academic culture misunderstands and distorts America's past" and how "historical gatekeepers such as professional journals" are "misshaping cultural memories to fit the ideological biases of the academic establishment" (8). Their basic contention is that a revisionist mafia not only dominates the dissemination of historical knowledge but also distorts that knowledge with the ultimate goal, they maintain, of "educating a new generation of radicals to the necessity of overthrowing American capitalism" (229).

Eric Foner emerges as exhibit A; not only does the nation's leading historian of the Reconstruction era combine the most prestigious academic credentials (DeWitt Clinton Professor of History at Columbia University and past president of both the OAH and AHA) with an unreconstructed red-diaper-baby background but, according to Haynes and Klehr, he also displays a "knee-jerk hostility to the United States" and has actually written sympathetically about American communism (49). While most of their other revisionists are considerably less eminent, the authors of *In Denial* invariably emphasize those people's connections with the academic mainstream (142). And whenever they catch sight of an admitted communist or ex-communist within the historical establishment, they point it out. Their treatment of Gerda Lerner is typical. Identifying her as both a "much-honored star of the contemporary academy" (41) and "a Communist Party activist for a decade," they claim that her elevation to the presidency of the OAH "was an early sign of the leading role achieved by radical historians in professional associations" (42). That it was, in fact, a recognition of her pioneering work in women's history is simply overlooked.

Red-baiting, however, has its intellectual limitations; and most of *In Denial* is devoted to pointing out how the revisionists distort the past. That distortion, it seems, comes from a failure to condemn communism with sufficient fervor, a flaw that characterizes what Haynes and Klehr consider the "overwhelmingly liberal and leftist academy" (82). They begin by pointing out how mainstream historians of the Soviet Union have paid inadequate attention to the horrors of Stalinism. Their main focus, however, is on those students of American communism who have either ignored and belittled Soviet espionage or else "have begun justifying or excusing those who engaged in it" (195). That kind of scholarship, *In Denial*'s authors insist, not only violates professional standards but also displays the "dishonesty, evasion, special pleading, and moral squalor" that distinguishes "far too much academic writing about communism, anticommunism and espionage." By refusing to face up to the evil of Stalinism, the revisionist historians of American communism are "like Holocaust deniers" (231).

These are strong words. To back them up, Haynes and Klehr put the scholarship they condemn under a microscope. They are relentless in their pursuit of unsubstantiated claims and careless phraseology, attacking admitted partisans and professional historians alike. Because *In Denial* does not acknowledge how quickly Venona and the Moscow archives changed the historiographical landscape, it grants its subjects little leeway for adjusting their interpretations.[14] Thus, although most serious scholars have accepted the new evidence, revised their earlier work when called for, and moved on, Haynes and Klehr do not allow for such revisions. On the contrary, they put a negative spin on anything that does not completely comport with their interpretation of the American CP and its history.

My own work can serve as an example. As the recipient of considerable attention in the book, I was both flattered and bemused by the authors' diligence in tracking down almost everything I wrote—including unpublished remarks at academic conferences. They did, I must admit, uncover some historiographical gaffs: in particular, the overstatements that characterized the last chapter of *Many Are the Crimes* where, at the urging of my editor, I reluctantly tried to assess the impact of McCarthyism on American society (50–51).[15] Were I to revise that chapter today, besides incorporating the scholarship that has emerged in the interim, I would certainly be more tentative in my judgments.[16] Surprisingly, however, given the authors' scrupulous concern with verification, I was puzzled by some of the statements attributed to me that, lacking citations, I could not track down.[17] In other places, Haynes and Klehr had twisted the meaning of what I had written or else simply misunderstood it.[18] Thus, for example, though they admit that my most recent book acknowledges the existence of Soviet espionage, they then state: "What Ellen Schrecker is still unable to understand is that American communism declined *because* of the determined campaign by anticommunists of every political hue."[19] Had they not read the book? Or had I failed to communicate my main point: McCarthyism (broadly defined) destroyed the communist movement?

More disconcerting than such misreadings, however, is the authors' refusal to accept a complicated view of the past. Haynes and Klehr are, in fact, so determinedly Manichaean in their approach that they actually devote an entire section of *In Denial* to countering "Nuanced Positions."[20] They cannot, or will not, recognize the contradictions within a communist movement that both promoted social justice and flacked for the USSR. Such a simplistic, black-and-white approach is profoundly ahistorical. Not only does it ignore years of serious scholarship; it also denies the complex reality of human activity in which, for example, the nation's founding fathers can create a framework for democratic freedom while, at the same time, holding nearly a million fellow beings in bondage.

A similar lack of sophistication surfaces in the authors' insistence that any attempt to understand the motivations of the KGB's American agents automatically translates into exoneration. Thus, when Bruce Craig, the biographer of Harry Dexter White, and I try to explain why people like White and Julius Rosenberg might have spied for the Soviet Union, we come under attack.[21] We have, it seems, "a dirty little secret"; our investigation of the motives of these Soviet agents means that we "applaud, albeit sometimes in camouflaged language, the assistance that American Communists gave to Stalin."[22] But trying to understand the motivations of historical actors is exactly what historians do. No one to my knowledge has accused either Christopher Browning or Daniel Goldhagen of condoning the Holocaust because they explored the motivations of the people who carried it out.[23] For Haynes and Klehr, however, explanation without condemnation does not suffice; it reeks of moral relativism.

We have seen such charges before. In labeling the scholarship of mainstream historians revisionism, Haynes and Klehr are repeating the main themes of the culture wars of the late 1980s and 1990s. Not only do they recycle the allegations that earlier critics had launched against the historical profession but they even select some of the same targets. Thus, to take one relevant example, they attack the authors of the National History Standards for downplaying Soviet espionage and the evils of Stalinism while reiterating Lynne Cheney's observation that the standards had overemphasized McCarthyism.[24] The terminology of Haynes and Klehr also harks back to the culture wars. Cheney had, after all, charged the historians who wrote the National History Standards with "pursuing the revisionist agenda."[25]

Revisionism is, of course, what most good scholars do as they engage new materials or ask new questions of old ones.[26] But the term now has a negative spin. Just as *multiculturalism*, *postmodernism*, and *feminism* were the epithets of choice for attacking literary scholars during the 1990s, *revisionism* became the main pejorative in the field of history. It got an especially bad rap during the *Enola Gay* controversy of 1994–95. Designed to commemorate the ending of World War II, the planned Smithsonian Institution exhibition came under attack in Congress and the media because its balanced approach to the atomic bombing of Hiroshima did not present a sufficiently celebratory view of the United States. It was, the exhibit's critics declared, "historical revisionism at its worst," a "revisionist and offensive" exhibition.[27] Since moderates as well as conservatives rushed to trash the proposed exhibit, it was clear that a serious gap had opened up between the expert knowledge of professional historians and the layperson's more simplistic take on the past.[28]

But what really damaged the historical profession with the general public was not its questioning of earlier interpretations, but its failure to offer a suitably heroic version of the nation's past. Such was Cheney's main beef against the National History Standards. Such was the main burden of the attacks on the *Enola Gay* exhibit. "We've got to get patriotism back into the Smithsonian," a Texas congressman explained. "We want the Smithsonian to reflect real America and not something that a historian dreamed up."[29] And again, it was not only conservatives who claimed that historians were unpatriotic and out of touch. "What I don't understand," David Brinkley complained about the *Enola Gay* exhibit, "is why a very strong element in the academic community seems to hate its own country and never passes up a chance to be critical of it." If someone like Brinkley, who surely should have known better, can disseminate such a distorted view of contemporary scholarship, it reveals how widespread the demonization of the historical profession has become.[30]

To a large extent, that demonization furthers the political strategy of a conservative populist movement epitomized by a president who does not "do nuance" and calls his critics "revisionist historians." Years of right-wing attacks on tenured radicals and other critical thinkers—"the scribblers, the ponderers, and the Smith College girls," in the words of Ann Coulter—have delegitimized much modern scholarship in the humanities.[31] Most ordinary citizens now view the denizens of academe as disgruntled feminazis, cross-dressers, or worse, dedicated to subverting traditional American values in the name of multiculturalism, political correctness, and incomprehensible prose. Those connections surfaced widely after 9/11, allowing Lynne Cheney and others to charge that the scholars who tried to explain the catastrophe were, in fact, supporting it. They belonged to, in the words of a notorious pamphlet by Cheney's American Council of Trustees and Alumni, a "blame America first crowd."[32] Though Haynes and Klehr refer only fleetingly to the World Trade Center terrorism, their allusion to "the deeply ingrained anti-Americanism" of the revisionist historians certainly resonates with that post-9/11 hostility toward the academic mainstream.[33]

The political agenda of *In Denial* is disturbing. Its authors are clearly trying to marginalize left-wing scholarship. Nonetheless, I do not think that Haynes and Klehr would openly call for a blacklist of anti-anticommunist professors. Nor do I think that their overly simplistic worldview makes them anti-intellectual. Even so, the tone of their oeuvre, with its demand for historians of American communism to toe the moral line, feeds into the kind of mentality that has produced Daniel Pipes's Campus Watch listing of supposedly deviant Middle Eastern scholars and David Horowitz's current crusade to impose political quotas on the nation's faculties. Although those two campaigns target experts on the Islamic world, the tropes are much the same: radicals have hijacked American higher education and must be balanced by scholars of a more traditionalist (or in the case of the Middle East, more pro-Zionist) orientation. Unfortunately, as the recent congressional attempt to regulate area studies reveals, Pipes and Horowitz are not just talking to themselves. Haynes and Klehr have yet to reach such a powerful audience. At this point, since the history of communism and anticommunism is still something of a backwater, the most serious damage that the two men's work can inflict is collateral, contributing to the broader project of delegitimizing the history profession by characterizing its denizens as soft on communism and thus obviously beyond the pale of respectability.

Institutional as well as ideological ties connect Haynes and Klehr to the conservative attack on the academy. The publisher of *In Denial* is Horowitz's long-time collaborator, Peter Collier. Haynes and Klehr would, no doubt, deny that such relationships matter; they did, after all, denigrate the significance of the funding they received from the John M. Olin and other right-wing foundations.[34] Nonetheless, it is clear that, whatever their conscious agenda may be, they are operating well within the world of conservative think tanks, foundations, and publications that has become an institutional alternative to the mainstream academic community.

. . . . .

Several years ago, Berkeley historian David Hollinger drew attention to a 1971 memorandum that Richmond attorney Lewis Powell had written at the request of a friend about to head the Education Committee of the National Chamber of Commerce. In it, the future Supreme Court justice recommended a multipronged campaign to offset what he believed was a massive attack on the American free enterprise system by left-wing academics.[35] Powell was not advocating a scatter-shot offensive, but rather a program that required "careful long-range planning and implementation . . . over an indefinite period of years, in the scale of financing available only through joint action, and in the political power available only through united action and national organizations."[36] Powell urged the business community to establish centers of scholarship outside the universities and to reward the amenable professors inside them. He also outlined a wide-ranging media campaign to counter the Left's alleged hegemony over the world of ideas. The profound shift to the Right in the nation's intellectual discourse that has occurred in the years since Powell wrote his memorandum attests to the efficacy of the program he outlined.[37]

It is not hard to see how *In Denial* fits into that program. Already the work of Klehr, Haynes, and their fellow traditionalists has influenced the reception of historical knowledge by the American public. Though they may complain about exclusion from the professional journals, their version of the history of American communism has taken hold within the media and the political establishment and has become the dominant interpretation outside of academe.[38] Its emphasis on an unsophisticated, black-and-white, good-guys-versus-bad-guys narrative reinforces the oversimplifications that pervade contemporary political discourse. This is a serious problem, for such oversimplifications debase our political culture, even if that may not be their stated function. Certainly, if nothing else, the delegitimizing of professional history, to which *In Denial* in its small way contributes, is narrowing the intellectual spectrum and helping to close the American mind.

Notes

I acknowledge the valuable assistance of Marvin Gettleman, Corey Robin, Carole Silver, and Lise Vogel.

1.   The most important materials from the archives of the former Soviet bloc have been collected and published in English by the Cold War International History Project of the Woodrow Wilson International Center for Scholars in Washington, DC, available at wwics .si.edu/index.cfm?topic_id=1409&fuseaction=topics.publications.

2.   John Earl Haynes, *Dubious Alliance: The Making of Minnesota's DFL Party* (Minneapolis: University of Minnesota Press, 1984); John Earl Haynes, *Red Scare or Red Menace? American Communism and Anticommunism in the Cold War* (Chicago: Ivan R. Dee, 1996); John Earl Haynes, *Communism and Anti-communism in the United States: An Annotated Guide to Historical Writings* (New York: Garland, 1987); Harvey Klehr, *Communist Cadre: The Social Background of the American Communist Party Elite* (Stanford, CA: Hoover Institution Press, 1978); Harvey Klehr, *The Heyday of American Communism: The Depression Decade* (New York: Basic Books, 1984); Harvey Klehr and Ronald Radosh, *The Amerasia Spy Case: Prelude to McCarthyism* (Chapel Hill: University of North Carolina Press, 1996); Harvey Klehr and John Earl Haynes, *The American Communist Movement: Storming Heaven Itself* (New York: Twayne, 1992).

3.   Harvey Klehr, John Earl Haynes, and Fridrikh Igorevich Firsov, *The Secret World of American Communism* (New Haven, CT: Yale University Press, 1995); and Harvey Klehr,

John Earl Haynes, and Kyrill M. Anderson, *The Soviet World of American Communism* (New Haven, CT: Yale University Press, 1998).

4. Daniel Patrick Moynihan, *Secrecy: The American Experience* (New Haven, CT: Yale University Press, 1998).

5. John Earl Haynes and Harvey Klehr, *Venona: Decoding Soviet Espionage in America* (New Haven, CT: Yale University Press, 1999); Herbert Romerstein and Eric Breindel, *The Venona Secrets: Exposing Soviet Espionage and America's Traitors* (Washington, DC: Regnery, 2000).

6. Allen Weinstein and Alexander Vassiliev, *The Haunted Wood: Soviet Espionage in America; The Stalin Era* (New York: Random House, 1999). Another product of the KGB archives is Nigel West and Oleg Tsarev, *The Crown Jewels: The British Secrets at the Heart of the KGB Archives* (London: HarperCollins, 1998).

7. For a sample of those memoirs, see Alexander Feklisov and Sergin Kostin, *The Man behind the Rosenbergs* (New York: Enigma, 2001); and Christopher Andrew and Vasili Mitrokhin, *The Sword and the Shield: The Mitrokhin Archive and the Secret History of the KGB* (New York: Basic Books, 1999). A more highly suspect publication is Pavel Sudoplatov and Anatolii Sudoplatov with Jerrold L. Schechter and Leona P. Schechter, *Special Tasks: The Memoirs of an Unwanted Witness; A Soviet Spymaster* (Boston: Little, Brown, 1994).

8. I have assessed that espionage in several articles. See Maurice Isserman and Ellen Schrecker, "'Papers of a Dangerous Tendency': From Major Andre's Boots to the Venona Files," in *Cold War Triumphalism: Exposing the Misuse of History after the Fall of Communism*, ed. Schrecker (New York: New Press, 2004); and Ellen Schrecker, "Stealing Secrets: Communism and Soviet Espionage in the 1940s," *North Carolina Law Review* 82 (2004): 1841–89.

9. John Earl Haynes and Harvey Klehr, *In Denial: Historians, Communism, and Espionage* (San Francisco: Encounter, 2003).

10. Having reviewed *The Soviet World of American Communism* for the *Journal of American History*, I am clearly one of the leading miscreants. I found the book useful, repetitious, and "a prosecutor's brief." Ellen Schrecker, review of *The Soviet World of American Communism*, by Harvey Klehr, John Earl Haynes, and Kyrill M. Anderson, *Journal of American History* 85 (1999): 1647–48.

11. Haynes and Klehr, *In Denial*, 7, 77–80, 232.

12. David Kaiser, "My War with the AHA," *Academic Questions* 13 (2000): 70–77.

13. Haynes and Klehr, *In Denial*, 232.

14. For example, the authors take Eric Foner to task for defending the Rosenbergs, but they do not cite anything he published after the Venona decrypts appeared. Ibid., 203, 293.

15. Ellen Schrecker, *Many Are the Crimes: McCarthyism in America* (Boston: Little, Brown, 1998), 368–415.

16. For some of the important new scholarship on the impact of McCarthyism, see Carol Anderson, *Eyes Off the Prize: The United Nations and the African American Struggle for Human Rights, 1944–1955* (New York: Cambridge University Press, 2003); Martha Biondi, *To Stand and Fight: The Struggle for Civil Rights in Postwar New York City* (Cambridge, MA: Harvard University Press, 2003); David K. Johnson, *The Lavender Scare: The Cold War Persecution of Gays and Lesbians in the Federal Government* (Chicago: University of Chicago Press, 2004); and Jessica Wang, *American Science in an Age of Anxiety: Scientists, Anticommunism, and the Cold War* (Chapel Hill: University of North Carolina Press, 1999).

17. Haynes and Klehr, *In Denial*, 207, states that I label Julius Rosenberg's "firing from
    a defense plant on security grounds an example of 'inquisitorial' tactics by American
    authorities." I do not recall ever making such a statement, and the citation that Klehr and
    Haynes give is to another quotation in the same paragraph.

18. Another example of a twisted statement, which they admittedly relegate to a footnote, is,
    "Regarding the regrettable effects of anticommunism on U.S. State Department efficiency,
    Schrecker specifically cited the removal of Carl Marzani, a former OSS official, from his
    State Department job" (260 n. 54). The statement they cite has to do with the fact that
    red-baiting affected the way in which the U.S. intelligence agencies operated after World
    War II. What I said was, "When the OSS folded right after World War II, many of its
    employees, Carl Marzani among them, transferred into the State Department. In 1946,
    a congressional attack on these former OSS officials and their 'strong Soviet leanings'
    forced the department to disband the intelligence-gathering unit these people staffed. The
    disappearance of that unit changed the nature of the federal government's intelligence
    setup, reorienting it from the relatively unbiased collection and assessment of information
    to a more cloak-and-dagger approach" (Schrecker, *Many Are the Crimes*, 370).

19. Haynes and Klehr, *In Denial*, 224.

20. Ibid., 206.

21. Ibid., 206, 208. For a thoughtful study of the Harry Dexter White case, see R. Bruce
    Craig, *Treasonable Doubt: The Harry Dexter White Spy Case* (Lawrence: University of
    Kansas Press, 2004).

22. Haynes and Klehr, *In Denial*, 208.

23. Christopher R. Browning, *Ordinary Men: Reserve Police Battalion 101 and the Final
    Solution in Poland* (New York: Harper Collins, 1992); Daniel Jonah Goldhagen, *Hitler's
    Willing Executioners: Ordinary Germans and the Holocaust* (New York: Knopf, 1996).

24. Haynes and Klehr, *In Denial*, 151; Gary B. Nash, Charlotte Crabtree, and Ross E. Dunn,
    History on Trial: Culture Wars and the Teaching of the Past (New York: Knopf, 1997),
    204. Even though I disagree with Haynes and Klehr about many things, I, too, felt that the
    National History Standards gave a disproportionate amount of attention to McCarthyism.
    Much as it would probably increase the value of my work on the subject to inflate the
    impact of the anticommunist furor, I did not find evidence that it was as important a factor
    as the National History Standards made it out to be.

25. Lynne Cheney, quoted in Mike Wallace, "The Battle of the Enola Gay," in *Hiroshima's
    Shadow*, ed. Kai Bird and Lawrence Lifschutz (Stony Creek, CT: Pamphleteer's Press,
    1998), 332.

26. "All good scholars are 'revisionists,'" Paul Boyer pointed out at the height of the culture
    wars, "continually questioning and revising standard interpretations on the basis of new
    evidence, deeper analysis, or the fresh perspectives offered by the passage of time." See
    Paul Boyer, "Whose History Is It Anyway? Memory, Politics, and Historical Scholarship,"
    in *History Wars: The Enola Gay and Other Battles for the American Past*, ed. Edward T.
    Linenthal and Tom Engelhardt (New York: Henry Holt, 1996), 131.

27. John T. Correll, quoted in John Dower, "Three Narratives of Our Humanity," in Linenthal
    and Engelhardt, *History Wars*, 74; Senator Nancy Kassebaum, quoted in Wallace, "The
    Battle of the Enola Gay," 324.

28. See Bird and Lifschitz, *Hiroshima's Shadow*, xliv.

29. Sam Johnson, quoted in Edward T. Linenthal, "Anatomy of a Controversy," in Linenthal
    and Engelhardt, *History Wars*, 59.

30. David Brinkley, quoted in Bird and Lifschitz, *Hiroshima's Shadow*, xliv.

31. Ann Coulter, *Treason: Liberal Treachery from the Cold War to the War on Terrorism* (New York: Crown Forum, 2003), 70.

32. Jerry L. Martin and Anne D. Neal, *Defending Civilization: How Our Universities are Failing America* (New York: American Council of Trustees and Alumni, 2001).

33. Haynes and Klehr, *In Denial*, 49.

34. Ibid., 63–65.

35. David A. Hollinger, "Money and Academic Freedom a Half-Century after McCarthyism: Universities amid the Force Fields of Capital," in *Unfettered Expression: Freedom in American Intellectual Life*, ed. Peggie J. Hollingsworth (Ann Arbor: University of Michigan Press, 2000); Lewis F. Powell, "The Powell Memorandum," August 23, 1971, reprinted in National Chamber of Commerce, *Washington Report* supplement, n.d., author's copy courtesy of David Hollinger.

36. Powell, "The Powell Memorandum," 181.

37. For an early overview of the campaign to create a conservative alternative to the academy, see Ellen Messer-Davidow, "Manufacturing the Attack on Liberalized Higher Education," *Social Text*, no. 36 (1993): 40–80.

38. For a recent example of the way in which Haynes and Klehr's emphasis on espionage has influenced popular writing about American communism, see Ted Morgan, *Reds: McCarthyism in Twentieth-Century America* (New York: Random House, 2001).

Civil Liberties in the Brave New World of Antiterrorism

Rogers M. Smith

Sadly, it's true: there is an undeniable tension between our desires to give governments power to protect rights and our hopes to deny them power to violate rights. And the ways of managing this tension have to change as conditions change. After the attacks of September 11, 2001, the United States began a sweeping restructuring and strengthening of the nation's intelligence-gathering and coercive institutions that is in some ways necessary. The Bush administration is not, however, paying any real attention to the other side of the challenge. It is not supporting any effective mechanisms to prevent its antiterrorist innovations from producing massive threats to civil liberties.

Instead, the measures underway appear to be creating three important patterns that combine to generate an even more significant one. First, partly for good reasons, the United States is severely eroding the Cold War distinction between foreign intelligence and security operations, on the one hand, and domestic criminal law enforcement, on the other. Second, and far more questionably, it is still seeking to breathe new life into the option of employing military instead of civilian criminal justice proceedings. And finally and equally dubiously, it has also begun to undercut the long-standing separation of immigration control from domestic criminal justice systems. The cumulative effect of chipping away at all these walls between traditional modes of governmental law enforcement, in the hope of combating terrorism more effectively, is to render all persons, citizens and aliens alike, vulnerable to the most draconian procedures the United States has ever adopted. Those procedures

Radical History Review
Issue 93 (Fall 2005): 170–85

were designed primarily to deal with alien saboteurs, but they were always applicable in theory, and they are now applicable in fact, to all Americans.

The New War for Freedom and the Reconstruction of Homeland Security

President Bush believes the United States is currently engaged in a new kind of war, one in which it has a clear calling to rid the world of those the president has termed evildoers and to spread democracy and freedom as widely as possible. This view is encoded in the Bush administration's revised national security strategy, which now holds that the United States must maintain undiminished its enormous military advantage over the rest of the world and that it is entitled to engage in unilateral preemptive wars whenever in its judgment the promotion of American values requires them, even if no threat to the country is imminent. As that document put it, the United States "must be prepared to stop rogue states and their terrorist clients before they are able to threaten or use weapons of mass destruction against the United States and our allies and friends."[1]

Knowing that this policy is likely to be answered with violent assaults at home as well as abroad, the administration has begun to reconstitute the four basic systems for exercising coercive force that the United States employs: the criminal justice system, the arena of coercion where the government is most bound by constitutional restrictions; conventional military operations, in which the United States is bound by its agreement to the 1949 Geneva Conventions; immigration control, where the courts have unfortunately said the United States is bound only by very minimal due-process guarantees; and its foreign intelligence-gathering and special operations agencies, which remain largely unconstrained by the Constitution and international law. Though the United States belongs to Interpol, it generally eschews a fifth set of coercive institutions, the developing system of international criminal law. Most notably, it has refused assent or recognition to the new UN International Criminal Court. The United States has thus far taken five major steps to enhance the nation's ability to detect and deter terrorist threats by restructuring these coercive systems.[2] These are:

1. The passage of the USA PATRIOT Act on October 25, 2001.[3]

2. The president's executive order issued November 13, 2001, authorizing detention and military trials for noncitizens suspected of terrorism.[4]

3. The opening on January 11, 2002, of a detention camp for unlawful enemy combatants at the U.S. naval base in Guantánamo, Cuba. Over seven hundred persons have been detained there, all declared by the United States to be not prisoners of war but "unlawful enemy combatants," without the individualized determinations of that status required by the Third Geneva Convention of 1949.[5]

4. The creation of a new Department of Homeland Security on November 25, 2002, which has absorbed a large number of federal programs and agencies, including the Immigration and Naturalization Service (INS) and its antiterrorist Special Registration Initiative targeted at keeping track of immigrants with Arabic and Muslim origins.[6] That initiative led to the questioning of roughly 130,000 male immigrants and alien visitors, the deportation of some 9,000 illegal aliens, the arrest of over 800 criminal suspects, as well as the detention of 11 suspected terrorists.[7] Though on April 30, 2003, the administration announced that the initiative was ending, in fact only requirements for annual reregistration have been modified.[8]

5. The signing on December 17, 2004, of the Intelligence Reform and Terrorism Prevention Act of 2004, extensively based on recommendations of the 9/11 Commission.[9] It created a new director of national intelligence with broad budgetary and personnel authority; a new National Counterterrorism Center, which absorbed the Terrorist Threat Integration Center (TTIC) created in May 2003 but never made fully operational;[10] mandated more extensive information sharing among federal, state, and local agencies; and created a Privacy and Civil Liberties Board with investigatory and advisory powers to ensure that civil liberties are not violated by executive branch antiterrorist measures.

These initiatives have sought chiefly to accomplish two purposes. Commendably, they seek to promote information sharing so that genuine threats to national security can be more readily identified and combated. Far more dangerously, they seek also to allow the government to detain, deport, and execute persons without adequate procedural safeguards.

Efforts to facilitate information sharing are warranted because it now seems clear that had there been sufficiently effective systems for intelligence sharing and assessment in place, U.S. agencies would have been able to use information they actually had in hand to prevent the terrorists who perpetrated the September 11, 2001, attacks from ever entering the country or staying long enough to complete their preparations.[11] Still, the sorts of information now shared pose new dangers to civil liberties. The USA PATRIOT Act, the Homeland Security Act, and the Intelligence Reform and Terrorism Prevention Act all corrode the barrier between foreign intelligence operations and domestic criminal law enforcement that formed a pillar of the structures the United States adopted to fight the Cold War. Under those arrangements, the CIA and National Security Agency were to operate exclusively overseas, while the FBI, the Bureau of Alcohol, Tobacco, and Firearms, and other federal criminal investigation bodies, along with state and local police, were to combat crime at home. Various federal laws and regulations prohibited the foreign intelligence agencies from carrying on their activities within the United States.

Now, sections 203, 507, 508, 711, and 903 of the USA PATRIOT Act authorize extensive information sharing among all agencies, whether operating at home or abroad, whether federal, state, or local—including educational records, immigrant histories, and the fruits of surveillance methods that would ordinarily be deemed to violate constitutional rights if employed by federal, state, or local criminal law officers in more routine investigations. Section 502 also authorizes coordinated action among these heretofore generally distinct agencies. The act authorizing the new Department of Homeland Security goes further yet by not only mandating information sharing and coordination but by also placing many intelligence-gathering and immigration law enforcement functions under this single new agency (e.g., sections 221, 471, 891–99). The Intelligence Reform and Terrorism Prevention Act mandates in section 1016 that the president appoint a "program manager" to work with a new Information Sharing Council to create policies and networks that will foster an "Information Sharing Environment" among "all appropriate Federal, State, local, and tribal entities, and the private sector." The information sharing mandates are pursued through a bewildering variety of new mechanisms, including the presidentially appointed Information Sharing Council, which remains exempt from the requirements of the Federal Advisory Committee Act; a Joint Intelligence Community Council, consisting of the director of national intelligence and the secretaries of state, treasury, defense, energy, and homeland security, along with the attorney general; and a Homeland Security Council that includes the secretary of defense, the director of homeland security, and the attorney general. It appears that the new National Counterterrorism Center is intended to serve as the central integrating institution in charge of analyzing threats and planning antiterrorist operations, even if just how it will do so remains unclear and information sharing and agency coordination remain problems. Though the director of national intelligence has a broad mandate to make it all work, critics contend that the position lacks sufficient budgetary, personnel, and operational authority to enable its occupant to succeed.[12]

Yet whatever inefficiencies persist, it is clear that under all these new information-sharing arrangements, classified data and foreign intelligence generally can now be made available to national, state, and local criminal law enforcement officials more extensively than ever before. Immigrant data is also now entered into the National Criminal Information Center (NCIC), even if it has not been checked for currency and accuracy. Instead, on March 24, 2003, the attorney general issued an order exempting the NCIC's Central Record System from national Privacy Act standards requiring those records to be "accurate, timely, and reliable."[13] The Justice Department is also involving state and local officials in enforcement of federal immigration laws for the first time.[14]

Though the need for better intelligence sharing is clear, it is also true that the old structures of law enforcement reflected important values now put at risk by these momentous transformations in national security institutions. Because the courts have long held that U.S. governmental agents of all types can take actions overseas, in regard to aliens, that would be unconstitutional if done to U.S. citizens, certainly if done within the jurisdiction of the United States, many agencies of the U.S. government are in the habit of regularly taking such actions, coercing witnesses, seizing evidence, and detaining suspects without the procedural protections provided to citizens at home. When agencies long accustomed to acting without regard to constitutional restrictions abroad become entitled to join much more fully in law enforcement efforts at home, there is clearly a danger that constitutional safeguards may be ignored here as well (especially when the administration is pressing to loosen those safeguards on a number of fronts). Even if intelligence-gathering agencies can merely make available data that could not be legally obtained by a domestic criminal justice agency, the practical result may be that domestic law enforcement becomes less bound by constitutional restrictions.

The increased intermingling of immigration law enforcement and criminal law policing raises similar worries. Some state and local police are concerned that if they get involved in immigration law enforcement, they will receive less cooperation from immigrant communities, who will fear that any contact with any sort of law enforcement agency might end in their deportation. Those fears are sustained, moreover, by the wealth of legal precedents holding that immigration officials can constitutionally take peremptory actions against aliens that other law enforcement officers cannot. If state and local police are simultaneously enforcing criminal laws and the more procedurally lax immigration laws, it becomes easier for them to act as though only the latter standards are binding on them. Thus when we break down the walls between foreign and domestic enforcement efforts, and between policing immigration laws and criminal laws, we risk increasing the ways in which domestic criminal policing efforts may veer into infringements on constitutional rights, for citizens and aliens alike.

Those risks are vastly increased by the government's multipronged efforts to conduct the war on terrorism without regard for the procedural safeguards provided by either the Constitution or international law. The president's order authorizing military tribunals, in particular, permits *anyone* suspected of having knowledge of terrorism or of being directly involved in terrorism to be arrested without the showing of probable cause to a neutral magistrate and with no opportunity to communicate with an attorney. Suspects can then be detained indefinitely, or tried in secret military trials with the aid of military defense counsel, on the basis of any evidence that military officials deem to have probative value, even if it is hearsay or has been illegally obtained. Detainees on trial can be denied the opportunity to see and hear all the evidence brought against them, convicted on a vote of two-thirds of a panel of military judges, without trial by jury, and sentenced to death without appeal to the civilian courts. The Defense Department has since added some additional proce-dural protections, such as the requirement that guilt be found beyond a reasonable doubt, but the basic structure laid out in the president's original executive order still remains in effect.[15] And even if persons are acquitted in such trials, the government can still incarcerate them indefinitely if it continues to see them as national security risks.

Under both section 412 of the PATRIOT Act and the Special Registra-tion Initiative, moreover, the administration has claimed similarly broad powers to detain indefinitely all persons suspected of involvement in terrorism or of being material witnesses in terrorist investigations, without ever filing criminal charges against them or permitting access to an attorney. The same treatment is of course accorded to those captured in Afghanistan and incarcerated at Guantánamo on the presumption that they are unlawful enemy combatants.

The United States has justified these stringent measures as within the war powers bestowed by the Constitution, though the country has not formally declared war on terrorists, and it is difficult to see just how it could do so. Wars are ordinar-ily declared against rival nations, not organizations or loose networks of organi-zations and individuals. As a result, the White House, the Defense Department, and the Justice Department have especially defended their actions by stressing the heretofore relatively obscure precedent of *Ex parte Quirin* (1942).[16] There the U.S. Supreme Court upheld secret military trials for Nazi saboteurs captured in Florida and on Long Island during World War II.

Though it has become common for both government officials and critics of current policies to refer to this case as validating severe measures aimed at "enemy combatants" or "enemy aliens," those terms are both too broad and too narrow to be accurate. *Quirin* does not focus on the powers of the U.S. government in relation to uniformed enemy combatants participating in a legal international war. It defines power over unlawful enemy combatants, which can reasonably be held to include participants in an undeclared war, though the opinion does not so specify. It also applies to those deemed unlawful enemy combatants regardless of whether they are aliens or citizens. Although the military trial upheld by the Supreme Court in *Quirin* did in fact take place in the context of a declared war, Chief Justice Harlan Stone's opinion stressed that secret military trials were appropriate only for persons accused of violating internationally recognized laws of war. "Lawful combatants," he wrote, "are subject to capture and detention as prisoners of war by opposing military forces" according to international law. "Unlawful combatants are likewise subject to capture and detention, but in addition they are subject to trial and pun-ishment by military tribunals for acts which render their belligerency unlawful." Such tribunals can, he made clear, be constitutionally conducted without the sorts of procedural safeguards, including Fifth and Sixth Amendment guarantees, ordinarily afforded to criminals and even to lawful enemy combatants. And though most of the saboteurs tried in *Quirin* were enemy aliens, Stone affirmed that, if the U.S. government deems a person to be an unlawful enemy combatant, it made no difference whether or not the person was a U.S. citizen. National security required that they, too, be subjected to arrest, detention, and secret military trials if the executive branch deemed such measures appropriate.[17]

The reason this ruling proves so significant is that even though it does not explicitly address combat outside the context of a conventionally declared war, it seems entirely plausible for the government to designate all those now involved in terrorism as new kinds of "unlawful enemy combatants" or "belligerents" since they clearly act in violation of international laws of war, as well as of domestic and international criminal laws. They are, after all, not conventional criminals, either in our eyes or their own, but they are also not lawful combatants, so what else can they be?

And if suspected terrorists can credibly be viewed as unlawful enemy combatants, then the *Quirin* precedent also makes it plausible to argue that they can indeed be arrested, detained, and secretly tried by military commissions without normal constitutional procedural protections, just as the Justice Department has been asserting, whether the suspects are aliens, dual nationals, naturalized citizens, birthright citizens, or anything else. Yet plausible as those positions are, in the current context they are fraught with broad-ranging implications. Since everyone even suspected of involvement in terrorism by this definition constitutes an unlawful enemy combatant or belligerent, every investigation of all possible terrorist activities can result in arrests, indefinite detentions, and secret trials on the basis of any sort of evidence that may give minimal credibility to allegations of such involvement.

Now consider what these legal powers mean in light of the necessary but heretofore largely unregulated new pooling of terrorist-related information among foreign and domestic security agencies, national, state, and local law enforcement bodies, and immigration officials that the United States is undertaking. The results of diverse forms of electronic surveillance, so-called sneak-and-peek searches for which warrants need not be shown in advance, questioning that occurs during indefinite detentions, and the mappings of the social networks of suspects are all bound to produce data on the activities of citizens with whom aliens communicate, as well as on their non-American connections. When international and domestic security agencies, national, state, and local police forces, and immigration officials are all entitled to share such information rapidly, even information that has not been checked for accuracy, on citizens and aliens alike, there is clearly enormous potential for both citizens and aliens to be subjected to coercive measures that would ordinarily be deemed unconstitutional on the basis of evidence that could not survive customary procedural safeguards. In sum, *Ex parte Quirin* provides the legal basis for treating even U.S. citizens as entitled only to rights of unlawful enemy combatants, the class of persons with the least rights when confronted by an accusing U.S. government; and the restructuring of American law enforcement institutions to conduct the war on terrorism more efficiently has greatly increased the capacities of American governments to designate persons as appropriate targets for such treatment.

The application of these draconian measures to American citizens has already begun, most notably in the cases of Yaser Esam Hamdi and Jose Padilla. The administration has repeatedly sought to justify these actions by again citing *Quirin* (e.g., *Hamdi v. Rumsfeld* and *Padilla v. Rumsfeld*).[18] Hamdi is a Saudi in his twenties born in the United States who was allegedly fighting on behalf of the Taliban and al-Qaeda when captured on a battlefield in Afghanistan. He claimed to be a noncombatant. He was held without formal charges in military prisons in Virginia and South Carolina for more than two and a half years and was not permitted access to lawyers seeking to act on his behalf until the Supreme Court agreed to examine his detention. In *Hamdi v. Rumsfeld*, the court affirmed the *Quirin* precedent in that the United States could seize and detain enemy combatants but held that Hamdi had a due-process right to a hearing by an impartial adjudicator and that this right was enforceable via a writ of habeas corpus. Rather than proceed with such a hearing, the U.S. government concluded that Hamdi was no longer a threat to the country and permitted him to return to Saudi Arabia on the condition that he relinquish his U.S. citizenship.[19]

Similarly, for well over a year the courts refused to offer any but the most limited judicial review of the conditions of confinement imposed on Jose Padilla, also known as Abdullah al-Muhajir, an American citizen and long-term resident arrested at O'Hare airport. He was detained incommunicado for some months as a supposed material witness to terrorist activities, and although officials then accused Padilla of having been sufficiently involved in a dirty bomb plot to qualify as an unlawful enemy combatant, he continues to be incarcerated in a military facility in South Carolina without formal charges. On December 18, 2003, two judges of the Second Circuit Court of Appeals ruled that the *Quirin* decision did not authorize the U.S. government to detain a U.S. citizen in this matter. Without addressing the merits of the case, the Supreme Court subsequently ruled five to four that Padilla's petition had been filed in the wrong federal court; but the *Hamdi* decision appeared to give Padilla a strong case on the merits. That appearance was reinforced by *Rasul v. Bush*,[20] which held that Guantánamo detainees also had a right to bring a habeas corpus petition to challenge their detentions, though whether any such challenges might actually be upheld remains uncertain. The Supreme Court has often firmly asserted its own jurisdiction to review executive actions, but historically it has rarely challenged the substance of executive measures taken in the name of national security.

Though *Hamdi* and *Padilla* are the most noted cases involving U.S. citizens, they are not the only ones. In the same manner, the FBI arrested Maher "Mike" Hawash, a Palestinian immigrant who is a naturalized U.S. citizen, in the parking lot of his Oregon employer in March 2003 and kept him in secret detention for forty days as a material witness. He was then charged in a federal civilian court with conspiracy to levy war against the United States via terrorist tactics.[21] The government chose at that point to end his secret detention and not to subject him to a secret military trial, but it continues to assert that it has the power to do so in all such situations.

Protecting Civil Liberties While Protecting against Terrorism
Still, the existence of legal claims and administrative capacities to take despotic measures does not mean that despotic measures will necessarily result. Principled, conscientious officials can ensure that even risky precedents, policies, and institutions do much more good than harm. And, again, threats of terrorism are real and require strong measures of some sort.

The pressing question is, what sort, and with what protections against abuse? So far governmental efforts have been devoted almost entirely to one half of the equation, the strengthening of government's coercive powers. That pattern does not seem to be changing: on September 11, 2003, President Bush urged additional powers to issue "administrative subpoenas" to detain suspects without advance approval from a judge or grand jury. Bush also proposed measures to make it more difficult for suspected terrorists to be released on bail and to expand the range of offenses punishable by death.[22]

Much less attention continues to be given to new mechanisms ensuring that all necessary security measures are accompanied by equally effective means of protecting civil liberties. Section 705 of the Homeland Security Act did provide for the creation of a departmental officer for civil rights and civil liberties and section 222 created a department privacy officer. In September 2003, the first civil rights and civil liberties officer, Daniel F. Sutherland, published his "Strategic Plan" for the new office. The plan, however, essentially constituted a promissory note. It contained no specifics concerning how information sharing would be accompanied by appropriate civil liberties protections.[23] In sections 8301–6, the Intelligence Reform and Terrorism Prevention Act added provisions for the officer for civil rights and civil liberties to assist in the development of appropriate policies, to report abuses to the inspector general of the Department of Homeland Security, and to work with the department's privacy officer; but at this writing their implementation is unclear.

Section 1061 of the Intelligence Reform and Terrorism Prevention Act also created a Privacy and Civil Liberties Board within the Executive Office of the President to oversee and advise on information-sharing practices on an ongoing basis, as well as to prepare an annual report to Congress on how well privacy and civil liberties were being protected. The chair and vice chair of the board are appointed by the president with the advice and consent of the Senate, and the president also appoints three additional members. The national intelligence director and the attorney general can, however, determine that information may be withheld from the board if they believe national security so requires. Still more fundamentally, all these institutions are structured as means for executive branch agencies to police themselves. They are essentially confined to investigatory and advisory functions, without any real decision-making or enforcement powers to use against those who both appoint and supervise them.

A variety of public and private agencies have provided somewhat more robust suggestions. The congressionally created Gilmore Commission, formally known as the Advisory Panel to Assess Domestic Response Capabilities for Terrorism Involving Weapons of Mass Destruction, recommended in its "Fifth Annual Report to the President and Congress" that the president "establish an independent, bipartisan civil liberties oversight board to provide advice on any change to statutory or regulatory authority or implementing procedures from combating terrorism that has or may have civil liberties implications (even from unintended consequences)."[24] Such a board would be less fully a creature of the president and the executive branch agencies than the bodies created so far, but its value still appears limited. The advisory board would have no enforcement powers to use if its advice were ignored and civil liberties invaded.

The panel also repeated a previous recommendation for "a separate domestic intelligence agency" that would be separated from the FBI's law enforcement activities "to avoid the impression that the U.S. is establishing a kind of 'secret police.'" The report argued that the "'sanction' authority of law enforcement agencies—the threat of prosecution and incarceration—could prevent people who have important intelligence information from coming forward and speaking freely."[25] This proposal in some respects appears more promising because this intelligence agency would have neither arrest powers nor immigrant incarceration or deportation powers. Its separation from those activities might help ensure that persons would not be subjected to coercion on the basis of unverified rumors alone. Still, if its information continued to be pooled without adequate checks for validity, the same dangers would still exist. At any rate, Congress has now moved in a different direction with the creation of the National Counterterrorism Center, which is to conduct strategic operational planning that encompasses "all instruments of national power, including diplomatic, financial, military, intelligence, homeland security, and law enforcement activities within and among agencies."[26] Though the center is not to constitute a secret police, it is likely to link a great many types of law enforcement activities in joint operations, with all the attendant advantages and risks.

Others are seeking to strengthen both antiterrorism operations and civil liberties protection via innovations not in the structure of the executive branch but in that of the judiciary. They propose building on the Federal Intelligence Surveillance Act and the Foreign Intelligence Surveillance Court that it creates. That court operates secretly and can issue secret warrants for intelligence operations. Both Harvey Rishikof, former FBI legal counsel during the Clinton administration, and Thomas F. Powers, a more conservative law professor writing in the *Weekly Standard*, have endorsed the alternative idea of a new specialized federal security court or terrorism court (possibly incorporating the FISC) that would be able to keep antiterrorist intelligence operations secret while also trying cases with greater procedural protections for the accused than secret military trials afford.[27] But those protections so far remain undefined; as long as this court acted secretly and continued to provide the virtual blank check for all types of intelligence gathering that the Federal Intelligence Surveillance Court has done, it, too, would not be much help in protecting civil liberties.

In December 2003, the Markle Foundation in New York City, chaired by former Clinton attorney general nominee Zoë Baird, issued its own task force report titled "Creating a Trusted Information Network for Homeland Security." This report focused throughout on the need to enhance information gathering and sharing capacities while also protecting civil liberties and privacy. It recommended the development of specific standards restricting the purposes to which data could be put, especially unchecked rumors; defining how long such data could be retained; providing for means of data authentication; and establishing regulations governing who had access to such data.[28] It urged the president to issue an executive order providing such guidelines.[29] While recognizing that "increased information sharing among law enforcement and intelligence entities is critical to the counterterrorism mission," the report expressed great concern that as 2004 began, "no clear government-wide direction has been established for appropriate handling of domestic information while protecting civil liberties."[30]

The Intelligence Reform and Terrorism Prevention Act responded in part by requiring in section 1016 that the president, in consultation with the Privacy and Civil Liberties Oversight Board, issue guidelines to protect privacy and civil liberties as part of the creation of an Information Sharing Environment (ISE) that the act mandates. Previously, the Bush administration had resisted such suggestions, and critics are questioning whether it will comply fully and adequately in the years ahead.

Time will tell if those criticisms are justified. But there is one further route toward protecting civil liberties while confronting terrorism more effectively that the United States has only begun to explore: enhanced legislative oversight. Executive agencies are not the most trustworthy candidates to watchdog themselves, however the boards are structured. Courts can insist on hearings and sometimes overturn abusive military and police practices, but litigation is far too slow, difficult, costly, and inefficient to serve as a potent vehicle for safeguarding civil liberties on a routine and continuing basis. As several recent reports argue, the logical location in a democratic society for ongoing oversight of executive branch operations is the legislature, the U.S. Congress. It is customary today to be cynical about whether these elected representatives of the American people can be expected to perform responsibly, for understandable reasons. But both in principle and in practice, to achieve greater democratic accountability and control over executive antiterrorist measures that may recurrently endanger civil liberties, there is no other place to turn. Congress must be reformed and pressured to do its job better.

Admittedly, that is a tall order. As the 9/11 Commission recognized, the current structure of congressional oversight of intelligence and counterterrorism is "dysfunctional."[31] Although the 108th Congress attempted reform by creating a new Select Committee on Homeland Security in the House and by designating the Government Affairs Committee as the lead committee for homeland security issues in the Senate, those innovations still distributed jurisdiction over various aspects of intelligence and security operations among seventy-nine committees and subcommittees. A task force cochaired by Thomas Foley and Warren Rudman argued in December 2004 that "very few members of Congress have any real incentive to acquire expertise on homeland security issues," while those who do find it hard to develop "a perspective that includes related concerns beyond their committee's or subcommittee's domain."[32] The task force endorsed the general thrust of the still-unheeded recommendations of the 9/11 Commission. It urged Congress to designate one committee in the House and the Senate to serve as the permanent standing committee that would be the single principal point of oversight and review for homeland security. It also called for the creation either of a congressional "Joint Committee on Intelligence," modeled on the old and successful Joint Committee on Atomic Energy, or the creation of separate House and Senate intelligence committees that would combine authorization and appropriation authority, so as to have the clout to make agencies pay attention. The 9/11 Commission recommended that within this committee structure, Congress should establish a relatively small special subcommittee dedicated to continuing oversight, and that the committee or committees have a bipartisan makeup in which the majority party had only one more member than the minority party. Members should serve indefinitely so as to develop expertise, but they should also have overlapping memberships on other committees with pertinent responsibilities to promote both coordination in oversight and breadth of view.[33]

These proposals are desirable means for Congress to take more responsibility in the conduct of the war on terrorism, but they do not include specific mandates for these oversight committees to ensure that civil liberties are protected in the course of intelligence gathering, intelligence sharing, and antiterrorist operations. Philip Heymann and Juliette Kayyem, professors at, respectively, Harvard Law School and

Harvard's John F. Kennedy School of Government, have coauthored a report sponsored by the National Memorial Institute for the Prevention of Terrorism that sets out two further ideas. They propose that Congress create a five-year nonpartisan commission, with members who have security clearance, to engage in a continuing review of impact on civil liberties of any "extraordinary measures" taken in counterterrorism operations, combined with annual reports to relevant congressional committees on any perceived problems. Heymann and Kayyem also recommend legislation that would build on the 1978 act that created fifty-six inspector generals within federal executive agencies. They would require all inspector generals to examine the efficacy and impact on civil liberties of the antiterrorist and intelligence activities of their agencies. Heymann and Kayyem further suggest the creation of an interagency committee of inspector generals to provide joint review and recommendations concerning information sharing and antiterrorist policies with implications for civil liberties.[34]

By recommending specifically that Congress focus not only on the efficacy of intelligence and counterterrorist operations but also on the protection of civil liberties, as a matter of ongoing oversight, the Heymann and Kayyem report goes beyond previous suggestions for congressional reform in a vital way. There is a risk, however, that a commission charged with addressing civil liberties concerns raised by extraordinary measures might fail to provide the continuing review of the impact on civil liberties of routine intelligence-gathering and intelligence-sharing operations likely to be needed. If such a separate commission were created at all, it would probably need to have overlapping membership with the pertinent congressional committees, which should in turn have sufficient power over appropriations to be effective. But whatever the particular structures adopted, Congress must assume a far more substantial role in overseeing and, where appropriate, guiding and restraining the executive branch officials involved in antiterrorism if Americans are to be sure that, in their quest for heightened security, they are not creating a new American KGB.

At present the Congress has failed to undertake such a sweeping restructuring and intensification of its oversight activities, and the Bush administration has hardly encouraged it to do so. The administration's emphasis has instead remained on expansion of discretionary executive branch powers. At the same time, it has repeatedly disparaged one further alternative for protecting civil liberties—an option that has, however, never been clearly discredited.

Though greater information sharing is surely required, it is unclear that, once we begin sharing data efficiently, we cannot then combat terrorism effectively while relying on domestic and international criminal justice systems. The administration insists that it is too dangerous to delay detentions and prosecutions of terrorists until law enforcement agencies can constitutionally obtain sufficient evidence of criminal conspiracy and other crimes to meet probable cause standards for arrest and beyond reasonable doubt standards for conviction. The Justice Department also contends that its covert intelligence operations would be seriously hindered if accused terrorists could see the evidence and witnesses against them. And Bush officials simply distrust international criminal justice institutions, feeling they will be used for political purposes against the United States.

Yet a variety of reports by congressional investigators and private news sources make it clear that, if U.S. agencies had effectively shared fully confirmed data held in various government hands, the terrorists who committed the September 11 attacks would never have been admitted to the country in the first place, much less allowed to stay for the time it took them to prepare. We also have ample precedents for conducting at least partly closed criminal trials, with the identities of undercover informants and the details of intelligence operations revealed to judges but not to the defense attorneys and the accused, when necessary to protect ongoing investigations. Perhaps even those procedures seem too risky at present, but there is no clear evidence to that effect, only speculation. And when we are undertaking to condemn persons to death, the burden of proof must fall on those arguing for abandoning the constitutional rights that have historically been the most effective, albeit still imperfect, bulwarks of justice in the use of coercive force.

So far, though the terrible failures of American intelligence and law enforcement agencies prior to September 11, 2001, show that we need heightened data sharing, no similar case has been made that those tragedies or others arose from any hindrances imposed by ordinary criminal justice procedures and guarantees. There is thus no clear and present need to suspend those guarantees. And without such suspensions, and with heightened congressional scrutiny, data sharing by itself would not increase dangers to civil liberties nearly as much. Similarly, the United States does not have the kind of negative experience with international criminal proceedings that might justify forgoing all efforts to see if they can work.

But if we continue to insist that ordinary criminal justice proceedings are inadequate to combat terrorism, and if we continue to restructure our institutions to promote information sharing and joint coercive action, we cannot in good conscience ignore the whole topic of what new devices we might adopt to ensure that civil liberties are protected in this brave new world of antiterrorism. If we do not establish such safeguards through some combination of congressional oversight, executive boards, and judicial review, many American citizens may increasingly come to feel that they are losing precious freedoms at home, even as Americans and innocent foreign civilians continue to lose their lives in wars that seek to establish freedom abroad.

Notes

1. These commitments are expressed in sections 3 and 5 of the Bush administration's September 17, 2002, national security strategy document, www.whitehouse.gov/nsc/nssall .html (accessed April 19, 2005). The language quoted comes from section 5. International relations scholars refer to wars not triggered by perceptions of imminent threat as preventive, not preemptive wars, and such wars are usually thought to violate international law.

2. In the immediate aftermath of September 11, 2001, the FBI, INS, and a variety of other law enforcement agencies, working in part through a New York joint terrorism task force (JTTF), arrested and detained 762 immigrants, none ever found to be connected to terrorism. The Justice Department's Office of the Inspector General issued a report in April 2003 finding that many of these immigrants were detained for needlessly lengthy periods and subjected to abusive treatment. Though it makes for a less significant innovation than the others listed, the administration has since created the National Joint Terrorism Task Force to assist the sixty-six JTTFs of this type that now exist. See "FBI War on Terrorism: Counterterrorism Partnerships," www.fbi.gov/terrorinfo/counterterrorism/ paternship.htm (accessed April 19, 2005).

3. Electronic Frontier Foundation, USA PATRIOT Act, www.eff.org/Privacy/Surveillance/ Terrorism/hr3162.php (accessed April 19, 2005).

4. "President Issues Military Order: Detention, Treatment, and Trial of Certain Non-citizens in the War against Terrorism," November 13, 2001, www.whitehouse.gov/news/ releases/2001/11/print/20011113–27.html.

5. Human Rights Watch, "United States: Guantanamo Two Years On," January 9, 2004, hrw.org/english/docs/2004/01/09/usdom6917.htm.

6. People for Internet Responsibility, Homeland Security Act of 2002, www.pfir.org/2002– hr5005 (accessed April 19, 2005). The Special Registration Initiative, with targeted nations and groups, is described at the U.S. Immigration and Customs Enforcement Web site, "Immigration: Special Registration," www.ice.gov/graphics/specialregistration/index.htm (accessed April 19, 2005).

7. Rachel L. Swarns with Christopher Drew, "Fearful, Angry, or Confused, Muslim Immigrants Register," *New York Times*, April 25, 2004, www.nytimes.com/2003/04/25/ international/worldspecial/25REGI.html.

8. American Immigration Network, "Special Registration has NOT Ended—Many Requirements Continue," December 4, 2003, www.USAvisanow.com/12–4–03.htm (accessed April 19, 2005).

9. U.S. House of Representatives Committee on Rules, Intelligence Reform and Terrorism Prevention Act of 2004, December 7, 2004, www.house.gov/rules/s2845crfulltext.htm (accessed April 19, 2005).

10. Information on the Terrorist Threat Integration Center can be found at the Central Intelligence Agency Web site, www.cia.gov/cia/public_affairs/press_release/2003/ pr05012003.html (accessed April 19, 2005). Authorization to transfer the TTIC to the new National Counterterrorism Center occurs in section 1092 of the Intelligence Reform and Terrorism Prevention Act.

11. See, for example, *Joint Inquiry into Intelligence Community Activities before and after the Terrorist Attacks of September 11, 2001*, 107th Cong., 2d sess., 2002, S. Rep. 107–351, H. Rep. 107–792.

12. Intelligence Reform and Terrorism Prevention Act, section 1021; Markle Foundation Task Force, *Creating a Trusted Information Network for Homeland Security* (New York:

Markle Foundation, 2003), 2 n. 2, 4 n. 7; Shannon McCaffrey, "FBI and CIA Unite for Antiterror Fight," *Philadelphia Inquirer*, May 1, 2003; Richard A. Posner, "Important Job, Impossible Position," *New York Times*, February 9, 2005.

13. "Order of the U.S. Attorney General," *Federal Register*, March 24, 2003, v. 68, no. 56, 14140–14141.

14. David Cole, "Driving While Immigrant," *Nation*, May 12, 2003, 6, 30.

15. Department of Defense, Military Commission Order no. 1, March 21, 2002.

16. *Ex parte Quirin*, 317 U.S. 1 (1942).

17. The full opinion in *Ex parte Quirin* can be found at the Constitution Society Web site, www.constitution.org/ussc/317–001a.htm (accessed April 19, 2005).

18. *Hamdi v. Rumsfeld*, 316 F.3d. 450 (4th Cir. 2003), 19; and *Padilla v. Rumsfeld*, U.S.C.C.A., 2d Cir. Docket # 03–2235 (2003) at FindLaw, news.findlaw.com/hdocs/docs/padilla/padrums121803opn.pdf (accessed April 19, 2005).

19. Joel Brinkley, "The Saturday Profile: From Afghanistan to Saudi Arabia, via Guantánamo," *New York Times*, October 16, 2004.

20. *Rasul v. Bush*, Supreme Court of the United States Docket #03–334 (2004), www.supct.law.cornell.edu/supct/html/03-334.zo.html (accessed April 19, 2005).

21. Jennifer Lin, "A Dual Image of Terror Suspect," *Philadelphia Inquirer*, April 30, 2003.

22. Donald F. Kettl, *System under Stress: Homeland Security and American Politics* (Washington, DC: Congressional Quarterly Press, 2004), 105–6.

23. Department of Homeland Security, "Strategic Plan for the Office of Civil Rights and Civil Liberties," www.dhs.gov/interweb/assetlibrary/CRCL_Strategic_Plan.pdf (accessed April 19, 2005).

24. "Gilmore Commission," Advisory Panel to Assess Domestic Response Capabilities for Terrorism Involving Weapons of Mass Destruction, "Fifth Annual Report to the President and Congress," December 15, 2003, 23, www.rand.org/nsrd/terrpanel.

25. Ibid., 31.

26. U.S. House of Representatives Committee on Rules, Intelligence Reform and Terrorism Prevention Act of 2004, December 7, 2004, www.house.gov/rules/s2845cdrfulltext.htm section 1021.

27. Harvey Rishikof, "A New Court for Terrorism," *New York Times*, June 8, 2002; Thomas F. Powers, "Due Process for Terrorists? The Case for a Federal Terrorism Court," *Weekly Standard*, January 12, 2004, www.weeklystandard.com/content/Public/Articles/000/000/003/562vydnj.asp?pg=1 (accessed April 19, 2005).

28. Markle Foundation Task Force, *Creating a Trusted Information Network*, 9, 15, 17.

29. Ibid., 19.

30. Ibid., 25.

31. *The 9/11 Commission Report: Final Report of the National Commission on Terrorist Attacks upon the United States* (New York: Norton, 2004), 420.

32. CSIS-BENS Task Force on Congressional Oversight of the Department of Homeland Security, "Untangling the Web: Congressional Oversight and the Department of Homeland Security," December 10, 2004, 2, www.csis.org/hs/041210_DHS_TF_WhitePaper.pdf.

33. *9/11 Commission Report*, 419–21.

34. Philip B. Heymann and Juliette N. Kayyem, "Long-Term Legal Strategy Project for Preserving Security and Democratic Freedoms in the War on Terrorism," National Memorial Institute for the Prevention of Terrorism, www.mipt.org/Long-Term-Legal-Strategy.asp (accessed April 19, 2005).

Back to the Future:
Antecedents of the Northern Command

Priscilla Murolo

Off and on for the past eighteen months, I have been researching federal military mobilizations within U.S. borders. Not state militia or National Guard actions, which have been much more common; just instances in which regular troops were deployed. Initially, I envisioned a book that looked at a dozen or so especially dramatic episodes that would raise red flags about the Pentagon's establishment of a Northern Command for military operations inside the United States. As it happened, however, my hunt for just the right episodes turned up such a surprising volume and variety of mobilizations that the Northern Command no longer strikes me as a new departure.

The Northern Command is the newest of five Unified Combatant Commands (UCCs) that oversee joint deployments of two or more of the armed services. The first three UCCs were established as World War II segued into the Cold War. In 1947, the Truman administration instituted the Pacific Command to take charge of operations in Asia and the Pacific, the European Command to cover Europe, the Middle East, and Africa, and the Caribbean (now Southern) Command to cover the Caribbean and Central and South America. In 1983, the Pentagon added the Central Command, initially responsible for the Middle East and now for the entire oil-rich region that stretches from Kazakhstan down to Kenya and Sudan. This is the so-called CentCom, whose spokespeople hold press conferences on the wars in Afghanistan and Iraq. Together, these four commands covered most of the world beyond North America. In October 2002, the Pentagon added the Northern Com-

Radical History Review
Issue 93 (Fall 2005): 186–91

mand with jurisdiction over North America, including the continental United States. The borders of the older commands, meanwhile, were expanded so that every inch of the globe is assigned to one or another UCC.[1]

The Northern Command—called NorthCom in military speak—was the brainchild of Donald Rumsfeld and the Joint Chiefs of Staff. It has a twofold mission: to "deter, prevent, and defeat" attacks on the U.S. mainland and to assist civil authorities as the president or secretary of defense deem appropriate.[2] NorthCom's creation generated surprisingly little controversy. The consensus in Congress was, and still is, that the Pentagon should play a central role in securing the homeland, and the press seems to agree. At the April 2002 briefing where Rumsfeld announced plans for NorthCom, reporters asked more questions about the search for Osama bin Laden than about the new UCC's role in civilian law enforcement. NorthCom's own news releases (online at www.northcom.mil) offer the only comprehensive coverage of its public activities, which have so far included fighting fires in California, conducting disaster drills in Nevada and Virginia and war games in Alaska, overseeing information sharing among agencies charged with homeland defense, coordinating military assistance to civil authorities, and working with the Georgia National Guard to protect the G-8 summit on Sea Island in June 2004. Although some members of Congress have balked at Pentagon demands for unrestricted intelligence gathering within the United States—and some journalists have paid attention—lawmakers and the press have scarcely acknowledged that NorthCom exists, let alone what it does or aims to do. But there it is, commanded by the Navy's vice admiral Timothy Keating, headquartered at Peterson Air Force Base in Colorado Springs, and involved in a national network of joint task forces with civilian agencies such as the Federal Bureau of Investigation (FBI), the Bureau of Immigration and Customs Enforcement, the Federal Emergency Management Agency, and the Drug Enforcement Agency. Officially, NorthCom leaves homeland security to civil authority and concentrates instead on homeland defense, but that is a distinction without a difference.

When my study of domestic military operations began, I saw the Northern Command as a dangerous violation of the long-standing principle that civilian law enforcement is a civilian affair. Dangerous it may be, but it is not exactly new—just the latest twist in a pattern that dates back more than two hundred years.

The Constitution, written in the wake of Shays's Rebellion, explicitly authorizes the deployment of troops to enforce federal law, to put down an insurrection against the federal government, or to stifle "domestic Violence" against any state whose officials request such intervention. This much I understood when I began my research. I knew as well that Congress subsequently expanded and reexpanded the government's authority to use military force against its citizens; that that force was often deployed in excess of the law; that just the opposite occurred when the

U.S. Army was charged with defending freedpeople's civil rights during Reconstruction; that what the Army called Indian Wars consisted mainly of attacks on civilian populations; that the 1870s ushered in six decades of military intervention in strikes; and that after World War II the pattern shifted toward the selective enforcement of civil rights legislation, the suppression of black rebellions, and the containment of the antiwar movement. *Radical History Review* readers who specialize in U.S. history are doubtless familiar with these trends and with special events such as the U.S. Army's assault on the Bonus Marchers in 1932 and its roundup of Japanese Americans a decade later.

The magnitude of domestic operations is hardly common knowledge, however. Counting the deployments is not a simple matter. By the most conservative standards—those used in histories published by the U.S. Army—the number of episodes since the 1790s hovers around one hundred. (Here I rely on an educated guess since the Army's Center of Military History has not yet issued the last of its three-volume series on "domestic support operations.") That figure is misleading, to say the least. For one thing, it erases operations aimed at Native Americans. Russell Weigley's *History of the United States Army* counts more than nine hundred forays against Native people between 1865 and 1898,[3] but Army historians of domestic operations mention not one. Nor do these historians consider operations in U.S. colonies overseas. Then there is the question of lumping. How should we quantify twelve years of continuous, multifaceted military action in connection with Reconstruction? When troops from the U.S. Army and Marines went to scores of cities to patrol black communities following the assassination of Martin Luther King Jr., was that one operation or many? What about military surveillance? In the World War I era, the Army's Military Intelligence Division spied on legions of U.S. civilians, from Socialists, Wobblies, and Garveyites to members of pacifist groups, ethnic clubs, and the National Association for the Advancement of Colored People. In the late 1960s, the Army maintained intelligence files on at least one hundred thousand political activists and kept some people under constant surveillance. These initiatives surely count as domestic military action, but as how many episodes? I have given up all efforts to pinpoint the number of times that federal armed forces have intervened in civilian life in the United States. I can tell you this, however: it has happened more than you think.

While many interventions have involved just a few troops, others have been large-scale operations. Some two thousand federal soldiers helped to break the Great Railroad Strike of 1877, for example, and more than twice that many suppressed the Pullman strike in 1894. Close to one thousand troops from the Navy and Marines patrolled Seattle following the general strike of 1919. More than nine thousand Army regulars policed Oxford, Mississippi, when the University of Mississippi was desegregated in 1962–63, and about five thousand were dispatched to subdue the black rebellion in Detroit in 1967. The following year, federal troops deployed in the aftermath of King's assassination numbered more than twenty thousand and came from the Army, Navy, and Marines. In 1992, when South Central Los Angeles exploded in response to the Rodney King verdict, fifteen hundred Marines and two thousand members of the Army Infantry went in. In these and other cases, moreover, federal forces operated in tandem with state units, including ten thousand National Guard troops in Detroit and ten thousand in Los Angeles. The most surprising thing about such numbers is how difficult it can be to track them down. Although troop deployments are a matter of public record, there is no cumulative tally, and statistics are remarkably rare in the historiography on domestic military action.

The most provocative facts my research turned up have to do with the variety of operations, not their numbers or scale. Unexpected patterns emerged, for instance, when I read about the military suppression of anti-Chinese riots in Wyoming and Washington during the late nineteenth century. The first of these interventions took place in September 1885, after a white mob in Rock Springs, Wyoming, attacked a settlement of Chinese coal miners, killed twenty-eight men, and drove the survivors out of town. At the behest of the Union Pacific Railroad, which owned the Rock Springs mines, the War Department sent three hundred infantrymen and a Gatling gun crew to escort the Chinese back into town and safeguard their return to work. By the end of the year, the troops had also helped the Union Pacific to bring in Chinese replacements for white strikers and break the Knights of Labor in southwestern Wyoming. Legal cover for these actions came from legislation that declared transcontinental railways military roads subject to federal protection.

In Washington, too, mining companies used Chinese workers in an effort to destroy the Knights; this provided the catalyst for anti-Chinese riots that brought federal troops to Seattle in November 1885 and February 1886. Here, however, the requests for troops originated with civil authorities—the territorial governor Watson Squire, staunchly backed by Seattle's mayor Henry Yesler—and President Grover Cleveland made a great show of adherence to the Constitution. Both interventions were preceded by presidential proclamations that warned rioters to cease and desist and cited Cleveland's statutory prerogative to send in federal forces at a governor's request. When the troops arrived, moreover, they policed the city with a much lighter hand than the Army used at Rock Springs. Their presence precluded a massacre, but, on strict orders from the War Department, soldiers in Seattle merely stood by as mobs forcibly shipped Chinese out of town.

If events in Rock Springs and Seattle illustrate variations in the military's domestic role, they also point to deeper continuities. While the Union Pacific's president Charles Francis Adams engineered the intervention in Rock Springs, corporate officials did not range among the major players in Seattle. Governor Squire and

Mayor Yesler had their own corporate agenda, however. Speaking primarily for local boosters, businesspeople, and real estate interests, they sought to contain chaos in order to keep Seattle attractive to investors and to put the Washington territory on a fast track to statehood, which came three years later in 1889. At its core, the goal of the Washington boosters was the same as that of the Union Pacific: a predictable, controllable environment for managing business enterprises and the larger society. In Rock Springs, that meant protection of the Chinese; in Seattle, it meant a bloodless expulsion.

As I survey histories of domestic military action, the search for stability strikes me as a common thread that must be recognized if we are to see clearly where we stand today. It certainly explains the legal gymnastics that have accompanied virtually every deployment of troops. Consider, for example, the repeated evasions of the Posse Comitatus doctrine, widely believed to outlaw the federal military's participation in civilian law enforcement. From its articulation in the Army Appropriations Act of 1878 to its most recent reiterations, this doctrine has always provided for exceptions; it permits the military to police civilians under any circumstances authorized by the Constitution or by an act of Congress. When Posse Comitatus has applied, moreover, military commanders have mostly honored it in the breach. Yet this doctrine remains a part of the U.S. Code. That makes sense only if we see military action as an effort to stabilize social hierarchies—a project that depends not just on force but equally on law.

The drive for stability has never precluded interventions that some progressives might endorse. A case in point is the U.S. Army's protection of freedmen's polling places during Reconstruction; another is its involvement desegregating southern schools in the 1950s and 1960s. For freedmen, however, the Army provided an inadequate shield—it never fully eliminated election violence or fraud, and it disappeared altogether once the Republican Party decided that white supremacy could best stabilize the New South. The desegregation crises, by contrast, had much happier endings: federal troops secured an uneasy peace after eight months in Little Rock, Arkansas, and ten months in Oxford, Mississippi. But these actions also deepened the Army's attention to domestic intelligence and cooperation with the FBI, setting the stage for mass surveillance of progressive movements in the late 1960s. Even the military deployment to Detroit in 1967 could be seen in a positive light, in that it ended shooting sprees by city police and Michigan Guardsmen, who together killed some thirty civilians—as opposed to the Army's toll of one. But the federal troops' success at pacifying Detroit also provided the pretext for an initiative that undercut public safety, not to mention democracy. Citing the Detroit body count, the Department of Defense organized a massive effort to train police and guardsmen in intelligence gathering, the suppression of civil disorder, and the use of military hardware. Counterinsurgency techniques developed for use overseas thus became a vital part of domestic law enforcement. This is not the only instance of synergy between military mobilizations at home and abroad. The Army's civilian surveillance system during World War I, for example, derived from prototypes designed to secure U.S. colonialism in the Philippines, Hawai`i, and Puerto Rico. Rising insubordination among U.S. troops in Vietnam gave the Pentagon a strong incentive to launch intelligence operations against the stateside antiwar movement. Similarly, the global crisis following 9/11 clearly catalyzed the Pentagon's decision to establish the Northern Command and seems likely to have an even larger ripple effect in years to come.

We should not mistake catalysts for root causes, however. Even before 9/11, the USA PATRIOT Act, and the creation of the Department of Homeland Security, a thoughtful student of domestic military operations might have predicted the development of the Northern Command. Signs pointing in that direction included two decades of military involvement in drug interdiction, border control, and tariff enforcement; the ten thousand troops deployed to Los Angeles in 1992 and during the Olympic Games in Atlanta four years later; the frequency by the year 2000 with which the domestic-security experts challenged the validity of the Posse Comitatus; and the debut in October 2000 of the *Journal of Homeland Security*, produced by a strategic research institute that services both the military and corporate sectors.[4] On this front as on so many others, 9/11 accelerated and consolidated trends that were already well underway. This brave new world of ours is not all that new.

Notes

1. See the map at www.defenselink.mil/news/Apr2002/020417-D-6570-003.jpg.
2. See the Northern Command's Web site, www.northcom.mil/index.cfm?fuseaction=s
    .who_mission (accessed April 20, 2005).
3. Russell F. Weigley, *History of the United States Army* (Bloomington: Indiana University Press, 1984), 267.
4. See the journal at www.homelandsecurity.org/journal.

"I've Got Something to Say":
The Public Square, Public Discourse,
and the Barbershop

Quincy T. Mills

We have always found barber shop forums interesting. Barbers who indulge
such gatherings may do their business no good but they themselves certainly
do become among the best informed persons to be found anywhere. They
store up as much ammunition for future forensic encounters a diversified
round of arguments on innumerable subjects gleaned from the cross-section
of individuals whom they serve from a scholarly Ph.D. to a son of the road who
has managed to scrape together change enough for a haircut.
—Enoch Waters Jr., "Barber Shop Forum," *Chicago Defender*, 1935

One Friday evening in fall 2003, I walked into Ron's Barber Shop on the West
Side of Chicago. I acknowledged the barbers and customers, all black and in their
thirties, as I walked into the shop. Customers waited their opportunity to get in
their barber's chair, while *Barbershop* (dir. Tim Story, US, 2002) was playing on
the DVD. A couple of customers I had never seen before held their hello-glance
a little long. After all, it did not look like I was there to cut my sixteen-inch locks.
After about five minutes, Ron turned off the DVD to the disappointment of many
customers. He announced the start of Café Society to a few perplexed faces. The
Café Society is a weekly public discussion forum sponsored by the Public Square,

Radical History Review
Issue 93 (Fall 2005): 192–99
Copyright 2005 by MARHO: The Radical Historians' Organization, Inc.

formally known as the Center for Public Intellectuals. He began, "Every Friday at 5:00 we take time out for an hour to talk about issues that affect our communities, our country, our world. We may not find an answer tonight, but we will have the opportunity to voice our opinions. It's alright to disagree, in fact that's expected, but let's respect each other's opinion."

Airing Dissent on the Big Screen

As I watched the movie with everyone else in those five minutes, I could not help but reflect on the controversy that resulted from the movie and the real and imagined portrayals of black barbershops as public spaces. In *Barbershop*, director Tim Story featured the barbershop and the potentially contentious debates that often arise. Eddie, played by Cedric the Entertainer, outrages the entire barbershop when he proclaims, "Rosa Parks ain't do nuthin' but sit her black ass down." The second, and more important, part of his monologue, though, marks his major point: "There was a whole lotta other people that sat down on the bus, and they did it way before Rosa did"—without subsequent NAACP (National Association for the Advancement of Colored People) or other organizational support. He suggests that the organizers of the Montgomery Bus Boycott needed and waited for a respectable, middle-class person to protest segregation on city buses, thereby bypassing working-class opposition and protest to Jim Crow transportation. This alternative view of the civil rights movement—which highlights the working-class base of the movement and usually remains missing from popular culture and collective memory—directly challenges the myth of the icon, the prophet, and the Moses-like figure leading his people. In this scene, the barbershop comes to life, illuminating the radical potential within this space for working-class black men to express dissenting views and rethink processes of struggle. The controversy that followed the movie was instructive because it brought different generations into dialogue about the civil rights movement, black leadership, and the question of who sets the boundaries of debate, comedic affect, and how history is remembered. Even more than upsetting every patron in the movie, this scene enraged many black movie goers and civil rights leaders. Jesse Jackson and Al Sharpton wanted this scene deleted from the DVD release arguing that Rosa Parks, Martin Luther King Jr., and other luminaries—otherwise known as the matriarchs and patriarchs of the modern civil rights movement—should remain off limits to comedic affect.

Jackson's and Sharpton's critiques centered on the statements made about Parks, yet they gave no attention to the class conflict between black working- and middle-class activists and leaders apparent in this controversial scene and in the movement itself. In much of black politics, the working class, feminists, homosexuals, and youth are too often marginalized for the purpose of some public face of racial unity and respectability. A black barbershop, via cinematic production, opened its doors for public viewing and presented fiery and contentious views. Although black barbershops are public spaces, the boundaries of race and gender characterize them more as private spaces. For many outraged leaders and moviegoers, the significance of the comments made about Parks in *Barbershop* were less about recentering the black working class in the collective memory of civil rights struggles and more about not making a profit from publicly denigrating a black leader, regardless of their iconography. Although the line between entertainment/popular culture and politics is often blurred, it was indeed fascinating to enter the barbershop and be entertained by public conversations and humorous reconstructions of its significance to black communities for the price of a movie ticket. I, too, am going to open the doors of a black barbershop: not for entertainment purposes, but for political purposes only.

The Public Square and Café Society

I entered Ron's barbershop every Friday night to facilitate discussions on predetermined topics as part of the Café Society. Café Society's sponsor, the Public Square, is a not-for-profit organization in Chicago that promotes participatory democracy by creating space for public conversations. Barbara Ransby, the executive director, and other members decided on renaming the Center for Public Intellectuals the Public Square because they believed it "reflected a more democratic process."[1] Based on the conviction that intellectual work is not reserved for the ivory towers of the academy, the Public Square fosters debate, dialogue, and exchange of ideas about cultural, social, and political issues to democratize intellectual engagement. This space for intellectual community and public engagement provides individuals a forum to share knowledge and ideas that concern people's lives. The Café Society is one project through which these public conversations take place. The Café Society is designed to foster a more robust civil society and engaged citizenry through weekly conversations about contemporary issues. As the title suggests, it captures the coffee shop culture, a more inclusive public sphere than Jürgen Habermas ever imagined. Yet, as many critics of public sphere theory have aptly pointed out, many public spaces, even if well crafted, are rarely totally inclusive. Few African Americans participated in the Café Society at coffee shops around Chicago. Ransby thus introduced Café Society into a black barbershop. Popular perception has it that barbershops are the kind of places in which you can find strangers and comrades willfully engaging in contemporary political, social, and cultural issues. Yet it is important to remember that people, not spaces, are active and radical. People in some barbershops may talk very little. Moreover, they may go against or with the status quo. Café Society at Ron's Barber Shop provides a unique forum where these black men and women might engage in issues they may otherwise not broach and get challenged on positions they themselves and others take for granted.

 I jumped at the opportunity to facilitate these weekly discussions in the barbershop. An obvious concern was how to attempt to infuse structured discourse in a space that normally fosters unstructured conversations. This did not ultimately prove to be much of a concern. The barbershop was fresh on my mind, despite the fact that I had not cut my hair in five years. In the summer of 2000, I completed an ethnography of a black barbershop for Melissa Harris-Lacewell's book, *Barbershops, Bibles, and BET: Everyday Talk and Black Political Thought*, in which she argues that African Americans develop their political thought and worldviews in collective dialogue with other African Americans.[2] As an ethnographer, I could not actively engage in the discussions and arguments, but it was enlightening to spend an election summer listening to various arguments about electoral politics, black nationalism, and other political worldviews. Additionally, my dissertation in progress illuminates the movement from black-owned barbershops with exclusively white patronage in the nineteenth century to black-owned and black-patronized barbershops as autonomous public spaces during Jim Crow.[3] It is necessary for me as a historian to step away from conversations with dead folks in the archives and engage in contemporary issues with everyday folks outside the academy. Carter G. Woodson said it best: "The cause of the Race can get a hearing in the Negro barber shop more easily than in a Negro school. In the barber shop the Negro has freedom; in the school the Negro must do what somebody else wants done."[4] So I spent some time in the barbershop.

Most exhilarating about these weekly Café Society discussions was the willing participation of the customers who thought they were just coming in for a haircut and maybe random discussion. They participated in something much more than a market exchange—an exchange of ideas. Although discussion topics ranged from the fine line between child abuse and discipline, the state of the economy, hip-hop in the twenty-first century, inequalities in health care, and same-sex marriage, several weeks were devoted to terrorism, security, and racial profiling in a post-9/11 America.

Racial Profiling and Homeland Security

Eager to get into the discussion, I questioned the folks in the barbershop, "what do you think of the current policy of racially profiling Middle Easterners in a post-9/11 America?"[5] One person argued, "It's not right, but that's just what we gotta do." The "we" in his statement stood in for America. This black male's identification with the state is more complex than a strict reading would suggest. Another person echoed the previous gentleman's patriotism, adding, "If we were stricter on immigration policy, we wouldn't have this problem." A third person jumped in the conversation to disagree as a "devil's advocate," as he called it, though I jokingly asserted, "You need not sleep with the devil and advocate on his behalf to disagree." He raised the point that by racially profiling one group, authorities might miss a potential terrorist—Timothy McVeigh, for example.

Somewhat startled at the unyielding sense of patriotism, I questioned the racial profiling of African Americans. I asked an open-ended question to see where participants would take the discussion: "What about racial profiling in black communities?" A black woman, one of three, in the barbershop blurted out, "You mean like those cameras on the poles at intersections?" She was referring to the police's "anticrime" cameras on the West Side of Chicago at supposedly high-crime intersections. Everyone in the barbershop argued that the Chicago police unfairly targeted African Americans. Many were reluctant to make the connection between the profiling of African Americans and the profiling of Arab Americans. For many customers in this barbershop, there was another racialized Other. For them, racial profiling might get national attention now that other groups were targeted. Yet still, they joined in the nation's ideological agenda of protecting the homeland (citizen versus noncitizen). And though they recognized their marginal status, they were unwilling to separate themselves from either the citizenry or the homeland. Historical parallels exist with African Americans' patriotism during wartime to highlight one side of their double-consciousness—their Americanness. During World War I, W. E. B. Du Bois argued that black soldiers should "close ranks" and support the war effort to prove black manhood and citizenship. He proclaimed, "Let, us, while this war lasts, forget our special grievances and close our ranks."[6] Although hopeful for better treatment in the postwar period, Du Bois anguished, "We return from fighting, we return fighting."[7] The so-called Double Victory campaign was no less patriotic during World War II. During the Cold War, the NAACP responded to McCarthyism by expelling its members who were, or thought to be, affiliated with the Communist Party.[8]

My role with the Public Square was to facilitate discussions, to move conversations in directions they may not have otherwise gone, and to illuminate contradictions and push them further, not only among the participants but in my own political thinking as well. The barbershop customers were willing to justify the racial profiling of Arabs and "Arab-looking" individuals because Arabs had killed thousands of Americans on September 11. In short, "that's just what we gotta do." However, they saw no contradiction in opposing the constant surveillance of African Americans because they had not committed such an act of terror. Quite frankly, African Americans have historically been the victims of terrorism—such as slavery, lynching, disfranchisement, and police brutality. My aim was not to alter their political views to coincide with mine, because many of them did not believe there was a contradiction here. But some men expressed views that others had not considered, and that was part of the objective in these public conversations. When we talked about terrorism and homeland security more specifically, folks in the barbershop seemed much less cozy with the state.

Terrorism and Homeland Security

At a different meeting, we spoke more explicitly about terrorism. I questioned, "Are you willing to give up some freedoms to make sure we're safe from terrorism?" One person replied, "No, because it's a trap. They're just trying to eliminate the Constitution." Many of the customers believed the new security measures would not stop terrorism, but would bog officials down with more information gathering. "Terrorists are smart," a customer yelled after the barber finished lining his hair along his ear. "They will not fall into security traps, but will change the way they do business." Citing numerous conspiracy theories, these men were suspicious of the Bush administration's motives. They referenced the Tuskegee Syphilis Experiment between 1932 and 1972, the counterintelligence programs designed to neutralize political dissent in the 1950s and 1960s, and the Florida electoral debacle of 2000.[9] We can also include the wanton destruction of civility and justice at Abu Ghraib and Guantánamo Bay in this list of governmental abuse and misuse of power that fuels conspiracy theories. These references and correlations of race and imprisonment invite us to redirect contemporary discussions of terror and terrorism from acts of unprovoked violence that happens *to* the homeland to acts of unprovoked violence that happens *within* and sponsored *by* the homeland. A black woman in the barbershop shifted our discussion in this very direction.

The woman, in her forties, argued, "Terrorist attacks will always happen. A lot of those folks from the KKK who fled from the South came north. You better watch out for *them*." This was an interesting shift from our discussion of terror and securing the homeland. She suggested that black folks were all too familiar with terrorism. Some customers even argued that those white sheets and hoods had been traded in for blue shirts, a badge, and a gun. While the United States is securing the homeland, can we get some security for young black men harassed by the police when they drive through affluent white neighborhoods or poor black neighborhoods? Can we get some security for undocumented Latino/as who are denied health care and public education? Can we get some security for gay, lesbian, bisexual, and transgender folks who constantly face harassment and violence? How about some security for the integrity of civil society, justice, and equality? The fight against terrorism and the new administrative capacity of homeland security are so laden with racial and nationally chauvinistic politics that the customers in the barbershop were quick to point out the flaws, historical connections, and scary possibilities the future may hold.

The owner of the barbershop astutely asked me, "What happens with these conversations? Where does the change come in?" At the beginning of an era in which dissent is considered unpatriotic and even worthy of surveillance, forums in which citizens can engage each other about the USA PATRIOT Act, the war on terror, and other issues seem quite radical and necessary. At the beginning of an era in which many Americans willingly and unconsciously forgo their civil liberties, forums in which citizens question the previously unquestioned seem to enable participatory democracy outside of random opinion polls that never seem to poll my home. But this question is indeed that radical question that scholars of discourse, identity politics, and the Public Square ask: what next? That bridge between theory and practice often remains rickety. Café Society does not sponsor any type of activism because its primary goal is to foster open discussion. Public conversations are not the answer, only part of the answer. If individuals are engaged in participatory democracy through public conversations, on one level, I hope for the sake of progressive and radical politics, these conversations lead to grassroots organizing. On another level, I hope individuals are empowered by these collective dialogues and transform their lives as they rethink the theory and practice of democracy and citizenship.

Notes

1. Ben Aaronson, "Expanding Chicago's Public Square," *Chicago Reporter*, May 2003, 7. The Center for Public Intellectuals was cofounded in 2000 by Lisa Yun Lee, the current board chair, Carl Nathenson, and Katrin Voelkner.
2. Melissa Harris-Lacewell and Quincy T. Mills, "Truth and Soul: Black Talk in the Barbershop," in *Barbershops, Bibles, and BET: Everyday Talk and Black Political Thought*, by Harris-Lacewell (Princeton, NJ: Princeton University Press, 2004), 162–203.
3. Quincy T. Mills, "'Color-Line' Barbers and the Emergence of a Black Counterpublic: A Social and Political History of Black Barbers and Barbershops, 1850–1970" (PhD diss., University of Chicago, in progress).
4. Carter G. Woodson, "Is the Educated Negro a Liability?" *Chicago Defender*, May 21, 1932.
5. I have removed all names for anonymity purposes.
6. W. E. B. Du Bois, "Close Ranks," *Crisis*, July 1918, 111.
7. W. E. B. Du Bois, "Returning Soldiers," *Crisis*, May 1919, 13–14.
8. Mary Dudziak, *Cold War Civil Rights: Race and the Image of American Democracy* (Princeton, NJ: Princeton University Press, 2000).
9. In 1933, the U.S. Public Health Service in Macon County, Alabama, enrolled four hundred African American men in a study to track the succession of untreated syphilis phases. The U.S. Public Health Service and scientists told these men they were being treated for "bad blood," a euphemism for syphilis. For forty years, they were never told they had syphilis and were never treated. By the time the study was exposed in 1972, twenty-eight men had died of syphilis, one hundred men had died because of syphilis-related complications, at least forty wives had been infected, and nineteen children had contracted the disease at birth. See Susan M. Reverby, ed., *Tuskegee's Truths: Rethinking the Tuskegee Syphilis Study* (Chapel Hill, NC: University of North Carolina Press, 2000). COINTELPRO is an acronym for the series of FBI counterintelligence programs of

1956–71, whose purpose was the neutralization of political dissidents. COINTELPRO targeted individuals including Martin Luther King Jr., Stokeley Carmichael, and Ella Baker and organizations such as Students for a Democratic Society, Southern Christian Leadership Conference, and the Black Panther party. COINTELPRO's tactics included infiltration, surveillance, and harassment. See Ward Churchill and Jim Vander Wall, *The COINTELPRO Papers: Documents from the FBI's Secret Wars Against Dissent in the United States* (Cambridge, MA: South End, 2002).

The Immigrant Workers Freedom Rides of 2003. All photographs by Jerry Atkin

The Immigrant Workers Freedom Rides of 2003.

We Make the Road by Riding (*Se Hace el Camino al Viajar*): Stories from a Journal of the Immigrant Workers Freedom Ride—Portland to New York, September 23 to October 4, 2003

Jerry Atkin

As we crossed state lines, generations, cultures, and languages, we came together in what Martin Luther King Jr. would have recognized as a temporary Beloved Community. Our signature chant changed from "Si se puede!" ("Yes we can!") to "Somos uno" ("We are one"). We were building the world we wanted, the world we deserved. We were making the road by riding.

The Immigrant Workers Freedom Rides of 2003

Answering the call of an organizing committee made up primarily of international unions and immigrant rights organizations, eighteen buses of Immigrant Workers Freedom Riders from across the country converged on Washington, DC, and New York in the first week of October.[1] Freedom Riders visited more than one hundred cities and logged more than twenty thousand miles along the way as they the demonstrated and lobbied for the rights of the 31 million immigrants, nearly one third

Radical History Review
Issue 93 (Fall 2005): 200–16
Copyright 2005 by MARHO: The Radical Historians' Organization, Inc.

of them without documents, who currently live in the United States. As we traveled across the country, we were not calling for specific legislation; our goal was to mobilize public support, including from Congress, for basic principles that could be used to shape changes in the current irrational and unjust immigration laws:

• *Reward work* by granting legal status to hardworking, taxpaying, law-abiding immigrant workers already established in the United States

• *Renew our democracy* by clearing a path to citizenship and full political participation for our newest Americans

• *Restore labor protections* so that all workers, including immigrant workers, have the right to fair treatment on the job and the right to organize

• *Reunite families* in a timely and humane fashion by streamlining outdated immigration policies

• *Respect the civil rights and civil liberties of everyone* regardless of immigration status

The Immigrant Workers Freedom Rides were modeled on the Freedom Rides of 1961. Challenging the segregated public transportation system, with separate waiting rooms and restrooms for white and "colored" people, the original Freedom Riders faced beatings and arrests. They took their lives in their hands when they boarded those buses. We did not face such dangers, though some of our immigrant riders did risk losing their jobs or being deported. What linked the two rides was that certain people in the United States were being denied their rights, and they wanted to bring this discrimination to the attention of the public.

This journal recounts the story of forty-seven Freedom Riders that rode the bus from Portland, Oregon, to New York City, a trip that spanned twelve days, a dozen cities, and more than three thousand miles. There were immigrants from Mexico, Guatemala, the Dominican Republic, China, Taiwan, Palestine, the Philippines, and Siberia. Anglos and African Americans rode along to support immigrant workers' rights. What made our bus unique was that we had five children with us, a lot of young organizers, and an age range from three years to seventy-six. We were multicultural and intergenerational, and somewhere out there in the middle of the country, in one of those flat places, we came together as a family.

My own participation on the Freedom Ride started with a phone call from the Rural Organizing Project (ROP), a statewide coalition of sixty human rights organizations. They asked if I would be interested in being one of five Anglo allies from small towns around the state. There was a pause of about fifteen seconds before I said yes. Before moving to a small village on the Oregon coast, I had been actively

Utah capital

involved with the Oregon Farm Workers' Union (PCUN: Pineros y Campesinos Unidos del Noreste) for about ten years, and as a representative of Portland Jobs with Justice had helped organize the Labor March for Amnesty in Portland in the fall of 2000. In truth, though, I had started getting on the bus in the mid-1960s, when I took my family to East Africa for three years while attending the University of East Africa in Uganda and teaching history and English in Tanzania. It was there that I began to see the world with new eyes. When I came back to the United States in 1967, those new eyes helped me see the war in Vietnam for what it was, and to see how racism affected the lives of my children. Later on, Karl Marx and Frantz Fanon would give me a framework for understanding what I already knew in my gut. Since that time, much of my political and work life has centered on building class consciousness (without ever using the words) and on developing labor/community coalitions. When the call from ROP came, I was ready.

As we crossed the country in a bus dubbed Soul Power, I came to understand the importance of every story that we told each other, and of the beauty of every life revealed in the stories. I learned that these beautiful strands of life could be, and were, woven into something far greater than the sum of the stories. Taken together, these stories make up the true history of this country. As we traveled, I also came to understand that there was power in the telling itself, in the act of being listened to. We were breaking a silence and staking a claim to our history. In the following pages I want to tell the story of our journey, but more than that I want to convey what it was like to be on that bus, to hear those stories, to make our way across this vast country to stand up for justice.

The Stories

How Much Does a Dream Weigh? (September 24, Caldwell, Idaho)

That night, outside Caldwell, we gather at Farmway Village, home to a thousand farmworkers and their families, home to a thousand stories. Five hundred people are waiting for us. Long tables groan under the weight of food and men and women from the Laborers' Union, in bright orange T-shirts, sweating over barbecues, grateful for the breeze blowing from the fields. The evening program, under towering trees and painted with a sunset, stretches far into the night with speakers from half a dozen countries and music from around the world. Mexican dancers with their colorful dresses, swirling movements, and radiant smiles steal the show. In the second ring of the circus, a cluster of children grace the stage as they chant, cheer, dance, and just generally bathe in the limelight. It is a true fiesta.

It is still hot at 9:30 in the evening when Michael, the immigrant rights attorney traveling with us, and I are greeted by our Mexican host family. We walk into a combination living room, dining room, and kitchen to the sound of soccer on the television. We are greeted by a smiling woman, her two oldest children, and her daughter's eighteen-month-old son. There are three other children in the house. The ten-year-old cannot speak Spanish or English, but greets us speaking a joyful language of her own invention that even her family does not understand, while her brother, with a deeply furrowed brow, has no words at all. The woman works seasonally, harvesting sweet corn, and the older daughter, perhaps twenty, works twelve hours a day riding a potato harvester, culling stones and clods from a conveyor belt on top of the harvester, in the dust, under the blistering sun, for $5.15 an hour, the federal minimum age. I am sure the potato growers would pay her less if they could.

I want you to be there with me. The room still throbs with the heat of the day, and Michael and I are sweating. Soccer teams from the Mexican league wage a mute struggle on the television while Michael talks about the Freedom Ride in Spanish and I watch the woman prepare *chichimanga*, red beans and tortillas, for us. At 10:00 p.m. Michael and I sit down to eat. Never mind that we have eaten our fill at the fiesta—we are required to eat until we are pleasantly uncomfortable and our smiling host is completely satisfied. What we do not eat, she uses to make *tortas* (sandwiches) for the next day. While we are eating, I watch the young mother wash her baby in the sink with an economy of movement and an effortless grace. There is great beauty here, and I am stunned by the beauty and poetry of everyday life.

Later the young mother, who suddenly speaks English, tells me her dreams. She says,

I want to be a doctor. I want to create a clinic, a place where homeless teenagers can get help so they will not end up in trouble. Sometimes they have to leave their homes because of alcohol and violence, and they have no where to go. I want to help them, but I cannot go to school because I do not have papers. My husband has papers and I hope I can get mine. I want to be a doctor very much.

But these words are only part of the story. I want you to be there, to see the gentle fire in her eyes as she speaks; know how completely good her heart is. There is earnestness and a purity of spirit here that takes your breath away—and breaks your heart.

This is only one of the tragedies of immigration policy: we are keeping out dreams; we are keeping out those who would be healers, who would use their lives to mend what has been broken. We are keeping out the beauty of the human spirit. The next morning on the bus I realize that this brilliant and beautiful young woman has given me her dream. That I have to carry it with me; carry it for her, on this Freedom Ride to Washington and New York City. There is no more precious cargo, no more urgent task. How much does a dream weigh? Sometimes it can be very heavy. I had already figured out that we were a caravan of a thousand stories making its way to Washington and New York. Now I realized that we were also a caravan of dreams. *Cuentos y sueños*, stories and dreams, crossing this country on a bus, trying to change the world a little. How can we possibly lose?

Coming Together (September 26, Denver, Colorado)

On our fourth day out, two events transformed us into a fledgling family. In the early afternoon we heard that the buses from Los Angeles had been stopped by the INS in El Paso and fourteen agents had come onto the buses demanding to see proof of citizenship. The keystone of all our security strategies was our constitutional right to remain silent. When confronted by the INS, people were to hand them a card informing them that they were exercising that right. On the Los Angeles bus they did not say a word to the immigration authorities, but they did, however, sing. "We Shall Overcome" was punctuated by the questioning and threats of the INS. They took people off the buses, and people went peacefully, and silently, into the interrogation rooms. No one broke, no one talked. After four hours, with groups of community leaders, politicians, and just plain folks all across the country ready to take action if any of the riders were detained, the buses were back on the road.

Because of the events in El Paso, we had to get serious about our own security plan. We had to confront the possibility that something like El Paso could happen to us. We stood in a vacant field in Fort Collins, Colorado, and tried to decide whether we would allow people to be taken off the bus and at what point we would engage in civil disobedience. We had to find a way to accommodate the different levels of risk, experience, and willingness to confront the authorities. And then there were the children. If Ramon and Paulina were arrested, their children would be taken into protective custody. Ramon spoke about what it means to be willing to put your children at risk, his voice cracking with emotion. People got it. After we agreed that we would allow people to be taken off the bus and only engage in civil disobedience if they were detained, John Cuff spoke, with deep passion and emotion. He said he accepted the group's decision, but his own instinct was to not let them touch anyone on the bus. As an African American veteran, he was willing to wrap himself in the American flag and make them come through him to get to the other riders. Descended from involuntary immigrants, he was willing to put his body on the line for the rights of immigrants who had come here seeking something better for themselves and their families. John's passion, Ramon's passion, passed through the group like an electric current, galvanizing us into something different.

Emotionally raw and vulnerable, we were more than an hour late arriving in Denver. No one knew how many people would still be there when we arrived. As we pulled up, people still lined the sidewalks waiting for us, and as we walked into the gymnasium of the Catholic high school, people lined the sides of the aisle three deep, applauding and yelling and chanting. They were reaching out to touch us as we filed in chanting "Freedom . . . Riders!" The five hundred people sounded like a thousand in the confines of the gymnasium. And for the first time we all felt as though we were doing something special. Over the next two days people would confess that they felt like rock stars when we walked in. I certainly felt it, but then I tried to imagine what it must have felt like for immigrant workers and their families to be welcomed with joy and love by strangers, Anglos and other immigrants. I couldn't.

The AFL-CIO had sent James Orange to be our keynote speaker. An associate of Martin Luther King's in Birmingham, an enormous and powerful man, he reminded us of our links to the Freedom Rides of the early sixties. The cadences of Martin Luther King Jr. and of the black church echoed through the hall. There was a palpable sense of joy and power in the room. We were on a mission for justice, part of the great unfolding story of America. We were America. We had started the day as acquaintances, and we ended the day as comrades. The next day we were on the path to becoming family.

We Make the Road by Riding (September 27, on the road)

As we traveled on toward Omaha, people took the microphone at the front of the bus and began to tell their stories. We trusted each other enough now to share some of the painful histories that had brought us together on this trip. They were stories of heartbreak, the courage of survival—and hope.

Olga, a union member working in a laundry and one of our younger riders, was an immigrant from Siberia. The youngest of fourteen children, she spoke of her persecution as a Christian in Siberia (the fines and the verbal, psychological, and physical abuse), as well as the pain of the separation of her family. It took her family six years to get permission to emigrate, and then they were told that no child over twenty-one would be allowed to come to the United States. For six years they have tried to reunite the family, without success.

Olga was shy. Telling her story was an act of great courage, and when it was later announced that she would be speaking at the rally in Omaha, the chant of "Olga! Olga! Olga!" echoed through the bus. I watched her turn red, pleasure and embarrassment fighting it out for control of her emotions. Pleasure won, but it was close. And then, when she rose to speak in Omaha, the same chant erupted spontaneously from the front rows. A local reporter noted that Olga seemed to be traveling with her own fan club, which was true. Olga's story rang out over the speakers, and she spoke with strength and passion. We hung on every word.

We make the road

Severo speaking at the Bible Way Temple, Washington, DC

Severo was our oldest rider at seventy-six. He came from Mexico and still worked in the fields and canneries, still being cheated by bosses and labor contractors. The first few days on the bus, he and his wife Miria sat quietly together, rarely speaking. Somewhere along the road Severo was encouraged to tell us his story. By this time he and Miria were being treated with the respect that elders deserve, and their body language had begun to change. Smiles became more frequent. One day Severo told us how he and Miria had been treated as workers in this country. It had been a hard life and, as his wife put it, they had paid with their hearing, their teeth, and their health. In Columbus, Ohio, supported by one of our *compañeras*, Severo was willing to speak at a Unity Breakfast, and in Washington he addressed more than a thousand Freedom Riders with passion.

Hamid, also in his seventies, told of his eviction from Palestine in 1948, of his fifty years as an undocumented worker in Lebanon, Jordan, and Syria. He spoke of the death of one of his sons caught in the cross fire of a civil war, and of his efforts to bring his remaining sons to this country to be with their mother who had suffered a stroke, leaving her unable to speak. As he found his place in the emerging family, he began telling jokes, singing songs, and leading us in games.

Many of the stories we told were filled with the pain of separation from family: funerals unattended, grandchildren never seen, children growing up without fathers. They were filled with the pain of mistreatment on the job, stolen wages, corrupt labor contractors, seven-day work weeks. But underneath it all were the dreams of a better world, and for all the sadness of these stories, they were told without self-pity or complaint. They were simply the stories that had happened, the reasons that things must change.

Trust grew. Faces relaxed into smiles, more laughter drifted up from the seats, we played music and sang. Children wandered the aisles looking for another lap to conquer, another heart to steal. We played music and sang. We looked out for one another. We were making the road by riding.

Grief (September 28, Des Moines, Iowa)

In Des Moines we attended a memorial service for eleven immigrant workers discovered dead in a railroad car. The Seattle and Portland Freedom Riders surged up the steps of the state capitol together chanting "Portland, Seattle / United in the battle." More than five hundred immigrant workers and their supporters roared their approval. The mayor spoke, the governor waved, the Catholic priest prayed. It was rally as usual, but something shifted when we began the actual memorial service. Freedom Riders had been chosen from both buses to place flowers in front of the white crosses as the names of the dead were recited. After a moment of silence, a rider from the Seattle bus came to the microphone. She said a few words, looked at the crosses, said a few more words, and then broke down in tears. She was immediately surrounded by riders from both buses supporting her in her grief. This was not a speech as usual.

Suddenly the tragedy of these deaths became real for me and for others in the crowd. These workers, men and women from five countries, died because they came across the border in a locked railroad car. The coyote who had taken their

Hope of the barrio

money to smuggle them into the country did not unlock the doors of the car when it arrived in Texas. Their bodies, what was left of them, were discovered four months later in Iowa, when the railroad cars were finally unlocked. They had died of exposure and dehydration, slow, painful deaths. For four months their families did not know what had happened to them. Were they in jail? Were they in the hospital? Were they locked in a railroad car dying by degrees, powerless to break out of their mobile prison? What was it like in that railroad car? Did people try to calm and comfort each other? Did they tell stories about their families? When did they give up hope, knowing that they would die?

As I sat there on the steps of the capitol in Des Moines, Iowa, I asked myself what kind of economic and immigration policies made deaths like these inevitable. Since 1998, two thousand immigrants have died in the desert trying to come into the United States, some of them murdered by vigilante ranchers. A close friend of one of our riders died that way. The rancher who murdered him was acquitted when he testified, "I saw an animal, and shot it when it came across the border."

While all this was unfolding in my head, three Latina girls, between the ages of five and eight, were playing in front of me. They had no idea what was happening. They were simply children, playing. My photographer's eye snapped away, catching them in the act of being themselves. They were laughing, filled with the joy of each other, the joy of being alive. And my photographer's eye saw them dying in the desert, or crying in despair when their mother or father went away and never came back. I did not imagine this. I did not think, "Wouldn't it be awful if . . ."; I actually saw it. I was there in the desert with them. My *compañero*, Jésus Morales, sensing that something was going on for me, came up to see if I was OK, putting his arm around my shoulder. I smiled at him and told him that I was fine, thinking that I was. But as he walked away I began, silently, to cry.

So, to our cargo of stories and dreams, we add grief. And determination to change this world so that no child here, or in any country, dies in the desert or grows up without parents. In this moment of stark clarity I wonder how we as a nation can tolerate these things. How I have tolerated them. Oh, right. That's why I am an organizer, why I write, why I am trying to take you on this bus ride with me so we can wake up a little and find the slow patient path of our growing power that leads to a better world than this.

The Freedom Riders Gather (October 1, Washington, DC)
More than nine hundred Freedom Riders on eighteen buses from ten cities, having traveled a cumulative twenty thousand miles and visited more than one hundred cities, converged on Bible Way Temple in Washington, DC. We had come to deliver our cargo of stories, dreams, grief, and hope. How radiantly beautiful we were. As we waited to go into the church, carnival broke out on our patch of the sidewalk. With the Miami bus we drummed and danced as other riders passed through. We

Outside the Bible Way Temple, Washington, DC

cheered each other, exchanged high fives and clasped hands. As we entered the church, the same energy of carnival that we had experienced on the streets was in the hall, only now there were a thousand of us. Banners, flags, and the Virgin of Guadalupe swayed above the crowd. The building pulsed with the energy of the Freedom Riders. It was amazing.

A swirl of important speakers addressed the crowd, and then the Freedom Riders spoke. Mako, from the Seattle bus, relived her experience as a five-year-old in 1942 as she watched the FBI arrest her father after the creation of the internment camps. She talked about the irony of learning "God Bless America" behind the barbed wire of Minidoka and finished her testimony with the thought that we should love America with all our hearts—but that our love should not be blind. And then our own Severo, our seventy-six-year-old farmworker, still working in the fields and canneries, addressed the crowd. He spoke about injustices in the fields, the attack on the farmworkers' union, and on our need to continue the struggle. The crowd rose to its feet to honor him, roaring its approval.

John Lewis, one of the original Freedom Riders, looking like a prizefighter past his prime with his shaved head and powerful neck, closed the event. After being beaten and arrested forty times between 1961 and 1965, he came by his prizefighter's looks honestly. He spoke about the beatings, the arrests, and the bus burnings that accompanied that first Freedom Ride. And he spoke about his own amazement that after forty-two years it was still necessary to take to the roads again to demand rights for the disenfranchised. He promised that when we left for New York, he would be on the buses with us. And he was.

Of the People, by the People, and for the People (October 2, Washington, DC)
The next day more than one thousand of us descended on Congress to lobby and educate our legislators. Our reception, as you might imagine, was mixed. My group was assigned to lobby a conservative Republican representing the eastern part of Oregon. Each of us had a part of the story to tell. The personal experiences of the immigrant workers were to form the centerpiece, but I would get to talk about worker protections. I would point out that immigrant workers, especially undocumented workers, constituted the most vulnerable workers in our workforce, often afraid to complain about unpaid overtime, unsafe working conditions, sexual harassment, or discrimination because they know they can be fired at the whim of the employer—or turned over to the INS. Because of their status, many have no access to the workers' compensation, unemployment, and retirement funds that they pay into. I would not point out, given who we would be talking to, that immigrant workers often felt too afraid to join in organizing campaigns, even though they saw the need to organize very clearly, and even though organizing immigrant workers is the future of the labor movement in this country.

Well, it was a moot point anyway, because the Congressman's schedule mysteriously changed, making it impossible for him to meet with us. His young aide was truly sorry about this, and she would be glad to talk with us here in the reception area or in the hall. The aide dutifully took notes as we talked. I asked her if it would be OK to take a picture, and she graciously said that it would be fine. Photo ops are something she understood. I had to back up into the interior hallway to get everybody in the picture . . . and saw someone looking suspiciously like the Congressman in his office leaning back in the chair with his fingers laced together behind his head. It felt like this was a cynical exercise in ignoring us, but the victory was still ours because we had come to the seat of political power and told our stories. We had brought some truth and some reality into the hollow deliberations of our lawmakers. We had come in good faith and we had served notice that we would not be silenced. We had spoken the truth to power, and we celebrated with ice cream in the congressional cafeteria.

Finale in New York (October 4, New York City)
Then we were there, in Queens, the most diverse borough of the most diverse city in our country. This was the final event of our journey, the rally to end all rallies: one hundred thousand people converged on Flushing Meadows to support the rights of immigrant workers and their families. I do not want to minimize the importance of this event. It was big. It made the news across the country, and the invisible issues of immigrant workers were, for a moment, raised up in the public eye, and there is

no way to be anywhere with one hundred thousand other people who support what you are doing and not feel strengthened. What I missed, over the roar of the crowd, were the kinds of conversations that had happened in the streets and in the community celebrations. There I had been able to make eye contact with people, touch them, talk with them; strengthen them in their work and be strengthened in return. I felt as though this was where the change was really happening.

Two things made this event more than the sum of the interminable number of speeches. There was the diversity and vibrant energy of who attended, and there was the music. For the Freedom Riders this held particularly true when the Mexican regional music supergroup Bronco appeared. Late in the afternoon, the Freedom Riders felt a little dulled after twelve days of travel and a lot of speeches, but when Bronco came on stage, everything changed. We were dancing in the streets. Well, aisles, actually, but the image works because it conveys the sense of excitement and release that good music always brings. This was the kind of music that anybody can dance to, music for and about us. We surged toward the stage. The end of the group's set came at the time we had to leave to meet our bus, and we danced our way out of the park. There are worse ways to end a long journey.

Visiting Ground Zero (October 7, New York City)
Many of the Freedom Riders made Ground Zero their destination on the first night we were in New York, and I wanted to see Ground Zero with their eyes, to see the power of the city all around me as a symbol of America, to see this tragedy as they saw it, but what I saw was a building site that had been fenced off with photo displays of New York City throughout its history. I did not see in my mind's eye the moment of impact, the towers collapsing, the people leaping to their death, those who gave up their lives to save the lives of others. So, honestly, I felt very little. I am not heartless, far from it, but while I mourn the death of thousands, I also mourn the death of millions: people who die every day in the wars that rage across our suffering planet. Immigrants flee these wars as refugees to chance their uncertain welcome here in the United States. They choose hope over the threat of death, over the pain of watching their villages and families destroyed. No one holds the American dream as purely as our immigrant population. They know the poverty and horror that they have left behind, and they see the great promise of America, even when it treats them badly.

Ground Zero. Where the bomb is dropped or, in this case, where the planes crashed, and the towers fell, and the people died. The center of a grief spreading out over New York, across the country, and around the world. Just as it did in Hiroshima, just as it did in Dresden. Our grief as a nation is not the alpha and omega of grief. It is just one more ground zero, one more place where the hooves of the Four Horsemen of the Apocalypse have touched down, shattering lives, scarring the earth.

As I walked around the site, I thought about all the immigrant workers whose lives are at risk in this country. Whose families are severed, whose voice is silenced by fear, whose work is hard, dangerous, and underpaid, whose rights are compromised because they are undocumented. People whose lives are at risk simply because their need to care for their families intersects with our demand for cheap labor. And it occurred to me that in terms of the bureaucratic and punitive immigration laws of this country, it is the family life of every immigrant that is at ground zero. This is where the shrapnel of our immigration laws and the economic realities of our world thrust into the lives of human beings who bleed when you cut them, cry when they are sad, who love their families—and who turn the wheels of our economy.

Sometimes it is difficult to see the reality of other people's lives. We are trapped in our own struggles to survive, our own families, and our own fears—and in the web of confusion spun by the mass media. Our empathy and compassion are dulled, and the stuff of life itself often passes unnoticed before us.

This Freedom Ride trip was about the stuff of life. About the struggles and sorrows of real people. About our ability to come together to love and support each other. And perhaps our little bus was a ground zero of another kind: the point of impact where good things happen and spread out into our families and communities as healing energy that can transform not just our immigration laws but our world as well. That transformation can only come from us. We, the people. The immigrants of generations past and generations to come. People of all races, cultures, genders, and ages. All of us seeking the good life, a life of safety and security for our families, for all families, everywhere.

Postscript (May 24, Wheeler, Oregon)

So what did it all mean, this Immigrant Workers Freedom Ride? Was it a turning point? Or an essay in futility in these dark times in which fear and intolerance distort everything in our collective life as a nation? We know that we will not see significant changes in our immigration laws any time soon. Employers will continue to exploit and abuse immigrant workers. The atmosphere of distrust that was ignited by 9/11 and fanned into flames by John Ashcroft and the induced and manipulated national obsession with homeland security is still with us, though it seems to be eroding some as the lies are exposed and as more people return to their senses. Under the circumstances, immigrant workers and their families will have to wait a little longer for anything like justice.

So if the Freedom Ride was not a quick fix, perhaps it was a catalyst for change. As we rolled across the country, communities came together to support the Freedom Riders in a way that had not happened since 9/11. Everywhere we went people seemed hungry for justice, and we gave them a chance to remember the power of their vision, the goodness of this work. Certainly no one who rode this bus for three thousand miles, through a dozen states, stopping in communities large and small, touching the lives of thousands of people, will ever be the same. We all carry the vision of the world we want, and we embody it in a new way because we know from our experience that another world is possible—and we have the blueprint for it.

Six months after the rally in Flushing Meadows thirty people from the organizations that work together around the PCUN gather for a day of leadership training and *conocimiento* (telling our stories to each other). Nine Freedom Riders are there: Ramon, the president of PCUN, recently honored by the Ford Foundation as one of seventeen new leaders for a new world; Samuel, our leader on the bus, guiding the training; Oskar, graduating from high school and ready to begin working with the youth group Latinos Unidos Siempre (Latinos United Always); José, graduating with a credential as a high school teacher; Severo and Miria, honored elders in this community; Damaris, now chief contract negotiator for PCUN; Laura, newly named as director of the Farm Work Education Center in Woodburn; Jésus, just back from the United Farm Workers convention in La Paz, California, on fire with his new vision for his community; and I. Our paths have only crossed a few times since we returned, but each time we feel the joy of our connection, retroactively missing each other and the time and miles we shared on a bus carrying stories and dreams—and a working model of the world we are trying to build.

The following week, at the Annual Caucus of the Rural Organizing Project, five more riders are present, including Cara, one of the organizers of the caucus, Pedro, starting a new job teaching popular education techniques to workers and community groups in five states, and Guadalupe, the current chair of the statewide immigrant rights organization CAUSA. At the caucus I have displayed some of my photographs, The Face of Immigration: The Face of America. People from ten member organizations sign up to have the exhibit come to their rural communities over the next year. A teach-in about immigration is tentatively arranged for the fall at a local college. I agree to record this journal for a local public radio station. The union, PCUN, asks me to prepare a longer illustrated version of my Freedom Ride journal for publication. The ripples spread out from the Freedom Ride in our lives and the communities around us.

As I worked on the revisions for this article, I traveled back to Ground Zero in my dreams. In the dream I turn slowly in a circle and watch as, across the centuries, wave after wave of immigrants, people of different colors, speaking different languages, break across the five boroughs of the city. Their ghosts lurk in all buildings: those that they created with their labor, the factories where they worked, the buildings they cleaned, the cramped rooms and houses they lived in. The city is translucent under the weight of so many ghosts, and then they disappear, nothing remaining of the city that immigrants built. Waking from the dream, I burn white sage to invite my ancestors, whose cousins welcomed the first European immigrants, to strengthen me as I continue on this journey. The swirling smoke of the sage rises into the sky.

Notes

The Spanish poet Antonio Machado, writing during the Spanish civil war, coined the phrase "Se hace el camino al andar" (We make the road by walking). We simply added a new wrinkle.

1. The national organizing committee included the American Federation of Labor and Congress of Industrial Organizations (AFL-CIO), the Hotel Employees and Restaurant Employees (HERE), the United Food and Commercial Workers (UFCW), the Laborers' International Union of North America (LIUNA), the Service Employees' International Union (SEIU), the National Immigration Law Center, the National Immigration Forum, the National Council of La Raza, the National Interfaith Committee for Worker Justice, and Jobs with Justice. This is but a partial list.

A View from the Galilee

Rachel Tzvia Back

The writer, a poet and professor of literature, lives in a small Jewish village in the western Galilee. This village was built beside the ruins of Mi'ar, an Arab village evacuated in Israel's 1948 War of Independence and eventually destroyed. The people of Mi'ar now live in neighboring Arab villages.

. . . . .

During these few and precious spring days in the Galilee, when the air is still cool, the hills still green from the winter's water abundance and the wild flowers still gracing the paths and stones with color before summer's killing heat sets in, we hardly have time to take note of the natural beauty. For as much as this is the season of blossomings, spring in Israel—for Jew and Arab alike—is the season of remembering. Land Day, Holocaust Memorial Day, Israeli Soldiers' Memorial Day, and Nakba (Memorial Day of the 1948 Palestinian Catastrophe) follow each other in rapid succession, each marked by its own yearly rituals: demonstrations, sirens, sad songs on the radio, memorial candles, visits to graves, the telling of stories, the loss. Of course, the Jewish/Israeli memorial days are nationalized and hence are more public in nature, with radio and television stations devoted to commemorating the days and places of entertainment closed. The marking of the Arab/Palestinian memorial days by Palestinian communities in Israel are viewed, still, as acts of sedition and political agitation. To every Land Day or Nakba memorial gathering, police and army forces show up heavily armed, prepared for riot and violence—replays of the very thing being memorialized.

But it is not about memorial days that I want to write—the memorial days

Radical History Review
Issue 93 (Fall 2005): 217–19
Copyright 2005 by MARHO: The Radical Historians' Organization, Inc.

merely serve as my backdrop. It was in the midst of these days of remembering—
our losses, our national and personal tragedies—that in my village we all received
the following notice in our postboxes: "During the spring vacation, groups of Mi'ar
descendents and the Islamic Movement weeded, cleaned, and painted the graves on
the southwestern and southeastern side of [our village]. People who see the activity of strangers in the area are requested to inform the office at once." The notice
was embedded in the weekly information sheet put out by the secretariat of our
village—an information sheet that informs us of a wide variety of communal issues,
from water stoppages to changes in Internet service. The information sheet sat on
our kitchen counter on the pile of that day's post, unread, until my almost thirteen-
year-old son pointed out to me the above passage. "Isn't this strange," he remarked,
"these two sentences don't seem to fit together. . . ."

Indeed, the two sentences of the notice do not fit together. One could lose
oneself—lose one's sanity—in the chasm between them. The first sentence, describing an act of respect and honor toward one's deceased ancestors, establishes an
expectation on the part of the reader that praise for the deed will follow. Instead,
the description of the grave tending is followed by a directive to report such deeds
in the future. The implicit warning is that we, the Jews of this village, must be vigilant, must look out for any Arabs who wander this hillside. Above all else, what we
must stay alert to are our Arab neighbors' expressions of belonging to this land in
general, and to our hilltop specifically.

The message emanating from the gap between the two sentences in the
notice on our village news sheet was upsetting enough. But what truly enraged me
was the use of the word *stranger* in the second sentence. The descendents of Mi'ar
came to the graves of *their* fathers and mothers, on land that once belonged to *their*
fathers and mothers, at the edge of what was once the village of *their* fathers and
mothers, to weed and tend *their own* neglected cemetery. The descendents of Mi'ar
are not "the stranger in our midst" that the Bible commands us to care for and protect. They are not strangers on this disputed territory that we both claim as homeland, where they and their ancestors lived for hundreds of years before we returned.
They are native, they belong, the land intrinsic to their individual and communal
selves. Saying they are strangers does not make them so.

Neither are they strangers, as in foreign and unfamiliar, or strange, to us—
their Jewish neighbors—in their losses, their fears, and their desires for safety. We
share similar experiences, similar emotions: terror of the violence at our thresh-
old, uncertainty about the future, traumas that will not let us think or act clearly.
Indeed, I know that the notice from the office was driven by fear, our own Jewish
fear of dispossession, of belonging nowhere. And in that place of fear, we refuse to
see another's legitimate claims to a small gathering of graves on the hillside—we
cannot acknowledge their loss, and we dare not acknowledge our part in that loss,
our homes built beside their ruins.

I am a poet—I know the power of words. Most of all, I know the power of words masquerading as neutral and transparent while they manipulate the ways we view ourselves and each other. In an insidious fashion, the note from our office promotes continuing animosity to and alienation from the descendents of Mi'ar who are more sibling to us than stranger. The note from the office insists on denying the rights of the other. To the people of my village I want to say the following: our small part in the greater conflict of this region demands of us to recognize the people of Mi'ar as native, not stranger, to acknowledge their rights and—in this season of remembering—remember also their own lost lives and homes.

Angelic States—Event Sequence

Matias Viegener

Connie Samaras's project, *Angelic States–Event Sequence,* began in October 1998, after she, like hundreds of thousands, witnessed the dramatic first demonstration of the "Star Wars" Strategic Defense Initiative (SDI) technology, first proposed by Ronald Reagan in 1983. Launched from Vandenberg Air Force Base in Santa Barbara, California, a specially equipped Minuteman missile intercepted and destroyed a test enemy missile launched by the American military from the South Pacific. The test occurred over Southern California, one of the most densely populated and most media-savvy areas of the United States, during the prime-time news hour while millions were driving home on the freeways. Thousands of people rushed outside to watch the spiral clouds glowing in the early dusk, the wispy curls an upbeat echo of the space shuttle Challenger explosion in 1980, but now boding American success triumphing over technological failure. "The thing about American success," said Gertrude Stein, "is American failure." The destruction of the World Trade Center, just as the subsequent explosion of the space shuttle Columbia, replays this dynamic of failure and success. Either result recapitulates the ideological dialectic of American superiority versus American victimization and does so within a paradigm of technology and empire.

In "Minuteman Missile over the Skies of Los Angeles" (1998), the missile's traces glow with an eerie romantic resonance like the dusk in a nineteenth-century Caspar David Friedrich landscape. While hardly the willful intent of the military planners, it nevertheless evokes their cinematic savvy in launching at sunset. Since the first Gulf War, all the images of battle have become filtered through the military's media department, all the reporters approved by their security, and many

Radical History Review
Issue 93 (Fall 2005): 221–26

"Minuteman Missile over the Skies of Los Angeles," Connie Samaras (1998)

of the animations and diagrams created with the military's design assistance. This aestheticized display of power, first described by Walter Benjamin during the rise of fascism in Europe, spreads its blanket over the entire sky.

Perhaps the best illustration of the peculiarly American, ever-thinning membrane between real world and fiction is the ongoing consolidation of military and entertainment technologies. Police surveillance becomes incorporated into urban design to both generate the appearance of security and suggest the potential for dan-

"NY Financial District (World Trade Center), November 2001," Connie Samaras

ger; power is integrated into systems of pleasure as obvious as the highly controlled amusement park and as subtle as a lone security light in an empty parking lot. There is no simpler way to imply the potency of transcendence than through remote light cast on an earthly site, a device employed for hundreds of years in cathedrals and churches. The clouds or rays of light in Samaras's photographs often echo religious greeting cards. As perfected by their predecessors in religion, surveillance technologies similarly deploy a secreted display of power, an illumination from afar that variously implies God, entertainment, or the state security apparatus. Klieg lighting works differently, by flattening everything with equal intensity, eliminating the play of light and shadow. While the klieg lights first surrounded the World Trade Center site to assist rescue operations, they remained lit weeks after they were needed. The glow of bleeding lights transforms night into timeless day and is likewise a symbolic reassurance of the triumph of our technology over our enemy's.

Samaras's photograph of the World Trade Center site, just days after its destruction, echoes the oft-repeated observation on how cinematic the collapse was, from the "special effects" explosion to the sculptural ruins. While not asserting that the destruction was art directed, "NY Financial District (World Trade Center), November 2001" does interrogate the cinematic sheen it acquires, and perhaps so

"Los Angeles Homicide," Connie Samaras (2001)

only through the eyes of an audience accustomed to Hollywood's staged disasters. In this respect the image also provides a psychological inquiry, asking how we have come to make our determination of the real and to what degree the so-called reality effect is implanted in us through the workings of power. Less a consensus of popular belief, much less one of material causation, this reality is produced through spectacle.

Like "Los Angeles Homicide" (2001), all of these images express heightened moments of the manifestation of power. Roused by the noise of police helicopters around her neighborhood, Samaras photographed the helicopter's surveillance lights searching for gang members who had just shot a woman in a nearby park. The lights cluster in the sky like a staged aurora borealis or the lights of an alien spaceship. Whether or not they actually work better than police in cars and on foot, the helicopters' overbearing lights and noise remind criminals and residents alike of the power of police surveillance, shining inside bedroom windows with all the persistence of Jeremy Bentham's Panopticon, whose power Michel Foucault describes as one of consciousness. Since subjects know they are at all times observable, they begin to monitor themselves; this self-implantation of surveillance makes the job of surveilling much easier—reduces it, in fact, to an effect. The *Angelic States* project

"Homeland Security Alert, Level Orange: Sahara Hotel, Las Vegas," Connie Samaras (2003)

investigates the persistence of self-consciousness and the intrusion of the state apparatus into every private space.

In the last years of progress toward a full surveillance society, there has been a turn in the symbolic valences of light and dark and a subsequent recalibration in the social meaning of the visible and the invisible. With new technology and shrinking cameras, evidence of surveillance is actually declining, while the display of surveillance power (the prime example being airport security) swells and grows. Display is effective, and so is invisibility. We are asked to trust a government unbridled by the USA PATRIOT Act and find ourselves labeled unpatriotic when we protest. Truth and good once again partake of the realm of faith and its transcendent displays of power. These displays are what Samaras calls techno-landscaping, the integration of surveillance policing and military and entertainment technology to construct the public face of a U.S. homeland paradoxically both in terrible danger and inordinately protected. Traditionally, God is everywhere, as is the devil, but God is idolized in the temples—the heightened security apparatus of the twenty-first century lies in the dark, and as cameras become ever more invisible, the devil appears with a beard and a turban.

On the side of "Homeland Security Alert, Level Orange: Sahara Hotel, Las

Vegas" (2003), in the desolate parking structure of the Sahara, one can discern a bulky, near-obsolete video security camera, almost a nostalgic embellishment of an earlier form of surveillance. The blank, yellow, polychromatic facade of the hotel reveals nothing but vague traces of curtains and hotel-room furniture, all alike and all available. The predominance of yellow highlights the colorlessness and strange emptiness of the orange alert. Taken during a survey of foreign-themed casinos during alert days, the project interrogates the workings of a government that has found a catch-22: whether terrorism actually occurs or not, either proves the necessity of the security alert. If an attack occurs we were right, and if one does not, we probably prevented it. Doubt is not a public option as the paradigm of security success and failure has been so completely appropriated by the mechanisms of neoconservative ideology.

Many of the images in *Angelic States–Event Sequence* remain noticeably devoid of people, which emphasizes the psychological workings of modern surveillance landscapes. The outer void projects an inner landscape of threats and protections, a teeming paranoia of power, victimization, and redemption. Samaras herself recedes into the darkness, often shooting these photographs in disguise, dressed as an undercover cop outside the 1999 Democratic Convention, a tourist, or as an insurance security specialist in Las Vegas, walking through a Middle Eastern–themed casino during the high-security alert at the time of the Iraq war. Occupying both the place of evil and of power, her positioning works to subvert the slick engine of contemporary sociopolitical ideology. Samaras's earlier work has concerned itself with the visibility and invisibility of the lesbian in the world, as well as the persona play involved in both the hiding and revealing of her body in space. The political assuredness of this work is a consequence of careful planning and thought, but also derives from a long experience of social and political strife. Despite their anxiety over the overbearing security apparatus surrounding us, the images of this series cling to a will to witness. Without a romantic faith in the transcendence of individual resistance, the photographs continually interrogate sociopolitical constructions of power and the potential for new lines of perceptual escape.

Statement on Recent Drawings

Conor McGrady

The core of my practice focuses primarily on painting and drawing, with, at present, a particular emphasis on drawing. All of the work is based on firsthand experience and oral histories of encounters with violence, ideological conflict, or low-intensity war. Largely executed in gouache, ink, and compressed charcoal, the drawings use an economical or distilled line to explore the impact of military control on domestic and public space, and the latent residue of fear or disquiet that resides in seemingly innocuous buildings and spaces. In these drawings violence becomes a form of omission, referring to the removal or containment of unwanted or subversive populations or individuals.

In the drawings I work almost exclusively from memory in an attempt to strip out all extraneous details and depict the residue or imprint of public and domestic spaces subject to every form of military control. The empty buildings and housing schemes in the drawings are not only subject to physical control by the military in the north of Ireland (where I am originally from) but in most cases were designed and planned with the help of military technicians to ensure containment of an insurgent population. In this situation the concept of private space does not exist, and these buildings and housing areas are subject to repeated military invasion, search procedures, and constant surveillance.

In the most recent work I have expanded the scale in order to investigate the impact of the drawings on physical space. Some of these drawings have been directly influenced by working for five months in Lower Manhattan through the Lower Manhattan Cultural Council's residency program in the Woolworth building. Here, issues of domestic control and security in the United States have fed into the

Radical History Review
Issue 93 (Fall 2005): 227–29
Copyright 2005 by MARHO: The Radical Historians' Organization, Inc.

"Enclave," Conor McGrady (2003). Gouache on paper

"Zone," Conor McGrady (2003). Gouache on paper

new work, in particular the impact of security zones on restriction of movement and access to so-called sensitive buildings. In these drawings architectural modifications to buildings and the sealing-off of streets in New York, dually aimed at protection and exclusion, take on the characteristics of similar structures in the north of Ireland and other police states, where attack from within the body politic is expected at any moment.

The aim of all the drawings is to raise questions relating to the control of space, to boundaries, and to ideas of how architecture is used as a divide to enforce social order.

Homeland Security, Surveillance, and the War in Iraq: An Interview with Christian Parenti

Lawrence Jones

The following telephone interview took place on January 29, 2004. Christian Parenti is an activist and intellectual who holds a PhD in sociology from the London School of Economics. He was recently Soros Senior Justice Fellow at the Open Society Institute and is currently a Ford Foundation Fellow at the Center for the Study of Place, Culture, and Politics, at the City University of New York Graduate Center. He has published *Lockdown America: Police and Prisons in the Age of Crisis* (2000), *The Soft Cage: Surveillance in America from Slavery to the War on Terror* (2003), and *The Freedom: Shadows and Hallucinations in Occupied Iraq* (2004). He has also been a regular contributor to several newspapers including the *Christian Science Monitor*, the *San Diego Union Tribune*, and the *San Francisco Chronicle*, among others. Most recently, he has reported from occupied Iraq for the *Nation*, and he has appeared on PBS's *NewsHour with Jim Lehrer* to discuss the current situation in Iraq. His other war reporting, in 1991–92, has included traveling with a guerilla unit in El Salvador in an FMLN [Farabundo Marti National Liberation Front]–controlled zone near the Honduran border. In the summer of 2003, Parenti was a fellow of the University of Minnesota Humanities Institute's working group, "Summer Institute: Policy and Ideas, a Think Tank for Social Change," where he and the interviewer met.

Radical History Review
Issue 93 (Fall 2005): 231–39
Copyright 2005 by MARHO: The Radical Historians' Organization, Inc.

231

Lawrence Jones: *Christian, as someone who has written extensively about the rise of the prison industry, its attendant incarcerating culture, as well as on the uses of surveillance throughout U.S. history, I'm wondering if you will talk about the extent to which the new security regime [instituted under the rhetoric of homeland security] represents a qualitative shift in kind, as opposed to a quantitative intensification of what existed previously?*

Christian Parenti: That's a very good question. I don't think there was a qualitative shift; it was merely a quantitative shift. Repression has always been very, very important, very central to capitalism and to American politics, particularly as regards managing race, class, and gender. Just look at our history of slavery, the Black Codes after Reconstruction, and lynching. The policing of the U.S.-Mexico border, for example, escalated into a small war, right around the time of World War I. Something like sixty American soldiers were killed, as were hundreds of Chicano and Mexican people.

So-called wayward young women were also subjected to extensive policing and even state violence during the Industrial Revolution. Single young women were deemed immoral and jailed with incredible ease up until at least the Progressive Era.

In your book, The Soft Cage, *it seems to me that one element of the quantitative intensification is the changing forms of technology that allow for ever-increasing and more effective forms of social control through surveillance. Take, for example, I-CLEAR (the Illinois Citizen Law Enforcement Analysis and Reporting System), a database that links 1,200 police agency data files in a comprehensive and searchable format. Can you comment on the genealogy of such efforts of mass surveillance, the uses these technologies have for homeland security, and the dangers they may pose for civil liberties and privacy?*

Well, in response to your previous question, I don't think there's a qualitative shift in the use of political surveillance, policing, and prisons, but I do think there's been a qualitative shift in the nature of routine surveillance that is brought about by electronic computing. This is what I argue in *The Soft Cage,* as others have argued elsewhere. Digital computing leads to such a large increase in the quantity of information that can be processed that there is in effect a political transformation of a qualitative sort, in that once meaningless information can now be digested in politically useful ways.

The origins of the database you describe could go back pretty far; it depends where you choose to start. In *The Soft Cage,* I take things back to slavery and the basic record keeping and identification that was essential to social control under the slave system. The first thing you need for a database of this sort is a unique personal identifier. An individual in a database needs to be identifiable in a way that separates him or her from all others in the database. Well, how does that start under slavery? It starts very informally: in documents such as the slave pass and manumission papers and wanted posters. From these documents come more formalized types of identification. Around the same time that these types of documentation are developing, we have the early formalization of passports, and also military passes. All of these make an attempt to fix the identity of the bearer of the pass usually through some biometric method, a rudimentary biometric method, that is to say, a description of their bodies. In a way, that's the earliest origins of these dossiers, within the ledgers of the plantation owners who noted the identities and behaviors of their slaves.

More specifically, you have the rise of formal record keeping by police officials with the advent of photography. The shift from a ledger-based type of dossier to more modern files comes into effect around the time modern policing really begins, uniformed policing, around the 1850s. Photography is essential in this transformation. Though the process takes place slowly, police move from ledgers, a fundamentally irrational way of keeping track of individuals, to modern files, where photographs are used to identify people, despite the use of aliases.

This led to the need to index these files, which at this point was accomplished with the rise of Bertillonage, developed in Paris by Alphonse Bertillon. He was put in charge of a police prefecture in Paris, and his father was a famous demographer and anthropologist who was using calipers to "scientifically" measure and define racial types. Young Bertillon used this same set of tools to measure individual bodies and create a systematized procedure of bodily measurements that could be used to numerically index police files. It was a way of fixing the identity to the photographs, regardless of the use of aliases or other means of subverting identification. The system was very complicated and began to break down due to a laxity in the use of standardization required for its effective application. So added to it is dactyloscopy, as they called it, or fingerprinting.

Though fingerprinting has earlier origins, by World War I [police and their states recognized] that fingerprinting was a superior form of identification, and that fingerprints were a unique identifier. This realization spreads quickly around the world, and a couple different systems for identifying fingerprints are developed. Then you have a push for creating national identification numbers of which Social Security is the first de facto one. The FBI pushed for the use of Social Security as a criminal justice national identification number. . . .

Really? What year was this?

From the end of the 1920s until the beginning of the 1960s the FBI pushed for a national ID. They were always defeated, legislatively, but in the early 1960s, the banking industry simply decided that it would de facto institute the Social Security number as a national identification number in that they would refuse services to individuals who would not give their number. They wrote about this quite openly. Of course, people were free to not give the number; just as they were (and are) free to not receive the services of a bank. As a result of this, the Social Security number's function begins to change. What is called function creep sets in, so this number for connecting and managing benefits, connecting individuals to benefits, suddenly becomes a national identification number.

At the same time, the Social Security number is legalized for use as a taxpayer identification number. In any case, this is all very technical and boring at a certain level, but the main point is not so much in this or that transformation in law or technology, but is rather the relationship between macrostructures of power and these capillary forms of power, to borrow from [Michel] Foucault. In this way, large institutions like banks are dependant on small technologies like Social Security numbers, the two levels of social phenomena developing in tandem.

Then we can talk about the war on drugs, coming out of the 1960s, and the creation of the LEAA, the Law Enforcement Assistance Administration, which gave massive impetus towards creating large computer databases. The first one, the NCIC, the National Crime Information Center, controlled by the FBI in Washington, DC, was set up in the late 1960s and lists all missing persons, wanted persons, stolen automobiles, firearms used in crimes. The NCIC served as a sort of federal model, but similar systems are set up at the state level, due to the efforts of the LEAA (first created in 1967 and coming into effect in 1968), a huge federal program designed to modernize American policing. One of the things the LEAA does is that it mandates the creation of state criminal justice planning agencies. So, for states to be eligible to receive federal funding, they have to have an agency of their own that is planning the transformation of policing; that also means spending state money as well. As part of these efforts, the states begin setting up statewide databases and begin advocating for the aggregation of what had heretofore been local collections of dossiers.

This is the origin of the current moment. In the 1980s and 1990s, there is a decline in the price of software and computers, a continued rightward movement in the politics surrounding issues of privacy, and more and more names and data items being added to these databases as the police are free to buy the mailing lists, etcetera, of the private sector. This is followed by intrastate agency database linking, then by interstate linkups creating regional networks of interlinked criminal databases. Prominent among these efforts are gang databases. One of the first and most sophisticated was Cal Gang, and the software developed for that program is now used all over the country. Cal Gang is interesting because it can either search for a name or a Social Security number, or for an alias, or for verbal descriptions of people. It can also search for images, or, rather, descriptions of images. And these different fields can be used in combination, so police can search for men named Joe who also have dragon tattoos on their arms, or whatever.

From all these multiple variables, they can get down to a couple possible identities with criminal dossiers. This system came online in the mid-1990s and has spread throughout the country, and we now see all the interagency linking I've mentioned. There are several regional gang databases at this point, and they're applying this same technology to dissidents and terrorists. In some of the more sophisticated versions, officers can actually search for digitalized images, though that is more difficult than one might think.

Whenever the topic of government surveillance is discussed, it is often assumed that the focus of these efforts is criminality or national security. And yet, as you have suggested, with the Social Security number's transition from benefits identifier toward national citizen identification number, systems of everyday surveillance have just as often emerged from seemingly more benevolent impulses, such as the social assistance infrastructure and social work. So it seems that the types of social control that might concern us aren't always going to look insidious at first glance.

A lot of routine surveillance is born from the helping professions, in particular social work, as you mentioned. At the turn of the last century, the early 1900s, some of the most detailed and extensive dossiers kept on people, and some of the most aggressive networking and sharing of files was done not by the state but by private institutions and social workers employed by them. Particularly, this was done by the scientific charity movement that sought to root out poverty by changing the behavior of the poor. They thought they could change the behavior of the poor by holding the poor accountable, which they attempted to enforce by close observation and record keeping, as well as by pressuring the poor to stop so-called destructive behaviors, which presumably made them poor, rather than the fact that the work was so badly compensated, or nonexistent. The scientific charity movement and its benevolent associations that gave alms to the deserving poor would share files quite aggressively. They inventoried the poor's possessions and wrote up life histories, and they would share this information with police, hospitals, and other social workers.

That's one example of how the helping professions have added to routine surveillance, but this should not be understood as always intentional. The Social Security number is a perfect example. Social Security is clearly a progressive innovation, yet the function of the number gets transformed by politics later on, thus function creep. This sets in with all these technologies. Take credit cards, for example: they're incredibly useful and incredibly convenient, but they also create electronic records of our locations in time and space. That information is then considered property that can be bought and sold by a variety of parties, and ends up in the hands of marketers, private investigators, the government, etcetera. There again you have function creep. The credit card was not introduced as a tag to track you with, or a method for analyzing your consumption patterns, but that's one of its primary functions now, an unintended consequence of these technologies.

Of course, the cell phone now is seemingly an even more effective tag, even to the point where individuals living in the West Bank, as you mention in your book, are being targeted and fired upon, actually based on the precise location of where their cell phone is being operated.

Yes, all of the latest wireless communication devices have GPS [Global Positioning System] chips in them that transmit their location to satellites quite regularly.

Leaving the United States for the moment, I'm hoping you could talk a bit about surveillance in Europe, in particular in the homeland of Bentham and his Panopticon. You mention in The Soft Cage *that the United Kingdom has set up around 1 million closed-circuit television cameras (CCTV). What were the rhetorical arguments marshaled to set this system up? Was there opposition to this development, or was it widely accepted by an ever-accommodating public?*

I am not an expert on this history of CCTV in England, but my understanding is it was very similar to the discourse we now find ourselves subject to here in America, the threat of terrorism. The resumption of the IRA's [Irish Republican Army] mainland bombing campaign, in the early to mid-1990s, that led to the rapid proliferation of closed-circuit television cameras. In that context, there was really not much of a debate at all. People were primed to hate the IRA; the IRA set off bombs in the city of London. One went off near LSE [London School of Economics and Political Science] when I was going to school there at the time, and people got very angry, so cameras, some of which were already up, proliferated rapidly and there wasn't much discussion about it. Also, a lot of these cameras are private initiatives; private institutions like a bank or school put up cameras outside their doors, but the police, of course, can get access to these tapes when they need them. What debate there was was often very technocratic, in part because although criminology in Britain has a very long tradition, it still has a heavily administrative element to its criminological studies. There was discussion, there was critique, but it remained largely academic, to the best of my knowledge.

Turning to popular culture, in recent years we've seen an explosion in voyeuristic/ exhibitionistic entertainment. I'm thinking about everything from nightclubs that feature controllable closed-circuit television camera systems for patrons to spy on other patrons, to nonactor television programs designed to give a glimpse of other people's reality, such as Cops *and* Cheaters *in the non- or semistaged variety, and* Survivor *and* Big Brother *in the game-show genre. What do you make of this seemingly visual turn in popular culture? Does this operate as anesthetic from the presence of the camera, does it make us more aware of surveillance possibilities, or is something else going on with this movement?*

I think that the proliferation of surveillance themes within entertainment habituates people to the gaze of authorities and that fame culture is very important to this habituation. The problem for many young people today is not *being* on camera, it is *not being* on it. There is a homemade fame culture on the Web, around Webcam communities, people who broadcast their lives, which all began with Jennicam in 1997, I believe. [The project actually began in 1996.] This was some young woman who put a Web camera in her college dorm room and never turned it off, so mostly it was just her on the phone, but occasionally she would take her clothes off, get into bed, and go to sleep. Voyeurs could wait for those moments of nudity, or whatever, and now there are whole communities of people who watch themselves, and watch each other, and it's a system of surveillance and narcissism.

Of course, there's nothing wrong with the surveillance in and of itself; it's not as if there are big secrets being broadcast over these Webcams. Friendster is another example of this culture; people essentially create dossiers of themselves and share them with other people. There doesn't need to be anything particularly interesting in these dossiers. But one might raise the question of how this may habituate us all to constant observation and monitoring. I think that this aestheticization of surveillance—surveillance-based entertainment—is as important to the legitimation of routine surveillance as are the arguments of state and corporate authorities which pander to our fears, making a direct assault on privacy, saying, "You must be protected from X, Y, or Z threat." The disenchantment of privacy, through entertainment and trivialization, is very important.

At the end of Lockdown America, *you hold out some hope that the dismal situation in this country's prisons, and the country's incarcerating culture, may be improved, and you cite the tireless work of activists, both on the inside and out, as your basis for this guarded optimism. What is the role of activists and engaged intellectuals in countering the surveillance regime being constructed under the aegis of homeland security?*

There is something of a movement [against the surveillance regime], and I actually don't pay as much attention to it in *The Soft Cage* as I should. There are organizations like EPIC [Electronic Privacy Information Center] out there that are lobbying, but there's no mass movement around privacy. There are specialized nonprofit liberal activists that are trying to problematize this issue. There's something so abstract about surveillance that it's hard to really get upset about it, certainly not the same way people got upset about prisons and policing. There is something so visceral about people being thrown in prison. Everybody being watched, well so what? Your behavior will not necessarily be impacted. The larger psychology and politics of society may be potentially impacted, but for most people that's fairly abstract.

Many people may think that as long as they are not doing anything wrong, it shouldn't matter for them.

Yeah, that's a key assumption, you're right, they often figure, "I have nothing to hide, so why should I care about privacy?" The fact of the matter is that, if viewed solely from the standpoint of the individual, that actually is a sound logic. If you're going to obey every law, and be totally obedient, then the authorities will probably not give you any trouble. If you view it more from a socially or politically oriented standpoint, then that's highly problematic; you have to ask what kind of society would we have if there was never any disobedience, and it would be a pretty grim picture. Most of what is considered social progress in the United States, from undoing Jim Crow segregation, getting women the right to vote, to ending child labor, involved people breaking the law, breaking rules, and disobeying. A culture where people are habituated to obedience, because they're habituated to surveillance, in a way precludes radical social change.

Since the Bush administration instituted a new homeland security/national security doctrine of preemptive strike, waged a war against Iraq, and occupied that country, you've had a couple of opportunities to visit U.S.-occupied-Iraq. Would you say a bit about the use of surveillance and other techniques of control being used in Iraq today, by U.S. forces, and then discuss the situation in Iraq more generally?

Well, essentially, there is a war still going on, and U.S. forces use aerial drones to watch the desert around military bases, a lot of forward-looking infrared to see at night, and all of this is done so as to increase security around bases, to prevent mortar fire and other attacks. They also engage in mass detention of people. There are thirteen thousand people currently held in Abu Ghraib prison, being interrogated and observed. However, to be perfectly honest, the situation in Iraq is rather chaotic. There isn't the kind of intense social control by the American authorities over the general population that they would like, or as exists here. Under Saddam, [the primary means of surveillance] was a Stasi-style low-tech system of snitching. Everybody was snitching on each other. That, of course, is less about the information collected and more about being obedient and maintaining social positioning. But that culture of snitching still exists. The Americans are picking it up and are using the cultural operating system left behind by Saddam to their own ends, and that's been very, very helpful in their fight against the resistance, in counterinsurgency efforts. I've interviewed members of the resistance, and have embedded with U.S. soldiers, and found that it's not so much surveillance but rather the culture of snitching that is really key in controlling Iraq.

It seems that this is ultimately what may have undermined Saddam, with a member of his family, so we are told, revealing information to the U.S. authorities that led to his capture.

Yes, you're right, that's a case in point. This snitch culture is also something that keeps the resistance from being able to unite, because they're so afraid that uniting their cells and coordinating their networks will be undermined by snitching. But people should not romanticize the resistance at all. It is by and large a pretty thuggish and religiously bigoted group.

One final question: What elements of the new surveillance regime, or even more broadly, homeland security apparatus, makes you most nervous for the future prospects of a progressive and democratic United States?

I guess the answer to that can be both technological and political. Politically, what bothers me most is the lack of political concern over this issue, and the way in which many people know about surveillance but lack the interest or will to do much about it. Like many other social problems of this kind, people really seem to not care. Which is not to say that they don't know; some don't, but many do know. They know what the war in Iraq is about, they know about the government's tremendous police power, they know that the government doesn't often respect the boundaries that it is supposed to be following, but they just figure, nothing is happening to me right now. I find that apathy most disturbing.

On the technological side, I guess it would be the proliferation of really cheap computing, but here's the contradiction, because there's usually some utility delivered by the device that can also be a tool of surveillance. It's not a Luddite kind of argument, which laments the arrival of new technology, but a more specific critique of the way in which surveillance potentials of new technologies are not addressed directly. There is no substantial legislative effort to intervene and limit that side of the surveillance society. So, there's a contradiction with the technology; it's useful, but there must be legislative protections put in place against abuse.

Academics and the Government in the New American Century: An Interview with Rashid Khalidi

Lori A. Allen, Lara Z. Deeb, and Jessica Winegar

While this article was going to press, versions of David Horowitz's Academic Bill of Rights were introduced in thirteen state legislatures and the U.S. Congress. The issue of academic freedom at Columbia University made national headlines and caught the attention of lawmakers, with most New York papers (including the New York Times) *and local lawmakers siding with the pro-Zionist critics of a Middle East studies professor who, despite abundant evidence to the contrary, was accused of anti-Semitism and intimidation of students in the classroom. Meanwhile, Rashid Khalidi was summarily dismissed from the New York City Department of Education's K–12 teaching development program, without any evidence of formal complaints against him and without any consultation with him or with Columbia University. For more information on these developments, see the special issue of the* Nation *on academic freedom, "Silencing Speech on Campus," April 4, 2005.*

Two years after 9/11, just as it seemed that pressure to refrain from criticizing U.S. foreign policy was beginning to wane, a series of events began to worry scholars. A subpoena was issued to Drake University in Des Moines, Iowa, to release records related to an antiwar event on campus. Republicans introduced a bill in the Colorado legislature that would require public universities to protect students

Radical History Review

Issue 93 (Fall 2005): 240–59

Copyright 2005 by MARHO: The Radical Historians' Organization, Inc.

from liberal political bias in the classroom. Several other states began to consider similar legislation based on conservative writer David Horowitz's "Academic Bill of Rights."[1]

But the most controversial scheme was the passage of HR 3077 in the U.S. House of Representatives, legislation that would amend the renewal of area studies funding by adding a government-appointed advisory board to oversee university centers that receive funding under the Title VI Higher Education Act. The goal, according to the legislation, was to ensure that area studies programs "reflect the national needs related to the homeland security, international education, and international affairs."[2] For the first time in nearly fifty years, academics found themselves faced with the prospect of direct government intervention into the content, shape, and direction of scholarship and teaching. Even those who were once content to hide out in the infamous ivory towers could do so no more. The relationship between academy and government—and scholarship and politics more generally—entered a transformative stage with an uncertain future. What was sure, however, was that scholarship threatened the neoconservative vision of the so-called New American Century. Indeed, the intensity of conservative attacks demonstrates that academics—despite claims to the contrary—possess real power to effect change in American politics and society.

Although the neoconservative assault was of broad significance, affecting a wide range of academics and intellectuals, many scholars of the Middle East experienced its effects most directly due to the region's significance to the United States' post–Cold War foreign policy agenda. At the end of his life, Edward Said had emerged as a favorite target of an ascendant group of Middle East strategists because of his scholarship and his criticisms of American and Israeli actions in the Arab world. Said's book *Orientalism* offered a devastating critique of the collusion between scholarship and political power—a collusion that neoconservatives openly advocated some twenty-five years later.[3] The same kind of virulent attacks as those directed against Said have been leveled at the historian Rashid Khalidi, whose professorship in Arab studies at Columbia University bears the late scholar's name. Khalidi also serves as the director of Columbia's Middle East Institute, which receives Title VI funding and has been accused of promoting anti-American views. Khalidi has written a new book in a style suitable for a broad audience, *Resurrecting Empire: Western Footprints and America's Perilous Path in the Middle East* (2004), in part to challenge the neoconservatives' assault on Middle East studies and their vision of the future.[4] It represents a significant challenge to the neoconservative viewpoint on the Middle East in public arenas. Khalidi imparts to U.S. readers his academic expertise regarding the modern history of Western imperialism in the Middle East, as well as its implications for America's new occupation of Iraq. He also offers readers evidence of the strong anti-imperial tradition in American culture. As a respected historian, program director, and scholar committed to public intellectualism—and as a prime target of the neoconservatives—Khalidi is in a unique position to shed light on the increasingly vexed relationship between the academy and the government in post–Cold War, post-9/11 America.

We decided to interview Professor Khalidi in New York in February 2004 to gain some insight into the situation in which we—junior scholars of the Middle East—suddenly found ourselves. While watching the troubling assaults on academic freedom unfold, we have become increasingly anxious about the future of research and teaching. Conversations with concerned colleagues in a variety of disciplines have revealed fears that our generation will fall victim to the surveillance and maligning of those academics who do not tow the line of whatever party is in power. As Khalidi suggests in the interview, the proposed changes to Title VI legislation mark just the beginning of what promises to be a long struggle in the fight for freedom from government control. But he also argues that a space exists for intellectual dissent.

HR 3077, Middle East Studies, and the Neoconservative Agenda

The bill HR 3077 was passed by the House Subcommittee on Education and the Workforce in September 2003. The bill, although a renewal of Title VI legislation dating back to the 1965 Higher Education Act, contained some significant revisions. The most important of these amendments was the creation of a new International Higher Education Advisory Board composed of seven members. Four of these would be appointed by Congress, three by the secretary of education. At least two members would represent elements of the U.S. government concerned with national security. This board would have the power to "monitor, apprise and evaluate a sample of activities supported under [Title VI] in order to provide recommendations to the Secretary [of Education] and the Congress for the improvement of programs under the title and to ensure programs meet the purposes of the title." Improvement was defined as making the programs "better reflect the national needs"—homeland security primary among them.[5] The board would also be mandated to make recommendations to recipient programs on how to encourage their students to serve the nation, including in the area of national security. Academics expressed concern about a requirement to allow government recruiters access to students and student recruiting information. But it was the advisory board itself that had academics deeply concerned.

Scholars of the Middle East could have seen such a move coming. After 9/11, a group of Middle East think tank "specialists," whose ideas about the region fit the ascendant neoconservative agenda, gained the attention of the Bush administration and the media. They began a concerted series of attacks on Middle East studies in the academy. One of the most infamous cases has been the Campus Watch Web site established by Daniel Pipes. Pipes, a Bush appointee to the U.S. Institute for Peace, founded the think tank Middle East Forum, whose mission is to "define and promote American interests" in the Middle East. The Web site invited college students to monitor their professors and report anything anti-Israel or anti-American.[6] Campus Watch created "dossiers" on eight scholars, but then removed them after facing a storm of criticism from academics who countered that classroom discussion of critical views about the Middle East made them neither apologists for terrorism nor unpatriotic. However, in 2004 the Web site continued to monitor professors' activities and report on various university departments and programs.

Middle East scholars have also come under attack in a book written by Martin Kramer, another conservative think tank member and the editor of *Middle East Quarterly*, a journal published by Pipes's Middle East Forum. Kramer's book, *Ivory Towers on Sand: The Failure of Middle East Studies in America*, published by the hawkish pro-Israel Washington Institute for Near East Policy just after 9/11, gained some notoriety as a result of often favorable reviews published in newspapers like the *New York Times* and the *Washington Post*.[7] The book also led to a spate of articles in more conservative publications that were similarly critical of Middle East studies. *Ivory Towers* argues that the field is a bastion of Edward Said acolytes who engage in fuzzy, fashionable theory mongering spurred by anti-Americanism and a radical political agenda. For these reasons and others, Kramer writes, academics have "failed to predict or explain the major evolutions of Middle Eastern politics and society over the past two decades."[8]

Despite the fact that neither academics nor policy makers predicted much that has come to pass in recent years, it was not only conservative columnists who picked up Kramer's criticisms of Middle East studies. Stanley Kurtz, the *National Review* editor and Hoover Institution fellow who testified before Congress in June 2003 about the "failures" of Title VI centers, also used them. His testimony included accusations that postcolonial theory was both anti-American and hegemonic in area studies. This hearing proved instrumental in prompting the House to write the disturbing revisions to the legislation.

Given that people like Kurtz, Kramer, and Pipes had been attacking Middle East studies in many prominent media outlets for two years, why were Middle East studies scholars not ready for the hearings on Capitol Hill? We began our interview by posing that question to Rashid Khalidi.

Rashid Khalidi: People claim that they weren't even given that chance [to discuss it]. No, not only were the academics caught on the wrong foot as it were, but I think also some people in the House who might have said something might have been a little surprised by the speed with which it was rushed through. On the other hand, it may be that people felt that discretion was the better part of valor, and that there's no capital in standing up and talking about an issue on which you may be on the wrong side of the supporters of Israel, in a situation where nobody had spoken up against the bill. Had a proper presentation of the utter falsehood of all the allegations that are being made been prepared and placed before enough members of the House, they might have seen this for the kind of partisan piece of chicanery that it really is.

Lori A. Allen, Lara Z. Deeb, and Jessica Winegar: *Do you think that the general academic view that people like Kramer, Pipes, and Kurtz are scholarly lightweights played any role in academics' lackadaisical attitude towards the legislation?*

I think it should be said that underestimating the new conservativism has now proven to be one of the stupidest things people could possibly do. People underestimate the president, they underestimate the people around the president, and they underestimate the whole radical revolutionary thrust of the core forces of this administration. This is something that is, to my way of thinking, a terrible, terrible strategic mistake: underestimating these people. They are trying to reshape American foreign policy. Some people are stuck in an analysis that says, "The United States through globalization is trying to dominate the world anyway. What's different about this?" Well, these are people who can't see the forest for the trees. They can't see that whatever forms of domination the United States exercised—whether in the Cold War or post–Cold War era, whether through globalization or otherwise—have very little to do with this new doctrine that this administration is putting forward. This is something different. There's a qualitative difference.

Why?

Well, the argument is that because of what happened in the United States, the United States is entitled to limit other countries' sovereignty. The United States acted in ways which limited other countries' sovereignty in the past, but it never really publicly and formally claimed that its security required that it make everybody else, if necessary, insecure. It never formally stated that nobody has sovereignty in the world but the United States. It never formally stated that the United States will not be bound by international law, will not be bound by multilateral institutions, which the United States created. The post–World War II structure is an American structure. Yes, it was created by many, many powers, but at its core, it is an American-determined structure. This administration is saying, "Ok, that era was then, this era is now. We do not need these things." And the president is saying, "We don't need a permission slip from anyone." That basically means, "We will not be bound by anything—morality, law, multilateral engagements, and this whole structure of international affairs as it has been created over the past sixty years."

Would you say that the terms of political legitimation are changing?

It's not just the terms of political legitimation. What this administration feels itself able to do in the world is different than what previous administrations have felt. Some people say it's only declaratory. But the war in Iraq showed that it's much more than a declaratory shift. That's my analysis. It's something that has to be worked out more, I think. But incidentally, I think that a lot of people should look very carefully at what the Bush administration says. It bears careful scrutiny. It bears careful textual analysis. And their actions should then be put in the context of their words, and the words of the Max Boots and the Admiral [James] Woolseys and the Richard Perles who swarm around them like a flock of gnats and whose ideas are the fertilizer for this evil, evil plant that's growing in Washington.

I've had arguments with people who say that intellectuals aren't important in this, and that the neocons are just window dressing for the sort of muscular nationalist military industrial complex types like [Dick] Cheney and [Donald] Rumsfeld. I actually don't think that's true. I think that as far as the president, the vice president, and the secretary of defense are concerned, these ideas are actually important.

Perhaps people did underestimate Pipes and Kramer. If so, they made a mistake. Because Pipes and Kramer are not operating on the level of their scholarship. They're operating on a different level. They're operating on a level of public discourse. They're operating on a level of a kind of slimy attack politics, which actually has become a very important part of the right-wing arsenal in the United States. Lee Atwater, back in the days of Ronald Reagan and George Bush Sr., pioneered some of these tactics of having absolutely no respect for the truth, taking things entirely out of context. Remember [Michael] Dukakis in the tank. You remember Willie Horton. That was Lee Atwater. He was a political genius. What kind of moral human being he was isn't the issue here. He was a political genius. Those techniques, those tactics, have been perfected by people like Karl Rove.

And this is where this should be situated. This has nothing to do with academia. This has nothing to do with truth, or what this guy published, or whether this guy got tenure. What's really important is that this is part of a broader tradition in American politics. It used to be a gutter tradition. It has been brought by the Republican Party in the eighties into the center. You know, [Richard] Nixon used it, [Joseph] McCarthy used it, other people used it, but it was discredited in some ways. It was perceived as shameful in some ways. It is now the machine of politics, especially as used by the Republicans. But everybody does it. [Bill] Clinton's people did it shamelessly as well. And that's what these people are doing. All you have to do is read their Web sites and compare the incredible bowdlerization of everything, or read Kurtz's testimony. You know, the reality bears no relationship *whatsoever* to the lies and falsehoods that they're putting out. That doesn't matter to them. This isn't about reality or scholarship. This is about politics. These are people going for the jugular. These are people who want to destroy things. These are people who want to win. And that's what we have to understand.

If academics stay back in their ivory tower, well, then they're going to be swept away by a political tide. They can babble on to their hearts' content after academia has been turned into some kind of ghastly right-wing vision. It's not these people [Kramer, Pipes, and the like] who are the guardians of this vision. It's Karl Rove, and the Christian Right, and the neoconservative right wing that really is behind this. The Middle East and the specific concerns of these people [Kramer, Pipes, and the like] have an important role. But this is bigger than that.

Are you suggesting that fire be fought with fire?

No, I don't think fire can be fought with fire for two reasons. First, we're never going to be as good at the kind of mudslinging and the kind of deceitfulness that these people are masters of. There's just no way that we can get so far down in the gutter as them successfully. Now that's not a very moral argument that I'm making, but it's an important point. You're not going to beat them at their game. The second thing is: if any of us have any authority, and I'm not talking about political operatives in the Democratic Party or people who are operating as political activists—they can do whatever they want, I'm not talking about them, I'm speaking now as an academic. If we have any authority, it has to do with *not* doing these kinds of things, but rather doing what we do, which is trying to figure out what's going on in the world, and using that information to explain things. Ultimately it has to do with some connection to truth. So that's the only role we can play. We can provide truthful material to people who are in politics, but it's a political game, and it has to be fought politically in some measure. We can't fight it directly. But we can help the people who are fighting it, by giving them stuff that's truthful.

Most of what's said about Title VI is a tissue of lies. It is claimed that the centers do not produce people who work for the government. There is not a center in this country that hasn't produced scores, if not hundreds of people, who work for the government. I come upon my own students who work for the government everywhere I go. It's a falsehood. It's a monstrous, enormous, colossal, deceitful falsehood. I mean, what can one say? You cannot fight this by saying something false about them, or false about the neocons. The only way to fight it is by producing lists. It may not work when the Senate finally considers this. It may or may not have impact. If we plunk on the table five pieces of data—chunks a hundred pages each—showing that this allegation is false, that allegation is false, it may have no impact. The political game may go somewhere else. That's another issue. But I think that's the only way that we can respond to this.

. . . . . .

Responses to the proposed advisory board had begun by fall 2003, first in the form of alarmed e-mails, then as petitions and phone calls to Congresspeople, and finally as an action alert put out by the Task Force on Middle East Anthropology.[9] Given the clear links between the changes to Title VI funding, the neoconservative agenda in the Middle East, and those critical of that agenda, it seemed apropos that scholars of the Middle East were among the first to react with concern. Articles on all sides of the issue were most often written with Middle East studies in mind.[10] We asked Khalidi whether he thought that Middle East scholars should be more concerned about the legislation than others.

Rashid Khalidi: No, I don't [think so]. Even though the attack is being motivated by people who have a particular Middle East ax to grind, ultimately, what it's aimed at is expertise of any sort. The neocons cannot hoodwink the American public if there are people out there who are capable of distinguishing between ideology and reality. And the targets of this are not just the people in the academy. The people in our government who are experts are also targets of the neocons. They are under attack. People within the intelligence community, within the uniformed military and within the State Department, are in fact even more important targets of a larger campaign of which this is only a part. And I know that many people in the academy shudder at the thought that in any way they and the CIA are on the same page. But, in fact, they are, whether they like it or not, in the sense that any form of advice from the real world, any form of grainy, detailed reporting of reality contradicts the faith-based approach that these people are dedicated to. They are operating in a world of illusion, created by this vision of culture, the [Samuel] Huntington vision of cultures and civilizations, which has no relation to reality.[11] And the only way they can sell this vision—whether it's of the Middle East specifically or the world more generally—is to rigorously fight any form of expertise. They have blocked off all the channels for advice getting up to the top in this administration. And there's a praetorian guard that keeps—I'm not saying truth, I'm just saying *fact*—from getting to the top.

We see it with weapons of mass destruction, because it's a scandal. That's true in every respect—everywhere within the government. Now I'm not saying that policy making is going to be good just because facts reach the top. That's a completely different issue. What I am saying is that I think that what is being attempted here is to install a political censorship over the academy such that certain unfiltered views about reality cannot be expressed without a cost being paid. And the same thing is being done within the government.

So you see the amendment to Title VI as part of a broader movement, also exemplified by things like the flagging of NEH proposals that contradict some political view?

Absolutely. And it's a little step towards that kind of thing. Family values. Abortion. Birth control. You name it. Wherever their agenda reaches—and it reaches quite broadly—they must fight against a whole realm of science, and a whole realm of empirically based research. We may not feel terribly committed to [empiricism]. We may feel that we're beyond that, but actually, if they knock that out from under us, we're in real trouble. I mean, we're almost back to witchcraft.

Do you see knowledge production within academia being particularly singled out?

Knowledge production in academia *is* singled out, because people in academia have a certain amount of authority. [The neocons] have cowed the people in the government. In a way, we're what's left. And they're going after us about the Middle East in particular because they have a particularly aggressive, particularly megalomaniac agenda in the Middle East. But I think it's true across the board. And I think this should not just alarm radical, left-wing, or liberal academics. I think that this is something that should alarm conservative academics. It should alarm *any* academic.

. . . . .

Khalidi alludes to a contradiction within the accusations of neoconservative supporters of the Title VI advisory board. This contradiction emerges between, on the one hand, the allegation that academics are not engaged enough in real-world issues, and, on the other, the attempts posed by this legislation to stifle such forms of engagement. The essential difference between supporters and opponents of the advisory board could be boiled down to the issue of whether scholarship exists in order to serve a narrowly and politically defined "national need" rooted in a broader neoconservative vision. Our conversation then turned to the possible outcome of this vision in the academic context, as we asked Khalidi about his expectations in the case that the amended legislation passes in the Senate.

Rashid Khalidi: It depends on its form and on control of the legislature in the future. Which means that even if this bill is not considered by the Senate, or if the Democrats torpedo it, it'll probably be back. It or another version of it. I mean, you're going to have to drive a stake through its heart to kill this one. I'm told that there are people on the Hill who want to prevent this from being adopted, who feel that Title VI is a well-run program, who feel that the proposed advisory board is a boondoggle and a witch hunt and a waste of the taxpayers' money. Will those voices be heard when push comes to shove? I don't know. Will that view command a strong enough range of support within the relevant committee? I don't know. We'll see. We don't want a politically determined committee looking into academia. God help us. I don't just mean about Title VI. I mean about everything.

Mobilization against the Advisory Board and Academic Censorship

Beyond the voices of those on the Hill who spoke against the amendments to Title VI and in defense of academic freedom, voices of opposition emerged from within higher education and the academy. One camp within this opposition—consisting mainly of institutional networks including the American Council on Education and the Council for International Education—worked through the higher education lobby to successfully introduce changes to HR 3077 while it was being debated by the House. Primary among these changes was the addition of language stipulating that the advisory board would not be allowed to control an institution's "specific instructional content, curriculum, or program of instruction."

These changes led some in the higher education community to insist that the continuing fuss was all much ado about nothing,[12] or to argue that the battle must be fought within the existing structure of the legislation itself. However, although this perspective was rightly concerned about ensuring renewal of Title VI funding, it did not represent many scholars—professors and graduate students alike—who thought it necessary to continue working toward eliminating the proposed advisory board altogether.

The concerns of those opposed to the board were multifarious. Among them were worries about its mandate to collect student recruiting information and its potential to foster elitism if area studies centers at private institutions, potentially less dependent on Title VI funding than those at public universities, chose to refuse funding under the new legislation. Yet the major issues were twofold: First, that the proposed advisory board represented unprecedented government microman-agement of scholarship and education and formed part of a broader attack on both academic freedom and public dialogue, especially about the Middle East. This per-spective viewed the legislation as part of a broader movement to attack those who expressed views about the Middle East and U.S. policy that contradicted the stance of the second Bush administration. And second, that an advisory board consisting of political appointees was primed to result in a partisan government structure, and a well-placed tool for a witch hunt. Essentially, these scholars held that if such a board were established, chances would be that many of its seven members would be appointed from those very neoconservative think tanks that spawned the idea in the first place.

Such fears prompted numerous actions across university campuses. For exam-ple, at Cornell University, a resolution was passed by the Graduate and Professional Student Assembly asking the university to take a stance against the advisory board amendment. Teach-ins and discussions were also held at the University of Chicago and at Berkeley. Several scholarly associations passed resolutions against the pro-posed amendments and in support of academic freedom, including the Middle East Studies Association and the American Anthropological Association. In addition to public commentary from the Left in the *Nation* and *Counterpunch*,[13] commentary against the proposed advisory board emerged from the Right as well. A piece in the *American Conservative*,[14] for example, argued that this sort of government regulation of academia would stifle public debate. These voices against the proposed amendments to Title VI were joined by various civil liberties, Arab American, student, and peace-and-justice organizations. The involvement of groups like Jews for Peace in Palestine and Israel, the American-Arab Anti-Discrimination Committee, and the U.S. Campaign to End the Occupation highlighted the recognition that this sort of legislation is directed at suppressing the possibilities for dissent and debate about Middle East policy and that it threatens to silence criticism of the United States and Israel.

Despite the efforts of these concerned scholars and organizations, a broad-based and organized movement against the legislation did not take shape. We asked Khalidi why a more broadly based political effort did not spring into existence in the academic community.

Rashid Khalidi: Part of the problem is that they [the neocons] are political, and we're not political. The people who are pushing this are not like us, in the sense that they don't represent this extremely disparate collection of private and public institutions, spread all over the United States, who have very little in common in many respects and who are all going off in different directions. Whereas they are a tightly knit, professional group affiliated with the party in power. They go into the Republican House leadership, and they are speaking the same language. They are on the same page. They believe in the same things. That's simply not true of the higher education community, where you have Republicans and Democrats, and neocons and liberals, and radicals and revolutionaries. It includes everybody. And the institutions are all cautious and conservative. And everybody is worried about alienating this senator, or that committee, or this department of government, because the universities are deeply dependent on the government. So why they didn't do what they didn't do, when we come to write the history of it? These will be some of the explanations. Should people be doing more? Yes. Who should be doing more? All the area studies associations should be doing more. All the professional associations, of all sorts, the American Historical Association (AHA), the American Political Science Association (APSA), the American Anthropological Association (AAA). All of the higher education bodies, all the provosts, in all of their configurations—the ones in the Midwest, the Ivies. They should all be taking this deadly seriously. Will they? It depends. You know, this university won't do it because the president feels this way, that university may not because they have a Republican governor who will be angry. . . . You know, there are all kinds of circumstances. But should more be done? Yes. Should it be done more quickly? Yes. Should it not be just a single effort? Yes. Because this is going to be with us. It's not going to die. No one is driving a stake through the heart of this vampire. It's coming back. If it doesn't get passed in this session, it will come back.

. . . . .

The issues Khalidi raises here regarding the obstacles faced by the higher education community and the importance of that community's engagement with politics are tied to broader questions about the relationships among the academy, public intellectuals, and the government. What role can or should the public intellectual play in our society, and what is the relationship of that figure to the academy and to politics? Is the public intellectual the gadfly, as Edward Said said, "whose place it is publicly to raise embarrassing questions, to confront orthodoxy and dogma (rather than to produce them), to be someone who cannot easily be co-opted by governments or corporations"? Is it the person who, in the words of Michel Foucault, questions "over and over again what is postulated as self-evident, to disturb people's mental habits, the way they do and think things, to dissipate what is familiar and accepted, to reexamine rules and institutions"?[15] Or is it someone who simply researches and presents basic facts about issues of political import to a public audience? Some argue that the quality of public intellectualism has declined in recent decades, in part as a function of increasing specialization of academic disciplines. Others contend that such a lack of intellectual clout is just another aspect of the infamous anti-intellectualism of the United States itself.

Public Intellectuals and the Academy

In the final portion of our conversation with Khalidi, he discusses his own efforts to contribute to public knowledge and political debate through his book *Resurrecting Empire*. We also discuss the question of whether or not the initiatives described above have succeeded in narrowing the purview, or deflecting the impact, of public intellectuals present and future.

Rashid Khalidi: One of the things I try and do in this new book, *Resurrecting Empire*, is to say that there is a strong anti-imperial tradition in American culture. In fact, it is the old republican tradition. It's been trampled on again and again. I mean, when the United States did what it did in the Spanish American war, not to speak of the way in which the United States was created at the expense of Native American peoples. You had expansion of various sorts, imperial and otherwise. But there is another tradition—which is represented by [Samuel] Adams and all the founding fathers—of not going abroad in search of monsters, that the empire will destroy the republic, that the United States should avoid entangling alliances. And that can go into a perverse isolationism. That can be reified and turned into some kind of silly, moss-covered memorial to the great founding fathers. But it can also be the source of a radical tradition which would argue against empire. Empire is not in the American psyche.

And as I argue in the book, there's a strong anti-imperial sense among Americans. This administration is having trouble dealing with that. Everybody should read very carefully the Bernard Lewis piece in the *Wall Street Journal*, where he ended up saying that the United States *should* support empire.[16] Well, I think we should have an argument about this. And I think that's an argument anyone could win with ordinary Americans, even Americans whose minds have been poisoned by CNN and have degenerated under the impact of Fox. Most Americans don't want to have an empire. You have to sell it to them in another way: "democracy," "a danger to the American people." Those are the things that Americans will go for. "If we're doing good things abroad then why should we oppose them? Because they're bad people. They shouldn't be there." Those are easy ideas for the deceitful empire builders in Washington to sell.

But the American people aren't stupid. They're beginning to figure out that there never was even the slightest, remotest shadow of a possibility of a threat in Iraq. The Iraqi regime threatened only its own people. Every neighbor of Iraq wasn't threatened by Iraq. If they weren't threatened by Iraq, why are *we* threatened? I mean, we're like an elephant up on a table howling and screaming because this half-dead mouse is on the ground. I mean it's a spectacle that the rest of the world cannot understand. And Americans are actually beginning to come out of this shell, this daze, that was created by 9/11 and then reinforced by the panic mongering of this administration—which it used to justify this adventure in Iraq. And public opinion has now, according to the last poll, actually turned against the war. The point is, there is space here in which a straightforward, simple, nonjargonistic, nonstupid, nonextreme critique can win over a large number of people.

Why isn't that space being claimed by more people with diverse views?

I don't know. You know, I'm a Middle East historian. All I can say is that there is lots of ammunition, lots of material in the public record of this administration and in the history of the modern Middle East that can be mined in ways which, I think, could be devastating in ordinary public debates over foreign policy. America is so far away that the world really doesn't impinge on Americans most of the time. That's not a willful ignorance; it's not a bad thing. It's not something we can fault people for. But that's the way American culture is. I think we should be trying to educate people. The international should be brought more to the center of people's consciousness. And you realize that young people understand that, by the overwhelming interest in courses on international subjects and foreign languages. In universities, you realize that young people are infinitely smarter than their elders. They sense that this is important. And, you know, there's a vast role for education in all of this. And it needs to be something that universities focus on.

At a recent lecture at New York University, you exhorted Middle East scholars to make their work more accessible. And your book is an effort to do just that. What is your experience with trying your hand at this kind of work?

Mostly we write for each other, and we write for a relatively narrow audience which understands the terms of reference, uses the same arcane language. And we're talking about complex things, and you couldn't sell five thousand copies of anything we write. And that's mostly what I do, that's what academics do, what we train our graduate students to do. What I suggest is that we should go a little further than that. We have an obligation to go a little further than that. By "we" I mean people who deal with the modern Middle East, or the Middle East generally, but also people who deal with the rest of the world. And it's particularly important now when the rest of the world is more important. The United States deserves to know about the rest of the world. What that involves for academics is learning how to do things that don't come naturally. We always attach qualifiers, we don't want to assert something that can't be proven, we tend to speak in long, complex sentences, we tend not to be able to sum up what we're saying in short, pithy, sound bites, and that's what is required for dealing with the media, for instance.

Your book is one aspect of your public intellectualism. Why do you think public intellectuals in this country have so little cachet, especially in comparison to Europe?

I'm not sure that they have no clout here. We just have to define public intellectualism a little more broadly. Unfortunately people thrown up by think tanks and the media have to be counted in some cases as public intellectuals. On the Right, largely. I don't think Ann Coulter is an intellectual, and there are many others like that—raving and ranting types. But, you know, there's a political debate going on. And for the first time in a long time, since the sixties, it's being joined from the other side. You go to the average airport bookstore, where all you used to find was Louis L'Amour—and Sarah Peretzky if you were lucky—diet books, and how to make a billion dollars. And [now] you find Noam Chomsky, Michael Moore, Al Franken, as well as books from the other side, Bernard Lewis, and a great deal of other material. I have to say, Bernard Lewis is a public intellectual. I don't agree with a lot of what he says. But there are actually people on both sides. A lot more now, I think, interestingly enough, perhaps now more than in recent decades. I think it's an entirely good thing.

You are part of a tradition, in line with Edward [Said], Eqbal Ahmed, and a number of others, some of whom have passed away recently. Do you feel that there are enough people coming after you?

I think one of the objectives of this offensive is to intimidate. They ask: "If we can do this to Edward Said, then what's going to happen to you, you poor, miserable, untenured faculty member? What's going to happen to you, you poor, miserable graduate student?" I think that's what they're trying to do. They're trying to mug you all, before you get to where they can't really touch you. To where you have tenure. They couldn't touch Edward. It enraged them that they couldn't touch him. They can't touch Chomsky. It enrages them. It drives them up the wall. That there are people who are, in some measure, unassailable. Whereas the Right has virtual control over a certain chunk of the media. There they can say anything they want—again and again and again. And it is not just repeated in the right-wing media but in the mainstream media. But there is in academia a corner where their writ does not run. It drives them absolutely batty. There are conservative and neoconservative students, and there are some faculty who resonate to those ideas. But, by and large, they don't get a lot of traction in the academy. In fact, they've become paranoid and talk about how persecuted they are. But it's a marketplace of ideas. It's not like there's any absence of those ideas out there. And the university is part of the world. In the media, the ideas mainly come from them, not from anything called the Left. Not from anything radical, or from even liberal sources, by and large. Regardless of what is said about the so-called liberal media. So, I'm not sure if there are enough people coming along. There probably are.

But the key thing to me is that we not just generate a culture that speaks only to itself. What happens in universities can be remarkably cut off from the world. And so much of what happens in the universities goes no farther. I'm happy when academics have an impact on public debate. Some of them I'm less happy about than others. But all too frequently we're just talking to ourselves. So what I worry about is people who can cross over. And talk in a sophisticated way to broader publics.

I don't think that's something that a young scholar should do for two reasons. It's not something that they should do because they first have to protect themselves from the kind of things that may happen if you ever say anything that people don't like—which is to say, you've got to get tenure. We're now, once again, for the first time in a while seeing why tenure exists. It tends to create a position where people don't teach a lot, don't administer a lot, and don't write a lot, and there's no way of dealing with them. That's a minority, fortunately, but it exists and tenure protects it. Tenure is primarily there to protect people who say things that are unpopular, things that are important to have said. So the first thing that a young scholar probably can't do is to risk their neck saying things that will imperil them in terms of the tenure process.

It's [also] probably something that a young scholar can't do because to talk in general terms that are accessible to a broad audience, you have to have a pretty wide base of expertise. You have to have done a lot of empirical or other kinds of work which establishes that you know what you're talking about such that you can talk in general terms. This is why some of the best work of academics, like [Fernand] Braudel or [Albert] Hourani, is "late" work, to use the term as it was used by Edward Said, that is accessible.

Are there other reasons why scholars do not do publicly accessible work? Perhaps because it is not validated in the institution?

Oh, of course. And it's not validated within the institution for two reasons: (1) because it would jeopardize tenure, but also (2) because there's a narrow vision of what a scholar and academic is. That you cannot be an activist. You cannot be a political person. And there's a huge wrangle over this in the academy. To what extent should political opinions be expressed in the classroom by the teacher who is in a position of authority? To what extent is the student's learning experience going to be affected by the fact that that student is aware that outside the classroom the professor, with all of her/his authority, has pronounced him/herself on this, that, or the other. I don't know where I come down on these things. But it has to be admitted that this issue of abuse of authority, which the Right is using as a stick to beat us up with, is not entirely illusory. I mean, there is an issue there. We've seen it in gender, and no one disputes it now. Relationships based on unequal power relations are no longer seen as appropriate.

Is it appropriate for a professor to use her/his authority to push opinions? Now, I'm with Edward Said. There's no such thing as opinionless, objective scholarship. Every piece of scholarship comes from somewhere. But I don't think that that means that anybody can say anything in the classroom with the authority of the teacher. You know, is it correct for me to hand out "Buchanan for President" tracts in the classroom as a professor? Obviously not. Should I be handing out revolutionary socialist tracts in the classroom? Obviously not. I mean, as a professor, is it legitimate?

My point is that there's probably a way in which the academy is forcing a kind of mindless conformity on students. But I think there are some legitimate questions to be asked here.

I can tell you that if you are engaged in any kind of politics as a student, you have to be exceedingly sure that the rest of your work is on extremely solid grounds. Because there are people in the academy who will penalize you for having any views, any opinions, any political life outside the academy. And that has to do with an old vision of the objective scholar. Mainly it has to do with the disapproval of the specific opinions expressed in many cases. But that's the way it is.

Do you think that can or should change?

Maybe it should. Can it? I don't know. Look, let's be frank. There's a ludicrous allegation that the universities are liberal. That allegation is ludicrous because huge chunks of the university which nobody ever talks about are extremely conservative by their very nature. Most law schools are conservative. Most business schools are conservative. Most medical schools, and the huge parts of universities that are involved with science, are neither liberal nor conservative. If anything, they might have a slight bent towards the status quo. And most schools of international affairs are conservative (i.e., security studies). They're not extremely conservative, necessarily, but they're certainly not left-liberal or liberal. I mean, where is there a business school that's liberal in the whole of the United States? Where is there a law school that's liberal? Well, there might be a couple law schools that are slightly liberal. Slightly. But there's a range of opinion in most of them, and most of them are quite conservative, and many of them are extremely conservative. The University of Chicago, for example. Nobody ever talks about that.

And even if you go further, where is there a nonconservative department of economics? Well, there are maybe one or two, but most of them are quite conservative. Even in some of the other social sciences, it's really hard to say that we are talking about departments, or fields, which as a whole are liberal. The only place where this ridiculous accusation has some traction is in the humanities. And only some parts of the humanities. So, yes, there is a liberal bias in parts of the humanities and some of the social sciences. Maybe history. Maybe anthropology. Maybe comparative literature. And what part of the academy is that? Well, it's a small part, albeit an important part. I wish it were more important. But actually, if you look at what most students study, they study accounting, they study business, they study engineering, they study law, they study science, they go into medicine. They may take a few humanities courses. Their minds, heaven forbid, may be poisoned by a liberal idea or two. But in the overall structure, universities are relatively conservative, with important liberal elements (to use that ridiculous terminology).

Do you have any evidence that these intimidation techniques are working, either among young colleagues or among students?

No. I doubt that they're working. I would be very surprised if they're working. You know, junior faculty have always kept their heads down. Rare is the junior faculty, the nontenured member of the university, who will contradict their seniors on anything of importance to them. Leave aside the politics and the real world. And there are understandable reasons for that, even if it's not always admirable. And, one way or another, that's not going to be changed by this. It has deep roots, the most important of which are internal to the universities. You have to have a process. If it's not the faculty who determines tenure, then you have an even worse body. And as long as you have that you have all kinds of problems of patronage and seniority. It is in some sense a corrupt system, but I can't think of what the alternative would be.

But there is another level at which this can work and may be working, which is at our level.

Graduate students.

. . . . .

Indeed, a number of young scholars have been explicitly advised not to study certain topics, especially Palestine. One respondent to an informal survey said that an advisor told him in 1996 to steer away from working on Palestinian issues as it would "affect [his] prospects for getting a job further down the road." On beginning graduate school in 1999, an anthropology student's advisor told her she had "counseled people against studying Palestinians until after the Oslo Accords, which she felt legitimized the identity of Palestinians on an international stage." Another respondent described her experience:

In 1994, I was talking with my advisor about potential fieldwork sites in the Middle East. There was a range of issues that I was interested in researching, and I thought that Palestine would be a fruitful place to explore them. She said it would be really hard for me to get tenure with a project in Palestine, because the academy, administrations, and trustees would always doubt one's allegiances. She said I should wait until I had tenure to start work in Palestine, which is what she had been planning to do since she started in academia.

Stories such as these are not uncommon. We asked Khalidi to comment.

People are being told, "Don't even touch Palestine. Go to Malaysia or anywhere else. The farther away you can get from Palestine-Israel, the better off you'll be."

I don't think it affects students. I think students are still adventurous and brave enough to do exactly the opposite of what they're told. If they're told to stay away, they say, "Why should I stay away? I want to see more about it." I detect a remarkable level of inquisitiveness and open-mindedness among students. I think that's one of the things that drives the other side crazy. They have cultivated a hothouse atmosphere where people will only get one view. Suddenly people are exposed to another view, and they lose people: people who actually get a chance to see alternative points of view. They say, "Yeah, maybe there is more to this than I was always taught in an isolated atmosphere." And that really scares the living daylights out of them. They have to maintain a closed system. Because much of what they're saying is false. There is a complexity to the conflict which, even if you are a committed Zionist and supporter of Israel, you can entertain. But they are the enemies of complexity. Because so much of the support they've developed is structured on the idea that there is only one way to see things. That there is no complexity. It's flat. It's a picture that does not stand up to any kind of scrutiny.

If students were staying away [from controversial issues], I wouldn't have so many people trying to work on topics related to Palestine-Israel. And it's not just me. Everybody who teaches these issues is besieged by students. The numbers of people interested—those who are committed one way, those who are committed another way, those who want to know, those with no views—are increasing.

. . . . .

There is no doubt that, within academia and the broader public, the Middle East, Islam, and area studies in general have gained increased attention—whether negative, positive, hysterical, paranoid, simply curious, muscularly intimidating, or otherwise. But it may be that this particular period of intense focus on these issues, sparked in part by HR 3077 and similar initiatives, has had quite the opposite effect than what may have been intended. Students have continued to be political and continue to be drawn to complicated, controversial issues. But they are wary. We close with an excerpt from an e-mail correspondence between two junior scholars who were part of a discussion we initiated on a Middle East anthropology listserv.

I do not feel cowed by the neoconservative critique, which is why I have publicly signed my name onto initiatives both within and outside of academia that aim to expose United States or Israeli or Arab government actions, and to analyze the effects that they have on social life and prospects for peace and prosperity. That said, I do feel like I'm treading on eggshells in the classroom and on the job market. I've been attacked a couple of times in the classroom for assigning certain readings (which are well-respected within the academy), or for using words like "occupation," which are agreed upon by the international community.

Her colleague responded:

Eggshells, glass, or burning coals, this ground needs to be tread. I won't be intimidated into silence, ignorance, or obfuscations. I refuse to wake up thirty years from now and ask myself, why didn't I say anything to people about what I knew of the brutalities of Israeli occupation and the criminal incompetence of the Palestinian Authority? Or why didn't I do more to learn about, and tell students about, what my government was doing in Iraq, or how Arab governments treat human rights activists? I have the abilities, facilities, and luxury to seek the facts and expose forms of oppression. That, therefore, is my responsibility. Advisors, granting institutions, editors and thought police may be trying to hide our shoes, but we have to continue to walk that bumpy path seeking out truth, no matter how hot the embers.

Notes

1. David Horowitz, "Academic Bill of Rights," Students for Academic Freedom, www.studentsforacademicfreedom.org/abor.html (accessed April 14, 2005).
2. From Sec. 633 of HR 3077, Library of Congress, thomas.loc.gov/cgi-bin/query/F?c108:2:./temp/~c108ETHkk4:e21036 (accessed April 14, 2005; this site is no longer active).
3. Edward W. Said, *Orientalism* (New York: Vintage Books, 1979).
4. Rashid Khalidi, *Resurrecting Empire: Western Footprints and America's Perilous Path in the Middle East* (Boston: Beacon, 2004).

5. From Sec. 633 of HR 3077, Library of Congress, thomas.loc.gov/cgi-bin/query/F?c108:2:./temp/~c108ETHkk4:e21036 (accessed April 14, 2005; this site is no longer active).

6. For analyses of how Campus Watch specifically targets professors seen to be anti-Israel and anti-America, see Scott Smallwood, "Campus Watch in the Media: Web Site Lists Professors Accused of Anti-Israel Bias and Asks Students to Report on Them," *Chronicle of Higher Education*, September 19, 2002, www.chronicle.com/daily/2002/09/2002091902n.htm.

7. Martin Kramer, *Ivory Towers on Sand: The Failure of Middle East Studies in America* (Washington, DC: Washington Institute for Near East Policy, 2001).

8. Ibid., as quoted in Zacharay Lockman, "Behind the Battles over U.S. Middle East Studies," *Middle East Report*, January 2004, www.merip.org/mero/interventions/lockman_interv.html. This article also contains a detailed critique of *Ivory Towers on Sand*, with a general overview of the battles described here.

9. This information can be found at University of California, Berkeley, Graduate Assembly, ga.berkeley.edu/academics/hr3077.html (accessed April 14, 2005).

10. For a collected sampling, see Social Science Research Council, www.ssrc.org/programs/mena/MES_Opinions/index.page (accessed April 14, 2005).

11. Here Khalidi refers to the so-called clash of civilizations thesis put forth by Samuel P. Huntington in *The Clash of Civilizations and the Remaking of World Order* (New York: Touchstone, 1997).

12. See, for example, an article by Diane Jones, director of the Office of Government Affairs at Princeton University, "House Bill Should Not Be Cause for Alarm," *Yale Daily News*, December 10, 2003, www.yaledailynews.com/article.asp?AID=24398.

13. See Vijay Prashad, "Confronting the Evangelical Imperialists, Mr. Kurtz: The Horror, the Horror," *Counterpunch*, November 13, 2003, www.counterpunch.org/prashad11132003.html. See also Kristine McNeil, "The War on Academic Freedom," *Nation*, November 11, 2002, www.thenation.com/doc.mhtml?i=20021125&c=1&s=mcneil.

14. Anders Strindberg, "The New Commissars," *American Conservative*, February 2, 2004, www.amconmag.com/2004_02_02/article.html.

15. Said and Foucault are quoted in Richard Posner, *Public Intellectuals: A Study of Decline* (Cambridge, MA: Harvard University Press, 2001), 30, 31.

16. Bernard Lewis, "Democracy and the Enemies of Freedom," *Wall Street Journal*, December 28, 2003, available at *Opinion Journal*, www.opinionjournal.com/extra/?id=110004478 (accessed April 14, 2005).

"We Can't Assume Our Alliances;
We Have to Work for Them":
An Interview with Angelica Salas

Enrique C. Ochoa

The scapegoating of immigrants during periods of national crisis has a long history in the United States. After September 11, 2001, under the guise of the so-called war on terror and homeland security, the Bush administration began a new crackdown on immigrant rights, pleasing well-organized anti-immigrant forces. At the federal level, the USA PATRIOT Act has been employed to target alleged terrorists, while the Immigration and Naturalization Service (INS) has been reorganized under the Department of Homeland Security, making all immigrants suspect. This has led to summary raids, detentions, and deportations throughout the country, instilling terror in immigrant communities. In June and July 2004, some immigrants avoided public spaces and kept their children home from school, while others openly protested INS raids at shopping centers and other public spaces in the greater Los Angeles area.

Immigrant rights activists and organizations are working to expose the contradictions of a U.S. policy that encourages immigration while simultaneously scapegoating immigrants. Over the past three decades, immigrant rights organizations have expanded throughout the nation. Despite post-9/11 setbacks, years of prolonged struggle have helped immigrants forge important alliances and develop legislative experience needed to continue the fight for justice and dignity.

Angelica Salas has been engaged in immigrant rights issues since her migra-

Radical History Review

Issue 93 (Fall 2005): 260–71

Copyright 2005 by MARHO: The Radical Historians' Organization, Inc.

tion from Mexico at the age of four. Salas is currently the executive director of the Coalition for Humane Immigrant Rights of Los Angeles (CHIRLA), a key organization in the struggle for immigrant rights. A graduate of Occidental College, she is the first immigrant to hold this leadership position.

The interview was conducted by Enrique C. Ochoa of the *Radical History Review* editorial collective.

Enrique C. Ochoa: *How did you get involved in immigrant rights activism?*

Angelica Salas: For me, it's very personal, in terms of the kind of work that I do. I came here from Mexico when I was about four or five years old. My father and mother actually came here first. My mom worked in garment factories, and my father worked different jobs. Both came without documents. After they were able to, they brought my sister and me to the United States. We crossed the border, like so many other people do, with an uncle who at the time was sixteen and an aunt who was fourteen, so we were very young kids. We came to Pasadena where our home still is. I grew up seeing what it was not to have documents in this country, seeing the kind of labor that my parents did, seeing how they were treated, how we were treated. Since I was the eldest, I had to do a lot of the translating for my parents, and I literally saw the interaction between our world and the outside world. I found out how our family members, most of whom were undocumented, were treated.

As I grew older, I became more politicized and more aware that something was wrong. I couldn't put my finger on it. Going through Pasadena High School was a different kind of world. I always felt that I lived in these two worlds. It wasn't really until I got to college that I became more aware, from the civil rights struggle to issues of discrimination, racism, and social class. I learned about the history of immigration and immigration law, and it just clicked for me in terms of my experience and the experience of so many other people.

Growing up, my parents were very strict in raising us to believe that it was not just about getting ahead, but it was about you and family and you and your place in the society. They taught us that if we were going to do something, it should be about helping others or about helping the family. Because it always starts with family. So there was always this sense that we had opportunities that they didn't have and we better appreciate them and we better make good use of them. I became aware of immigrant rights organizations such as CHIRLA, El Rescate, and the Central American Refugee Center (CARECEN), groups that were doing a lot of work in the Central American community in terms of really fighting against the death squads. I became fascinated with it and wanted to do something that related to me and my life.

In college, were you involved in organizations that addressed these issues?

Yes, I was involved with MEChA (Movimiento Estudiantil Chicano de Aztlán), and I volunteered with the communities surrounding Occidental College. I had a friend who was very involved with El Rescate. In 1986, during the time of the limited amnesty connected with the Immigration Reform and Control Act (IRCA), I volunteered to help people with their paperwork. I helped family members and then other people in the community. I was excited that organizations such as CHIRLA existed. When I was in college, I thought this was an example of the type of place that I would like to work, and I feel lucky that I am able to work here.

Can you talk a bit about CHIRLA, its origins and aims?

CHIRLA was formed in 1986 as a volunteer organization. It was composed of different activists in the community who really felt that it was important to have an organization whose main focus and mission was immigrants and refugees from a multiethnic perspective, as opposed to one that was ethnic-specific, such as Latino, Asian, etcetera. Those organizations existed already. There were certainly a lot of *Mexicano* groups, Central American groups, and Asian groups at the time that had been around for thirty-plus years. But no single organization was really looking at the issue of immigrant rights more holistically. The heads of different organizations, such as the Mexican American Legal Defense and Education Fund (MALDEF) and the Asian Pacific Education Center (APEC) met to create CHIRLA, along with members of the clergy, including Father Luis Olivares from La Placita who was very engaged in this work. They brought these organizations together to form a coalition to advance the civil rights and human rights of immigrants and refugees. Through a multiethnic perspective, CHIRLA was to be part of improving relations among different groups. What was happening at the time was the passage of the Immigrant Reform and Control Act of 1986, which provided amnesty for the undocumented. As a result, 2.7 million people received amnesty. So CHIRLA played a very large role in educating people about how they could actually process their paperwork, what they needed to do in order not to miss the deadlines, and how they could meet the requirements of the amnesty program.

The other part of CHIRLA's work was advocacy. Since IRCA mandated sanctions on employers who hired undocumented workers, CHIRLA worked to stop employer sanctions. CHIRLA believed, correctly, that employer sanctions were going to create more worker abuses and that it was also going to create discrimination at the time of hiring. So employers opted not to hire people, even if they were qualified, if they had an accent or looked foreign. CHIRLA believed that people have a fundamental human right to work and that right should not be penalized. So that is how CHIRLA was formed.

CHIRLA was initially a volunteer organization formed with steering committees. But as time went by and resources became available, there was money to hire a staff. Three major programs have always been part of CHIRLA: immigration and citizenship; workers' rights; and community education. The immigration and citizenship project advocates for humane immigration law and monitors the fair implementation of immigration policy. Our belief is that we may not agree with the laws that we have, but let's see if we can implement them fairly by working directly with the INS.

Our Worker's Rights Program, which is our largest program, is making sure that immigrants are educated about their rights in the workplace. We are vigilant about exposing exploitation and actually engaging policy makers to do something about it. The Worker's Rights Program organizes the community around citizens' rights, working with different groups of immigrants and around particular industries. We mostly work in the informal economy and among the nonunionized workforce. That's how our work with day laborers began back in 1989. We also have worked with household workers or domestic workers, and have engaged sidewalk vendors, gardeners, and a slew of other workers. We support the initiation of new organizations and engage with those groups that don't have union affiliation.

Our other program is community education. This entails literally going to places where immigrants gather—churches, schools, and businesses—and creating educational materials that we can distribute to help people become knowledgeable about their rights and responsibilities. That has led us to start an immigrant assistance hotline that takes in over twelve thousand calls a year. Immigrants call to ask questions and many times to complain or to denounce abuses in the workplace and also in the community.

In terms of the Worker's Rights Program, you mentioned the gardeners who underwent a large campaign to organize. Do workers as they begin to organize come to CHIRLA? How does this all work?

Well, it happens in different ways. In the case of day laborers, there was major conflict, which is where human relations work comes in. There was major conflict between the day laborers, businesses, residents, and policy makers, including city council members and county supervisors. We engaged in this mediation process saying that we will be part of the mediation but that we are also biased as advocates for the workers. So we literally went to the hot-spot corners and talked to the men about what they thought a solution for this particular situation might be. Everyone agreed that the current situation wasn't working, and it certainly wasn't working for the day laborers. They were being ticketed and picked up by the police. Our organizing was aimed at getting the day laborers engaged in the discussions about how to remedy this particular situation so that their voices would be heard. So in that particular case we went directly to the workers, but to a certain extent they also came to CHIRLA to denounce the abuse that they were suffering at the hands of the police and business owners.

This also occurred when domestic workers began reporting abuses in the workplace. There were cases where people would report that they were being paid far too little for their labor. There was one woman who was earning $150 a month and who found out, after five years, that she was owed quite a bit of back pay. This is just one example of how we started to organize workers so that they know their rights.

Recently we started organizing immigrant youth. We did this intentionally because we started having parents and kids coming to our offices and asking about how they could legalize their status so that they can go on to college and pay in-state tuition fees. But when the question begins, "How can I fix my legal status?" you see that there may be no remedy based on the current laws. You begin to see patterns and realize that we need to get together a group of people who are willing to take on this issue.

The gardeners' movement was a different situation, because they organized themselves. They had leadership and were working with others, such as the group Communities for a Better Environment. What they needed was a place to meet and gather, to get some support and advice, and they knocked on the doors of different organizations. And everyone told them that CHIRLA does this particular kind of work. One of the things that I feel very proud about is that we said, "Okay, you guys are organizing, but you need a meeting space. You need someone to help out in these initial stages. Well, we are here for you. It doesn't mean that we are going to take over or anything like that, but that we are offering you a place where you can meet." The gardeners' association met on Saturdays. They were doing it on their own, but they knew that we were a resource. The director of worker's rights worked closely with them and was available for advice and support. That helps them much more since they took their organization and what they wanted to do seriously. So, we can't take credit for all the hard work they do; we just supported them.

In describing your interactions with the different community groups that come to you, it sounds like you use methods of popular education. Can you talk about the role of popular education in CHIRLA?

It all goes through a process. To be honest with you, some of the meetings deal with how one runs a meeting, the very basics: how you chair a meeting, how you facilitate a meeting. Just developing those skills, I think, is so important. Maybe not enough attention is given to it, but it is important to have people feel comfortable being in a group and having a couple of folks who assist in the facilitation. So it is not just us leading the meeting. The other part is that we have had some really good organizers, especially who in their home countries were themselves organizers, who used popular education methods. People who know how to develop materials, flyers, and other things like cartoon magazines that are not super wordy but that really make sense to people. You have seen *Super Doméstica*, a cartoon magazine that apprises household workers of their rights. We also did a book on legalization and the history of migration that was distributed at the national level. The migration book was based on fictional characters, but it used real moments in history to discuss how we arrived in this place now. It's not that we suddenly have this slew of immigrants that we never had before, but that their experiences are part of a larger history of the United States and the U.S. and its interventions abroad.

We have worked with other mediums for educating the public. For example, we are part of MIWON (Multiethnic Immigrant Worker Organizing Network). One thing that has been very helpful has been the creation of art and posters and designs used to talk about the immigrant experience. And then music is also very important. With the day laborers there was the formation of the Day Laborer Band, Los Jornaleros del Norte. They play at a lot of different social and organizational events, not just for CHIRLA, but all around Los Angeles. They play music that tells about our story: songs about learning English, about trying to get a driver's license, using popular music that people enjoy listening to. But they also become connected to it. So there are different ways to connect so that we are not just always on a soapbox talking.

I think it is very important to see our engagement beyond CHIRLA and facilitating connections to other realms in our society. An example of this would be the day laborer marathon team that has run now for six years in a row in the Los Angeles Marathon. This year, the press picked twenty-six different runners in the 2004 marathon and for each of the miles decided to highlight the life story of that particular runner. One of the runners they chose was a day laborer who was a runner in his home country. What's really exciting is that the press is going to be paying more attention to this group of folks who has really made running another aspect of the way they connect and build communities and relate to each other. They also make their community proud and so especially day laborers are excited when the marathon comes around because they know that they will see them.

Before 9/11, it looked like there was movement in terms of immigration reform. Both President Bush and President Vicente Fox of Mexico were talking about some sort of limited amnesty dealing with undocumented Mexicans in particular. But then 9/11 happened.

After 9/11 happened. I think that the Right and anti-immigrant groups took advantage of the situation to say, "We told you so." There was a sense that 9/11 happened because of immigrants. This really set us back. Because before that, for the first time in several years, there was discussion about the contributions of immigrants. Right before September 11, *U.S. News and World Report* came out with a list of how different industries have gained from immigrant labor, and Alan Greenspan came out saying how important immigrant labor was to economic growth. These very positive conclusions were all of a sudden negated because of what happened on September 11.

The whole framework changed. The Immigration and Naturalization Service system changed and was placed under the new Department of Homeland Security. Now immigrants were seen first and foremost from the perspective of terrorism and the desire to control international criminal activity. That continues. There has been a major historical change in immigration law policy. What is difficult for us is that our immigration and citizenship project used to engage with just one department, the INS. There was one director, and if we had problems with enforcement, we talked to that person and with Doris Meisner [the director of the INS in the Clinton administration], who we met with several times in Washington, DC. After September 11, the INS was divided into three departments. The Bureau of Citizenship and Immigration Services is willing to meet with us on a monthly basis. However, the Bureau of Immigration and Customs Enforcement, the ones who are involved in the raids and detentions, are not willing to engage with us in the same way, and it is very hard to penetrate this organization. They say, "We don't have to tell you anything, these are national security issues." So the whole bureaucratic framework around immigration has changed.

This has altered the mode that we were in prior to September 11, when we were working toward a legalization program. In July and August 2001, President Bush had come out talking about a legalization program that would help Mexicans, and he indicated that he would make it possible for people from different countries to legalize their status. The difference between then and now is that now we start with the premise of controlling the borders against terrorism. After 9/11, Bush says that we can no longer talk about legal status: we now create distinctions between the legal track and the illegal track. The legal track as it currently is—family petitions, asylum seekers, and employment-based visas—is very difficult for anybody to get on. And the illegal track—which includes guest workers and temporary visas—is really about controlling the borders and knowing who is here and having oversight. That kind of policy creates two sets of folks: those who are integrated, who have opportunities to be citizens, and those who will forever be temporary in the country. Because of September 11, what we have as a solution from the administration is 180 degrees from what was initially proposed.

Because of the work of the organizing efforts that immigrant rights groups have been engaged in on a number of fronts, I am very encouraged that we can push the administration and Congress to developing something that is more meaningful and fairer for our communities. That for me is where I begin, that is where I start, because there is a lot of organizing and energy around the country on this issue. There is a very deep sense that things cannot remain as they are, that these guest-worker programs are not acceptable and we have to do something to remedy them. I am encouraged by this. I am very confident. The organizing that has emerged from our efforts to get driver's licenses and access to higher education, while not entirely successful, has led to significant mobilizations, and that is what is most powerful. The Immigrant Worker Freedom Ride, we have been engaged with that as well. Without the organizing, legislative change can't take place.

You spoke about what 9/11 meant for the overall immigration picture. Could you say what it meant specifically for immigrants in Los Angeles?

Well, right away the major change was the lack of work. The economic devastation was very difficult on immigrant workers. The second thing was the rise in discrimination and the lack of protection. Because what also came with September 11 was the push for local law enforcement to be more involved in identifying terrorists. Immigrants were seen as potential terrorists. Arab, Muslim, and South Asian communities were targeted by the FBI and other law enforcement agencies. And generally, there was a green light to push for these kinds of anti-immigrant reforms with a sense that law enforcement should be participating with the immigration enforcement arm to do this work.

There was also a perception of heightened security, a sense that certain places should be off limits to the general public. This contributed to, for example, work-site raids at airports, and identification became required to get into some places of business, government resources, and buildings such as the Sears Tower. This suddenly excluded a whole population of undocumented people. Not only that, but if they were working as janitors or in restaurants in these buildings, the message sent was that these workers now posed a terrorist threat. That was very difficult because we saw that people were not just being deported because of their immigration status; now they were being named felons and criminals because they were working at places that were determined to be a high security risk. We worked with a lot of the peopled that were affected by Operation Tarmack at the Los Angeles International Airport and at other local airports because those places were also raided. People who had the cleanest records were all of a sudden being told that they might have to spend fifteen years in jail and pay a $250,000 fine because they had used false Social Security numbers. They were no longer seen as just falsely documented; they were now seen as violating a security regimen, violating national security.

We had housekeepers and cooks facing felony charges. As we were moving forward in negotiations with the district attorney and the U.S. attorney general, their spokespeople would say "OK, they won't spend any time in jail, but they will have to accept a felony charge." We said that was unacceptable, because as soon as they accept a felony, if they are legal permanent residents or in the process of legalizing their status, they will never be able to legalize their status because they will be felons. So what we fought was to reduce these charges from felonies to misdemeanors or to completely eliminate the charges. After 9/11, we saw the lack of due process. People were being detained for long periods of time on minor immigration violations that equated civil immigration violations with terrorist and criminal activity. These are two very different things.

The other thing that happened right after September 11 was an effort to sift out terrorist elements using no-match letters. Seven hundred and fifty thousand letters went out in 2002 telling employers that the Social Security number of a given employee did not match the number on his or her personnel record. So, mass dismissals of individuals occurred with very little protection for workers. All of a sudden there was a green light to do all these things that many had wanted to do for a long time, and 9/11 was just the perfect excuse. For us, it was so overwhelming. I felt each day that there was some new policy coming down the pipe. It wasn't even laws that we were trying to fight against; it was policy. Administrative policies were created that would change from one day to the next. There was no process to challenge these changes.

These new policies and laws fell under the PATRIOT Act?

With the PATRIOT Act, individuals were being detained for up to seven days without being charged. The act itself created an atmosphere of fear and suspicion but also vigilance within the community. One case in particular illustrates this. A man was videotaping in a building in Santa Ana because he wanted to show his family where he lived. All of a sudden, he was picked up by the FBI and faced possible deportation. I later found out that the same thing was happening in many places across the country. Individuals that were out on a family outing were looked upon with suspicion because they were South Asian or Muslim or Middle Eastern in appearance. And, of course, the whole special registration process illustrated this new atmosphere. It was just chaos, absolute chaos. Individuals who were asked to willingly go and represent themselves to federal authorities were all of a sudden being detained and deported.

Isn't there also a gendered impact to the ways in which these policies have been implemented?

Oh yes. Men and boys had to register. I went to a town-hall meeting put on by the Council on American Islamic Relations and IMPAC (the Muslim Public Affairs Council) where there were a number of women who were now sole providers in the family. There were families who saw their family members get picked up, or who did not return. It was an awful situation. I think that history will show that this is a huge blemish for the U.S. in terms of the ways it treats people. Just hearing the wives and children of these men and how they were impacted. And the fact of the matter is that there is this deep suspicion of the men and boys. Through our hate-crimes program, we have heard just the utter nastiness of the way people have been treated since 9/11. There has been so much rhetoric by public officials (such as George Bush) about how we should all get along, while at the same time the Department of Justice is implementing all of these programs. So the rhetoric doesn't match the actions.

You have talked about coalition building and you mentioned MIWON. Can you say something about how it originated?

MIWON began in 2000. It was a coming together of KIWA (Korean Immigrant Work Advocates), the Pilipino Workers' Center, and CHIRLA. We came together as advocates for low-wage immigrant workers. At the time, KIWA had a fight with a restaurant owner in Koreatown in Los Angeles, and MIWON emerged as a result of the solidarity that developed in support of a particular fight and through that base sort of connected with each other. What struck us was that there was no real sense that low-waged immigrant workers were working together with a common strategy. But 2000 was also the time when we were seeing a historic change in policy around immigrant workers in support of legalization laws. We also saw that the protagonists were not necessarily the low-waged immigrant workers that were going to be directly impacted by bad laws we had. It was really important to us in Los Angeles that there be a presence of the leadership of immigrant workers, and that they were at the forefront of this fight. Since that time, we have a worker board made up of representatives of the different workers' organizations, and the leadership has become solidified. Now each organization (including a newly founded Garment Worker Center) sends representatives to MIWON for the worker board in order to develop leadership among the workers. Their discussions concern advocacy around pieces of legislation, though first and foremost it's about legalization and driver's licenses and mass mobilizations. They have an annual May Day march that brings together fifteen thousand people in downtown Los Angeles. While we are sometimes criticized for not inviting elected officials to speak, we see it as an opportunity for immigrant workers to speak for themselves. They actually take leadership and the stage. They're the ones who are in charge. It's Workers' Day, so it should be about the workers. For MIWON, it is very important for a multiethnic collaboration among all these other organizations.

I've been to the last two May Day marches, and they were amazing. MIWON really recaptured the importance of May Day for workers and, specifically, for immigrant workers.

It's so important because, in Latin America, if someone is a *trabajador* [worker], it's a big day. Labor Day, which is celebrated in the U.S., is to celebrate the work you do; on May Day, which is an international workers' day, it's about the laborer; it's about the person and the class. You don't just have value in terms of producing products. It has to be about the worker, who she or he is. For us, it's important that there be a visible street presence because of the invisibility of immigrant workers in this society. They labor in the shadows. But I think I wouldn't say even in the shadows. Literally, you aren't considered a person. Certain jobs that people do are closed off to the rest of society. They are done outside the gaze of public view, dishwashers, busboys, cooks at restaurants, hotel housekeepers, janitors.

So it's all about visibility?

Yes, especially in places where they are supposed to be invisible. That's why day laborers are so attacked. They stand out on the street corners. They are not hidden away in the sweatshops, and that annoys the American population. "How can they be so visible on the street corners? In *our* neighborhoods?"

They're visible not just in working-class neighborhoods but in middle-class neighborhoods, visible in front of places like Home Depot.

Especially middle-class neighborhoods. That is why I think to a certain extent laborers are so targeted by the anti-immigrant forces and by their neighbors who can't ignore them.

Can you talk a bit more about the different connections CHIRLA has made nationally with other immigrant rights groups?

One of the things about CHIRLA is that we have to be involved nationally and statewide. We are regionally based—our name says we work in Los Angeles—but we have the largest number of immigrants and undocumented immigrants in Los Angeles, more than in most other states combined. Because immigration policy is a federal issue, Congress is ultimately the body that moves this forward. There is no way that we can do our work without having national connections and a national presence. So part of what we do is engage with other similar organizations. So we have sister coalitions in New York, Massachusetts, Illinois, Florida, Tennessee, Nebraska, and Oregon. At one point there was one in Texas, but that no longer exists. In California there are organizations in San Francisco, San José, and Los Angeles. We connect with these different organizations and try to coordinate actions and polls and develop joint work plans. We also try to connect with national partners. Organizations like AARP [American Association of Retired Persons], for example, are involved, but they serve more as an independent advocacy organization with a board that has representatives from different sectors, even though all the sectors are just necessarily involved in immigrant rights. So it is a very interesting setup. Other organizations are ethnic-based national organizations. As a collective of coalitions, we engage in that nationally. We are also part of the Immigrant Organizing Committee out of the Center for Community and Change that we helped to initiate in 2000. There we bring together different organizations. Most of them are immigrant rights organizations; many are not, but they have constituents who are immigrants. The Immigrant Organizing Committee connects antipoverty groups with immigrant rights groups. It encompasses approximately twenty-five organizations from across different parts of the country, including Kansas, Georgia, places where all of a sudden there is a much greater presence of immigrants.

To really understand the nature of the society in which we live requires forming broad alliances that are enduring. For example, people tell us that a particular issue is a "Latino issue" or it is an "Asian issue," rather than identifying it as an immigrant issue. It is easy to think that our allies are within the larger community of Latinos and among Latino politicians, but that is not necessarily so. The immigrant community is not monolithic. We can't assume our alliances; we have to work for them.

The Aftermath of September 11:
A Radical Transformation or
Old Bottles for New Wine?

Burçak Keskin-Kozat

Mary L. Dudziak, ed., *September 11 in History: A Watershed Moment?*
Durham, NC: Duke University Press, 2003.

A watershed moment implies a rupture in time, one after which things no longer exist as we know them. Our norms, rules, and institutions become obsolete because they cannot fully account for the transformed conditions of life. Such a moment urges us to redefine the foundations of our social existence, of our relationship to others, as well as to ourselves. Nevertheless, attempts at redefinition are always imbued with power inequalities, and the perceived exigency of transformation may legitimize violations of previously achieved guarantees against abuses of power. It is therefore extremely crucial to critically reflect on (what is claimed to be) a transformative moment and on which parts of our social, political, and legal ideals it demands to redefine.

The ten essays in Dudziak's edited volume take issue with the portrayal of the September 11 attacks as a watershed moment in the history of the United States, of Islam, and of international relations. Authors do not dispute that the attacks affected existing social, political, and legal structures, but they do question that the

Radical History Review
Issue 93 (Fall 2005): 273–76
Copyright 2005 by MARHO: The Radical Historians' Organization, Inc.

273

ensuing changes were unprecedented. In other words, 9/11 did not bring about a paradigmatic shift in policy making, identity formation, and jurisprudence. Instead, it reframed existing paradigms so as to now more easily justify the dismissal of democratic, egalitarian, and nonviolent means in resolving domestic and international conflicts.

The first set of essays evaluates September 11 as a continuation of American imperial pursuits, political culture, and racial practices. The only change the authors observe lies in the intensity of measures taken against suspected terrorists and rogue nation-states: the Bush administration suppresses domestic and international opposition more aggressively than any U.S. government has ever done before. As Marilyn Young's essay shows, it threatens the sovereignty of other nation-states and of the international rule of law to unprecedented degrees. The post-9/11 era entails a revival of World War II and Cold War political practices, albeit with a shift in the targeted objects of action. Elaine Tyler May makes clear that the administration now persecutes people of Arab descent instead of those of Japanese origin, endorses a nationwide neighborhood watch against terrorists instead of against communists, and encourages Americans to buy consumer goods instead of government bonds. Similarly, in Leti Volpp's work, noncitizen Arabs replace African Americans in racial profiling incidents, although these practices invoke Orientalist images that are gendered and racialized in a different way. The administration also uses Cold War categories of space—such as Ground Zero and Pearl Harbor—but it hollows out the U.S. role in their initial constitution. In this respect, as Amy Kaplan writes, it reclaims an "American innocence" by projecting its illegitimate activities onto anomalous spaces such as Guantánamo Bay.

The second set of essays investigates the meaning of September 11 for the Islamic communities abroad and within the United States. Authors point out that the attacks have required Muslims to distinguish themselves from their terrorist coreligionists and to reconcile their religious identity with non-Islamic realities. Such a quest is by no means novel. On the contrary, from the very beginning of their encounters with the West, Muslims were forced to reshape their belief system in response to the latter's advanced technology. Many social movements—such as Wahabbism (which prescribes a total return to the ancient Islamic tradition), Salafism (which endorses reformation of the tradition in line with contemporary developments), or Salafabism (which dictates the destruction of contemporary forms without any reconstruction)—tried to accommodate differences between Islam and the West, but none of them succeeded in offering an effective scheme for peaceful coexistence.

The 9/11 attacks urge Muslims more urgently than ever to find a viable alternative that will decrease the popularity of violent strategies. To accomplish this formidable task, Khaled Abou El Fadl suggests reforming the tradition in such a way that it addresses Islamic grievances of (post)colonialism, corporate capitalism, and imperialism. Sherman A. Jackson, on the other hand, points out possible false universals that such a solution may justify. He instead argues for the existence of multiple alternatives allowing every Islamic community to reflect its distinct historical experiences onto the present and hence resist violent means in its interaction with non-Muslim groups or nation-states.

The third set of essays investigates repercussions of September 11 on both American and international law. Authors assert that the attacks have not only obscured the boundaries between domestic and international jurisprudence but have also led to increasing violations of civil and human rights. Ruti Teitel views these developments as a direct consequence of "security sovereignty," an understanding that emerged at the end of the twentieth century and justified "intervention in states that are in already recognized conditions of diminished sovereignty" (198). Although intervention may be absolutely necessary in certain circumstances, the right to intervene has, as both Ruti Teitel and Laurence Helfer assert, enabled the Bush administration to introduce extensive executive controls over legislature, militarize the American legal system, and justify its unilateral, violent actions in the name of national security. This situation calls for a new framework that can simultaneously address concerns for civil rights, legitimate government, and national security. Christopher Eisgruber and Lawrence Sager offer one possible solution: to strengthen the gatekeeping role of domestic courts and strictly regulate the procedural content of executive actions.

The book ends with Mary Dudziak's reflections on 9/11 at its first anniversary. She argues that memories of the event became a way to negotiate one's relationship with the United States, whether one sees it as one's own homeland or as a violent actor launching unjust wars across the globe. Because "constructing a memory involves forgetting" (213), Dudziak reminds us of the need to pay attention to what is suppressed and what is remembered in these recollections.

The collection is significant in bringing together different disciplinary perspectives, from legal studies to history, linguistics, and American studies. More important, authors supplement their critiques with concrete proposals for social, political, and legal reform. Their arguments are well supported with examples drawn from immediate history, court proceedings, witness testimonies, and newspaper reports. Their theoretical and methodological astuteness renders the book an excellent source for both undergraduate- and graduate-level courses.

It is, however, crucial to note two inadequacies of the book. First, the authors primarily focus on the experiences of the U.S. administration, the American public, and American Muslims and Islamic communities. Failing to present a full-fledged comparative perspective on the attacks, they underestimate the global scope of post-9/11 developments. Is 9/11 only an American event? How do the Bush administration's responses influence interactions among nation-states or social groups in the non-West? How do Western states other than the United States negotiate their role in the post-9/11 world? What do the attacks mean for immigrants and refugees outside the United States? What does the existence of international antiwar demonstrations imply for contemporary social movements?

Such omissions are understandable given that the essays originated at a conference held in March 2002, when the events did not necessarily call for these particular inquiries. Yet these issues should be raised, perhaps in the introduction, especially when the book was published as part of a series titled American Encounters/Global Interactions. In its current form, the collection successfully illustrates American experiences of 9/11; it, however, depicts the rest of the globe not as an actor but as a passive space on which American imperialism becomes more vehemently inscribed every day.

Second, it is necessary to ask whether September 11 constitutes a watershed moment for things other than American politics, Islamic communities, and international law. For instance, is it a watershed moment in the history of terrorism, secularism, or the nation-state? How does it affect social identities not based on ethnic or religious attributes? How does it shape the future of American class relations when people from upper and lower classes lost their jobs as a result of the ensuing economic crisis? What does it imply for American women who are now called on both as mothers and wives and as soldiers?

Despite these unanswered questions, the book occupies an admirable place among those that tackle the aftermath of the September 11 attacks. A sellout or traitor status is usually attributed to those who criticize their governments and/or cultural communities in emergency situations. Dudziak's edited volume successfully challenges such a rationale and explores the possibility of peaceful coexistence at the beginning of the twenty-first century. The book's emphasis on historical contextualization and critical reflection points to democratic and legitimate courses of action, which are always difficult to speak of or to achieve during times of escalating physical and symbolic violence.

Note

This review was initially prepared for circulation in the H-USA network of the Humanities and Social Sciences Online Database (www.h-net.org/~usa).

Sexual States and National Insecurities

Marc Stein

David K. Johnson, *The Lavender Scare: The Cold War Persecution of Gays and Lesbians in the Federal Government*. Chicago: University of Chicago Press, 2004.

Eithne Luibhéid, *Entry Denied: Controlling Sexuality at the Border*. Minneapolis: University of Minnesota Press, 2002.

What links the Arab, Muslim, and Middle Eastern terrorists who bombed the Alfred P. Murrah Federal Building in Oklahoma City in April 1995 with the sinners, secularists, abortionists, feminists, gays and lesbians, and civil libertarians who caused the attacks on the World Trade Center and the Pentagon in September 2001? Both were political fantasies created in the immediate aftermaths of U.S. national traumas, both constituted outsiders within as major threats to the body politic, and both temporarily directed blame away from what were simultaneously being produced as more appropriate targets of opportunity (homegrown antigovernment reactionaries in 1995 and foreign anti-U.S. al-Qaedians in 2001).[1] These fantasies and targets had something else in common: whether imagined as the products of dysfunctional families, failed fathers, or monstrous mothers; whether constructed as ascetically asexual, inappropriately homosocial, or inadequately heterosexual; whether depicted as gender inverts or gender extremists; and whether portrayed as patrons of prostitutes, promoters of pedophilia, violators of virgins, or vectors of vice, they were all represented as gender and sexual deviants who, in threatening national patriarchal heteronormativity, also threatened the nation.

Radical History Review
Issue 93 (Fall 2005): 277–84
Copyright 2005 by MARHO: The Radical Historians' Organization, Inc.

David Johnson's new book, *The Lavender Scare*, and Eithne Luibhéid's new study, *Entry Denied*, are strikingly different on theoretical and methodological levels, yet both successfully explore significant historical antecedents of today's sexualization of U.S. national insecurity. Offering compelling challenges to scholarship on the state that ignores sexual matters, they are important additions to a growing body of work that examines the significance of sexuality in the histories of three overlapping and intersecting formations: the national security state, the police state, and the welfare state. In Johnson's study, which focuses on U.S. federal government campaigns against gay and lesbian citizens (principally civil servants in the 1940s, 1950s, and 1960s), we see national-security and police-state mobilization, with links to the growth of the New Deal welfare state. In Luibhéid's work, which investigates the policing of female aliens (principally immigrants of color constituted as prostitutes, lesbians, wives, pregnant women, and raped and abused women in the late nineteenth and twentieth centuries), we see the interpenetration of the police and welfare states, with links to the growth of the Cold War national security state. Both monographs are major contributions to ongoing discussions about the history of "sexual citizenship" and the "straight state."[2]

In comparative terms, Johnson's book is more methodologically and theoretically traditional (relying principally on the approaches of social, political, and cultural history), more deeply researched and intensively focused, more interested in those who claimed alternative or oppositional sexual identities, and more concerned with relationships between state repression and social movement resistance (in the sense that one of the book's major arguments is that Cold War state repression helped inspire the growth of gay and lesbian movements). Luibhéid's book is more methodologically and theoretically innovative (relying principally on the approaches of cultural, ethnic, and feminist studies); more broadly conceived; more focused on intersections of sexuality with class, ethnicity, gender, nationality, race, and sex; and more committed to examining the ways in which the state produced the very sexualities that it then proceeded to regulate. Read together, these books help expose one another's limitations, but they are first-rate accomplishments and suggest exciting possibilities for future research.

The Lavender Scare offers a fundamental challenge to any histories of McCarthyism, the Red Scare, domestic anticommunism, the national security state, or the Cold War at home that ignore the federal government's antihomosexual campaigns. More than twenty years ago, John D'Emilio issued an earlier version of this challenge, and among Johnson's many contributions is that he provides a more richly detailed book-length consideration of developments considered more briefly by D'Emilio.[3] According to Johnson, a "lavender scare," which he defines as "a fear that homosexuals posed a threat to national security and needed to be systematically removed from the federal government" (9), began in the late 1940s and came to significant public attention in 1950, when congressional testimony revealed that ninety-one State Department homosexuals had been fired as security risks. Soon the scare spread to other components of the federal bureaucracy and the federally controlled local government in Washington, DC, and within a few years, it was institutionalized in the federal loyalty/security system, the capital's sexual psychopath law, and the activities of the Metropolitan Police, the U.S. Park Police, the Federal Bureau of Investigation, and the Civil Service Commission. Until the 1970s, gay and lesbian federal employees were constituted as security risks on the basis of generally unsubstantiated allegations that they were blackmailable, cliquish, cowardly, ill, immoral, maladjusted, neurotic, secretive, unstable, vulnerable, and weak. Targeted by the executive and legislative branches of government, thousands of accused homosexuals lost their civil service jobs (far more than accused communists), thousands of area residents were arrested on sex-related charges, thousands more were included on lists of homosexual deviants compiled by government agencies, and countless others lived in fear of these disasters and related troubles.

Johnson's discussion of the euphemisms and innuendos used in antigay campaigns (which often relied on coded references to misfits, moral weaklings, security risks, and undesirables) is particularly interesting, as is his analysis of convergences, divergences, connections, and disconnections between campaigns against homosexuals, campaigns against communists, and campaigns against the State Department, the civil service, the federal bureaucracy, the New Deal, the city of Washington, DC, and the national government. Also fascinating are Johnson's explorations of allegations about the homosexuality of various well-known figures, including Dean Acheson, Charles Bohlen, Whittaker Chambers, Walter Jenkins, Adlai Stevenson, Sumner Welles, and U.S. senator Lester Hunt's son, whose arrest may have contributed to his father's suicide (and whose story was the basis for Allen Drury's 1959 best seller *Advise and Consent*).

Building on D'Emilio's work (but with less of an emphasis on what D'Emilio referred to as "a widespread effort to reconstruct patterns of sexuality and gender relations shaken by depression and war"),[4] Johnson attributes the intensity of the antigay campaign to two primary factors (beyond the Cold War itself): partisan politics and the growth of the gay and lesbian subculture in Washington, DC. Several chapters discuss the motivations and actions of frustrated Republicans and fearful Democrats. While the former lost five consecutive presidential elections from 1932 to 1948 and were determined to discredit both the Truman administration and the expanded federal bureaucracy, the latter believed it necessary to respond to allegations of national security weakness through demonstrations of manly resolve. Several other chapters discuss the growth of the gay and lesbian subculture in Washington, DC, the employment of homosexuals in the civil service, the responses of gay men and lesbians to the lavender scare, and the emergence of local homophile resistance led by Mattachine Society activist Frank Kameny.

Important gay and lesbian victories began in the late 1940s and 1950s, when court rulings placed new limits on the activities of the local police, and continued in the early 1960s, when homophile leaders, allied with the American Civil Liberties Union, demanded full civil and citizenship rights. After pursuing several civil service discrimination cases in court and organizing picketing demonstrations at the White House, the Pentagon, the State Department, and the Civil Service Commission, homophile activists began winning government employment discrimination cases in the 1960s. In 1975, the Civil Service Commission finally announced that it had removed the words *immoral conduct* from its list of disqualifications for federal government employment and that it would now apply "the same standards in evaluating sexual conduct, whether heterosexual or homosexual" (210). Johnson's work is especially effective not only in exploring the complex dynamics of partisan conflict but also in describing the distinctiveness of the local gay and lesbian subculture in the nation's capital, the uniqueness of the work cultures forged by gay men and lesbians in the federal civil service, and the special features (and national significance) of the DC homophile movement.

While *The Lavender Scare* focuses on the sexual policing of U.S. government workers and public officials, Luibhéid's *Entry Denied* examines the sexual policing of U.S. national borders. In so doing, it offers a fundamental challenge to histories of U.S. immigration that ignore sexual issues. Convincingly arguing that "the U.S. immigration control system has served as a crucial site for the construction and regulation of sexual norms, identities, and behaviors since 1875," Luibhéid proceeds through a set of case studies demonstrating that "laws and procedures granted 'preferred' admission to wives, while mandating the exclusion of lesbians, prostitutes, and other 'immoral' women" (x–xi). These preferences and exclusions invariably had class and racial dimensions, so that women constituted as middle-class and white were more likely to be considered sexually acceptable, whereas women constituted as poor and nonwhite were more likely to experience sexual exclusion. As Luibhéid concludes, immigration control has been "integral to the reproduction of patriarchal heterosexuality as the nation's official sexual and gender order" (xviii), "race and class distinctions have further determined whose heterosexualities become valued" (xix), and these dynamics have produced "particular visions of the U.S. nation and citizenry" (xi).

After a first chapter that provides a broad overview of the regulation and production of women's sexualities within the federal immigration-control system, Luibhéid turns to four major examples. The Page Law of 1875, she argues, established "a blueprint for exclusion" (31) by targeting Asian prostitutes and regulating the sexualities of Asian immigrant women more generally. The Gentlemen's Agreement of 1907–8, which permitted Japanese men residing in the United States to send home for wives, privileged heteropatriarchal family formation, but it then led white supremacists to constitute Japanese American reproduction as a racial and economic threat to the nation. The 1952 Immigration and Nationality Act, which excluded male and female homosexuals as "psychopathic personalities," was enforced in sexed, gendered, classed, and racialized ways at the U.S.-Mexico border. And the refugee/asylum and border-patrol systems that took shape in the 1980s and 1990s reinscribed exclusionary heteropatriarchal racist nationalism in their responses to (and implication in) migrant women's experiences of rape. Luibhéid also discusses various other immigration laws and practices that favored heteropatriarchal white family formation and excluded women on the basis of intersecting sexual concerns related to crime, illness, immorality, insanity, interracial sex, lesbianism, polygamy, poverty, pregnancy, prostitution, transgenderism, and violence.

One of the many key (and, arguably, Foucaultian) insights of Luibhéid's book is that immigration authorities were not necessarily responding to "preexisting identities that immigrant women already had," but, rather, were involved in "constructing the very sexual categories and identities through which women's immigration possibilities were then regulated" (xi). So, for example, rather than attempting to answer the question of whether particular Asian immigrants were prostitutes, Luibhéid shows that the United States regarded all Asian immigrant women as suspect, and she thereby challenges the notion that absolute differentiations can be made between prostitutes and nonprostitutes. Similarly, rather than dealing with the issue of whether particular immigrants were actual lesbians, she focuses on what "looking like a lesbian" meant to immigration authorities at the U.S.-Mexico border (77). Luibhéid also puts Michel Foucault to good use in her analysis of the "microphysics of power" (38), exploring the disciplinary technologies used by immigration officials to question, interview, interrogate, photograph, examine, monitor, and put under surveillance female aliens. Transformed into cases, immigrant women were subject to regulation and control by the Immigration and Naturalization Service, the border patrol, and a network of embassies, consulates, visa and passport systems, border control checkpoints, and social welfare agencies.

In each section of her book, Luibhéid establishes disturbing links between sexual exclusions in the past and the present. While many of the specific exclusions discussed are no longer in force, family reunification preferences within U.S. immigration policies and practices continue not only to reproduce national heteropatriarchal hegemony but also favor ethnic and racial groups already resident in the United States in large numbers. Resident aliens remain deportable for consensual sex crimes and for "crimes of moral turpitude" (xvi). Women categorized as prostitutes are still excludable and deportable. The same-sex partners of U.S. citizens and residents are not entitled to immigration preferences based on heterosexual marriage (unless they marry heterosexually). Exclusions based on HIV and AIDS remain in force. Women of color and poor women who are considered likely to become public charges on the basis of real or perceived reproductive sexual behaviors are stopped at the border and targeted for deportation once on U.S. territory. Immigrant women continue to be demonized and denied public services on the basis of sexual and reproductive racism. And the refugee/asylum and border-control systems continue to deal inadequately with women's experiences of rape.

Luibhéid's analysis suggests several questions for those interested in pursuing new research related to Johnson's topic. First, how did sexuality intersect with class, ethnicity, race, and sex/gender in the campaigns against homosexuals in the federal government and the responses of lesbians and gay men? Johnson addresses very briefly the quantitatively greater victimization of gay men in the lavender scare, and he includes several lesbian examples, but there is much more that could be said about how the antihomosexual campaigns differentially affected lesbians and gay men, African Americans and Euro-Americans, and Jews and Christians; how class, ethnic, race, and sex/gender relations of power in the federal civil service mattered in these campaigns; and how various social differences and hierarchies influenced the lesbian and gay subcultures and movements that responded. Second, how did the lavender scare produce the sexualities that it then regulated? Johnson briefly mentions that the antigay campaigns "did not just affect people who self-identified as 'gay' or 'lesbian'" (12), and he points out that the campaigns contributed to the production of more rigid distinctions between homosexuals and heterosexuals (in part by promoting the notion that one drop of homosexuality made one a homosexual), but these are topics worth pursuing in greater depth. Third, in what ways did the lavender scare produce normative sexualities in the course of demonizing deviant ones? Again, Johnson briefly discusses this issue, mentioning that the antihomosexual campaigns encouraged civil servants to more actively police their homosocial relations and gender presentations. Johnson also opens up a fascinating discussion of how the civil service handled allegations of heterosexual immorality. But there is more work to be done about the place of heteronormative civil servants and government officials in the history of the straight state. Fourth, in what ways have campaigns against homosexuals in the federal government continued long after the lesbian and gay movement won its formal victory against the Civil Service Commission in the 1970s? Johnson's book concludes with this episode, but there are good reasons to believe that the campaigns have not ended. Beyond the avenues of investigation suggested by *Entry Denied* lie a number of other areas worthy of future research attention: state and local dimensions of the campaigns against gays in government; cultural representations of DC deviants; the roles of antihomosexual government queers (especially Roy Cohn, J. Edgar Hoover, and Joseph McCarthy); and links between local and national homophile resistance.

In turn, Johnson's work raises questions for scholars interested in exploring topics related to Luibhéid's project. First, how did various types of sexualized aliens respond to and resist the policing of immigrant sexualities in the United States?

Luibhéid admits that she "did not attempt to theorize immigrant women's multiple forms of agency, except to the extent that it is visibly inscribed in official documents" (xxv), and she returns to this issue in her conclusion. As she acknowledges, this is "a task for future research" (xxv). Second, while there are compelling political reasons to focus on immigrant women's sexualities, Johnson's work on state campaigns that targeted male deviance and Luibhéid's interest in the construction of heteropatriarchal sexualities raise questions about Luibhéid's justification for her focus, that "women's bodies historically serve as the iconic sites for sexual intervention by state and nation-making projects" (xi). Third, is it possible to reach any quantitative conclusions about the effects of the policies and practices described by Luibhéid? Johnson attempts to do this type of work in his monograph, carefully qualifying his conclusions, and it would be similarly helpful to have a sense of the extent of the exclusionary dynamics considered by Luibhéid. In Luibhéid's case also, there are additional productive possibilities for future research, including cultural representations of sexual exclusion and the roles of immigrants themselves in policing alien sexualities.

What links the political dissidents who were targeted by Cold War campaigns against subversion with the working-class people of color who emerged as the focus of nativist campaigns against immigration? Both are partial constructions of history that correspond to major historical developments in the twentieth century, but as Johnson's and Luibhéid's outstanding works suggest, both also became the basis of desexualized accounts that were publicized and promoted by historians and became part of the standard narrative of U.S. history. Federal antisubversion campaigns, however, did not only (or principally) target communists in the 1940s, 1950s, and 1960s; they also (and principally) targeted homosexuals. Anti-immigration campaigns across the late nineteenth and twentieth centuries did not only focus on race, ethnicity, and class; they also focused on sex, gender, and sexuality (as these intersected with race, ethnicity, and class). Working together, the U.S. national security state, police state, and welfare state developed classed, gendered, racialized, and sexed visions of heteronormative citizenship, purging and excluding those positioned outside of these visions but paradoxically producing the return of the oppressed.

Notes

1. See, for example, Emily M. Bernstein, "Fear About Retaliation among Muslim Groups," *New York Times*, April 21, 1995; and Gustav Niebhur, "U.S. 'Secular' Groups Set Tone for Terror Attacks, Falwell Says," *New York Times*, September 14, 2001.
2. On the latter, see Margot Canaday, "Building a Straight State: Sexuality and Social Citizenship under the 1944 G.I. Bill," *Journal of American History* 90 (2003): 935–57. On the former, see Lauren Berlant, *The Queen of America Goes to Washington City: Essays on Sex and Citizenship* (Durham, NC: Duke University Press, 1997); Lauren Berlant and

Michael Warner, "Sex in Public," *Critical Inquiry* 24 (1998): 547–66; Cheshire Calhoun, *Feminism, the Family, and the Politics of the Closet: Lesbian and Gay Displacement* (New York: Oxford University Press, 2000); Margot Canaday, "'Who Is a Homosexual?': The Consolidation of Sexual Identities in Mid-Twentieth-Century American Immigration Law," *Law and Social Inquiry* 28 (2003): 351–86; *Citizenship Studies* 5, no. 3 (2001); Lisa Duggan and Nan D. Hunter, *Sex Wars: Sexual Dissent and Political Culture* (New York: Routledge, 1995); Michael Warner, ed., *Fear of a Queer Planet: Queer Politics and Social Theory* (Minneapolis: University of Minnesota Press, 1993).

3. John D'Emilio, *Sexual Politics, Sexual Communities: The Making of a Homosexual Minority in the United States, 1940–1970* (Chicago: University of Chicago Press, 1983).

4. John D'Emilio, "The Homosexual Menace: The Politics of Sexuality in Cold War America," in *Passion and Power: Sexuality in History*, ed. Kathy Peiss and Christina Simmons (Philadelphia: Temple University Press, 1989), 236.

"Active Measures"; or, How a KGB Spymaster Made Good in Post-9/11 America

Joseph Masco

In August of 2003, a rather extraordinary event went largely unnoticed by an American news media transfixed by escalating violence in postwar Iraq and the domestic terrorist warnings issued by the new Department of Homeland Security. Oleg Kalugin, the former head of KGB operations in the United States, an acknowledged handler of Cold War spies, and a key player in the four-decades-long covert war between the CIA and KGB, was granted U.S. citizenship.[1] Unlike most immigrants to the United States, Kalugin's newly professed "love of America" thus comes at the end of a career explicitly devoted to overthrowing the government. His 1994 autobiography details an energetic career of recruiting U.S. spies, directing espionage activities against the United States, managing anti-American propaganda campaigns around the world, and participating in at least one political assassination involving a poison-tipped umbrella.[2] Given the number of recent high-profile cases in which merely the appearance of espionage has accelerated the classification of government information and the lockdown of U.S. facilities, Kalugin's new legal status makes for a provocative post–Cold War development.[3] Similarly, the lack of widespread media coverage of his story seems remarkable in a country fascinated with espionage that is also at war.

What intrigues me most about Citizen Kalugin's recent career, however, is what it reveals about the ongoing transformation of the United States from a coun-

Radical History Review
Issue 93 (Fall 2005): 285–300
Copyright 2005 by MARHO: The Radical Historians' Organization, Inc.

Figure 1. Oleg Kalugin giving a tour of KGB espionage sites in Washington, DC.
Photograph by the author

tercommunist to a counterterrorist state. Kalugin's shift from anti-American KGB agent to pro-American celebrity spy participates, I believe, in a larger domestic project to recalibrate historical memory of the Cold War in order to enable a specific vision of American power in the twenty-first century. Specifically, the Cold War no longer constitutes an episode in U.S. history from which we all narrowly escaped, but rather provides the structural model for how to wage an unending global war founded in secrecy and covert action.

From Russia, with Love

I first encountered Oleg Kalugin on a bus tour of Washington, DC, in July 2003 (fig. 1). Teamed with Connie Allen, a former U.S. Army counterintelligence special agent, Kalugin was on board to provide tourists, ex-military personnel, former members of the security state, and at least one anthropologist with a tour of the U.S. capital. The presence of retired (counter)intelligence agents from both the United States and the former USSR promised a firsthand look at the covert terms of the Cold War as fought in the nation's capital.

The Centre for Counterintelligence and Security Studies (CI Centre), founded in 1997 by two former FBI counterintelligence agents, was responsible for organizing the tour. The CI Centre is part of an evolving set of private institutions created by former Cold Warriors to capitalize on their expertise, tell their story, and advocate a specific role for spies and counterintelligence in the post–Cold War, post-9/11 world. Allen and Kalugin are both listed as professors at the CI Centre, which has amassed an impressive array of security experts drawn from the CIA, FBI, U.S Air Force, U.S. Navy, the Canadian RCMP, and the KGB. The CI Centre provides training to government agencies and corporations about counterintelligence techniques and offers a variety of espionage-themed travel excursions, including SpyDrives of Washington, DC, and Moscow, a luxury SpyCruise, and a four-star SpyRetreat.

Part autobiography, part historical analysis, part propaganda, the bus tour was designed not only to entertain and educate but, more importantly, to expose a field of invisible yet constant threat and subversion. Kalugin, for instance, who was presented as the proverbial man behind the curtain in advertisements for the tour, was on the bus to share with us some of the covert methods and practices used by Soviet intelligence operations in the United States during the Cold War. Allen, by contrast, offered a historical counternarrative that focused on how domestic intelligence agents had caught spies in America, detailing the damage done by, as she put it, the "traitor bastards" (e.g., John Walker, Aldrich Ames, and Robert Hanssen) who helped the Soviets. Taken together, Allen and Kalugin presented an image of a nation-state under unending assault from spies, saboteurs, and enemy agents. Moreover, their respective narratives highlighted that it has always been, and always will be, this way. The Cold War does not emerge as an exception—a mutation in global affairs caused in large part by the development of thermonuclear weapons—but rather seems part of a seamless history of intelligence gathering, espionage, and the counterpursuit of traitors and spies. The specificity of the Cold War in fact dissolves under the weight of Allen and Kalugin's narrative, becoming simply a distinct configuration of an ongoing battle against the combined assault of subversive agents, foreign and domestic. Counterintelligence and espionage are, for these professionals, a forever project.

The bus tour begins in downtown Washington, DC, where we drive by the offices of the FBI and the State Department while hearing tantalizing tales about compromises and listening devices, packet exchanges and recruitments. Allen points out the Mayflower Hotel where Aldrich Ames received his first payment for spying. Kalugin then shows us his old spy haunts: the Occidental Club on Pennsylvania Avenue, and the National Press Building at the corner of Fourteenth and F Streets. He tells us a story about electronically intercepting a phone call between then secretary of state Henry Kissinger and his wife in which Kissinger repeatedly asks his wife for reassurance about how good he looks on television. Kalugin tells us that the information, though strategically useless, was nonetheless sent right to the top of the KGB to demonstrate the degree to which Soviet spies had penetrated U.S. institutions. The intimacy of the Cold War struggle becomes revealed here in the everyday details of surveillance, recruitments, and counterespionage.

Moving into Georgetown, we stop in front of seemingly innocent restaurants, homes, and side streets. We hear about covert meetings between "handlers" (man-

Figure 2. Site of the U.S. Postal Service mailbox in Georgetown used by Aldrich Ames to send signals to his Soviet handlers. Photograph by the author

agers) and their "assets" (spies) while looking for "dead drops" (information drops) and "signal sites" (covert messages). At Chadwick's pub on K Street, where I like the burgers, we learn that Aldrich Ames sold the names of scores of CIA and FBI assets over a meal (leading to the prompt execution of several individuals within the USSR). We stop in front of Au Pied de Cochon, the French bistro where KGB defector Vitaly Yurchenko gave his CIA handlers the slip in 1985. We drive by Alger Hiss's house, and then stop at Thirty-seventh and R Street in front of a blue U.S. Postal Service mailbox (fig. 2) used by Aldrich Ames as a signal site for communication with his Soviet handler. We learn that the mailbox is a new one, the original now housed in the International Spy Museum, a hugely popular institution that opened in downtown DC in 2002 with Kalugin sitting on the board of directors.

Despite its appeals to contemporary cloak-and-dagger intrigue, much of the tour focuses on the trade in secrets during World War II, a time when the United States and Soviet Union actually collaborated as allies. This is because it is the most publicly documented era of spying, thanks in part to the declassification of the Venona transcripts in 1995.[4] This means that much of the content of our tour took place decades before our tour guides entered into the (counter)intelligence game. The slippages that begin to emerge in their presentation over expertise, historical context, and firsthand knowledge are, however, irrelevant to the larger mission of the tour—that of documenting threat and vulnerability on an invisible but totalizing scale. Given this ideological project, much of the tour appears, nonetheless, anticlimactic: after all, the stuff of spying is not rooted in architecture but information, and the act of spying is ultimately not something you can document for a tourist audience from the comfort of an air-conditioned bus. We stop, for example, in front of public parks in DC and are informed about the various covert conversations, exchanges, and recruitments that took place in their open spaces. The empty park bench (fig. 3), in fact, becomes a prime site of espionage in the tour, making the claims that spying can take place anywhere, while proliferating the point to near absurdity.

Allen and Kalugin's narrative of constant vulnerability and threat falters most when we arrive at the Soviet (now Russian) embassy (fig. 4). Built in the 1980s on one of the highest peaks in the District, we learn that the embassy offered a perfect site for Soviet electronic surveillance of the nation's capital. The U.S. embassy in Moscow, built at the same time, was famously compromised by KGB electronic devices; as Kalugin put it, "the entire building was a transmitter," leading to one of the most contentious international incidents of the late Cold War. We learn, however, that the United States was not so naive. Allen informs us that superspy Robert Hanssen told the Russians about one of the most secretive projects of the Cold War: the construction of a tunnel underneath the Soviet embassy in Washington, DC, allowing U.S. agents to place taps on the phone lines and install other information-gathering technologies. Within the intelligence community, rumor has it that privileged members of Congress would get tours of this several-hundred-million-dollar operation to eavesdrop on Soviet conversations and witness America's Cold War tax dollars at work.

For the first time on the tour, the United States is presented not as a victim of espionage but as one of its many practitioners. But it is also the last. No one mentions again the role of espionage, misinformation, and spying in U.S. foreign

Figure 3. Park bench in Washington, DC; possible espionage site. Photograph by the author

Figure 4. The former Soviet (now Russian) embassy in Washington, DC.
Photograph by the author

and domestic policy on the SpyDrive. The covert U.S. actions in Iran, Afghanistan, Guatemala, and Chile, for example, go unmentioned. Similarly, there is no mention of the revelations in the Church and Pike Committee hearings of the mid-1970s, which led to new laws regulating the domestic power of the CIA and FBI.[5] We hear nothing about the scale of U.S. intelligence gathering on U.S. citizens, the secret program to read citizens' mail, the FBI harassment of civil rights leaders like Martin Luther King Jr., or the infiltration of activist groups like the Black Panthers and the American Indian Movement by covert U.S. agents.[6] Similarly, the McCarthy era is not mentioned until the end of the bus ride, when I have the following exchange with Allen and Kalugin. "I have to ask," I say, "how do you both now see the McCarthy period—looking at it from a contemporary perspective with the end of the Cold War?" Allen responds:

We always say that McCarthy was right for the wrong reasons. We certainly had the penetration [by a foreign intelligence service]. He just didn't know why we had the penetration. It was an unfortunate time, where people got wrapped up in something that was sometimes beyond their control. There were a lot of allegations made that were never proven, and a lot of people suffered. But at the same time, there were people denounced as communists who were communists and were also spies, and got away with it as well. It was just a very difficult period of time for us. We hope we have learned as a society, at many levels, about that kind of thing. Oleg would you like to respond?

Kalugin then offers the following perspective:

It is not an easy question to answer. From the standpoint of America's democracy it was an anomaly. It was a distortion of American values. That's what McCarthy means to me, absolutely nothing other than a distortion. On the other hand, it alerted the United States, and particularly the government of the United States, to some of the dangers that they either ignored or did not understand. So there was a value: as a result of McCarthy's attacks on America's democracy, the U.S. had to take measures to purge its institutions from potential risks. And in that sense, well, there was some progress made. So it was not just one line—either very good or very bad. It was both. Well, the Cold War is over, and hopefully we will never experience McCarthy or anything of that kind again in our lives.

In her account, Allen presents the McCarthy period as ultimately a problem of professional expertise. The senator had identified the problem correctly but simply did not know the counterintelligence trade. The unresolved aspect of her narrative is drawn not only from the damage done to innocents but also to the spies that got away with it. But the lack of commentary here on abuses of power within the U.S. (counter)intelligence community is telling, especially in our contemporary moment in which the USA PATRIOT Act revisits most of the concerns of the McCarthy period about civil rights within a national security state. The call by these counterintelligence experts to learn from the past is, thus, made impossible by their strategic avoidance of it. But then again, to acknowledge the U.S. security scandals of the 1950s, 1960s, 1970s, 1980s, or 1990s would be also to invite questions about the status of intelligence operations under the so-called war on terror, which might undermine the value of the renewed counterintelligence project stressed so explicitly at each step in the tour.

Kalugin's narrative is even more surprising in that he does not gloat over the fear of the communists in 1950s America, or tell stories about how McCarthy's theatrics played in the Kremlin—no, he speaks as an American. This might be simply amusing if Kalugin's role in contemporary American political culture were more neutral. But Kalugin's immediate value in the United States rests on his ability to leverage his résumé as a KGB spymaster in order to validate a specific narrative of the Cold War for an American security audience. His version of the Cold War confirms, rather than complicates, American perceptions of the Soviet Union, thus enabling a purification of history in the midst of the call for a resurgent U.S. counterintelligence mission in the twenty-first century. The SpyDrive tour, while entertaining and led by highly charming and polished professionals, is in this regard not history at all; it is public relations. More precisely, it is what Kalugin calls "active measures."

KGB 101

My second encounter with Oleg Kalugin came a week later at the International Spy Museum, which opened in July 2002 just a few blocks from the Mall. The museum has become one of the most popular tourist venues in Washington, smashing all box-office expectations during its first year of operation. Founded by former members of the intelligence community, the International Spy Museum offers an innovative answer to the problem of commemorating a covert war. Unlike previous generations of soldiers, who could expect national recognition on Veterans Day, as well as monuments to their bravery installed in public spaces across the country, Cold Warriors were left in the dark in the 1990s. Deprived of a victory parade—a moment of national celebration and recognition for "winning" the longest war in U.S. history—Cold Warriors are also not likely to receive a memorial on the Mall in Washington commemorating their service and sacrifice to the nation. Indeed, because the vast Cold War security apparatus remains intact and still grounded in secrecy, the contribution of America's spymasters is likely never to be officially acknowledged or publicly remembered. At the International Spy Museum, the intelligence community gets its space near the Mall, but it does so on completely privatized terms. The purpose of the museum is simple: to communicate the huge contributions that spooks have made to the United States. In doing so, the International Spy Museum capitalizes on the popular fascination with spies both for profit and for the good of the security state. It is a history museum, war memorial, and recruiting center all in one; it is both an effort to tell the covert story of the nation and an explicit attempt to reproduce a new generation of intelligence specialists (see fig. 5).

On entering the exhibit space, for example, one is asked immediately to select a new identity and "cover story," allowing visitors to enter the exhibits literally as undercover agents. A melodramatic film presentation then lays out the risks of spying and asks each audience member directly, "Do you have what it takes to be a spy?" The subsequent exhibits present the history of spy culture through a complex blurring of historical fact and popular fantasy—James Bond's Aston-Martin (complete with machine-gun headlights) is on display, as are images of television spies like Mrs. Peel from *The Avengers* and Maxwell Smart from *Get Smart*. These fictional icons are blended with artifacts and stories from World War II and the Cold War espionage trade: visitors can inspect listening devices used by both the CIA and KGB, Minox spy cameras, and weapons disguised as ordinary household items (a lipstick gun!), as well as view exhibits on covert communications, code breaking, and surveillance techniques (fig. 6). The museum is designed like a maze, forcing visitors through a historical survey of spying dating back to biblical times before providing access to exhibits on the Cold War. A small exhibit on the McCarthy period acknowledges that innocent people were accused of being spies, but the intelligence reforms of the 1970s, and the decision-making processes behind these reforms, are not mentioned in any of the museum's exhibit texts. The final exhibit spaces then become deadly serious, detailing the crimes and captures of Aldrich Ames and Robert Hanssen, before ending with a chilling film that argues that future terrorist attacks, like those on September 11, 2001, can only be prevented with a rejuvenated and globally aggressive covert intelligence campaign. The museum that begins with spying presented as a game, supported by nostalgic images from Cold War popular culture, ends with a ruthless contemporary pitch for expanding intelligence budgets to meet an expanding global mission. When the lights come up, visitors are then delivered directly into a large, and extremely well-stocked, espionage-themed gift shop.

On this particular July night in 2003, however, I visit the International Spy Museum not to see the exhibits but to hear a two-part lecture by Kalugin on the Soviet security state titled, simply, "KGB 101." Speaking to a packed house, Kalugin is introduced by the director of the museum (a thirty-five-year CIA veteran) as well as by the president of the CI Centre (a twenty-five-year FBI counterintelligence man), which cosponsored the talk. Kalugin's impressive résumé is the immediate focus of the presentation. We learn via a PowerPoint presentation, choreographed to Stalin's national anthem, that Kalugin was the youngest officer in KGB history to attain the rank of general. His successful career of espionage in the United States

Figure 5. *School for Spies* exhibit. Photograph courtesy of International Spy Museum

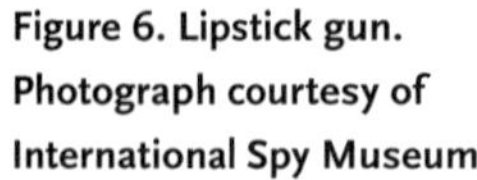

included recruiting John Walker, the U.S. Navy intelligence officer alleged to have given the Soviets the codes for all Pacific communications, including the nuclear launch commands for U.S. submarines. We learn that Kalugin first arrived in the United States in 1959 as a twenty-four-year-old KGB officer and Fulbright exchange student. His success in recruiting spies, as well as his skill in spreading Soviet misinformation and propaganda, took him from undercover journalist to acting chief of the Soviet embassy in Washington, DC, and eventually back to the Soviet Union in the 1970s to head the KGB's foreign counterintelligence operation. In his autobiography *The First Directorate* (1994), Kalugin identifies his return to the Soviet Union as politically transformative. Having spent much of his adult life in the United States, Kalugin describes really seeing the Soviet system for the first time as the head of the KGB counterintelligence project, and being shocked by its corruption, cruelty, and inefficiency. By 1990, he had denounced the KGB leadership and was officially stripped of his rank. He was then elected to the Soviet parliament before watching the USSR come apart, and immigrated to the United States in 1995. In 2002, Russian president Vladimir Putin ("my former KGB subordinate," as Kalugin reminds us) convicted Kalugin of treason in absentia, citing evidence from Kalugin's 1994 autobiography. If Kalugin were ever to return to Russia, he would face immediate arrest and quite likely a long prison sentence.

Kalugin begins his KGB 101 lecture by describing himself as a true believer in the Soviet system, a person who genuinely believed that communism would deliver "paradise on earth in our lifetime." He underscores that he has never been a defector, presenting himself more as a disillusioned believer living on the other side of history. Indeed, his narrative of professional accomplishment and moral conviction within the KGB, followed by resistance to the Soviet system, makes for an impeccable résumé for a person wishing to be embraced by the U.S. intelligence community. At each step, Kalugin counterbalances historical evidence of his professional duplicity with overtures to his authentic patriotism and personal character. His charm lies in precisely the ability to be pitch perfect in his delivery, with just the right touches of humor and gravitas to deflect attention away from the sordid business of professional lying and espionage.

The most interesting aspect of Kalugin's talk is his discussion of the KGB's training program for its intelligence agents. Years of language training in local dialects, as well as a focus on the philosophy and literature of target countries, formed the center of the program. It was training designed to enable small talk, allowing the recruitment of potential assets to be on casual and local terms. The United States, in this regard, was not just Kalugin's assignment; it was always a serious object of study, one that he embraced with obvious enthusiasm. He notes that as a young KGB trainee, he had access to the world's news media and literature, texts denied to citizens of the USSR. It is here that one can sense the slow seduction the United States held for Kalugin. In his autobiography, he describes arriving in Manhattan and being shocked both by the size and texture of the city (its architecture, arts, and the freedom of movement of its citizens), as well as by the extreme poverty that seemed unaddressed by the state.

Kalugin follows these personal epiphanies with a detailed description of the organization of the Soviet security state, emphasizing the infiltration of the KGB into every institution of Soviet society. He states that at the height of the Cold War there were nearly five hundred thousand KGB agents in Russia, in stark contrast to the tens of thousands of FBI and CIA agents in the United States. A discussion of the purges within Soviet society, the mass murders, leads into a discussion of KGB techniques for dealing with internal dissent. Kalugin describes several episodes in which the KGB detonated a bomb in the name of a dissent group to enable violent regional reprisals by the state. He describes the eighty-six fake CIA groups the KGB formed in Afghanistan in the 1980s to draw out the Mujahideen fighters for execution. The foreign and domestic duplicity of the KGB within Soviet society was matched by KGB propaganda efforts against the United States. Kalugin describes organizing mass protests of U.S policies overseas—stating that for a mere five thousand dollars one could manufacture tens of thousands of protestors in front of the U.S. embassy in India, for example—demonstrating how easily one could create an international anti-American incident during the Cold War. Here, Kalugin describes the active measures taken to defeat the West:

At the heart and soul of Soviet intelligence operations were active measures aimed at, well, the eventual destruction of the Western societies—through disinformation, through subversive actions, through guerilla warfare, through terrorism, through civil war, whatever. That was part of the program. Let me give us some innocuous figures from the Russian KGB top-secret report for 1981. In that year alone, the KGB reported to the Party Central Committee, to Mr. Brezhnev, that it financed, produced, or in one way or another, was involved in the publication of 70 books and brochures worldwide, 66 documentary and feature films worldwide, 4,800 articles published in various newspapers worldwide, 3,000 conferences and exhibitions worldwide, 1,500 radio and television programs, and finally, 170,000 lectures—like the one I am delivering tonight—across the county, across the world. That was the total of KGB active measures that year.

A week earlier, on the SpyDrive, Kalugin had made a similar point directed specifically at the United States:

We launched a major liberal magazine in New York City. Two Nobel laureates were on our editorial board—Linus Pauling and Bertrand Russell. None of them knew that the magazine was funded by the KGB, that the editor was a KGB guy. And then one day you open the *New York Times* and find an advertisement saying, "Down with the United States' involvement in Vietnam. It is high time to withdraw U.S. troops—it is a shame and a disgrace," signed by hundreds of luminaries in science and the arts. They did not know that I paid $10,000 for that advertisement, and that they were dupes in a sense.

As tantalizing as these personal stories are, they come mixed with wild pronouncements unsupported by any firsthand evidence. Kalugin tells us, for example, that J. Robert Oppenheimer and Enrico Fermi were Soviet agents and that they provided secrets to the USSR about how to build an atomic bomb. We hear that it was the KGB that started the rumors that the CIA was involved in the assassination of John F. Kennedy, and it was the KGB that was responsible for spreading the idea that J. Edgar Hoover was a closeted transvestite. We are told that, indeed, it was Ronald Reagan's Strategic Defense Initiative that broke the will of the Soviet state and precipitated the end of the Cold War. In short, we learn from Kalugin that the KGB was precisely as monstrous as the United States always said it was, that the domestic critique of the U.S. intelligence service during the Cold War was largely the product of the KGB's active measures, and that it was only the confrontational toughness of the U.S. military state that defeated the Soviet Union.

Thus Kalugin confirms exactly—without deviation—the narrative U.S. Cold Warriors produced about the Soviet Union during the Cold War. He does not challenge their assumptions; instead, he reinforces them. And in so doing, he provides the rationale for dismissing all (post–)Cold War critique in the United States as simply a product of KGB machinations. We hear nothing, for example, about how U.S. espionage campaigns were interpreted by the KGB, or about the errors made by the CIA in its estimates of Soviet capabilities, from the famous bomber and missile gaps of the early Cold War to the agency's inability to even imagine the end of the USSR in the 1980s. Indeed, the heroes of the story are implicitly the U.S. intelligence officers who, outnumbered and outmanned, were able to beat the KGB at its own game. Kalugin concludes by stating that if the United States had installed human agents in Saddam Hussein's Iraq, president George W. Bush would not have had to go to war with Iraq, arguing that a single bullet could have prevented the U.S. invasion in 2003. Thus Kalugin ends his talk with an explicit call for U.S. sponsored espionage and assassination. In this way, Kalugin's "KGB 101" lecture primarily offers a narrative useful to past and present U.S. intelligence officers. It purifies the past by documenting the brutality and active measures of the Soviet regime and dismisses many of the internal criticisms of the FBI and CIA as Soviet propaganda. It also argues for the centrality of spooks in the modern world, making members of the intelligence community the true brokers of both history and security. Kalugin's own ideological makeover, therefore, enables a more profound ideological makeover of the U.S. security state as covert agent.

The success of this ideological program was brought home to me later in the year, when I was conducting archival research on the U.S. nuclear program at several government institutions near the West Coast. In Las Vegas, I spoke to a career Nuclear Test Site (NTS) worker who brought up the large-scale antinuclear protests staged at the site through the 1980s. These protests, which involved a vast range of groups from the environmental, peace, antinuclear, and Native American activist communities, formed part of a global effort to confront the terms of the escalating Cold War arms race and to recognize its foreign and domestic costs.[7] Stating baldly that the protests were funded by the Soviets, this NTS worker dismissed the activists' political critique of environmental contamination and militarism within the U.S. nuclear program. He then asked if, by chance, I had ever heard of a KGB spymaster named Oleg Kalugin. Kalugin, the life-long student of America, has identified and understood his audience all too well and delivered precisely the narrative they needed at this historical moment.

The intelligence community has always argued that only its failures become part of the public record: the Iran-Contra affair; Soviet spies Walker, Ames, and Hanssen; or the successful terrorist attacks on Washington, DC, and New York in 2001. However, now that same professional community has some very public, and in some cases very profitable, institutions to spread the good word about U.S. (counter)intelligence. They have their own privately held museum near the Mall (the International Spy Museum); they have a new pedagogical and lobbying institution (the CI Centre), and they have their man from Moscow in America to confirm their version of history. Untouched by historical review or political critique, Kalugin and the institutions that engage him are now reconfiguring the story of the Cold War in order to reinvent the national security state for the twenty-first century on covert, explicitly antidemocratic, terms.

What Is "New" about the New Normal?

In the immediate aftermath of the terrorist attacks on New York and Washington, DC, political commentators in the United States eagerly identified 9/11 as the start of a new American epoch, one that replaced the inherited logics about security and global order gained from the forty-plus years of the Cold War with new understandings of American vulnerability and power. But even as policy changes—from the USA PATRIOT Act to the execution of preemptive war in Iraq—seem to support the claim that the United States has made a radical break with its past, the terms and logics of the war on terror remain understandable precisely because they are so familiar. Within weeks of the attacks, Vice Present Dick Cheney, for example, declared the new security measures (already codified in the USA PATRIOT Act) as the "new normal," mobilizing to solidify the terms of the counterterrorist state for the foreseeable future. But what is actually new about the new normal? When were Americans ever presented with a global U.S. military campaign—fought largely on covert terms—that did not merge an apocalyptic notion of everyday domestic threat with an expansive use of government secrecy and a demand for ever-increasing military budgets? The structural logic of total war that defined the Cold War remains the defining principle of American security policy, linking the foreign and the domestic under a highly reproducible logic of imminent threat. From this perspective, the war on terror is a global project that seeks to perfect, rather than replace, the structural logics of the Cold War.

This regeneration of the covert security state was well underway before the attacks of September 11, 2001. Here, we might follow Kalugin's lead and interrogate the active measures of the U.S. security state. Within weeks of the 9/11 attacks, President Bush sent his advisor Karl Rove out to meet with Hollywood executives and producers to discuss the production of patriotic entertainment, vehicles that would communicate, as well as promote, the risks and dangers of the war on terror for the American public.[8] But the intelligence community was already way ahead of him, having sent representatives out to Hollywood since the mid-1990s to provide technical advice. The results were spectacular: already in production as the 9/11 attacks occurred were three television shows about terrorism and the heroic exploits of the CIA/FBI to combat it: CBS had *The Agency*, ABC had *Alias*, and FOX had *24*. The CI Centre, also an energetic consultant to the entertainment industry, has participated in a British television production called *MI6* and a television miniseries about the Robert Hanssen case. And this year we will see the network television arrival of *D.H.S.: The Series*—an action drama about homeland security that has the formal backing of the Department of Homeland Security. On the series Web site (www.dhs.tv) one finds a sepia-toned image of President George W. Bush, Secretary of State Colin Powell, and Secretary of Defense Donald Rumsfeld, heads bowed in prayer, with the words "How do we know that we are truly safe?" superimposed over their image. Cabinet members and homeland security personnel have been promised cameos in the television series, yet again blurring the distinction between fiction and reality also evidenced at the International Spy Museum. What links these productions is not only their constant recitation of vulnerability and threat but also the assumption that the only way of producing security in such a climate comes through state-sponsored covert action.

What we are seeing in the United States right now is not only a regeneration of a security state founded in secrecy and covert action but also a rescripting of history to enable that mission. The newness of the war on terror is primarily an invention, a means of separating it ideologically from the past in order to force the dialogue away from the known costs and consequences of total war. The goal of this strategy is twofold: First, to enable a national regeneration through violence, allowing the war on terror to become an ideological construct based on, but publicly disconnected from, past U.S. policy; and second, to make it all but impossible for citizens to argue for less militarism or to demand from officials a basic definition for the concept of security that they so pervasively evoke. Linked to this rejuvenation of the covert security state is, thus, an implicit argument that democratic process and security are ultimately incompatible. This is an old Cold War line, used for generations to validate both an expansion of the military state and an increasing manipulation of public media to produce consent.[9] One way to resist the curtailing of civil liberties, the aggressive global military campaign, and the ever-expanding use of state secrecy to prevent debate and avoid international law is to historicize these very logics as long-standing American Cold War strategies. In order to understand the new normal, it may well be that we need to shed more light on the terms, costs, successes, and failures of the Cold War security state. Actively engaging the historical archive may well be the best tool today for showing the consequences of unrestrained American power and for demonstrating the foreign and domestic costs of allowing officials to define the United States as a counterterrorist state.

Notes

1. See David Stout, "Former Top Russian Spy Pledges New Allegiance," *New York Times*, August 24, 2003.
2. Oleg Kalugin with Fen Montaigne, *The First Directorate: My Thirty-Two Years of Intelligence and Espionage against the West* (New York: St. Martin's, 1994).

3. See, for example, Joseph Masco, "Lie Detectors: On Secrets and Hypersecurity in Los Alamos," *Public Culture* 14 (2002): 441–67.

4. John Earl Haynes and Harvey Klehr, *Venona: Decoding Soviet Espionage in America* (New Haven, CT: Yale Notebene, 1999).

5. The fourteen volumes of the Church Committee's 1970s investigation into the CIA and FBI are available at the Assassination Archives and Research Center, www.aarclibrary.org/publib/church/reports/contents.htm (accessed September 6, 2004). See also Lawrence E. Walsh, "Final Report of the Independent Counsel for Iran/Contra Matters," Federation of American Scientists, www.fas.org/irp/offdocs/walsh/ (accessed September 6, 2004).

6. See also Ward Churchill and Jim Vander Wall, *The COINTELPRO Papers: Documents from the FBI's Secret Wars against Domestic Dissent* (Boston: South End, 2002); and Kathryn S. Olmsted, *Challenging the Secret Government: The Post-Watergate Investigations of the CIA and FBI* (Chapel Hill: University of North Carolina Press, 1996). Finally, a useful text for evaluating the social and political consequences of secrecy during the Cold War is Daniel Patrick Moynihan, *Secrecy: The American Experience* (New Haven, CT: Yale University Press, 1998).

7. For a detailed analysis of the complexity and history of the antinuclear movement, see Lawrence S. Wittner's three-volume history: *One World or None: A History of the World Nuclear Disarmament Movement through 1953* (Stanford, CA: Stanford University Press, 1993); *Resisting the Bomb: A History of the World Nuclear Disarmament Movement 1954–1970* (Stanford, CA: Stanford University Press, 1997); and *Toward Abolition: A History of the World Nuclear Disarmament Movement 1971 to the Present* (Stanford, CA: Stanford University Press, 2003).

8. See Rick Lyman, "Hollywood Discusses Role in War Effort," *New York Times*, November 12, 2001.

9. See, for example, the arguments about the problem of public dissent raised in "NSC 68: United States Objective and Programs for National Security (April 14, 1950)," a core planning document of the Cold War; reprinted in Ernest R. May, *American Cold War Strategy: Interpreting NSC 68* (New York: St. Martin's, 1993). See also Olmsted, *Challenging the Secret Government*, on U.S. media coverage of intelligence activities during the Cold War.

The Abusable Past

R. J. Lambrose

No Experts Need Apply

History job candidates have frequently complained about the multiplication of requirements for teaching jobs. In a tight job market, universities are often unembarrassed to advertise for a "nineteenth-century U.S. historian who can also teach the Ancient Middle East and Modern East Asia, coach the men's lacrosse team, and change the toner in the photocopier. Significant publications and teaching experience required."

Those historians frustrated at their ineligibility for such positions may want to look into alternative careers as expert witnesses in legal cases. Consider this recent solicitation forwarded to us from the Round Table Group (RTG), which is seeking on behalf on an attorney client "an historian, highly credentialed and at a prestigious university, to perform some historical research and instruct a lay jury on what was known about a particular occupational hazard (lead paint contamination) between 1950 and 1980." Most of us would naively assume that historical research on the history of occupational hazards might be a prerequisite for this assuredly lucrative gig. But we would be wrong. The RTG quickly reassures us that "the historian need not be a subject matter expert; our client is mainly interested to find an historian who is a good communicator; someone who can easily communicate a story to a lay jury."

For the RTG and its clients, the model of the historical witness is surely Philip Scranton, University Board of Governors Professor of History of Industry and Technology at Rutgers University (remember: "highly credentialed" and "prestigious university") who has signed on as an expert witness for twenty major chemical companies. These firms, which include Dow, Monsanto, and Union Carbide, are fighting

Radical History Review

Issue 93 (Fall 2005): 301–306

Copyright 2005 by MARHO: The Radical Historians' Organization, Inc.

the claim of a former chemical worker who says that his liver cancer was caused by exposure to vinyl chloride monomer at his job. Crucial to the worker's case is the historical research of David Rosner and Gerald Markowitz, whose book, *Deceit and Denial: The Deadly Politics of Industrial Pollution* (2002), exposed, among other things, the paint industry's cover-up of white lead's toxicity and the chemical industry's cover-up of the hazards posed by vinyl chloride and other substances.

In an effort to impeach Rosner and Markowitz, the chemical companies engaged Scranton to write a forty-one-page critique of *Deceit and Denial*. Yet, as Jon Wiener reports in the *Nation* (February 7, 2005), while "Scranton is serving in this case as an expert witness for the chemical companies, he's not an expert on cancer-causing chemicals; he's best known for his prizewinning book on the textile industry in Philadelphia." But following the RTG script, he has a "story" (really, a tall tale) to tell, rather than any expertise to offer.

Scranton's story is that Markowitz violated "basic principles of academic integrity, historical accuracy, and professional responsibility" and engaged in "sustained and repeated violations" of the official standards of the American Historical Association. Sounds disturbing, no? But when we get to the fine print, it turns out that these egregious ethical violations consist of things like the fact that Markowitz knew the names of the outside reviewers of *Deceit and Denial* for the University of California Press and, indeed, suggested some of the names to the publisher. "Such practices," Scranton writes, "subverted confidential, objective refereeing of scholarly manuscripts."

Setting aside the fact that the evaluation of book manuscripts rarely involves the sort of blind review given to refereed articles, Rosner and Markowitz's book turns out to be one of the most heavily vetted manuscripts in the annals of history publishing. The Milbank Memorial Fund, which copublished the book, paid for eight people to review the manuscript (including the former head of the National Cancer Institute) and then brought them to a two-day conference to review it in detail. And even if the outside evaluators' names had once been confidential, the chemical companies have ensured that they will no longer be, for they subpoenaed and deposed all the reviewers; the writ also demanded that the reviewers produce "any original written, typewritten, handwritten, printed or recorded material . . . now or at any time in your possession, custody or control," e-mail included.

So there you have the chemical industry's approach to history: carrots and sticks, roundtables and subpoenas, greased palms and slapped wrists, warm invitations and chilling effects. Only time—and historians—will tell if this will prove a winning formula.

A Fish Tale

Those who carefully save their copies of the *Smithsonian Magazine* might want to blow the dust off the August 1998 issue. That's the one with Michael Kernan's article ("Sharing the Gift of Music") that begins: "A few months ago a remarkable man named Herbert Axelrod donated two Stradivari violins, a Stradivari viola and a Stradivari cello to the Smithsonian, creating what is now known as the Axelrod Quartet." Savor that word *remarkable.*

What Kernan found most remarkable was Axelrod's extraordinary generosity. The musical instruments he donated "have been appraised at $50 million, though Axelrod has turned down offers as high as $55 million." And that was not all. "A self-taught ichthyologist," Axelrod, Kernan explained, had "made a fortune publishing handbooks on pets, especially tropical fish." After selling the business for "a reported nine figures," Axelrod was now occupying himself by giving "money away to various music institutions and museums, including a $1.5 million endowment to the national Museum of Natural History's Division of Fishes." A few years later, in another issue of *Smithsonian Magazine*, the Smithsonian's secretary, Lawrence Small, joined in the celebration of Dr. Axelrod's generosity.

The Smithsonian was not alone in fawning over Axelrod. In August 2003, the *New Jersey Monthly* profiled him as having risen from modest circumstances in Depression-era Bayonne to become "the philanthropist who endowed the New Jersey Symphony Orchestra (NJSO) with an unprecedented collection of rare instruments." The "instruments were appraised for $50 million," and the Vienna Philharmonic had offered $55 million. (Sound familiar?) But for the New Jersey Symphony, Axelrod had been willing to let them go for "the bargain price of 18 million." Why? "Because he loves the orchestra and wanted to help it distinguish itself."

Alas, there are a few remarkable wrinkles to this Carnegie-esque saga of the self-made man turned philanthropist. Take, for example, Axelrod's credentials as "self-taught ichthyologist." As the *Newark Star-Ledger* pointed out in a long, revealing article, Axelrod's first connection to the Smithsonian came in 1955 when he coauthored *The Handbook of Tropical Aquarium Fishes* with one of its scientists. Unfortunately, as a lawsuit later revealed, Axelrod had stolen the color plates for the volume from the work regarded as the bible of the field. Moreover, although he told everyone he was a medical doctor, Axelrod had a PhD in Education from NYU.

Still, an acquaintance with Herbert Axelrod *is* an education. Consider the "nine figures" that he claimed to have received for the sale of his company, TFH Publications (that's Tropical Fish Hobbyist, for the uninitiated). He had been rounding up, it turned out. The actual figure was eight figures, or $80 million, and even at that, the buyer, Central Garden and Pet Company, now thinks that they were scammed. In their lawsuit (one of many trailing the good doctor), they claim that

Axelrod engaged in a long-term pattern of deceit, including "siphoning of more than $3 million into bank accounts in Switzerland and the Cayman Islands; illicit business deals in Cuba; payments to support a longtime extramarital relationship that were recorded as author's fees; at least a quarter of a million dollars in charitable contributions falsely booked as advertising expenses; and the wide-scale concealing of books in warehouses to fraudulently boost sales figures."

But what about the largesse that landed Axelrod on the *Chronicle of Philanthropy*'s annual list of the nation's sixty top charitable givers and among the Smithsonian's distinguished benefactors? That's what the chairman of the Senate Finance Committee, Charles E. Grassley (R-Iowa), has started to ask after reports that $50 million might be a tad inflated valuation for his Smithsonian gift—a scheme to get a massive tax deduction. Independent appraisers contacted by the *Newark Star-Ledger* called the $50 million figure "ludicrous," "preposterous," and "a joke." "It is troubling that the Smithsonian may be turning a blind eye to tax mischief. . . . Donors shouldn't be able to get away with playing the taxpayers like a fiddle," said Grassley. Meanwhile, Small, the Smithsonian secretary, pulled a Rumsfeld by professing ignorance about any wrongdoing: "It is not the responsibility of any museum to do any appraising or tax evaluation. We do not know what any donor does in the way of tax deductions at all." At last report, however, the Smithsonian was backing away from its plans to rename the National Museum of American History's Hall of Musical Instruments after Axelrod.

But it is the NJSO that finds itself most embarrassed, since it actually paid for the instruments after a desperate fund-raising campaign that included substantial borrowing. The *Newark Star-Ledger* published a long (eleven thousand–word) investigative report in August that raised questions about the authenticity of several of the instruments. At best, it appears the instruments may be worth the $18 million paid for them. But so far, the NJSO is sticking to the $50 million figure. They have insured the instruments for that sum and insist that they reached that number after an appraisal by "one of the top people in the business." Yes, and also a long-time business partner of Herbert Axelrod. Indeed, it now appears that at the same time that Axelrod was pressing the NJSO to seal the deal for the musical instruments and, thereby, to fill his (offshore?) bank account with a large wad of cash, he was also liquidating most of his other holdings. Not a bad strategy when you know that federal investigators are closing in. The NJSO was Axelrod's exit strategy.

On April 12, 2004, the government filed tax-evasion charges against Axelrod. When he failed to show up in court for his arraignment two weeks later, authorities learned that he had fled to Marina Hemingway in Havana. Although reporters found him happily at work on a new pet book, he also told them that he would like to return to New Jersey some day. That return came perhaps sooner than he hoped when federal authorities caught him on the lam in Germany and had him extradited back to the United States. In December, he agreed to plead guilty to aiding and abetting the filing of a false tax return for a former employee in return for authorities dropping charges that he conspired to defraud the IRS. He still awaits sentencing.

In his complex negotiations with federal authorities, Axelrod might like to lean on his good friend Larry Small, who has made a specialty of problematic donors in his tenure as Smithsonian secretary. As our faithful readers (see *RHR* 82) will recall, Small had a run-in with the feds over his illegal purchase of a set of Amazonian tribal objects that included body parts and feathers from protected and endangered species of birds. Small's violation of the Federal Migratory Bird Treaty Act could have gotten him six months, but instead he plea-bargained his way to two years' probation and one hundred hours of community service.

No word yet on what Secretary Small will be doing for his community service. We would suggest a stint cleaning up Maryland's beloved Rosa Bonheur Pet Cemetery.

Discounted Dreams

It's beginning to look as if Wal-Mart's four-decade-long honeymoon with the American media is coming to an end. Revenues are down, local resistance is up, and reports of employee abuse (e.g., unpaid overtime, locked-in immigrant night workers, etc.) are percolating through the pressrooms and chat rooms. A year ago last April, labor historian Nelson Lichtenstein organized a conference on Wal-Mart at the University of California, Santa Barbara, and last fall PBS ran a *Frontline* special titled "Is Wal-Mart Good for America?" To viewers accustomed to PBS's kid-glove treatment of potential corporate donors, the question mark stuck out like an awkward crack in the golden bowl (Special: $6.99) of Wal-Mart's carefully burnished reputation.

How galling it must have been, then, for Wal-Mart heirs Nancy and Bill Laurie, when they were compelled last November to remove their daughter's name from the new basketball arena at the University of Missouri, Columbia (UMC). The Lauries, already owners of the Saint Louis Blues, a (locked-out) professional hockey team, had generously picked up a third of the tab ($25 million) for UMC's huge sports complex in return for premium tickets, a midcourt luxury suite with complimentary food and beverages, and, not least of all, the naming of the arena after their daughter, Elizabeth Paige Laurie, then a student at the University of Southern California (USC).

What a thoughtful commencement gift—we hear you saying—for a young woman starting out in life. Her very own hoop dream realized—at age twenty-two. And yet, as almost always happens with such up-from-the-playground fantasies, Laurie's dream was immediately crushed last November, when her first-semester roommate, Inez Martinez, revealed to the hosts of ABC's 20/20 news magazine how she had been paid for four years to do Laurie's homework assignments, write her papers, and answer her e-mail correspondence with professors. Though there was no indication that the Wal-Mart heiress had actually locked her roommate in while the assignments were being completed, Martinez did reveal that after tuition costs forced her to drop out of USC in her freshman year, her ex-roomie continued to send her books and assignments, along with sharply worded memos reproaching her independent contractor for sloppy typing or disappointing grades. "She was pretty picky," Martinez recalled. "She was a very demanding, expect-the-best boss." Though tempted to quit many times, Martinez needed Laurie's checks. The payments, totaling some $20,000 over four years, allowed Martinez to take classes at the University of California, Riverside. Private vices are public virtues, as Bernard Mandeville—or was it Jude Wanniski?—once said.

To be sure, USC's vice president of student affairs, Michael Jackson, was not so taken with young Laurie's four-year venture into supply-side economics. Talking with a *Los Angeles Times* reporter, Jackson confessed that in twenty-five years in academia, he had "never heard of possible cheating of this magnitude." But then what is Wal-Mart about if not orders of magnitude? And entrepreneurial outsourcing? And expect-the-best management? Why, then, stigmatize the same resourcefulness that would win Elizabeth Paige Laurie a spot on *The Apprentice* or, at the very least, a cabinet appointment? The question mark runs across UMC's newly renamed Mizzou Arena like a hidden crack in the gleaming edifice of American higher education.

Barbara Abrash is a curator, teacher, and independent producer. She is associate director of New York University's Center for Media, Culture, and History and the Center for Religion and Media. Recent publications include a special issue of the journal *Wide Angle* (edited with Cara Mertes and Lynne Jackson) on the work of media activist George Stoney. Productions include *Indians, Outlaws, and Angie Debo* (1988), which received the Organization of American Historians Erik Barnouw Award for historical documentary.

Lori A. Allen is a PhD candidate in the anthropology department at the University of Chicago. She is currently completing her thesis, titled "Suffering through a National Uprising: The Cultural Politics of Violence, Victimization, and Human Rights in Palestine," as a Peace Scholar at the United States Institute of Peace. She is also a founding member of the Task Force on Middle East Anthropology.

Jerry Atkin is a longtime labor and social justice activist. A cofounder of the Center for Working Life, he has worked with active and inactive workers on issues of plant closings, mass layoffs, and worker education for more than twenty years. He has been involved in campaigns with the Oregon Farm Workers' Union, PCUN, since 1993.

Rachel Tzvia Back, a poet, translator, and professor of literature, has lived in Israel since 1980 and in the Galilee since 2000. She was part of the successful community activism to stop planned building on the ruins of the Palestinian village of Mi'ar. Her latest collection, *The Buffalo Poems* (2003), tracks the cycle of violence defining the lives of Palestinians and Israelis these past years. Her translations of the important modern Hebrew poet Lea Goldberg are forthcoming in *Lea Goldberg: Selected Poetry and Drama* (2005).

Francisco E. Balderrama is a professor of Chicano studies and history at California State University at Los Angeles, where he was selected outstanding university professor. He is coauthor, with Raymond Rodriguez, of *Decade of Betrayal: Mexican Repatriation in the 1930s* (1995), which the Gustavus Myers Center for the Study of Human Rights proclaimed an outstanding work on intolerance in North America.

Beatriz da Costa is an interdisciplinary artist and researcher. She works independently as well as collaboratively. From 2000 to 2005 she worked in collaboration with the Critical Art Ensemble and is a cofounder of the Preemptive Media Arts Collective. Her interests include social robotics, biopolitics, and the politics of surveillance. She has recently joined the faculty of the University of California at Irvine as an assistant professor in the Graduate Program in Arts, Computation, and Engineering.

Lara Z. Deeb is a cultural anthropologist and an assistant professor in women's studies at the University of California at Irvine. She is the author of *An Enchanted Modern: Gender and Public Piety in Shi'i Lebanon* (forthcoming). She is also a founding member of the Task Force on Middle East Anthropology and the Radical Arab Women's Activist Network.

Eric Hiltner, cofounder of the Bolozone, Dreamtime Village, and Urbana IMC, is a multi-skilled philosopher of action, design, and multiplicity. He is currently working on a manuscript titled "Auto Free Design," which focuses on setting up cities in ways that allow people to meet needs within walking distance. His video, building, and writing projects explore progressive, radical, and sustainable alternatives to the dominant codes.

Martha Howell is Miriam Champion Professor of History at Columbia University. She specializes in the social, economic, and legal history of northern Europe between about 1300 and 1700, with particular interest in gender relations. Her publications include *Women, Production, and Patriarchy in Late Medieval Cities* (1990), *The Marriage Exchange: Property, Social Place, and Gender in Cities of the Low Countries* (1998), and, with Walter Prevenier, *From Reliable Sources: An Introduction to Historical Methodology* (2001).

Lawrence Jones is senior research analyst at a Chicago-based economic consultancy and an associate editor for the interdisciplinary humanities journal *Common Knowledge*, where he also serves as director of the journal's Subscription Dissemination Project. Formerly a fellow of the University of Minnesota Humanities Institute, he has recently contributed several entries to *The Encyclopedia of American Counterculture* (2005).

Burçak Keskin-Kozat is a PhD candidate in sociology at the University of Michigan at Ann Arbor. Her dissertation explores the influence of local, translocal, and global dynamics in the implementation and reception of the Marshall Plan in Turkey (1948–52). Her research interests include modernities/modernization, the cultural politics of the Cold War, nationalism, religious movements, and gender.

R. J. Lambrose has been honored with a lifetime skybox at the annual American Historical Association convention, complete with exam copies and complimentary tote bags.

Jorge Mariscal is director of the Chicano/a-Latino/a Arts and Humanities Program at the University of California at San Diego. His *Aztlán and Viet Nam: Chicano and Chicana Experiences of the War* (1999) was the first anthology of Mexican American writings about the war. His *Brown-Eyed Children of the Sun: Lessons from the Chicago Movement* (forthcoming) will explore Chicano/a radicalism during the Vietnam War era. He is an active member of Project YANO, an organization working to demilitarize California public schools.

Joseph Masco is an assistant professor of anthropology at the University of Chicago. He has recently published essays in the journals *Public Culture*, *American Ethnologist*, and *Cultural Anthropology* and is the author of *The Nuclear Borderlands: The Manhattan Project in Post–Cold War New Mexico* (2006).

Conor McGrady received his MFA at the School of the Art Institute of Chicago and is the recipient of two Community Arts Assistance Program Grants from the city of Chicago. Most recently, his work has been exhibited at the Chicago Cultural Center, White Columns in New York, and Ratio 3 in San Francisco. In 2002 he was selected to participate in the Whitney biennial. He is a member of the Culture and Conflict Group and currently lives and works in New York.

Quincy T. Mills is a PhD candidate in the history department at the University of Chicago. He coauthored "Truth and Soul: Black Talk in the Barbershop" in Melissa Harris-Lacewell's *Barbershops, Bibles, and BET: Everyday Talk and Black Political Thought* (2004). He is currently working on his dissertation, "'Color-Barbers' and the Emergence of a Black Counterpublic: A Social and Political History of Black Barbers and Barbershops, 1850–1970."

Priscilla Murolo teaches history at Sarah Lawrence College. She coauthored *From the Folks Who Brought You the Weekend: A Short Illustrated History of Labor in the United States* (2001) and has started research for a book on federal military interventions into civilian affairs in the United States.

Kevin Noble is an artist from New York who works primarily in painting, drawing, and photography. He is a founding member of the Culture and Conflict Group, which explores the role of culture in conflict and military occupations. His recent series of photographs, *Irish Republicans: Ireland and America*, was shown at the CEPA Gallery, Buffalo, New York, at the Glucksman Ireland House at New York University, and as part of the Terrorvision exhibition at Exit Art in New York. He lives and works in New York.

Enrique C. Ochoa is a professor of history at California State University at Los Angeles and a member of the *Radical History Review* collective. His publications include *Feeding Mexico: The Political Uses of Food Since 1910* (2000) and *Latina/o Los Angeles: Migrations, Communities, and Political Activism* (forthcoming).

Claire Pentecost is an artist, writer, and associate professor at the School of the Art Institute of Chicago. Recent projects include VisibleFood.org, an open-content database and Web site exposing the global corporate system that produces our food with inherent but invisible social and environmental damages, and publicamateur.org, promoting the work of artists and activists who traverse disciplinary boundaries to produce knowledge usually conceded to professionally imbedded experts.

Kavita Philip is an associate professor of women's studies at the University of California at Irvine. Her articles in colonial environmental history, technology and globalization, and new media studies have appeared in *Cultural Studies, Postmodern Culture,* and elsewhere. She is the author of *Civilizing Natures* (2004); coeditor, with Neil Englehart, Mahmood Monshipouri, and Andrew Nathan, of *Constructing Human Rights in the Age of Globalization* (2003); and coauthor, with Terry Harpold, of *Going Native: Cyberculture and Postcolonialism* (forthcoming).

Vivian H. Price, a former union electrician, teaches in the Department of Interdisciplinary Studies at California State University, Dominguez Hills. Her work has appeared in *Feminist Economics, Film Appreciation,* and *Women in Construction,* and she is a coeditor of *Labor versus Empire* (2004). She produced the films *Hammering It Out* (2002) and *Pride and Politics* (2004), and her new documentary, *Transnational Tradeswomen* (in progress), is about the effects of globalization on women construction workers in Asia.

Jasbir K. Puar is an assistant professor of women's and gender studies at Rutgers University. She works on queer globalizations, South Asian diasporas, gay and lesbian tourism, and sexual scripts of terrorism. Her articles have appeared in *GLQ, Signs, Society and Space, Feminist Studies, Social Text, Antipode,* and *Gender, Place, and Culture.*

Eliza Jane Reilly is the director of the Center for Liberal Arts and Society at Franklin and Marshall College, where she also teaches in the American studies program. She is a member of the *Radical History Review* editorial collective.

Natsu Taylor Saito is a professor of law at Georgia State University College of Law and an associate professor in the Department of Ethnic Studies at the University of Colorado–Boulder. She is coeditor, with Ward Churchill, of *Confronting the Crime of Silence: Evidence of U.S. War Crimes in Indochina* (2005).

Connie Samaras is based in Los Angeles and is a professor in the Department of Studio Art at the University of California at Irvine. She has extensively exhibited and lectured on her work both nationally and internationally. She recently returned from the South Pole, where she was a National Science Foundation grantee for the artists and writers program. Her project was photographing the liminal space between life-support architecture and extreme environment.

Ellen Schrecker is a professor of history at Yeshiva University who has written extensively about the Cold War red scare. Among her books are *No Ivory Tower: McCarthyism and the Universities* (1986), *The Age of McCarthyism: A Brief History with Documents* (1994), and *Many Are the Crimes: McCarthyism in America* (2001). She is currently collaborating with the political scientist Corey Robin on a general study of political repression in the United States.

David Serlin is an assistant professor of communication and science studies at the University of California at San Diego and the author of *Replaceable You: Engineering the Body in Postwar America* (2004). He is a member of the *Radical History Review* editorial collective.

Rogers M. Smith is the Christopher H. Browne Distinguished Professor and chair of political science at the University of Pennsylvania. He is the author of *Stories of Peoplehood: The Politics and Morals of Political Membership* (2003).

Marc Stein is an associate professor of history at York University in Toronto, the author of *City of Sisterly and Brotherly Loves: Lesbian and Gay Philadelphia, 1945–1972* (2000, rev. ed. 2004) and the editor-in-chief of the *Encyclopedia of Lesbian, Gay, Bisexual, and Transgender History in America* (2003). He is currently working on a manuscript titled "The U.S. Supreme Court's Sexual Revolution? 1965–1973."

Matias Viegener teaches in critical studies and the MFA writing program at the California Institute of Arts. His criticism has appeared in the anthologies *Queer Looks: Perspectives on Lesbian and Gay Film and Video* (1993) and *Camp Grounds: Style and Homosexuality* (1994). He is the editor and cotranslator of Georges Bataille's *The Trial of Gilles de Rais* (1991). He has most recently published fiction and criticism in *Bomb*, *Artforum*, *Art Issues*, and *Artweek*.

Kath Weston is an anthropologist who teaches at Harvard University. Her most recent book is *Gender in Real Time: Power and Transience in a Visual Age* (2002). She and her partner, Geeta Patel, were married under Massachusetts law in 2004.

Maurice B. Wheeler is an associate professor of library and information sciences in the School of Library and Information Sciences at the University of North Texas. He is an authority on public library management and organizational development issues such as leadership development, change management, and workforce diversity. He has served as director of the Detroit Public Library and has held various posts at the University of Michigan Library.

Jessica Winegar is an assistant professor of anthropology at Fordham University. She writes and teaches on cultural politics in the Middle East, with a focus on visual art in Egypt. She is a former Middle East Section board member of the American Anthropological Association and a founding member of the Task Force on Middle East Anthropology, dedicated to enhancing public awareness of Middle East anthropological knowledge.

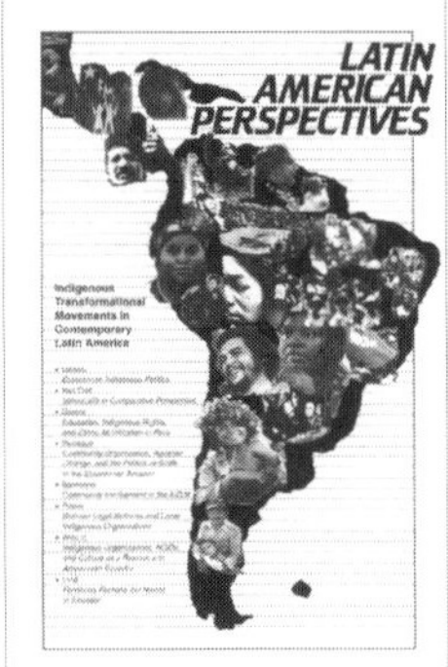

LATIN AMERICAN PERSPECTIVES

A Journal on Capitalism and Socialism

Managing Editor
Ronald H. Chilcote
University of California, Riverside

Join a forum for discussion and debate on the political economy of capitalism, imperialism, and socialism in the Americas. A theoretical and scholarly journal, **Latin American Perspectives** provides you with an in-depth look from participants and scholars throughout the Americas, with issues frequently focusing on a single problem, nation, or region.

LAP offers a vital multidisciplinary view of the powerful forces shaping the Americas, such as:

- Economics – and the study of the moral, political and social desirability of economic policies
- Political Science – and the patterns of social action that underlie the operation of nations, the competition for power, and the conduct and misconduct of governments
- International Relations – particularly as they affect the nationalist movements and internal problems of Latin American countries
- Philosophy – theoretical and applied to the hard realities of developing nations
- History – a critical view, with frequent inside views of history in the making
- Geography – the environmental condition, ecology, and exploitation of resources
- Sociology – organized groups, social institutions, and the new social movements, including feminism, ecology, and urban and rural labor
- Anthropology – the culture, ethnicity, and resistance of peoples of the region
- Literature – the personal poetic comments of activists and revolutionary scholars

Bimonthly:
January, March, May, July,
September, November
ISSN: 0094-582X